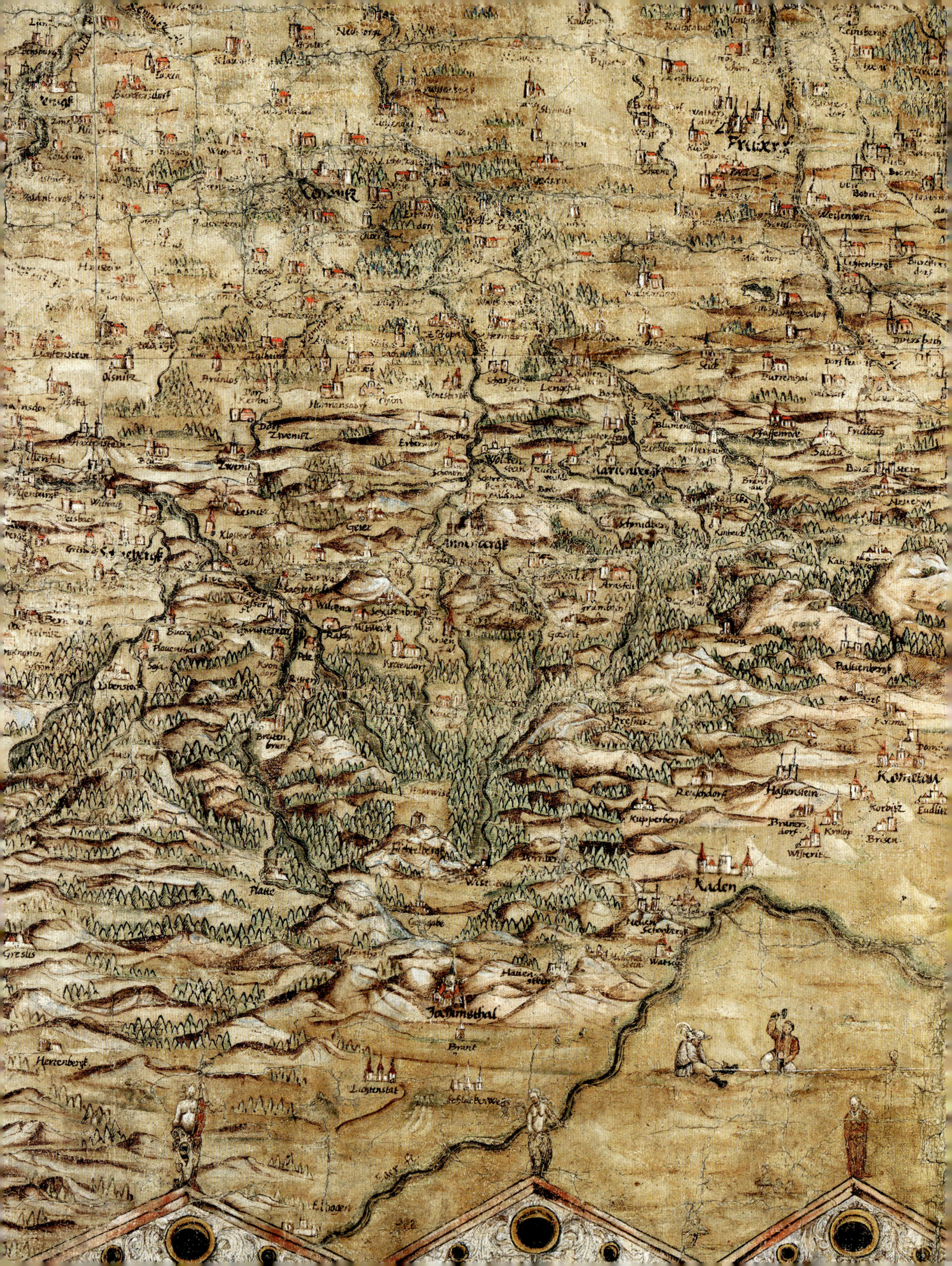

Fruxer
Zwenitz
Dorf Ziveniz
Hermansdorf
Scharfenstein
Lengefelt
Blumenau
Pfaffenrode
Saida
Wolkenstein
Marienbergk
Brandau
Schmidberg
Kinbeut
Annabergk
Geier
Zell
Wilkena
Arnsfelt
Preßnitz
Reischdorf
Hassenstein
Komotaw
Korbitz
Eudlitz
Brunersdorf
Krolop
Brisen
Wisterit
Kupperbergk
Wise
Kaden
Gotsgabe
Hauenstein
Watscz
Joachimsthal
Brant
Lichtenstat
Schlackenwerd
Hertenbergk

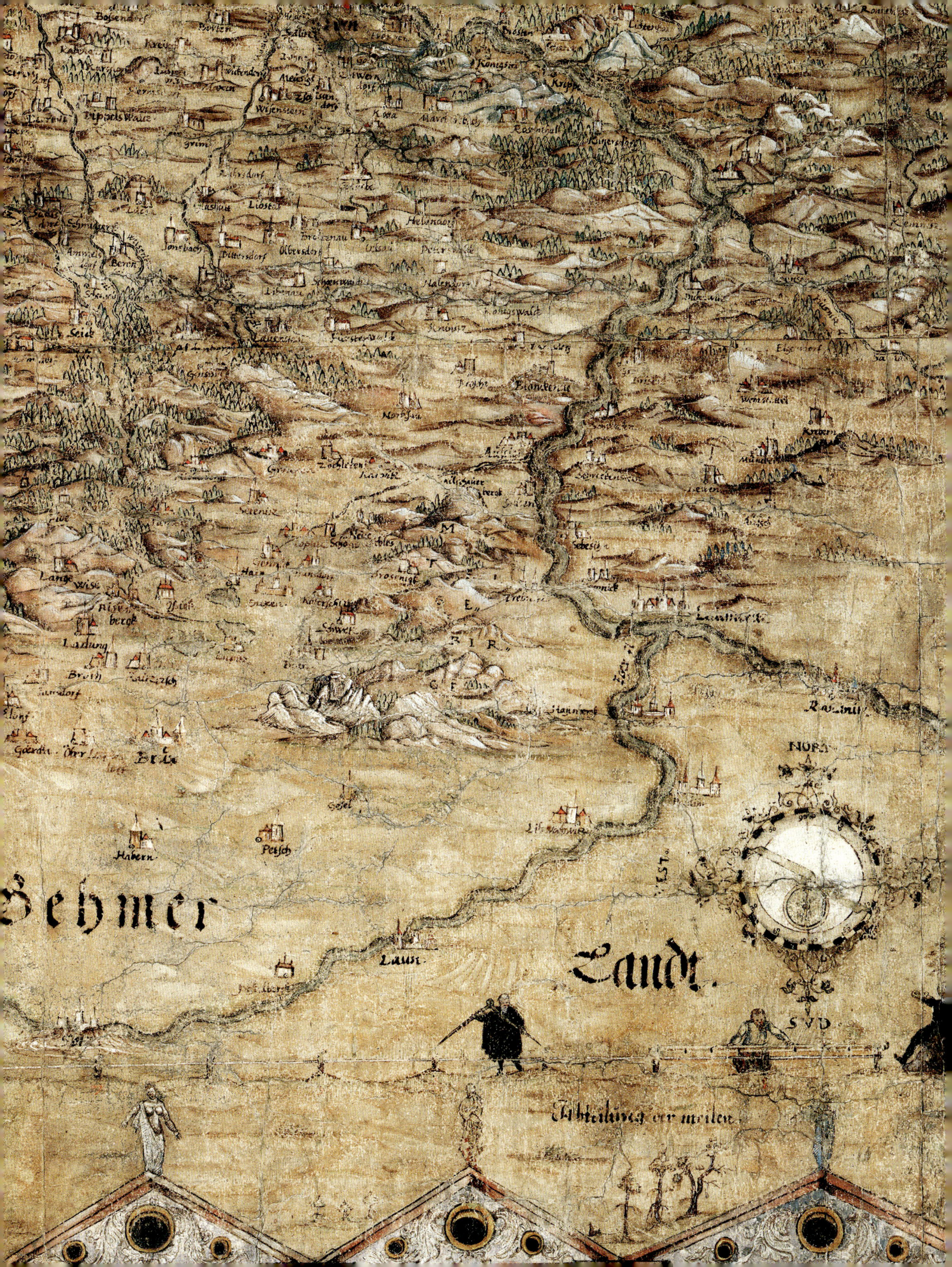

Behmer
Landt.
NORT
SVD

Ordenũg des freyen vnd loblichē berckwergks in Sandt Joachims thal.

S. Anna. S. Joachim.

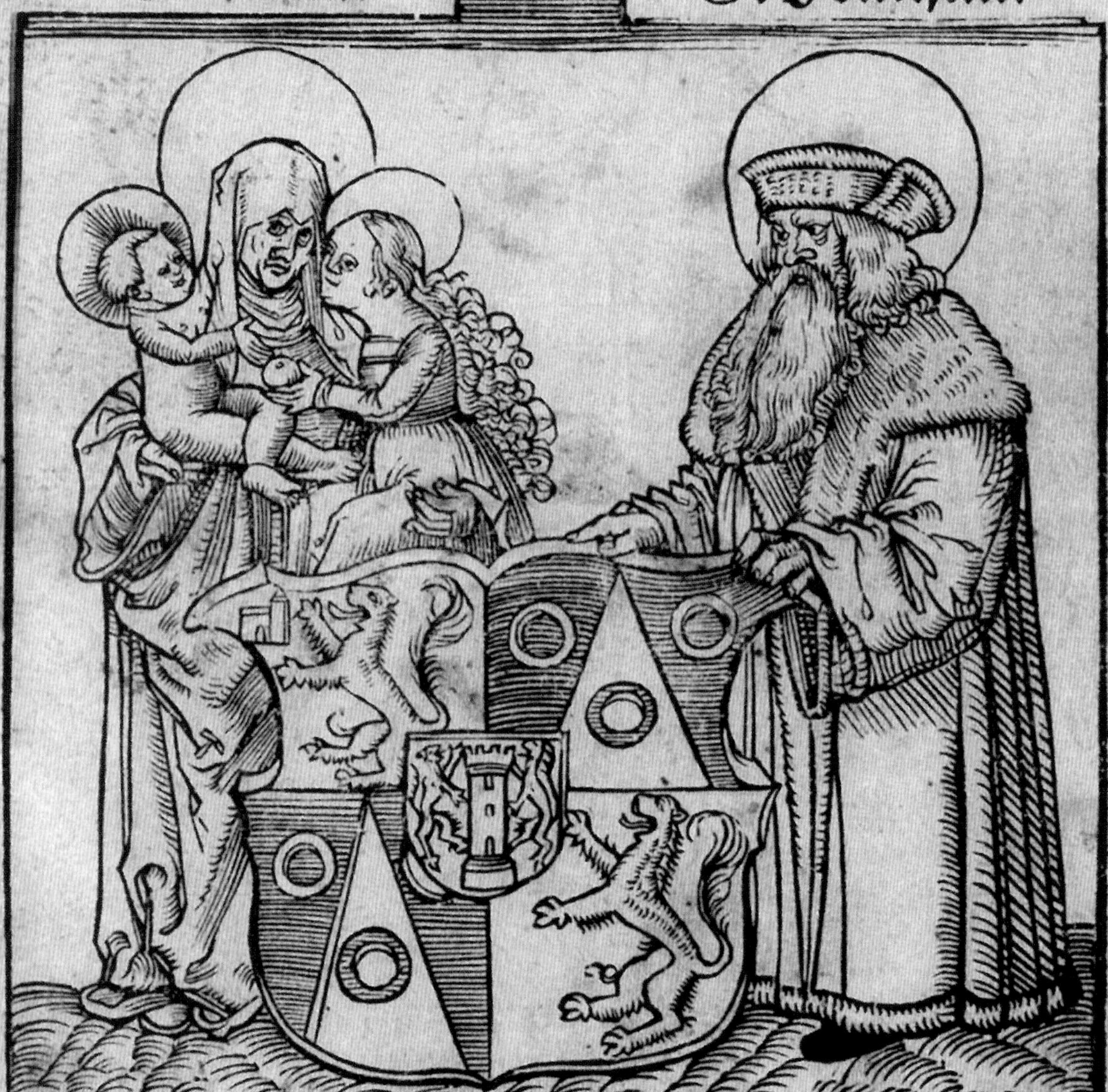

THE MINING TOWNS OF THE BOHEMIAN ORE MOUNTAINS

in the Early Modern Period and Their Impact on Cultural History

MICHAELA HRUBÁ
JAN ROYT
TÁŇA ŠIMKOVÁ

Charles University – Karolinum Press
Jan Evangelista Purkyně University – Faculty of Arts
2023

KAROLINUM PRESS
Karolinum Press is a publishing department of Charles University
Ovocný trh 560/5, 116 36 Prague 1, Czech Republic
www.karolinum.cz

Jan Evangelista Purkyně University in Ústí nad Labem
Pasteurova 3544/1, 400 96 Ústí nad Labem
www.ujep.cz

Layout by Zdeněk Ziegler
Set by DTP Karolinum Press
Printed in the Czech Republic by Těšínské papírny, s. r. o.
First English edition
A catalogue record for this book is available from the National Library of the Czech Republic.

The book has been published with the institutional support for long-term conceptual development of the research organization of Jan Evangelista Purkyně University in Ústí nad Labem.

ISBN 978-80-7561-375-2 (Jan Evangelista Purkyně University in Ústí nad Labem)
ISBN 978-80-246-4144-7 (Charles University)

The original manuscript was reviewed by
doc. Dr. et Ing. Jiří Fajt, Ph.D. (Staatliche Kunstsammlungen Dresden);
PhDr. Jan Klípa, Ph.D. (Institute of Art History, Czech Academy of Sciences)

TABLE OF CONTENTS

AUTHORS OF FIGURES

18a – Albertina, Wien
42 – Bayerische Staatsbibliothek
35 – Deutsche Fotothek
1, 58, 61 – Diocese of Litoměřice
8 – Geolab FŽP UJEP
11 – HU AV ČR
18 – Kunsthistorisches Museum Wien
25 – Moravské zemské muzeum
21 – Münchener DigitalisierungsZentrum, Digitale Bibliothek
7 – Münchener Staatsbibliothek – Digitale Bibliothek
13 – Museum in Karlovy Vary – Jáchymov branch
107 – Museum of Religious Art of the Plzeň Diocese
99 – National Archives
3 – National Gallery Prague
6, 19, 69, 73, 100 – National Heritage Institute
4, 17, 23, 24, 26, 28, 39, 40, 48, 52, 53, 54, 56, 57, 59, 62, 63, 64, 65, 66, 67, 70, 71, 76, 78, 79, 80, 81, 83, 85, 86, 87, 88, 89, 90, 91, 92, 93, 94, 95, 96, 97, 98, 101, 102, 104, 105, 106, 108, 109, 111, 112, 113 – J. Peer
16 – Rijksmuseum Amsterdam
5, 22, 27, 29, 74, 75, 77 – J. Royt
30, 31, 32, 33, 36, 37, 38, 43, 44, 49, 50, 55, 60, 84 – T. Šimková
9 – SLUB Dresden
14a – SOA in Plzeň
14 –SOA in Zámrsk
46 – SOkA Karlovy Vary
20 – M. Vorel

LIST OF FIGURES

Back matter:

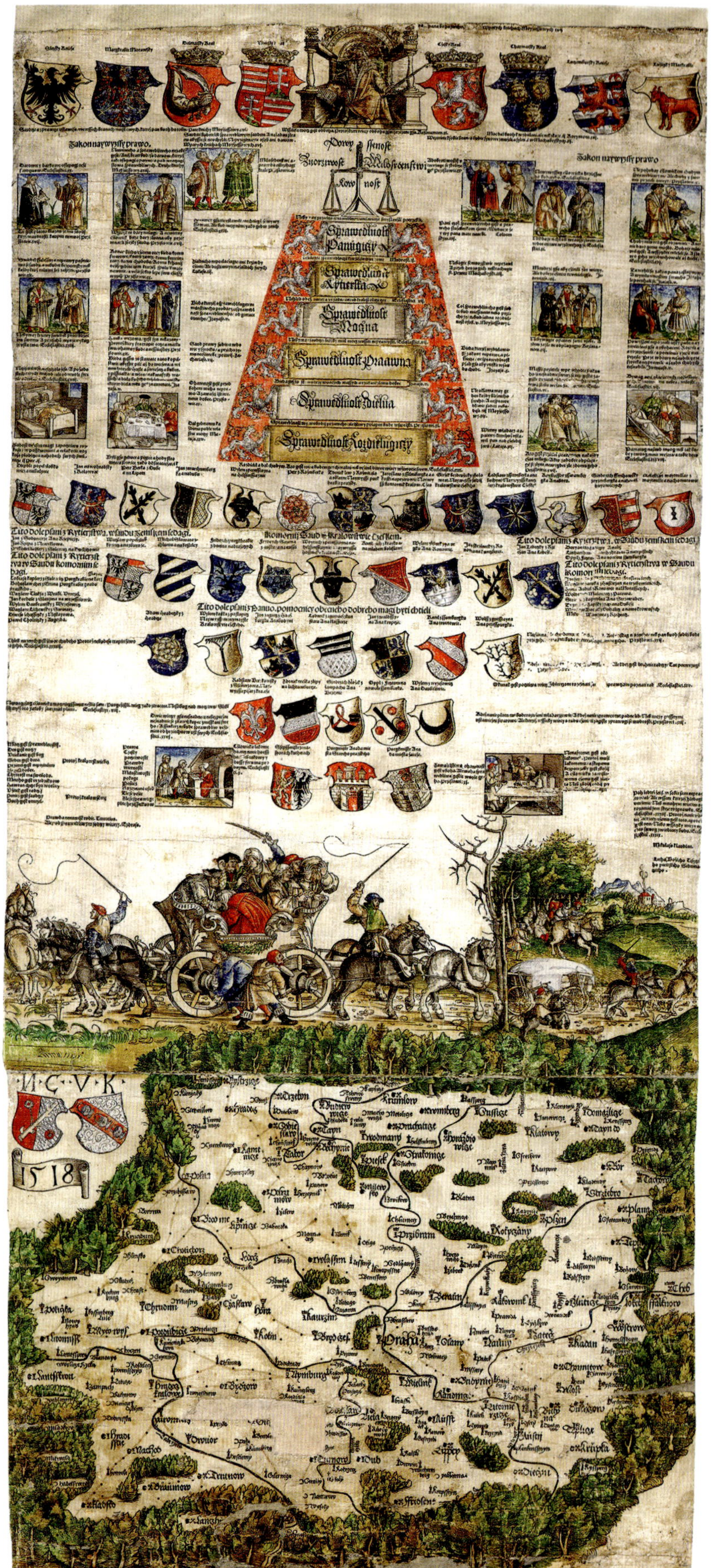

Fig. 1 A section of Klaudyán's map showing the border mountain belt of the Ore Mountains. Photo © Diocese of Litoměřice.

INTRODUCTION

The cultural heritage of the mining towns in the Ore Mountains is as rich and varied as their history. The buildings, monuments, and artworks that speak to the wealth and art of their population testify to the growing prosperity of the individual towns, symbolize pivotal moments in their history, and demonstrate the mutual cross-border influence in art and culture between the regions on the Bohemian and Saxon sides of the Ore Mountains. The knowledge of cultural monuments and of foreign influences and local developments in construction, architecture, and art, helps visitors to the towns and cities of the Ore Mountains gain better insight into the remarkable history of a significant part of the former Kingdom of Bohemia. In addition, it is a helpful tool in exploring the close relationship developed over the centuries between the two sides of the Ore Mountains, where both ordinary people and mining specialists saw the border as merely a formal concept from the realm of high territorial politics, rather than a dividing line between two countries.

The origins and growth of many mining towns and villages, accompanied by active building, happened over a long period of time – from the 13th to the 16th century. The driving force behind the development of the settlements in the mining region was, particularly in the 15th and subsequent centuries, nobility from Saxony, who brought with them the material culture of their homeland, new and unusual to the Kingdom of Bohemia.

In terms of architectural history and a history of visual culture in general, the period coincides with the age of late Gothic and early Renaissance, which took on a different form in the wide strip of land that is today northwest Bohemia than it did in the art and architecture of Prague. Construction projects and art works in the mining towns, financed by the nobility or mining entrepreneurs from the revenues of mining extraction, soon became a major presence that became an equal partner and competitor to the existing royal, municipal and aristocratic endowments in the centre of the kingdom.

The objective of this book is to introduce the most important mining centres and their historical monuments, to help answer the question about what made the Late Gothic and Renaissance in northwest Bohemia so unique and distinctive relative to the architectural and artistic tastes that were prevalent in the rest of the country, and to confirm the theory that has been supported by research evidence to date: specifically, that at the end of the mediaeval period, i.e., around the turn of the 15th and 16th centuries, a unified economic and cultural space was formed in the Ore Mountains irrespective of the Bohemian-Saxon border, united by mining activities, language, art, and the Lutheran faith.

The first non-selling edition of the book was created as a result of research within the cross-border project *Naše světové dědictví – Hornická kulturní krajina Krušnohoří/Erzgebirge* (Our World Heritage – Mining Cultural Landscape of the Erzgebirge), in which the Faculty of Arts of J. E. Purkyně University cooperated with the Institute of Industrial Archaeology, History of Science and Technology at the Freiberg University of Mining and Technology and other partners. The project was implemented within the framework of the cross-border co-operation programme financed by the European Regional Development Fund and the Ministry for Regional Development of the Czech Republic (no. 100283089). The book was published in Czech and German in 2020, immediately after the inscription of the Erzgebirge region on the UNESCO World Heritage List. The expanded English edition of the book is motivated by the desire to introduce this exceptional region to all visitors, tourists and those interested in the history of Central Europe and its cultural heritage who come to this area to learn about the unique mining landscape on the border between the Czech Republic and Saxony, whose character was shaped from the 12th to the 20th century and is characterised by historic mining towns and a large number of preserved monuments.

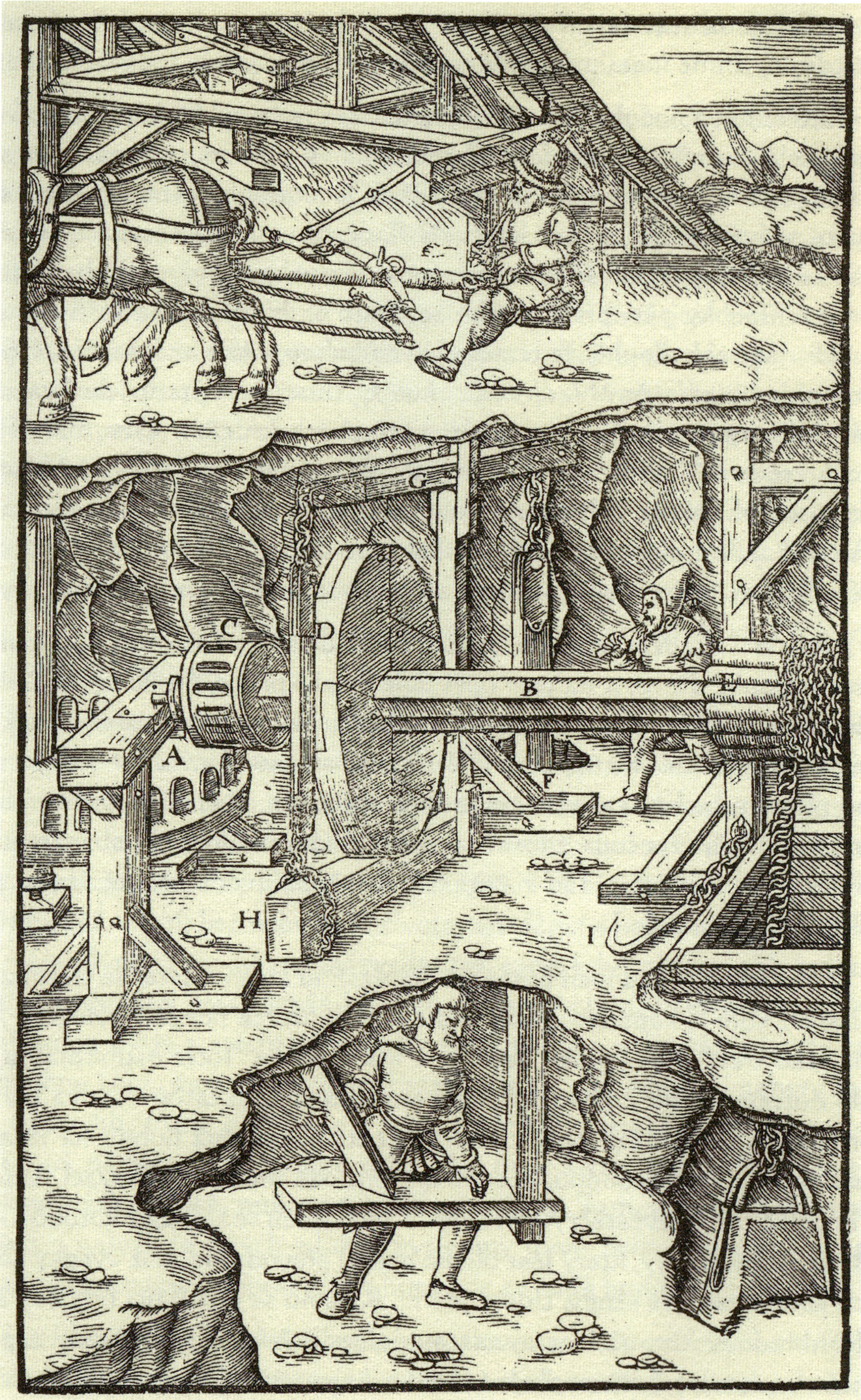

Fig. 2 Graphics from Georgius Agricola's *De re metalica (Twelve Books on Mining and Metallurgy)* showing a horse-driven mining machine for extracting water and ore from shafts. Reproduction from the book by Agricola, G., *Jiřího Agricoly Dvanáct knih o hornictví a hutnictví: Georgii Agricolae De re metallica libri XII*. Ostrava 2001.

ORE MINING IN THE ORE MOUNTAINS AND THE ESTABLISHMENT OF MINING TOWNS

"If God gave his blessing and ore was struck, it was the custom of the old miners to have the Te Deum laudamus sung in honour of God..."
Johannes Mathesius, Bergpostill, Nuremberg 1564[1]

The development of mining was certainly a watershed moment in the economic and cultural development of mediaeval society in the Ore Mountains.[2] Ore also gave these border mountains between Bohemia and Saxony their name. The Germans say *Erzgebirge*, which directly translates to Ore Mountains, while the Czechs say *Krušné hory*, derived from the word *krušec*, meaning a rock containing ore.[3]

People have been processing ore since prehistoric times. Its impact on economic activity, craftwork innovation, social structure, living conditions, and cultural production has been fundamental. Since the mediaeval era, mining had formed the basis of the wealth and power among many royal families. In Central Europe, mining activity was most intensive in the regions of Meissen and Saxony, and later also in the Kingdoms of Hungary and Bohemia, and the Duchy of Austria. One of the most prominent mining centres was Freiberg in Saxony, producing silver, which supported the power ambitions of the House of Wettin. The mining towns in Upper Hungary were also rich in ore deposits. Other mining regions included Transylvania, Cracow and, from the 15th century onwards, Schwaz in Tyrol.[4]

Disregarding the use of the land's ore wealth in prehistoric times, which has been documented by archaeological excavations in some locations of the future Kingdom of Bohemia to have existed since the Bronze Age, the oldest mining centres can be found in the dominion of the Slavník dynasty with its mining township of Kaňk (Gang), located near the later-founded

1) Jan Urban (ed.), *Jan Mathesius, Hornická postila s krátkou jáchymovskou kronikou* (Praha: 1981), 126.

2) Marian Małowist, "Górnictwo w średniowiecznej Europie Środkowej i Wschodniej jako element struktur spoleczno-gospodarczych w XII–XV wieku," *Przegląd Historyczny* 63/4 (1972): 589–604.

3) Michaela Hrubá, "Horní města v Krušnohoří a počátky reformace", in: Jan Klípa – Michaela Ottová (ed.), *Bez hranic. Umění v Krušnohoří mezi gotikou a renesancí* (Praha: 2015), 647–649; Idem., "Historie Krušnohoří mezi středověkem a raným novověkem", in: Michaela Hrubá – Michaela Ottová – Jan Royt, *Ars Montana. Umělecký a kulturní transfer v otevřeném prostoru česko-saského Krušnohoří na prahu raného novověku* (Praha: 2016), 13–45.

4) Jan Klápště, *Proměna českých zemí ve středověku* (Praha: 2005); Josef Žemlička, *Království v pohybu. Kolonizace, města a stříbro v závěru přemyslovské epochy* (Praha: 2014).

town of Kutná Hora. In the 13th century, this mining district became the most important source of silver on which the Přemyslids built their glory and supported their power aspirations. From the beginning of the 13th century, mining settlements were built in the Highlands (Vysočina), where the mining town of Jihlava (Iglau), an important centre of silver mining, was later established. Silver mining has been associated with western Bohemia since the late 12th century, where silver ore gave its name to the town of Stříbro (meaning 'silver'). Gold deposits were actively exploited by the Luxembourgs. Closer to Prague, gold mining in the district of Jílový goes as far back as the Celtic period, where the Přemyslids were later also heavily involved. Gold from this area, apart from being used to craft the Crown of St. Wenceslas, primarily provided revenue to support large construction projects, including Karlštejn castle, the Charles Bridge, and Prague's New Town. Gold was also mined in the Kašperské Mountains (Bergreichstein), and in the Zlaté Mountains (Zuckmantel) within the larger Jeseníky (Gesenke) mountain range.[5]

The greatest share of profit from the mining of precious metals and ores was secured by the monarch on the basis of the right of ownership known as the Bergregal. In the High Middle Ages, the monarch founded most mining towns. These towns were governed by specific laws and enjoyed the special favour and protection of the ruler. At this point, however, extraction and processing of ores was also carried out by some monasteries – for example, Osek (Ossegg) and Sedlec (Sedletz) – and, more rarely, with the monarch's permission, by some noble families.[6]

The exploitation of ore deposits has been documented in the Ore Mountains since the Bronze Age – particularly tin, which, along with copper, was the main ingredient for the production of bronze. Archaeologists assume that the tin deposits near Krupka (Graupen) and Bohosudov (Mariaschein) were already being mined at that time, along with some of the deposits on the Saxon side of the mountains. At the turn of the millennium, iron deposits were probably being used by people living in hill forts in the foothills of the Ore Mountains. The first evidence of tin trading in Bohemia comes from the report of Ibrahim ibn Yaqub, who travelled via Prague to the imperial court in Magdeburg.[7] It is highly probable that this was tin from Ore Mountain deposits.

In the early Middle Ages, silver became a priority in the Ore Mountains. The earliest reports of silver mining date back to the second half of the 12th century in connection with the settlement of the area and the building of roads that traversed the mountain ridge.[8] The

5) Petr Morávek – Jiří Litochleb, *Jílovské zlaté doly* (Jílové u Prahy: 2002); Petr Morávek et al., *Jílovské zlaté doly* (Praha: 2018); Karel Neuberger, *Stříbrský rudní revír od minulosti po současnost* (Stříbro: 2018); Bohumil Toms, "Historické důlní revíry na těžbu zlata a stříbra na Šumavě a v Pošumaví," in: *Zlatá stezka* 16 (2009), 201–232; Wolfgang Schwabenicky, "Mittelalterlicher Silberbergbau in Sachsen: Forschungsstand – Probleme – Fragestellungen," in: *Aufbruch unter Tage. Stand und Aufgaben der montanarchäologischen Forschung in Sachsen, Arbeits- und Forschungsberichte zur sächsischen Bodendenkmalpflege*, Beiheft 22 (Dresden: Landesamt für Archäologie, 2011), 7–36; Petr Hrubý, "Středověká těžba stříbronosných rud ve 13. a 14. století na českém území," in: Kryštof Derner (ed.), *Středověké hornictví a hutnictví na Přísečnicku ve středním Krušnohoří* (Dresden: 2018), 31–37.

6) Kateřina Charvátová, "Hospodářství oseckého kláštera v první polovině 14. století," *Československý časopis historický* 28 (1980), 239–258; Jaroslav Čechura, "Velkostatek kláštera Osek v letech 1310–1419," ČNM 160, No. 1–4 (1991), 20–46; Norbert Krutský, "Hornická činnost kláštera Osek. K historii těžby a zpracování nerostných surovin," in: *800 let kláštera Osek* (Osek: 1996), 314–328.

7) Dušan Třeštík, "Cesta Ibrahima ibn Jakuba do Prahy v roce 966," *Dějiny a současnost* 5 (1992), 9–13.

8) Ladislav Hosák, "Mitellalterlische Straßenverbindungen von Böhmen nach Sachsen und in die Oberlausitz," *Säch-*

Přemyslids were encouraged by the example of the Wettins, who – starting from 1168 – were profiting from mining around Freiberg, which soon became an important mining centre and symbol of wealth. The expensive construction of the local church testifies to that; its remarkable Golden Gate is one of the most noteworthy monuments of early Gothic architecture in the German lands.[9]

In the Bohemian part of the Ore Mountains, metal mining was initiated by the monarch, as well as by the nobility, especially the powerful Hrabischitz family, later known as the Lords of Riesenburg. Mining was also carried out by the local Cistercian monastery in Osek, founded by the Hrabischitz family. The monastery owned extensive estates in the Ore Mountain foothills. The Hrabischitz family also helped develop the Bohemian and Saxon sides of the Ore Mountains. As early as 1302, an agreement between Boresch III of Riesenburg and Gerwicus, Abbot of the Osek monastery, stipulated an equal division of profits from ore mining.[10] Silver was probably mined on the Osek estate as early as the 14th century, and intensive prospecting was carried out simultaneously with developing the area.[11] It is also possible that the granting of town rights to the monastic village of Hrob may have been linked to silver mining.[12] Colonizing activities of the Cistercians also came from the monasteries in Saxony; in particular the Altzelle monastery, involved in the extraction and processing of silver ore. Its mining activities have been associated by German scholars with the beginnings of mining in Freiberg.[13] In addition to silver deposits, there were most likely also iron deposits on the Osek monastery estates.[14] The monastery served as a prominent example of landed elite in northwest Bohe-

sische Heimatblätter 11/1 (1965); Ivan Vávra, "Mostecká cesta," *Historická geografie* 18 (1979): 351–382; Idem., "Osecká cesta – hrobská cesta," *Historická geografie* 20 (1982): 187–201; Tomáš Velímský, "Studium středověkých cest a problematika vývoje osídlení levobřežní části oblasti Labských pískovců," *Archeologica Historica* 17 (1992): 349–364; Eva Černá – Tomáš Velímský, "Výsledky rekognoskace cesty z Mostu do Freibergu," *Archeologica Historica* 15 (1990): 477–487; Idem., "Česko-saské kontakty a problematika středověkých cest přes Krušné Hory a Děčínské stěny," *in:* Kristina Kaiserová (ed.), "Čechy a Sasko v proměnách dějin," *Acta Universitatis Purkynianae. Philosophica et historica. Slavogermanica* 1 (Ústí nad Labem: 1993), 359–372. Most recent: Hauke Kenzler, "Bergbau und Kolonisation. Die Rolle des Montanwesens innerhalb der mittelalterlichen Besiedlungensgeschichte des Erzgebirges/Hornictví a kolonizace. Role hornictví ve středověkém osídlení Krušných hor," in: *Krušná krajina/Erz(gebirgs)landschaft – Ore Landscape* (Archeomontan: 2013, Dresden: 2014), 157–167.

9) Otfried Wagenbreth, "Die bergrechtliche Situation in der Frühzeit des Bergbaus von Freiberg in Sachsen, 1168 bis etwa 1350," in: *Dolování stříbra a mincování v Jihlavě* (Jihlava: 1999), 64–68; Uwe Richter – Wolfgang Schwabenicky, "Der Beginn des Freiberger Bergbaus, die Grenzbeschreibung des Klosters Altzelle und die Entstehung der Stadt Freiberg," in: Ed., *Burg, Straße, Siedlung, Herrschaft: Studien zum Mittelalter in Sachsen und Mitteldeutschland* (Beucha: 2007), 311–330; Yves Hoffmann – Uwe Richter, *Entstehung und Blüte der Stadt Freiberg: die bauliche Entwicklung der Bergstadt vom 12. bis zum Ende des 17. Jahrhunderts* (Halle: 2012).

10) Tomáš Velímský, *Hrabišici páni z Rýzmburka* (Praha: 2002), 154; Josef Emler (ed.), *Regesta diplomatica nec non epistolaria Bohemiae et Moraviae II. (1253–1310)* 1913, 823 (Praha: 1882), available at https://sources.cms.flu.cas.cz.

11) Jan Kořán, Přehledné dějiny *československého hornictví I.* (Praha: 1955), 103; Norbert Krutský, *Hornická činnost kláštera Osek*, 315; Petr Plachý – Michal Soukup – Josef Večeřa, "Stopy středověké těžby v horách nad Osekem, okres Teplice," *Arbeits- und Forschungsberichte zur sächsischen Bodendenkmalpflege* (ArchaeoMontan: 2013), 137–145.

12) Jitka Budinská – Petr Jančárek – Jiří Procházka, *Hrob. Dějiny města* (Teplice: 1982), 10.

13) Karlheins Blaschke, "Altzelle – ein Kloster zwischen Geistlichkeit und Herrschaft," in: Martina Schattowsky – André Thieme, *Altzelle, Zisterzienserabtei in Mitteldeutschland und Hauskloster der Wettiner* (Leipzig: 2002), 92–93; André Thieme, *Kloster Altzelle und die Besiedlung im mittleren Erzgebirgsvorland*, ibid., 101–139; Martina Schattowsky, "Die böhmischen Besitzungen des Zisterzienserklosters Altzella (1162–1540)," in: *Folia historica Bohemica* 6 (1984), 221–234.

14) Petr Meduna, "Archäologische Forschung im Raum des Klosterbesitzes von Ossegg," in: *Cisterciáci ve středověkém*

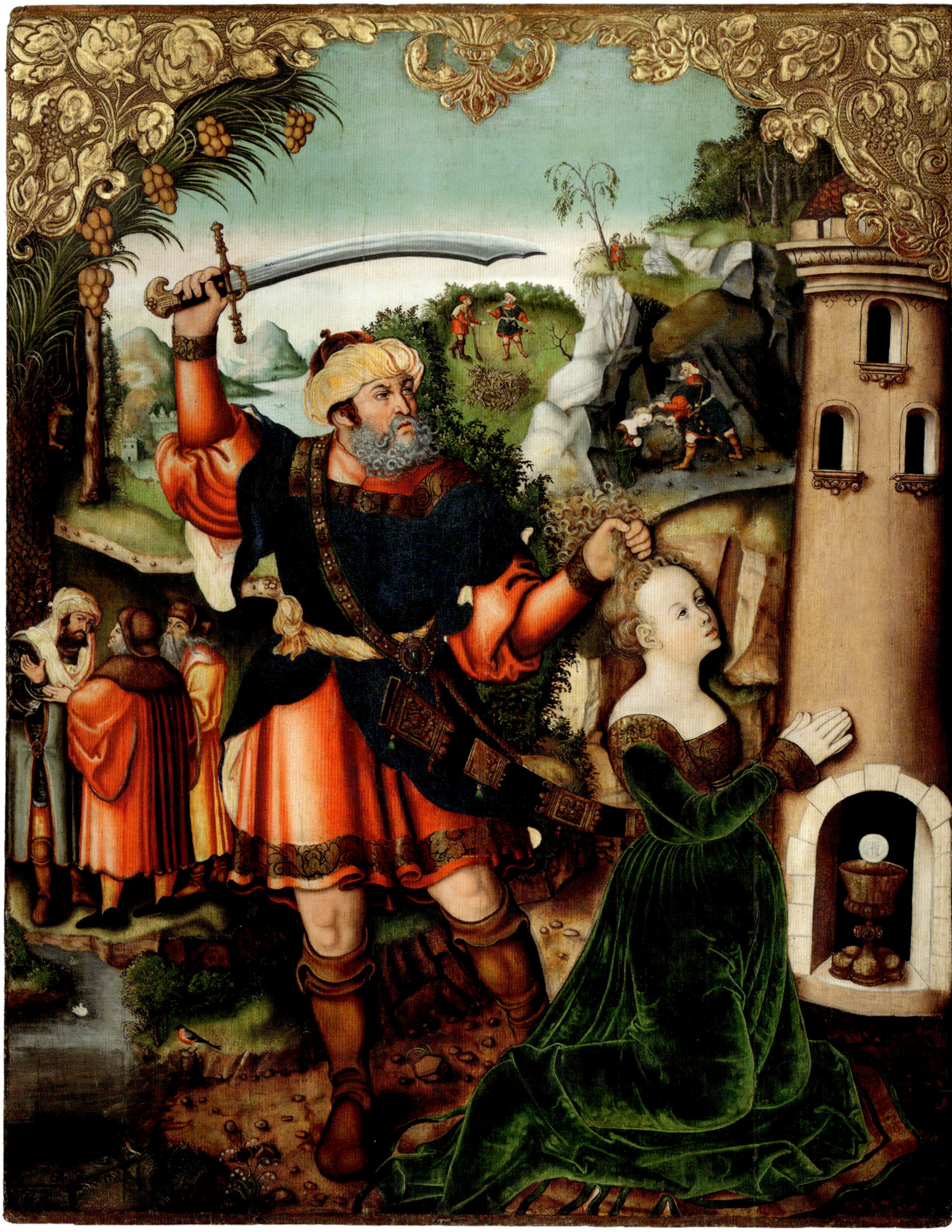

Fig. 3. The central panel with the scene of the Decapitation of St. Barbara on the altar triptych from Osek, Master IW, after 1546. Photo © National Gallery Prague 2022.

mia.[15] It had a functioning farm, and its prospecting and metal mining activities undoubtedly played an important role in its economic affairs.[16]

Execution of St. Barbara, St. Barbara Altarpiece from Osek (Fig. 3)
A triptych altarpiece with the image of the Execution of St. Barbara is related to the donor activities and decoration of the monastic church in Osek. In addition to the works of art, the preserved mining register of the town of Hrob provides direct evidence of the monastery's mining activities. The list of the first mine owners includes the Abbot of Osek, probably Abbot Jacob, who was granted the use of the Tunnel of Corpus Christi in 1547. The triptych is attributed to the Monogrammist IW. National Gallery, after 1546.

During the reign of the last Přemyslid kings, an increasing number of noble families owned estates – like the powerful Riesenburgs – on both sides of the Ore Mountain border. Among them were families originally settled in various parts of the Saxon borderlands, especially the regions of Pleissenland and Vogtland, which were in the Přemyslids' sphere of interest. Newly arriving families thus enjoyed the favour of the Bohemian kings.[17] The most prominent among them were the lords of Plauen, Kolditz, and Schönburg.[18] Cross-border contacts intensified thanks to ties between the noble families.

Throughout the Luxembourg period, the Ore Mountain region received a great deal of attention. The interests of the royal family were, here as elsewhere, at odds with the expansive ambitions of the lordly families. The latter benefited from their extensive land holdings, from the transit-route character of the region, and from the region's mineral wealth. Among the most powerful families were the lords of Riesenburg, who continued to focus their economic activities on ore mining. This is evidenced by a charter from 1354, by which Charles IV granted the brothers Boresch and Slavkov the right to free mining and precious metal mining on their estates for 12 years, on condition that their weekly profits would not exceed 50 threescore of Prague groschen.[19]

českém státě, Les cisterciens dans le royaume médiéval de Boheme, Sborník z kolokvia v Kutné Hoře, Actes du colloque de Kutná Hora, Cîteaux, Commentarii cistercienses 47 (1996), 193–202.

15) Jan Royt, *Gotické deskové malířství v severozápadních a severních Čechách 1340–1550* (Praha: 2015) 183–186; Norbert Krutský, *Hornická činnost kláštera Osek*, 314–316.

16) Kateřina Charvátová, "Hospodářství oseckého kláštera v první polovině 14. století. (The Cistercian abbey of Osek and its economy during the first half of the 14th century)," *Československý časopis historický* 28 (1980), 239–258; Jaroslav Čechura, "Velkostatek kláštera Osek v letech 1310–1419," *ČNM* 160, No. 1–4 (1991), 20–46.

17) Sabine Brunner, "Beziehungen zwischen Böhmen, dem Egerland und dem Vogtland vom Mittelalter bis zur frühen Neuzeit," in: Kristina Kaiserová (ed.), *Čechy a Sasko v proměnách dějin, Acta Universitatis Purkynianae, Philosophica et Historica I., Slavogermanica II.*, (Ústí nad Labem: 1993), 75–88.

18) Kurt Truöl, "Die Herren von Colditz und ihre Herrschaft," in: *Mitteilungen des Geschichts- und Altertumsvereins zu Leisnig*, No. 15 (Leisnig: 1927), 1–136; Walter Schlesinger, *Die Landherrschaft der Herren von Schönburg. Eine Studie zur Geschichte des Staates in Deutschland. Quellen und Studien zur Verfassungsgeschichte des deutschen Reiches in Mittelalter und Neuzeit IX/1* (Münster – Köln: 1954); Lenka Bobková, "Sasko v teritoriální politice českých králů do roku 1459," in: Kristina Kaiserová (ed.), *Čechy a Sasko v proměnách dějin, Acta Universitatis Purkynianae, Philosophica et Historica I., Slavogermanica II.*, (Ústí nad Labem: 1993), 49–67.

19) Kaspar von Sternberg, *Umrisse einer Geschichte der böhmischen Bergwerke, Band 2*, (Prag: 1838), 149; Johann Fridrich Böhmer – Alfons Huber (ed.), *Regesta imperii VIII*, no. 1898, (Innsbruck: 1877), 151.

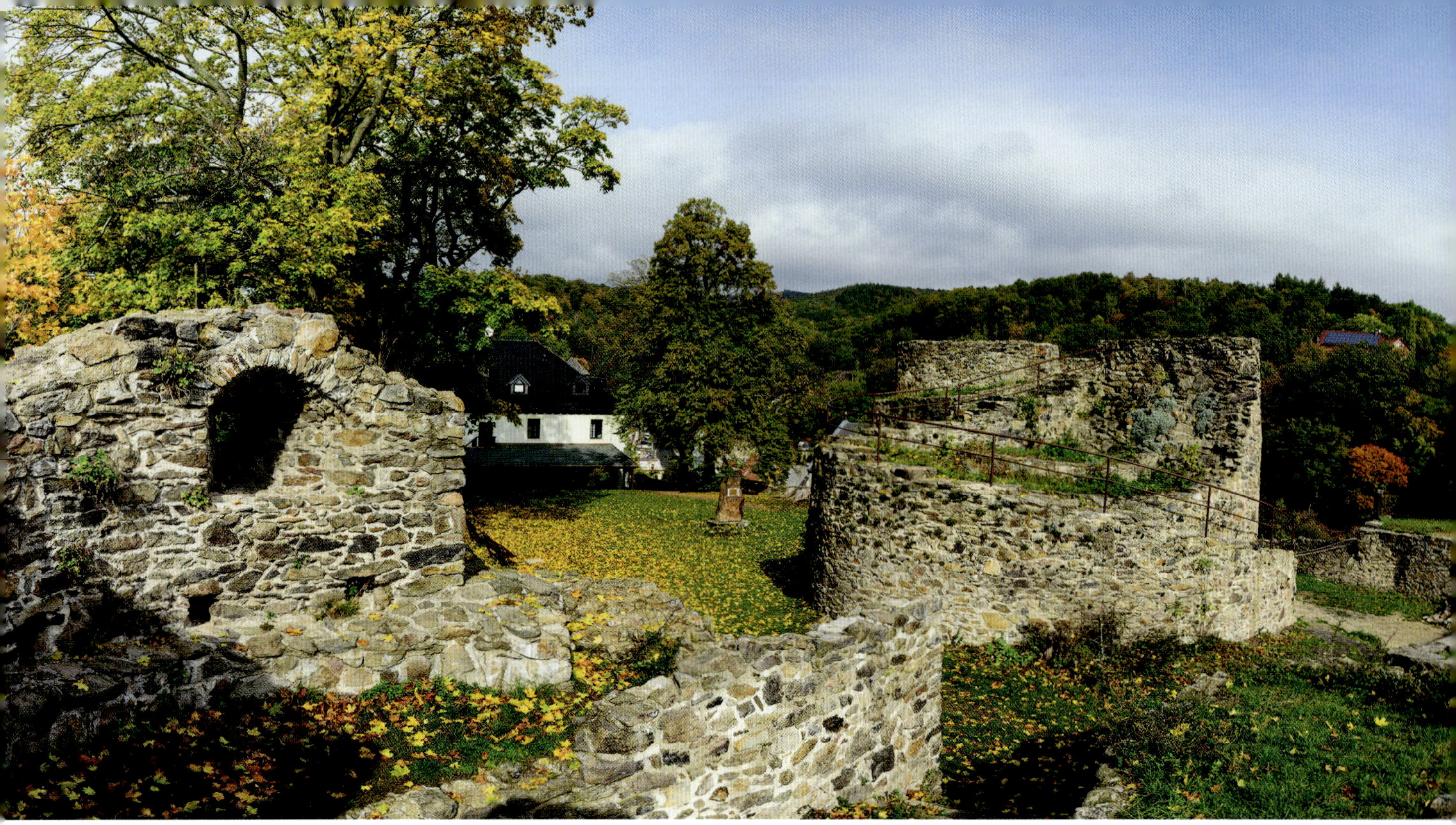

Fig. 4. Gothic castle in Krupka called Rosenberg from the beginning of the 14th century, originally built as a royal guard castle. Photo by J. Peer (2019).

By this time, according to reports from mining sites, ore mining had gradually become a key industry for the Bohemian-Saxon border region. At the very end of the Přemyslid period, sources mention tin mining in Krupka for the first time. (Fig. 4) In 1305, King Wenceslas II granted a tin mine called Krupá to Zvěst of Trmice (Türmitz). The existence of the Miners' Church of St. Prokopius, founded by miners as early as 1204, also testifies to the long tradition of tin panning in this location. The miners came to the Ore Mountain foothills from Jílové and founded the settlement of Kirchlice (Kirchlitz) which disappeared in the 17th century. Tin panning in the area was carried out in the alluvial deposits of the Zalužanský Stream.[20]

Among the oldest iron and silver mining sites is Přísečnice (Preissnitz), located on the old trade route from Bohemia to Saxony. A charter of Charles IV from 1352 lists Přísečnice as a mining town with a customs house, but the first mention of the town dates back to 1335.[21] After the mid-14th century, copper mining began under the royal castle that protected the road from Loket to the empire. That activity spurred on the establishment of the town of Kraslice (Graslitz), granted city rights by Charles IV in 1370. As early as 1340, the town of Nejdek (Neudek) is mentioned for the first time, where a tin mining site was established. Nejdek became a mining town in 1410. Mining is also mentioned in the first references to other locations that later became mining towns or cities. For example, silver and lead mining was report-

20) Ludomír Kocourek – Květoslava Kocourková – Karel Vilím – Jindřich Körschner, *Krupka z cínu zrozená* (Teplice: 2005); Táňa Šimková, *Stavebně-historické zaměření kostela sv. Prokopa v Krupce* (Ústí nad Labem: 2012), manuscript.
21) Zdena Binterová, *Přísečnice zatopená, ale nezapomenutá* (Chomutov: 2004); Zdena Binterová, *Zaniklé obce Chomutovska V., Přísečnicko* (Chomutov: 1996), 15.

ed near Jindřichovice (Heinrichsgrün) as early as 1314.[22] Mining at this time was probably not large-scale and had little economic impact. Some sites even disappeared during the Hussite wars, to be settled again from the Saxon side at a time when the area was under the influence of the Wettins. The Wettins' ambition to expand across the border was already in full force during the reign of Wenceslas IV. In 1397 they were granted the important royal towns of Most (Brüx) and Louny (Laun).[23] Two years later (1398) they widened their influence when Boreš (IX.) of Riesenburg needed to pay off his debts and sold the Riesenburg castle and the town of Duchcov, along with 25 manors and other property, to William I, Margrave of Meissen. The transaction took place without the permission of King Wenceslas IV, who called into question the status of the sale.[24]

The mining of precious and non-ferrous metals, as well as iron ore, had a tradition in the Ore Mountains starting from the 14th century, probably interrupted in most areas by the Hussite wars. The Hussite army, led by Žižka, reportedly destroyed a large mining settlement near Přísečnice and plundered other mining settlements.[25] Experts on the history of mining in the mediaeval period, however, speak of a general crisis of mining, which in the second half of the 14th century also affected mining centres outside of Bohemia. The crisis has been attributed to an extended period of cold climate or obsolete technology.[26] Although sources are scarce, we know that mining in the Ore Mountains was probably resumed around the mid-15th century.

St. Wenceslas Chapel at Prague Castle, detail of decoration (Fig. 5)
Since the Middle Ages, the Ore Mountains have also been mined for precious stones, primarily minerals such as amethyst, agate and jasper. Rich deposits were found in the vicinity of Ciboušov (Zibich) near Klášterec nad Ohří (Klösterle an der Eger). Amethysts and jaspers from this area were used to decorate the St. Wenceslas Chapel of St. Vitus Cathedral at Prague Castle between 1372 and 1373, and Emperor Charles IV also had them placed in the chapels of Karlštejn and Tangermünde castles.

New mines were opened during the second half of the 15th century in Měděnec (Kupferberg), which eventually became the centre of copper and iron mining. Intensive prospecting also began near Krupka (Graupen). Dozens of new mines were opened in the area between Krupka (Graupen), Cínovec (Böhmisch Zinnwald) and Telnice (Tellnitz), and ore processing and smelting plants were set up in the Mohelnice (Müglitz) River valley. Most likely, these were

22) Václav Kotěšovec, *Pohledy do historie měst a obcí Kraslicka: Bublava, Jindřichovice, Kraslice, Oloví, Přebuz, Rotava, Stříbrná, Šindelová, Dolní Nivy* (Praha: 2011).
23) Lenka Bobková "Územní politika prvních Lucemburků na českém trůně," *Acta univerzitatis Purkynianae, Philosophica et Historica I. Studia Historica I.* (Ústí nad Labem: 1993), 101.
24) Hans Beschoner, *Die Herrschaft Riesenburg und ihre Besitzer bis zum Übergang in wettinischen Besitz im Jahre 1398, Forschungen zur Geschichte Sachsens und Böhmens* (1937), 92–128; Tomáš Velímský, *Hrabišicové, páni z Rýzmburka* (Praha: 2002), 205; CDS I B 2, No. 153, 92–93 (electronically available at http://codex.isgv.de/).
25) Bořivoj Lůžek, *Po stopách husitství v Ústeckém kraji* (Ústí nad Labem: 1959).
26) Petr Hrubý, "Středověká těžba stříbronosných rud ve 13. a 14. století na českém území," in: Kryštof Derner (ed.), *Středověké hornictví a hutnictví na Přísečnicku ve středním Krušnohoří* (Dresden: 2018), 31–37; Jiří Majer, *Rudné hornictví v Čechách, na Moravě a ve Slezsku* (Praha: 2004), 64–66.

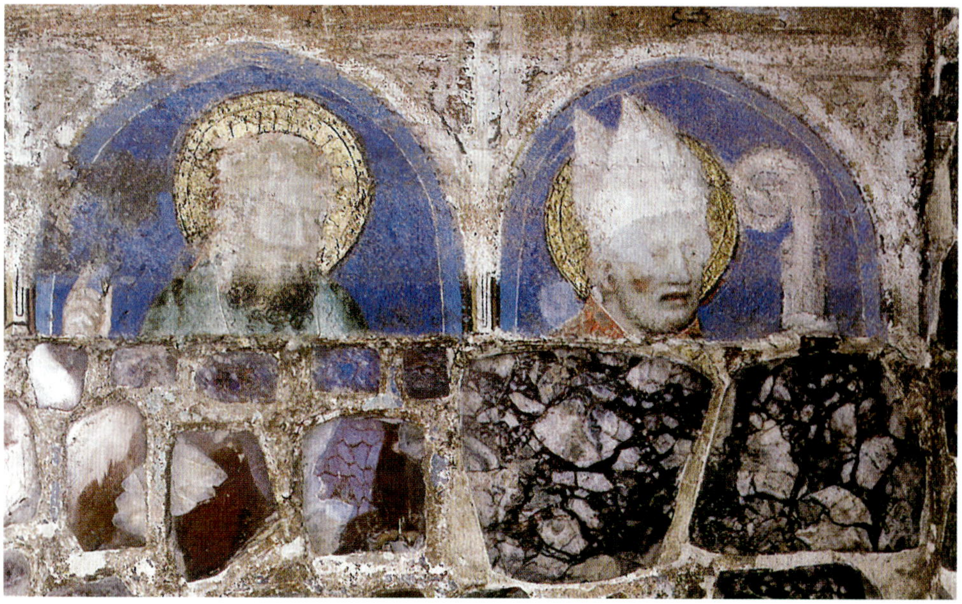

Fig. 5 Chapel of St. Wenceslas at Prague Castle, detail of decoration, 1372–1373. Photograph by J. Royt (2019).

not newly-discovered deposits but rather previously-established sites, where mining was resumed after the troubled Hussite times when the demand for precious and non-ferrous metals resumed. The fast-developing Krupka, a town which was quickly growing rich, was promoted to a mining town in 1487. Local miners also had shares in mines in Altenberg, Geising, and other places in Saxony. The construction and renovation of the Church of the Assumption of the Virgin Mary and the Hospital Church of the Holy Spirit near the city walls, built in a style indicating the end of the 14th century, was a reflection of the town's representation.

The new owners of the local estates, often the *nouveaux riches* who had made their fortunes during the Hussite wars, plunged into the mining business and often made large profits from it while the monarchy was unstable. Among them were the Lobkowitzes, whose star quickly began to rise following the Hussite wars. In 1459, King George of Poděbrady granted Nicholas of Lobkowitz and his son the Bergrecht (the privilege of free mining) for the gold and silver mines within a three-mile radius of their castle of Hasištejn (Hassenstein). This privilege revived intensive mining activity, especially in the mines around the town of Přísečnice. In 1473, the right was extended to the brothers, Johann and Jaroslav Lobkowitz von Hasištejn (Hassenstein), and the three brothers were able to exercise it for the rest of their lives, in keeping with the customs of the mintmaster of Kutná Hora and the local miners.[27] (Fig. 6)

The House of Schlick (Šlik) also began to assert its position in the area at this time. They had earned a considerable fortune and the imperial title of count for their services at the court of Sigismund of Luxembourg. Mates Schlick, the brother of the Emperor's Chancellor Kašpar, who had managed to consolidate the family's assets, was not yet involved in mining; but on his land, especially on the Schöneck estate in Saxony, he had become active in the timber business, and timber was a strategic raw material for mining. (Fig. 7) The Schöneck estate was a point of dispute between the Schlick family and the Saxon Elector Johann Friedrich of

27) Jaroslav Bílek – Ladislav Jangl – Jan Urban, *Dějiny dolování na Chomutovsku* (Chomutov: 1976), 26; Listina z 12. března 1473, original: NA, České gubernium – guberniální listiny, No. 289.

Fig. 6 Tombstone of Jan Hasištejnský of Lobkovice. Ulrich Creutz, around 1516, monastery church of the Fourteen Holy Helpers in Kadaň. Photo © National Heritage Institute.

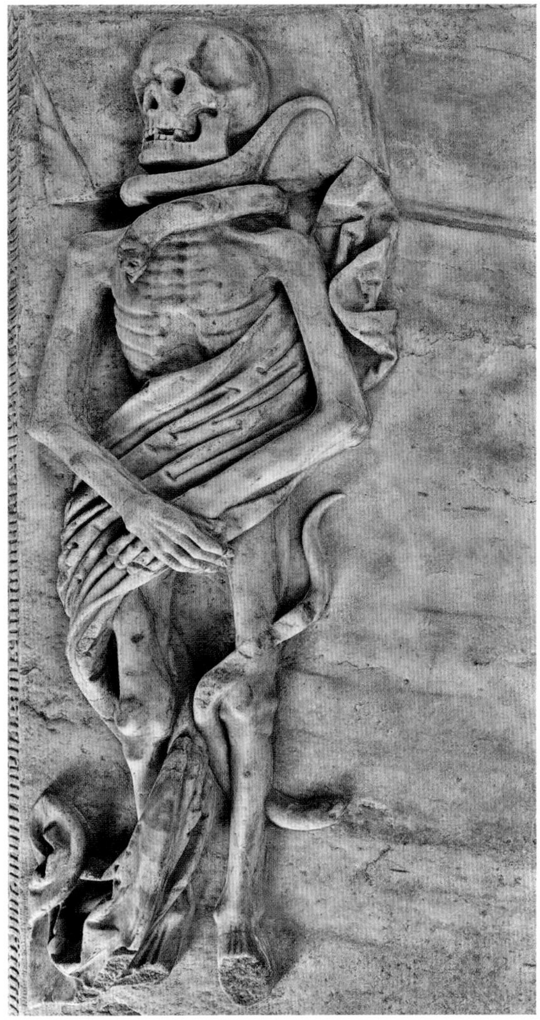

the Ernestine branch of the House of Wettin, who saw the region as having key importance for the burgeoning mining industry in the Ore Mountains.[28] First, the Schlick family probably reopened the older mines in Nejdek (Neudek), but a major breakthrough in their involvement in mining came in the early 16th century, when silver ore was struck near Konradsgrün, later renamed Údolí (Tal), or Údolí sv. Jáchyma (Sankt Joachimsthal). Prospecting began in the area around 1510 and mining was launched around 1512. The business activities of the local nobility went hand in hand with the influx of foreign capital, which was tied to the imperial cities of Nuremberg, Augsburg, and Leipzig in Saxony.[29] The growing interest in mining and intensive prospecting inflamed disputes over the course of the border between Bohemia and Saxony. As in other border areas, the border line had not yet been properly demarcated, and consisted only of a large strip of forest. It was there that disputes over so-called forest mining occurred.

In the first decade of the 16th century, a conflict erupted between the Bohemian king and the Saxon Elector, Johann Friedrich, over the newly-established mining sites of Horní Blatná

28) Michal Novotný, "Šlikové. Majetková struktura panství a společenské postavení rodu do roku 1487" (diploma thesis, Charles University, 2007), 135–137.
29) Josef Janáček, "Die Fugger und Joachimstal," *Historica* 6 (1963): 109–144.

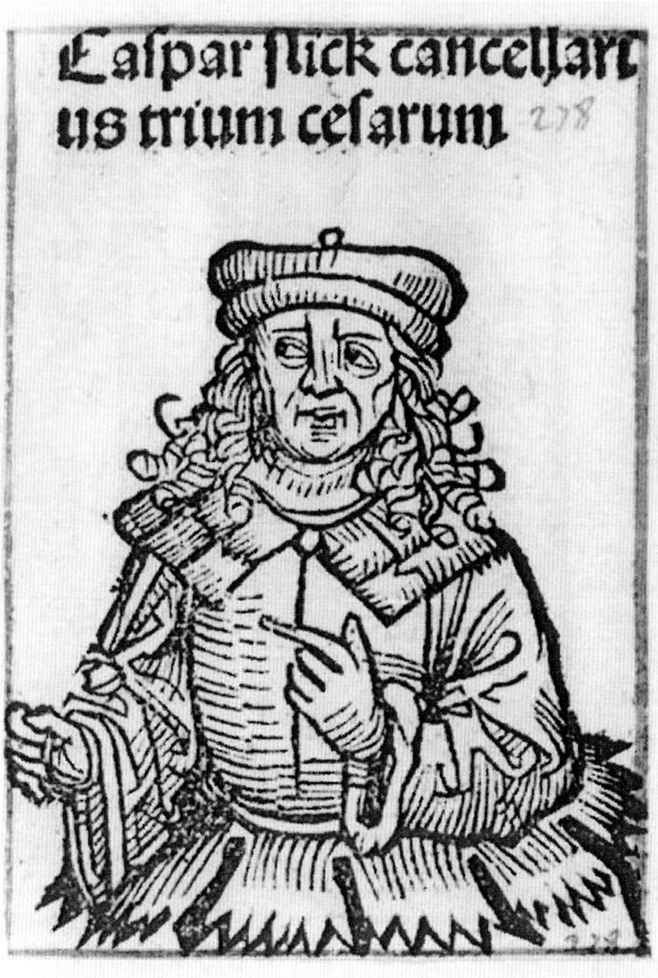

Fig. 7 Kaspar Schlick. Depiction in Schedel's Nuremberg Chronicle (Schedelsche Weltchronik) from 1493. Reproduction © Münchener Staatsbibliothek – Digitale Bibliothek.

(Bergstadt Platten, 1532), Boží Dar (Gottesgab), and Bludná (Irrgang, 1533). (Fig. 8) In the end, after the defeat of the Saxon Elector in the Schmalkaldic War, these areas came under the sovereignty of the Bohemian king and were promoted to free mining towns after 1547.[30]

The border forest was guarded more and more tightly, for reasons to do both with the prospecting activities as well as the revenue generated by tolls and customs tax on goods and raw materials, which were transported abundantly over the Ore Mountain ridge as a result of the flourishing economic activity in the region. King Vladislaus of Bohemia banned the export of unprocessed ore beyond the national border, as a concession to the Krupka (Graupen) miners, who had unfavourable conditions for processing ore on site due to insufficient water supplies. The king eventually permitted this method of ore processing in 1499, but imposed a toll on the transportation of ore. Systematic import and export checks were not introduced until the reign of Ferdinand I, when an organised network of customs offices was set up.[31] By this time, however, the prosperous Ore Mountain region was on its way to becoming econom-

30) Walter Schlesinger, "Entstehung und Bedeutung der sächsisch-böhmischen Grenze," *Neues Archiv für Sachsiche Geschichte 59 (1938), 6–39.*

31) Marie Buňatová, *Pražští kupci na cestách* (Praha: 2013), 93; Josef Jireček, "Celnictví české za 16. věku," *Časopis muzea Království českého* 41, no. 1 (1867), 3–32.

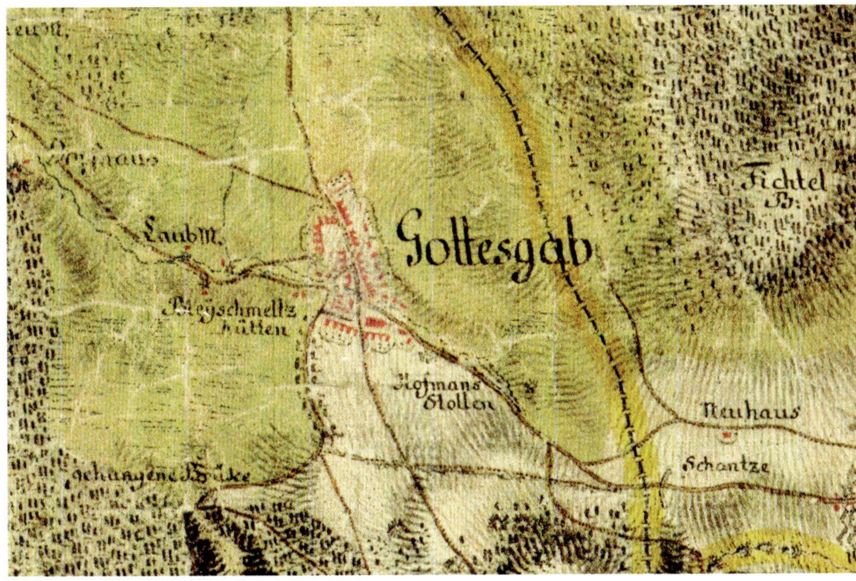

Fig. 8 Detail from the 1st military mapping showing the mining town of Boží Dar/Gottesgab. Reproduction © Geolab FŽP UJEP.

ically coherent and not significantly limited by the border, despite efforts to make the latter a profitable source of royal income.[32]

The fact that the mining industry was alrealy bourgeoning on the Bohemian side of the border in the second half of the 15th century, even if not quite apace with the Saxon side, is evidenced by the first codified mining laws. The oldest ones, originating from Krupka (Graupen, 1464) and Nejdek (Neudek, 1494), serve as evidence that mining at that time was still fully under the legal influence of the local Kutná Hora law. It was only later that legal practices from neighbouring Saxony took hold.[33]

Through the end of the 15th century, the mining industry in the Bohemian part of the Ore Mountains underwent no major development. Mining mostly took place in older locations. No new large deposits were discovered, and few new mining sites were created. A turning point came with the discovery of silver lodes near Konradsgrün on the Schlick estate. This find caused a large influx of miners and specialists from the Saxon mining centres of Freiberg, Annaberg, Marienberg and Schneeberg. A new mining settlement was built, which had over 400 houses soon after its foundation in 1516. In 1520, the settlement was promoted to the free mining town of Jáchymov (Sankt Joachimsthal).[34] (Fig. 9)

The discovery of a massive lode of silver ore in Jáchymov unleashed what could only be described as "The Ore Mountains silver rush". Other mining sites, which from a legal point of view could be described as mining towns, began cropping up or growing very quickly. These included Měděnec/Kupferberg (1520, owned by the Lords of Vitzthum), Oloví/Blei-

32) Josef Janáček, *České dějiny. Doba předbělohorská (1526–1547) I/1* (Praha: 1968), 114.

33) Hermann Hallwich, *Geschichte der Bergstadt Graupen in Böhmen* (Prag: 1868), 21; Petr Jančárek, *Města českého Krušnohoří v předbělohorské době. Příspěvek ke studiu jejich sociální struktury* (Ústí nad Labem: 1971), 39–40; Michaela Hrubá, "Tradice horního práva v českých zemích a právní rámec těžby v Krušných Horách," in: Michaela Hrubá – Michaela Ottová – Jan Royt, *Ars Montana. Umělecký a kulturní transfer v otevřeném prostoru česko-saského Krušnohoří na prahu raného novověku* (Praha: 2016), 47–52.

34) Pavel Kašpar, "Šlikové a počátky dolování stříbra v Jáchymově," *Bulletin mineralogicko-petrologického oddělení Národního muzea v Praze 12* (2004), 22–24; Andrea Huczmanová, "Začátky dolování v Jáchymově, založení města a mincovní práva Šliků ve světle politických jednání a písemných pramenů," *Herditas minariorum* 3 (2016), 9–24.

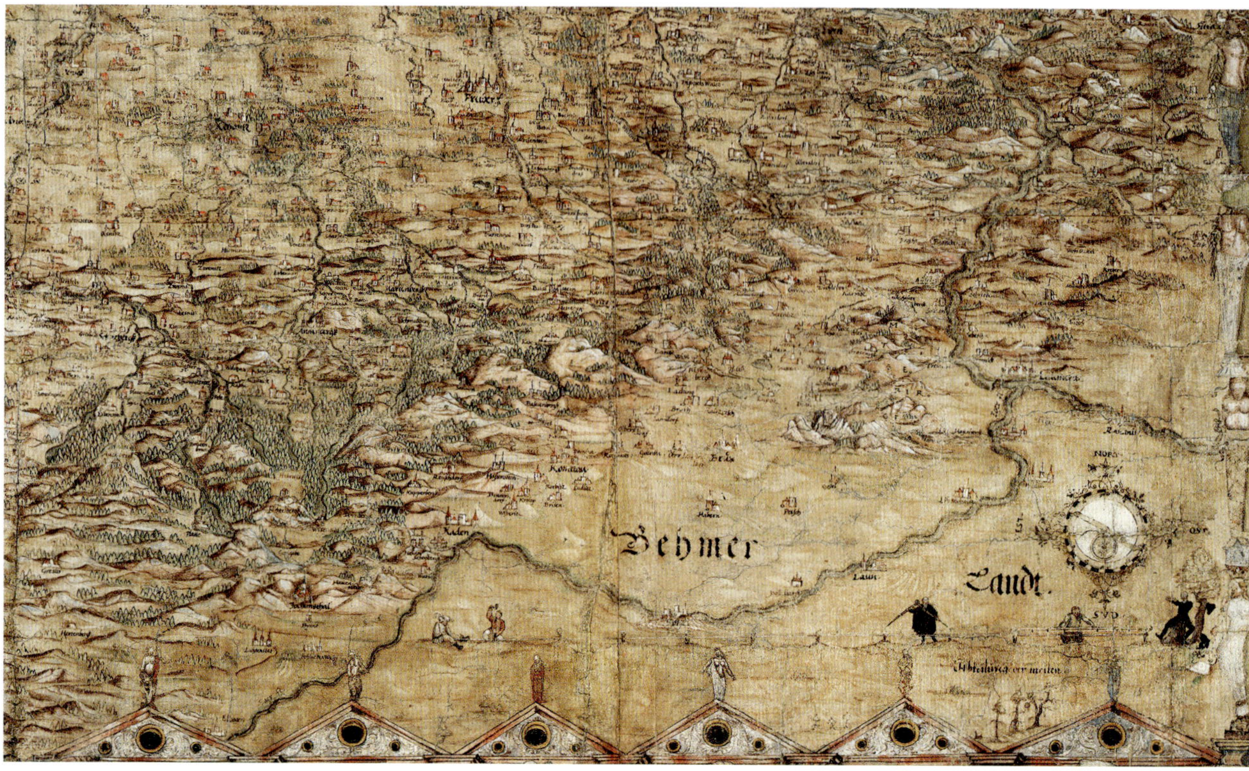

Fig. 9 Map of Thuringia and Meissen with the provincial boundary. Hiobus Magdeburgus, 1566. Reproduction © SLUB Dresden.

stadt (1523, Counts of Schlick), Loučná/Böhmisch Wiesenthal (1527, Counts of Schlick), Hora sv. Kateřiny/Katharinaberg (1528, Lords of Veitmile/Weitmühl), Hora sv. Šebestiána/ Sebastiansberg (1529, Lords of Veitmile/Weitmühl), Abertamy/Abertham (1529, Counts of Schlick), Vejprty/Weipert (1532, Lobkovic/Lobkowitz), Pernink/Bärringen (1532, Counts of Schlick) and, after the land border hed been fixed on the Saxon side, Boží Dar/Gottesgab (1533, Saxon Elector) and Horní Blatná/Bergstadt Platten (1532), which only came under the sovereignty of the Czech king in 1547. Other mining sites acquired the attributes of towns after the mid-16th century, and included: Přebus/Frühbuss (1553, Schlick), Mikulov/Niklasberg (1554, Lobkowitz), Výsluní/Sonnenberg (1562, Lobkowitz), Hora sv. Šebestiána/Sebastiansberg (1563, Lords of Veitmile/Weitmühl) and Místo/Platz (1572, Lobkovic/Lobkowitz).

The rapid urbanization of the Ore Mountains reached its peak in the 1620s and 30s. The network of mining towns and settlements essentially followed the earlier development on the Saxon side of the border. As a result, there were more than twenty mining towns or settlements in the Ore Mountain mining area by the middle of the 16th century, and in terms of urbanisation, the region had no equal in the Kingdom of Bohemia and beyond. The noble families involved in setting up the mining sites usually owned large estates in the foothills. The Schlicks settled in Ostrov nad Ohří (Schlackenwerth) and Loket (Elbogen), the Lords of Weitmühl owned Chomutov (Komotau), the Lobkowitz family owned Kadaň (Kaaden) and later Bílina (Bilin), and the Pflugs of Rabenstein owned a residence in Bečov (Petschau). Their estates grew richer and their mansions slowly acquired a Renaissance look. The monarchs, both

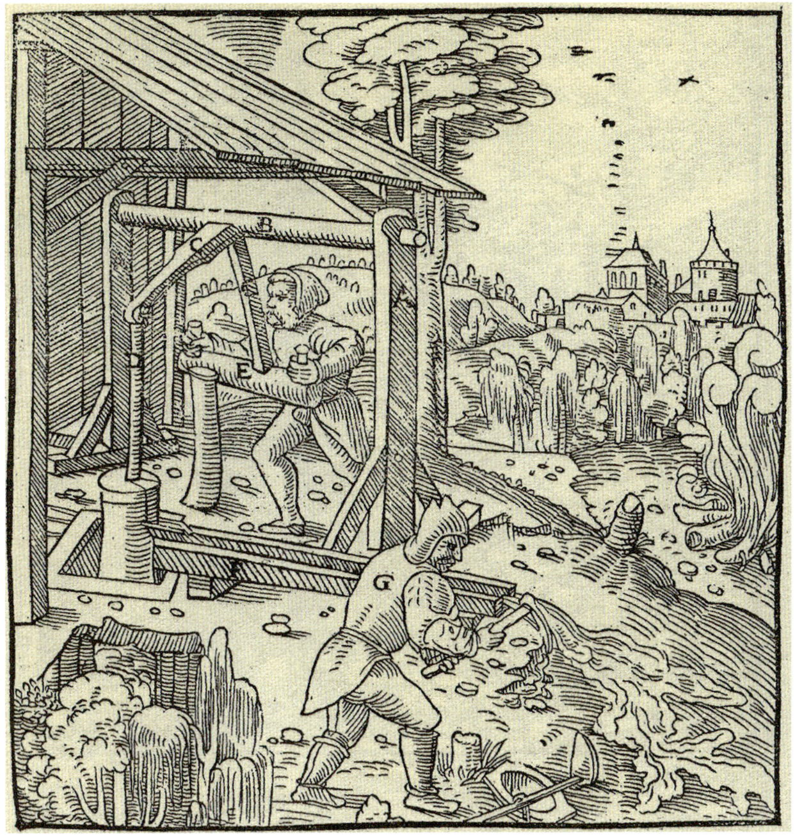

Fig. 10 Graphics from Georgius Agricola's *De re metalica (Twelve Books on Mining and Metallurgy)* showing water being pumped from the mines with the city skyline in the background. Reproduction from Agricola, G., *Jiřího Agricoly Dvanáct knih o hornictví a hutnictví: Georgii Agricolae De re metallica libri XII*. Ostrava 2001.

of the Jagiellonian and later the Habsburg dynasties, were also interested in the development of mining as it brought them large profits.[35] (Fig. 10)

Mining towns were also built in the highest elevations of the Ore Mountains. They either developed spontaneously, as in the case of the rapidly growing Jáchymov, or they were constructed on a regular ground plan with a large rectangular square and a network of streets, following the example of older Saxon towns. To this day, one can admire the generous design of towns such as Boží Dar, Horní Blatná, Hora sv. Šebestiána, and Výsluní. Life in the mountains was not easy. The harsh climate was not favourable for any agricultural production, and at first, virtually all resources had to be imported from inland, which naturally affected their price, including the price of food products. The lords in power who invested in mining needed to bring in miners, as well as various specialists and craftsmen, without whom the towns could not function; they therefore granted a number of rights and privileges to the newly-established settlements. But from the start, mining towns had a specific socio-economic makeup that lacked the diversified structure of crafts that was standard in other towns, and their inhabitants largely depended on the import of products from the Lower Ore Mountains. Even ore processing was dependent on the import of raw materials and special products. The Ore Mountains became a very large area of consumption. In addition to mine owners, mining entrepreneurs and miners, the merchants and the craftsmen from the towns under the Ore Mountains also

35) Jan Kořán, *Přehledné dějiny československého hornictví* (Praha: 1955), 79; Pavel Trnka, "Finanční situace českého krále Vladislava Jagellonského v letech 1471–1490" (diploma thesis, Charles University, 2008), 58–68.

expanded their wealth, as their towns formed the broader base for the mining activity in the mountains. Most (Brüx) was such a town on the Bohemian side, while on the Saxon side there was Chemnitz. The agriculatural base extended to the Eger and Elbe valleys, from whence local traders supplied the towns in the Ore Mountains and also transported grain and malt to Saxony across the mountain passes.[36]

What can we say in summary about the development of the mining towns and settlements in the Bohemian part of the Ore Mountains? The earliest mining towns dedicated to the extraction of silver and related precious metals such as copper and tin, first began to emerge in the eastern part of the mountains, where the lower altitude ensured easier access to ore deposits in the passes and deep-cut valleys. Despite significant spatial constraints, these locations allowed for the building of technical infrastructure, burgher houses and public buildings. At the same time, they were often strategic passage points for long-distance roads and trade routes, which also played an important role in provincial politics and were therefore closely watched over by fortified castles. (Fig. 11)

However, prospecting activity was not significant, in contrast to the Saxon side, where silver mining boomed as early as the second half of the 12th century. Therefore, only a handful of mining towns were founded on the Bohemian side before 1450, of which only Krupka was of any significance. Apart from Krupka, mining activity as a primary reason for building an urban agglomeration can only be demonstrably documented at Nejdek and Jindřichovice. With other towns and villages founded during the 13th and 14th centuries, the influence of mining activities on their formation is either questionable, as in the case of Hrob (Klostergrab) and Krajková (Gossengrün), or it can be completely ruled out, as in Luby (Schönbach), Hroznětín (Lichtenstadt), Kraslice (Graslitz) and Přísečnice (Preßnitz). In the 14th century, the stunted urban development that occurred in the entire Ore Mountains region may have been due to the more general crisis of mining, which widely affected the already established mining towns in the Kingdom of Bohemia.[37] More favorable conditions for the founding of mining towns only came with the universal mining boom in the Ore Mountains, which began in 1450. Still, only a handful of new towns were founded there between 1450 and 1515.

The heyday of mining town expansion in the eastern and chiefly the western part of the Ore Mountains, which brought settlement to the higher, less accessible mountain areas, occurred mainly in the 16th century, with the Schlick-owned Jáchymov in the vanguard. Its foundation in 1516 was followed in quick succession by the development of Oloví (Bleistadt), Měděnec (Kupferberg), Loučná (Böhmisch Wiedenthal), Hora Svaté Kateřiny (Katharinaberg), Abertamy (Abertham), Vejprty (Weipert), and Pernink (Bärringen), and the towns of Horní Blatná (Bergstadt Platten) and Boží Dar (Gottesgab), both of which lay in Saxon territory at the time, and only became part of Bohemia after the border change of 1547. Moreover, the establishment of new mining localities was accompanied by massive colonisation and migration to the Ore Mountains from the neighbouring Saxony, particularly strong during the Jagiello-

36) Jančárek, *Města českého Krušnohoří v předbělohorské době*, 16.

37) Michaela Hrubá, "Historie Krušnohoří," in: Michaela Hrubá – Michaela Ottová – Jan Royt, *Ars Montana. Umělecký a kulturní transfer v otevřeném prostoru česko-saského Krušnohoří na prahu raného novověku* (Praha: 2016), 41.

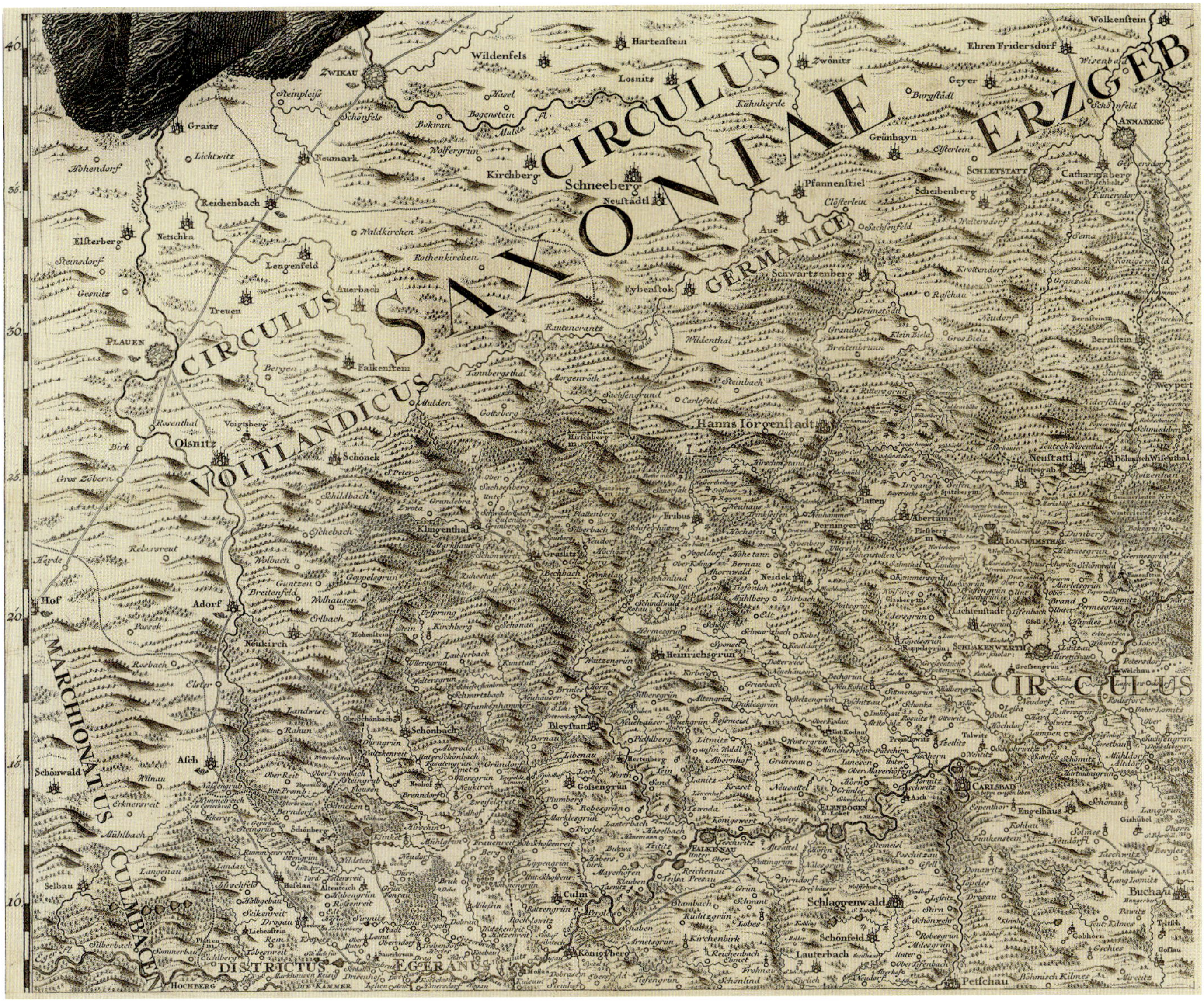

Fig. 11 Müller's map of Bohemia from 1720. Reproduction © HU AV ČR.

nian period. Mining activity played a crucial role in these migratory movements, as the newly arriving experts from Saxony made up for the shortage of mining experts from the inland Bohemia. The importance of attracting mining workers and experts from Saxony is particularly highlighted by the fact that their presence and settlement near the existing mining villages could result in the promotion of the site to a mining town. This is exactly how Oloví (Bleistadt) was granted town privileges by Stephan Schlick in 1523.

Settlement activity continued unabated through the second half of the 16th century, when Přebuz (Frühbuss), Mikulov (Niklasberg), Kovářská (Schmiedeberg), Hora Svatého Šebestiána (Sebastiansberg), Výsluní (Sonnenberg) and Místo (Platz) were established. Thus, a relatively dense primary network of mining towns was completed. The dynamic urban activity began to wane dramatically after 1550, when rare ore reserves in some areas of the Ore Mountains were depleted and the mining industry went into decline.

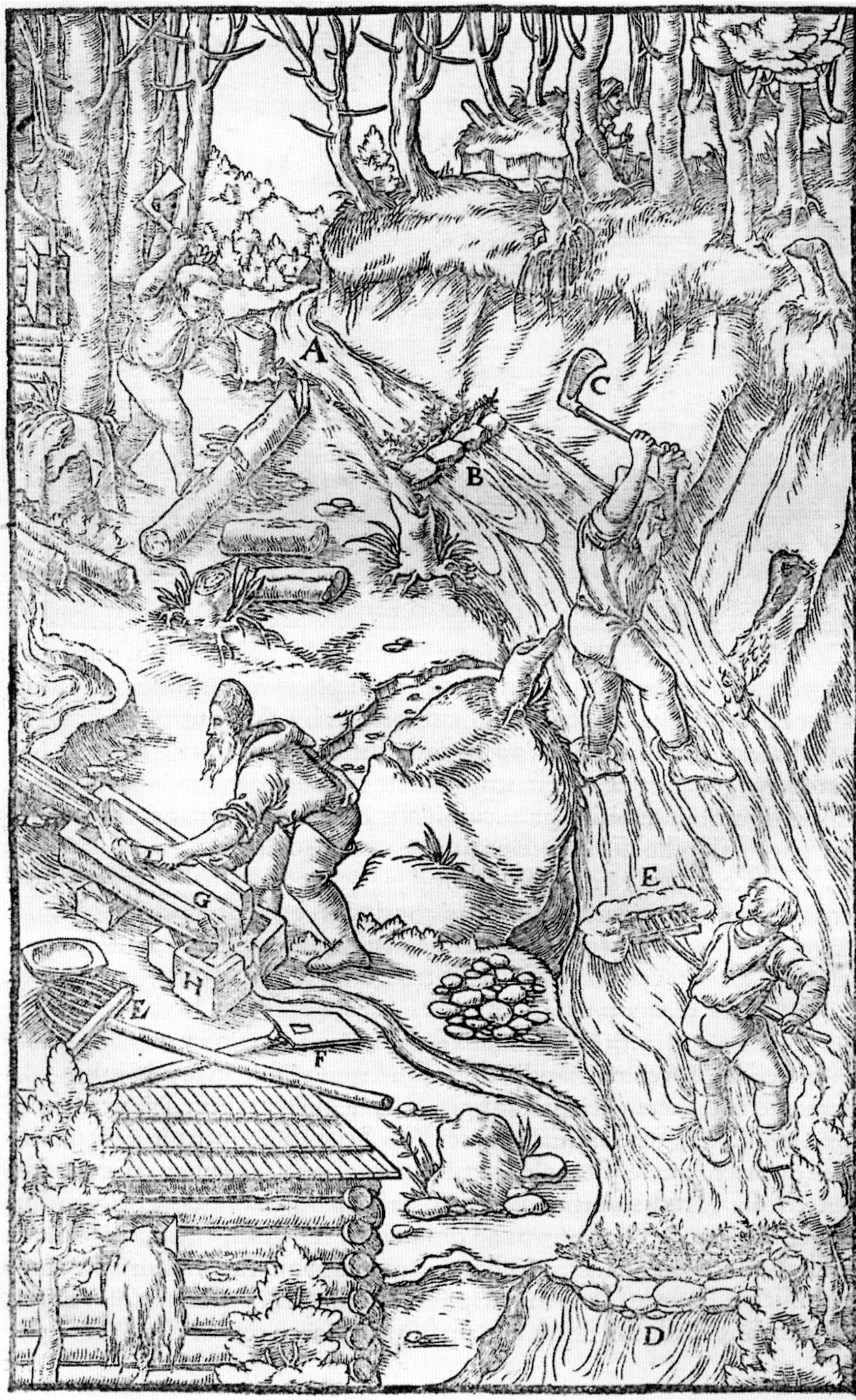

Fig. 12 Graphics from Georgius Agricola's *De re metalica (Twelve Books on Mining and Metallurgy)* showing the washing of tin ore on a stream. Reproduction from Agricola, G., *Jiřího Agricoly Dvanáct knih o hornictví a hutnictví: Georgii Agricolae De re metallica libri XII*. Ostrava 2001.

THE MINING PROFESSION AND MINING LAW

In the Middle Ages in particular, mining was undoubtedly one of the most prestigious and technically and technologically complex pursuits. It had the best legislative backing but was also the most dangerous, and as such required divine protection. High demands were made on the miners' expertise, as Georgius Agricola aptly described in the introduction to his book *De re metallica libri XII* (Twelve Books on Mining and Metallurgy), which was published in Basel in 1556: "*Furthermore, there are many arts and sciences of which a miner should not be ignorant. First there is Philosophy, that he may discern the origin, cause, and nature of subterranean things; for then he will be able to dig out the veins easily and advantageously, and obtain more abundant results from his mining. Secondly, there is Medicine, that he may be able to look after his diggers and other workmen, that they do not meet with those [Pg 4]diseases to which they are more liable than workmen in other occupations, or if they do meet with them, that he himself may be able to heal them or may see that the doctors do so. Thirdly follows Astronomy, that he may know the divisions of the heavens and from them judge the direction of the veins. Fourthly, there is the science of Surveying, that he may be able to estimate how deep a shaft should be sunk to reach the tunnel which is being driven to it, and to determine the limits and boundaries in these workings, especially in depth. Fifthly, his knowledge of Arithmetical Science should be such that he may calculate the cost to be incurred on the machinery and the working of the mine. Sixthly, his learning must comprise Architecture, that he himself may construct the various machines and timber work required underground, or that he may be able to explain the method of the construction to others. Next, he must have knowledge of Drawing, that he can draw plans of his machinery. Lastly, there is the Law, especially that dealing with metals, that he may claim his own rights, that he may undertake the duty of giving others his opinion on legal matters, that he may not take another man's property and so make trouble for himself, and that he may fulfil his obligations to others according to the law.*"[38] Given the technological complexity of ore mining and processing, mining towns needed comprehensively educated people and began opening town schools with well-stocked libraries, the

38) Bohuslav Ježek – Josef Hummel (ed.), *Jiřího Agricoly dvanáct knih o hornictví a hutnictví* (Ostrava: 2001), 45–46; *De Re Metallica*, translated from the first Latin edition of 1556 by Herbert Clark Hoover and Lou Henry Hoover (New York: Dover Publications, 1950). Available online at: Project Guttenberg.

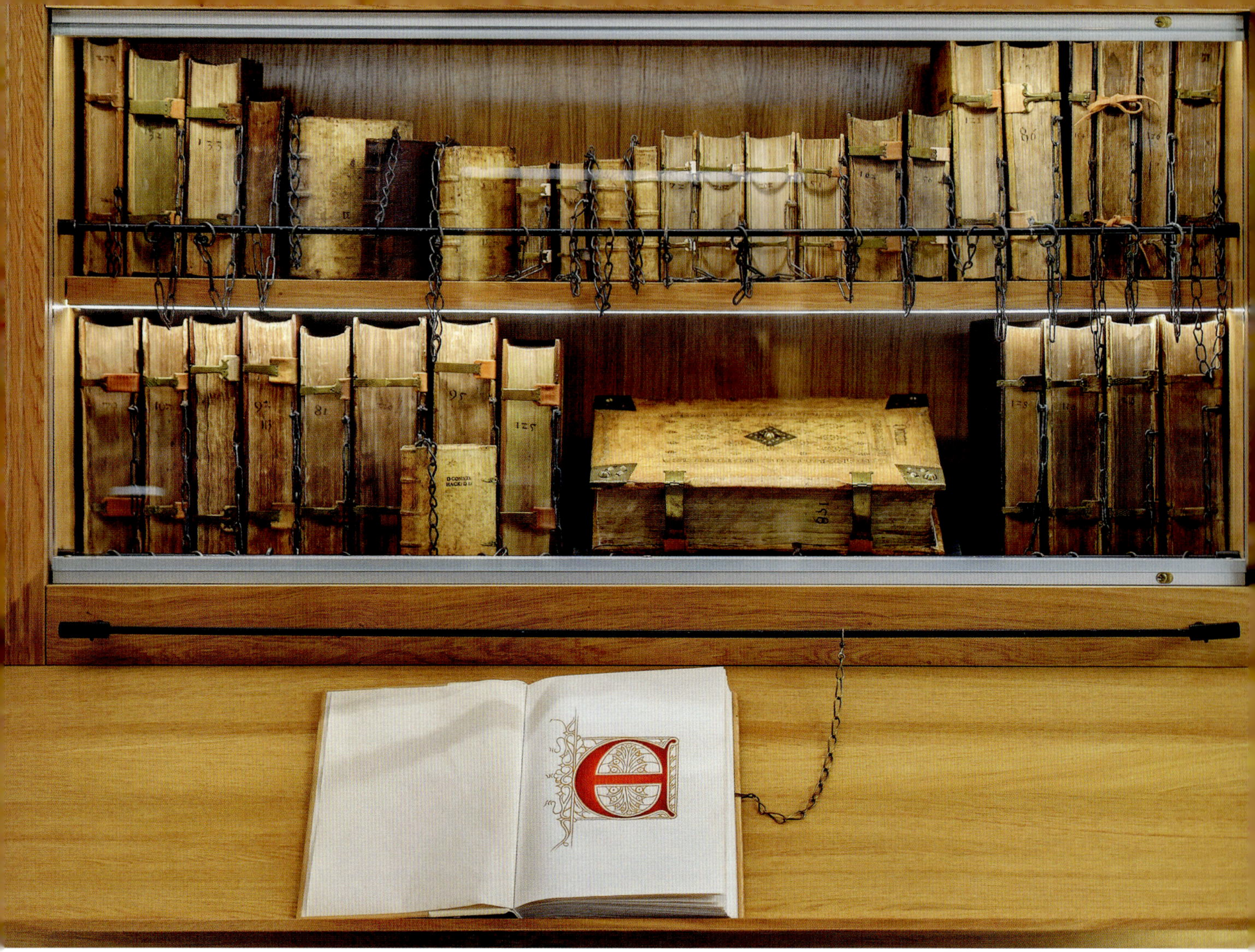

Fig. 13 The library of the Latin school in Jáchymov. Photo © Museum in Karlovy Vary – Jáchymov branch.

most famous of which was in Jáchymov (Sankt Joachimsthal), but they are also known to have been in Abertamy (Abertham) and Oloví (Bleistadt). The increasingly wealthy mining towns could afford to support them, as the best students often proceeded to the top universities in Europe and were able to return as distinguished specialists.

The Latin School and Library of Jáchymov (Fig. 13)

The Latin school of Jáchymov was established soon after the town was founded. Its most renowned rector was Johannes Mathesius, who worked there during his first stay in Jáchymov between 1532 and 1540. His educational concept had a lasting influence on the school. His motto was the phrase with which he opened his rectorial address: "The love of Christ is better than all knowledge." The introduction of catechism into the school curriculum by this staunch follower of Luther was initially questioned by the town council as Jáchymov was predominantly Catholic, but Mathesius persisted and succeeded. Emphasis was placed on the teaching of Latin and the reading of the classics, and the older students also learned Greek. A long-time friend of Mathesius,

Nikl Hermann, was cantor at the school from 1518. As a skilled composer, he was in charge of music instruction, including lessons of sacred music composition. The school was financed and supervised by the city. Not only did it serve the youth of Jáchymov, but also children from the surrounding towns and villages (Abertamy/Abertham, Pernink/Bärringen, Horní Blatná/Bergstadt Platten, Boží Dar/Gottesgab, Vejprty/Weipert, and Přísečnice/Preßnitz). Mathesius made the Jáchymov school the leading educational institution in the country. He described the school's activities, including performances of Latin and Greek comedies, in the Jáchymov Chronicle, of which he was the author. A school for girls was also established in the town. An important part of the school was a library, a part of which survives to this day. A total of 232 books have been preserved, 52 of which were printed before 1500, which makes them rare first editions. The library primarily contained theological writings and works of classical authors written in Latin and Greek, but also many German books, dictionaries and maps. Natural history, astrological writings and calendars made up a significant part of the collection. It was expanded through financial contributions and donations from formerly private libraries. It was not only school children who used the library, but also local doctors, mining specialists and officials. After the enactment of the Renewed Constitution in 1627, both the school and the library were closed on the basis of being a 'centre of Protestantism'. It was only in the 19th century that the library books were found in the attic of the Jáchymov town hall.[39]

The Latin School of Abertamy

Another school in the area that was famous for the quality of its teaching was the Latin school in Abertamy. The school (cantoria) was also a municipal institution where the cantor (Schulmeister) taught alongside a Lutheran pastor. The languages of instruction were German and Latin, and the educational goals included piety (pietas) and eloquence (eloquentia). Catechism classes were conducted by the pastor, and the cantor taught reading, writing, arithmetic, choral singing, and music. The school in Abertamy had close links with the Latin school in Jáchymov. The first cantor appointed from Jáchymov was Kurt Balden (until 1562), followed by Andreas Kreutzinger, who worked there for six years. His successor was the humanistically educated Augustin Rappolt (1568–1570), who had previously worked in Jáchymov, where he taught the 'artes liberales', or the seven liberal arts (trivium: geometry, arithmetic, grammar; quadrivium: dialectics, rhetoric, astronomy and musica). Arcana Arcanorum, a rare text on alchemy, also comes from this period, and probably used to be part of the Abertamy school library (source: State District Archive in Karlovy Vary/Karlsbad, Abertamy Parish Office Collection), It was written in Latin and German and accompanied with some Greek markings. The fourth cantor was Wenzel Huber of Annaberg (1575–1577), who also worked as a scribe. The last Lutheran cantor, Elias Steiniger, worked in Abertamy for 37 years (1583–1630). He is known to have been proficient in the construction and adjustment of clockworks.[40]

39) Josef Hejnic, "Jáchymovská škola v 16. století. Problémy a úkoly," *Historie* 40/1 (Sborník Národního muzea v Praze, 1986), 29–40; Josef Hejnic – Peter Thiergen – Ludger Udolph, "Die St. Joachimsthaler Lateinschulbibliothek nach dem Jahre 1620," in: *Res slavica: Festschrift für Hans Rothe zum 65. Geburtstag* (Schöningh: 1994), 529–535.

40) Josef Rödig – Eduard Porkert, *Abertham und seine Schule* (Abertamy: 1938).

Lazarus Ercker (1528/30–1594)

The leading mining specialist, Lazarus Ercker, who worked in Bohemia, also came from Annaberg in Saxony. A mathematician educated in Wittenberg, he worked first in the mint in his native town and later as an assayer at the Electoral Court in Dresden, where he was also promoted to the position of assayer general. He gained work experience during his travels to the mining areas of Tyrol. He tried to find new methods to improve the utilising of ores, in which the content of silver and other metals was gradually decreasing. His efforts were not appreciated in Saxony, so he moved to Bohemia, where he worked in Jáchymov (Sankt Joachimsthal) and, from 1568, as a control tester in Kutná Hora (Kuttenberg). The results of his many years of research were published in his book entitled *Beschreibung Allerfürnemisten Mineralischen Ertzt und Bergkwercksarten* (1574; "Description of Leading Ore Processing and Mining Methods"). He also prepared a Czech edition of this book, but the manuscript has been lost.

In 1577, he was appointed the highest mining master of the Kingdom of Bohemia; he oversaw all ore mining in Bohemia and also made efforts to consolidate the mining law. In 1583 he was appointed master of the mint in Prague. Emperor Rudolf II knighted him with the title of Lord of Schreckenfels. After his death, his widow Zuzana ran the Prague mint until 1600.[41]

No other profession in the Middle Ages had such a firm legal basis as mining. The oldest mining law in the Kingdom of Bohemia was the Jihlava Law. The Ius regale montanorum – the Mining Code issued by Wenceslas II in 1300 – was a significant step in the legal management of metal mining. It was not only the oldest mining code, but also the oldest written code in the history of Bohemian law. The code was written in Latin and divided into four books. The first book was focused on the workers in the mining industry, the second and third on the 'mines' and the fourth on legal disputes. The Code regulated the conditions for the mining and processing of silver. It specified the king's share of profits from the mining and minting of silver and marked the beginning of the use of the Prague grosz. Individual articles also set out the rules for occupational safety, the payment of wages, and the length of working hours. The Code prohibited miners from organising guilds and unions. This mining code was in force throughout Bohemia until the 16th century and was regarded as the basic norm for all mining districts. After the Hussite wars, following changes in the ethnic composition of the mining towns, the code was translated into Czech, whereby Czech terminology relating to the operation of mines and mining authorities was created.[42] In the Jagiellonian period, in view of the changing economic situation, amendments to the law were made regarding the purchase of silver ores, and new measures were introduced in the organisation and financing of mining operations. A crucial change in the traditional form of mining in the Bohemian lands, including the mining law, came with the rapid development of the Ore Mountain mining district at the beginning of

41) Jiří Majer, "Lazarus Ercker (1528/30–1594) a české hornictví," *Dějiny věd a techniky* 27/3 (1994), 129; Ludmila Kubátová, *Neznámý rukopis Lazara Erckera 1569* (Praha: 1996); Ludmila Kubátová, "Účast žen na dolování v Horní Blatné," *Studie z dějin hornictví* 35 (Praha: 2006), 48–57; Ludmila Kubátová, "Zuzana Erckerová – paní mincmistrová a mincmistryně," in: *Studie z dějin hornictví* 22 (1993), 26–28; Jaroslav Jiskra, *Těžba stříbrných rud v Jáchymově v 16. století s jáchymovskými osobnostmi a první báňskou školou: Georgius Agricola, Johannes Mathesius, Lazarus Ercker* (Plzeň: 2008), 100–106.
42) František Hoffmann, "Rukopisné sborníky horního práva," *Studie o rukopisech* X (1971), 65–137.

Fig. 14 Jáchymov Mining Rules – title page.
Reproduction © SOA in Zámrsk.

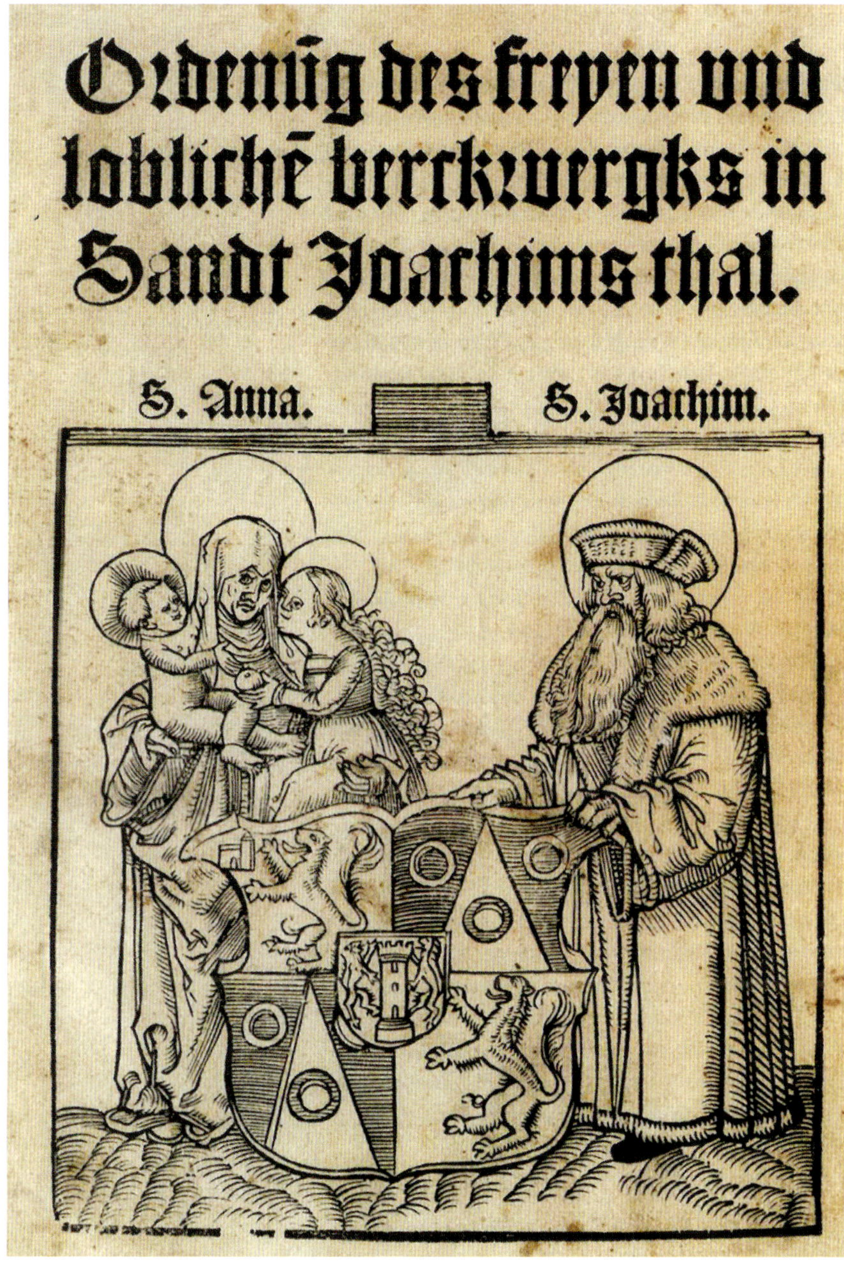

the 16th century. The proximity of the Saxon border, the large influx of miners from Saxony and the inflow of foreign capital, created very specific conditions in the region, which required a new approach to organising and managing mining activities. Most mining regulations issued by the mining authorities were therefore based on models from neighbouring Saxony.

The Mining Code of Jáchymov (Fig. 14)

The so-called Joachimsthaler Bergordnung (The Mining Code of Jáchymov) issued by Stephan Schlick in 1518 and based on the model from Annaberg, became the fundamental legal basis for mining in the Ore Mountains. It was comprised of 106 articles and printed in Leipzig under the title *Ordnung des freyen und löblichen Bergwerk in Sankt Joachimsthal*. In 1526, it was expanded by

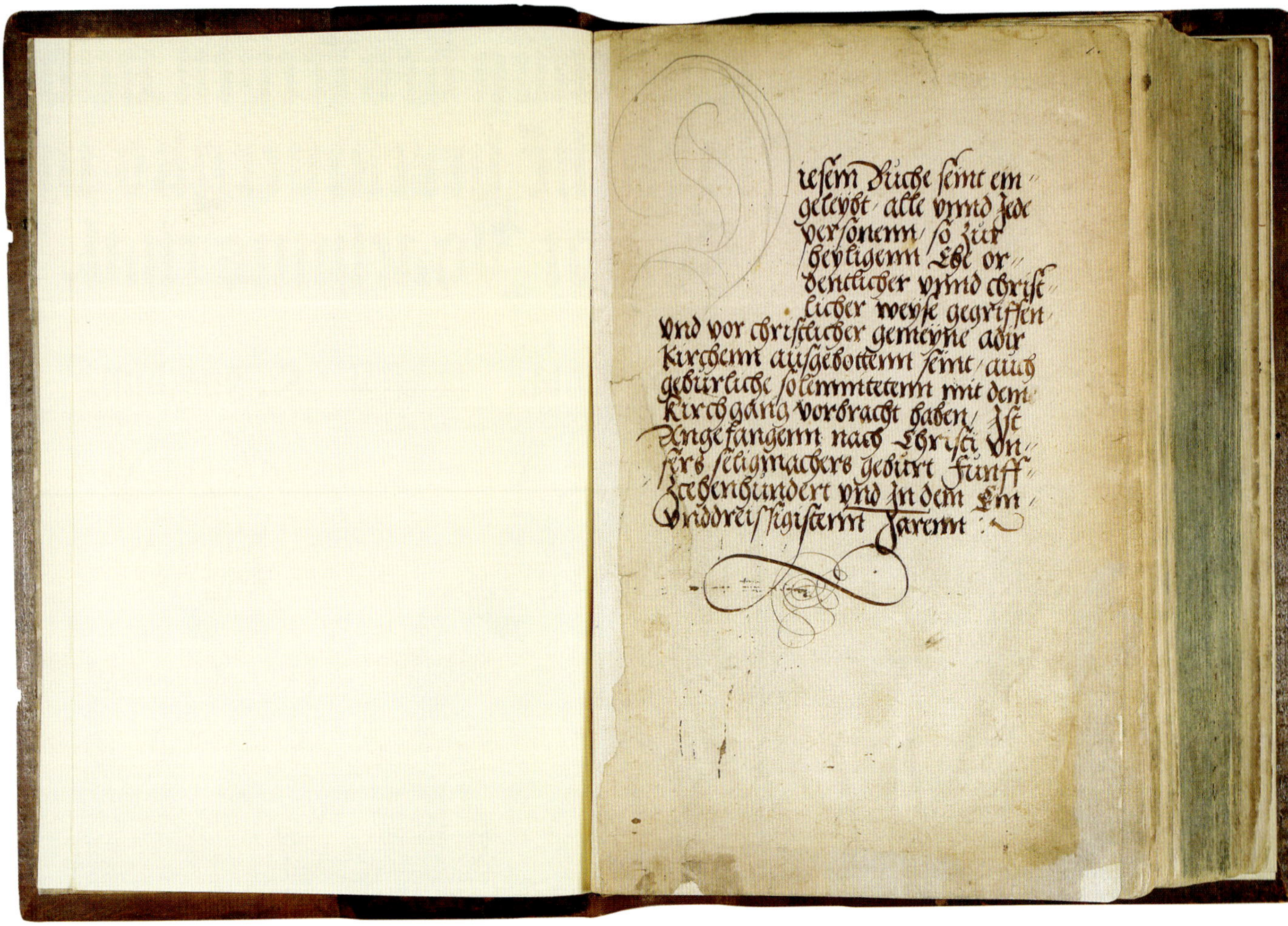

Fig. 14a Introductory sheet of the Jáchymov Marriage Register with an outlined initial D. This is the oldest civil registry kept in the territory of the present-day Czech Republic, it is an archival cultural monument now preserved in the State Regional Archive in Plzeň. The registry was kept between 1531 and 1623 and besides records of marriages, it also contains records of breaking the marriage vows, cases related to premarital sexual intercourse, etc. Registries appear in the Czech lands in the first half of the 16th century in the mining towns of the Ore Mountains. These sources illustrate, above all, the great geographical dispersion of the betrothed and thus the influx of population into the developing mining towns through marriage. Other surviving registers include three registers of Horní Blatná, namely the registers of deaths and marriages established in 1541 and the register of baptisms from 1542. Another town in the Ore Mountains, Abertamy, has a marriage register from 1544 and a baptismal register from 1545. In the Czech language environment, the oldest registers are from Prague from the turn of the 16th and 17th centuries. Photos © SOA in Plzeň.

32 new articles in response to rapid developments in the mining industry. This legal norm was gradually adopted by other mining towns and cities, especially in the Ore Mountains. Essentially, a parallel mining code began to emerge in Bohemia.
Schlick Family Archive, State Regional Archive in Zámrsk

Introductory sheet of the Jáchymov Marriage Register with an outlined initial D (Fig. 14a)
This is the oldest civil registry kept in the territory of the present-day Czech Republic, it is an archival cultural monument now preserved in the State Regional Archive in Plzeň. The registry

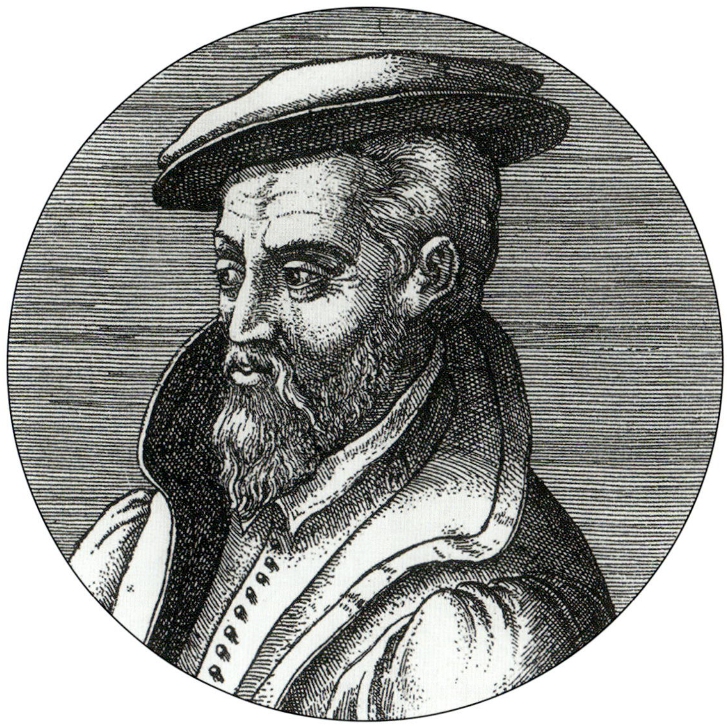

Fig. 15 Georgius Agricola (1494–1555).
Reproduction from Hentzen, A. – von Holst, N., Die grossen Deutschen im Bild. Olympia 1936.

was kept between 1531 and 1623 and besides records of marriages, it also contains records of breaking the marriage vows, cases related to premarital sexual intercourse, etc. Registries appear in the Czech lands in the first half of the 16th century in the mining towns of the Ore Mountains. These sources illustrate, above all, the great geographical dispersion of the betrothed and thus the influx of population into the developing mining towns through marriage. Other surviving registers include three registers of Horní Blatná, namely the registers of deaths and marriages established in 1541 and the register of baptisms from 1542. Another town in the Ore Mountains, Abertamy, has a marriage register from 1544 and a baptismal register from 1545. In the Czech language environment, the oldest registers are from Prague from the turn of the 16th and 17th centuries. Photos © SOA in Plzeň.

Georgius Agricola (1494–1555) (Fig. 15)

This versatile scholar, expert in philosophy, theology, natural sciences (especially mineralogy) and medicine, studied at the University of Leipzig and worked as a doctor and pharmacist in Jáchymov. Later he lived in Chemnitz, where he also died. He is the author of important texts about mining. He probably wrote Bermannus, or a Dialogue on Mining (Bermannus, sive de re metallica dialogus) in Jáchymov. His best-known work is undoubtedly "Twelve Books on Mining and Metallurgy" (*De re metallica libri XII*), in which he summarised the contemporary knowledge on ore mining and processing. It became an authoritative text on mining for centuries to come.[43]

43) Bohuslav Ježek – Josef Hummel (ed.), *Jiřího Agricoly dvanáct knih a hornictví a hutnictví* (Praha: 1933); Hans Prescher, "Georgius Agricola und St. Joachimsthal/Georgius Agricola a Jáchymov," in: *St. Joachimsthal in der Zeit Georgius Agricola. Zur Geschichte einer Bergstadt im 16. Jahrhundert/Jáchymov v době Georgia Agricoly. K dějinám horního města v 16. století* (Schneeberg – Karlovy Vary: 1994), 23–24, 73–74; Jiří Majer, "Georgius Agricola (1494–1565). Život a dílo," *Dějiny věd a techniky* 27/11 (1994): 1–19.

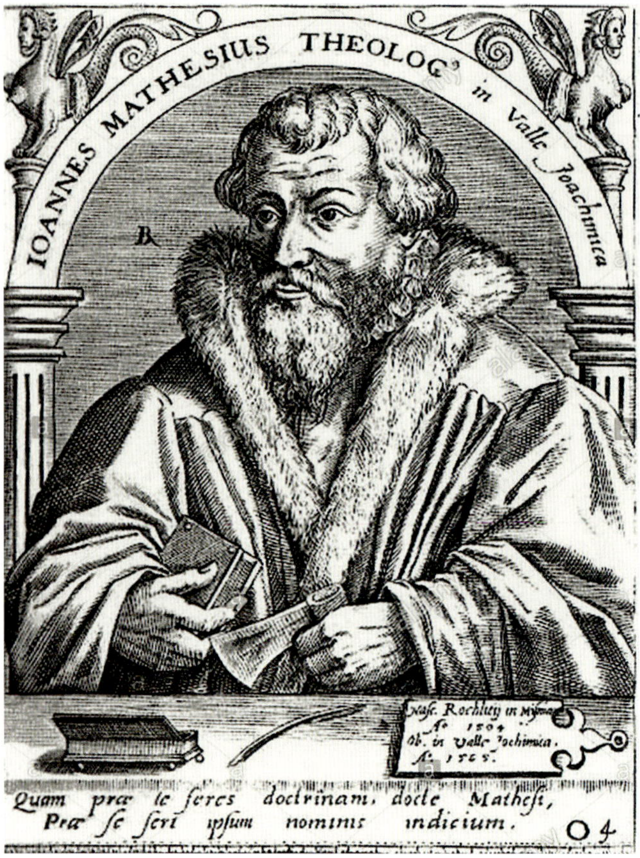

Fig. 16 Johannes Mathesius (1504–1565).
Reproduction © Rijksmuseum Amsterdam.

Johannes Mathesius (1504–1565) (Fig. 16)

Mathesius can undoubtedly be considered one of the most prominent intellectuals associated with the mining towns in the Ore Mountains. Through his contribution, Jáchymov became a centre of mining business as well as humanistic education. He studied in Nuremberg, Ingolstadt, and in 1529, he came to the University of Wittenberg, inspired by the teachings of Martin Luther, whose faithful follower and lifelong friend he became. Soon after the foundation of the Latin school in the rapidly-growing town of Jáchymov, Mathesius was asked to serve as director of the school. He never lost contact with Luther or Wittenberg, and returned to this centre of the new faith. While there, he was visited by a seven-member delegation of mining masters and representatives of Jáchymov, where the Lutheran faith had taken root among the population. They offered him the position of spiritual administrator. On this occasion, the Jáchymov delegation also met with Luther, presented him with the gift of the famous Jáchymov medals, sang some mining songs and discussed the mining trade with him. After arriving in Jáchymov, which was referred to as the Valley (Údolí, or Thal in German) at the time, Mathesius started as an assistant pastor and later became a spiritual administrator and a respected leader. In 1542, his wedding to Sibyla Richter (†1555), the daughter of a metallurgical official, was attended not only by the local notables, but also by Jeroným (Hieronymus) and Jáchym (Lorenz) Schlick, who were the nobility of Jáchymov. Mathesius served as pastor of Jáchymov from 1545 until his death. His sermons, in which he addressed more than merely spiritual matters, became legendary. He was able to speak to the problems and needs of the everyday life of the town's population, and especially to the unique character of the mining community, to which he had formed a close attachment. More than 1,500 of Mathesius' sermons have survived and were published. The best known is a collection of sermons on the various aspects of mining and life in Jáchymov, published under the title Sarepta, or Bergpostill in Nuremberg in 1562. It is a very important source of information about the mining profession and life in the mining towns. Mathesius was also the first biographer of Martin Luther. His popular account of the reformer's life and teachings was published in sermon form a year after Mathesius' death and twenty years after the famous reformer's death. This volume became an important source of disseminating Luther's legacy.[44]

44) Petr Hlaváček, *Johannes Mathesius. Opomíjený příběh z dějin wittenberské reformace* (Praha: 2019); Jan Mikschik, "Johannes Mathesius a Jáchymov," (bachelor thesis, Charles University, 2014).

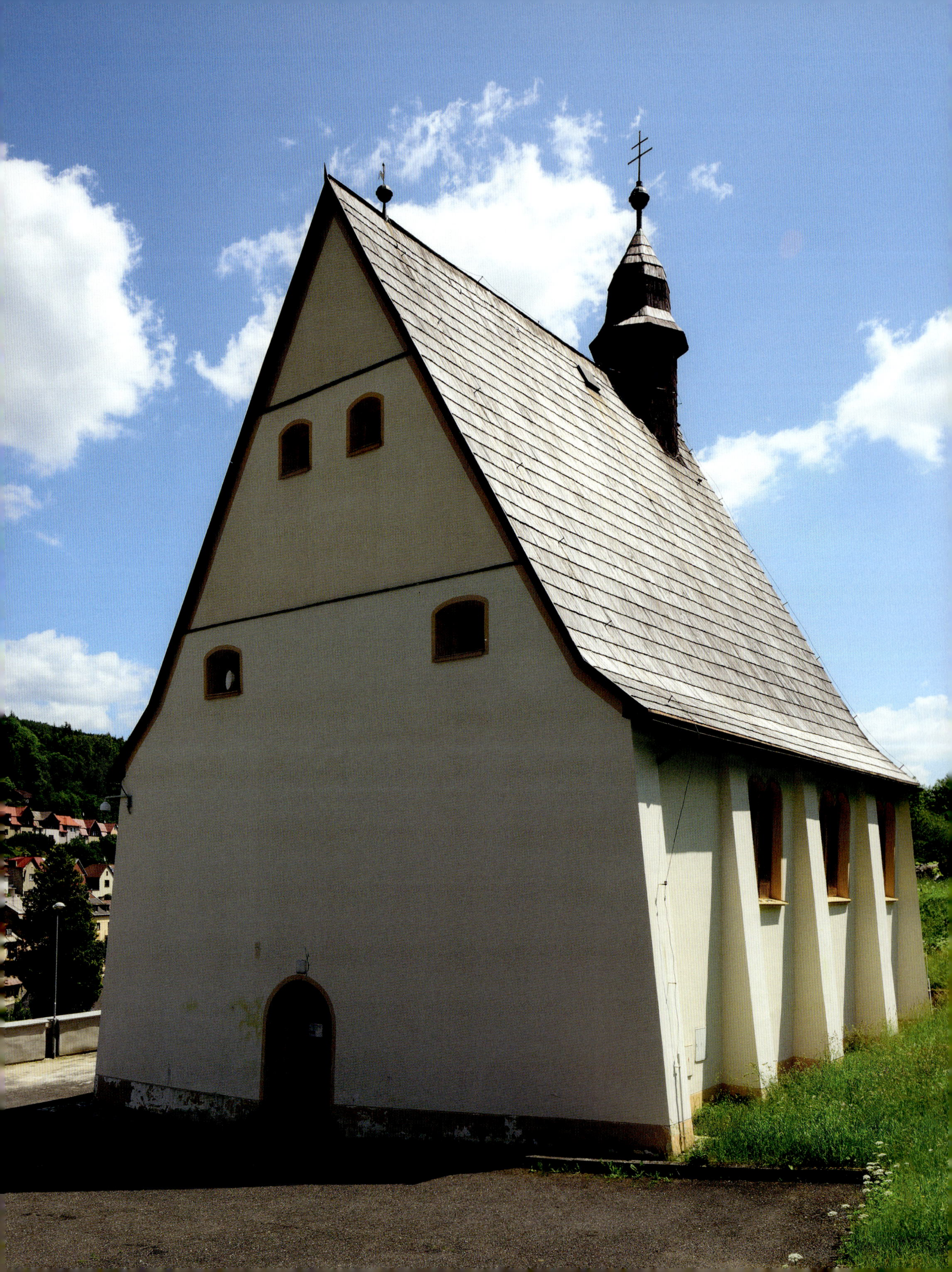

MEDICAL CARE, HOSPITALS, AND SOCIAL SOLIDARITY

The mining profession was highly specialised and quite arduous. The miners digging for ore underground were exposed to health risks on a daily basis and needed special care. Physicians were therefore an integral part of the community of mining towns, including Jáchymov, where the first medical doctor arrived soon after it was founded. There was a hospital attached to the Church of All Saints, founded by the mining foreman Wolf Sturz. The pastor Christoph Ering built a new hospital building near the church. The hospital was a rectangular building with a portal built in 1566, located on the northwest façade. The building was demolished in the 1970s.

There was also a pharmacy, one of the oldest in Bohemia, available to the local residents. The first apothecary there was Georg Sturz, son of the founder of the hospital. A number of prominent physicians worked in the mining towns, specialising in mining medicine and helping ailing or injured miners. The physician Václav Payer of Loket (a.k.a. Wenceslas Payer de Cubito, 1488–1537) was the first to describe what became known as the Jáchymov mining diseases; Payer also studied the curative effects of the Carlsbad springs, based on the findings of the physician and theologian Magnus Hundt (1449–1519), who was also in the service of the Schlick family.[45] In Jáchymov, distinguished figures of Renaissance medicine took turns as town physicians. They included Johannes Naevius (1499–1574) and Johann Kopp von Raumenthal (1487–1558), but the most famous Jáchymov physician and pharmacist was certainly Georgius Agricola (1494–1555).[46] An example of the importance and wide-ranging expertise of medical doctors in mining towns was the multitalented Ulrich Rülein von Calw (1465–1523). He was a physician, mathematician, geologist, mining specialist, astrologer and builder from the Saxon side of the Ore Mountain border, who lived in the notable mining town of Freiberg, where he also headed the town council for several years.[47] It is thus necessary to consider the doctors

45) Vladimír Křížek– Josef Sajner – Bohumil Ryba (ed.), *Václav Payer, Pojednání o Karlových Varech z r. 1522* (Praha: 1984).
46) David Tomíček, "Jáchymovští horníci a medicína první poloviny 16. století ve světle vybraných spisů Georgia Agricoly a Jana Koppa z Raumenthalu," in: Michaela Hrubá – Michaela Ottová – Jan Royt, *Ars Montana. Umělecký a kulturní transfer v otevřeném prostoru česko-saského Krušnohoří na prahu raného novověku* (Praha: 2016), 253–269.
47) Jentsch Frieder, "Rülein von Calw, Ulrich", in: *Neue Deutsche Biographie* 22 (Berlin: 2005), 222.

Fig. 17 Jáchymov, Church of All Saints. Built in 1516–1520, later it served as a hospital and cemetery church. Photo by J. Peer (2019).

of mining towns as polyvalent personalities with extensive knowledge that was required and expected in this context. The aforementioned Renaissance personalities are clear evidence of this.

We have also mentioned hospitals, where old or ailing miners found refuge, often with their dependent families in tow. If a miner died or was injured on the job and was unable to provide for his loved ones, his entire family were left in social distress. The mining town authorities anticipated this and devised ways of providing for the miners' widows, so as to protect them from destitution. Nuremberg poet and Lutheran Hans Sachs (1494–1576) wrote poems about death from poverty, such as the one containing the lament of an impoverished widow: *Jak jsme chudí, ubohé děti / Bída s nouzí a hlad je ten třetí* [How poor we are, oh children of mine / Poverty, hardship, and hunger combine].[48] Widows' requests for help submitted to the town hall are also documented in the upper Ore Mountain towns, where women tried to earn a living by renting the municipal kitchen, salt shops, or town baths. [49] The widows who failed to acquire a trade or otherwise secure their livelihood were considered *Hausarmen*, i.e. the deserving poor. They did not live directly in the hospital, but received regular support from the town, including bread, firewood, grain, or flour. They might also receive rental assistance from the town if they lost their house and had to find accommodation elsewhere. They could also borrow money from the hospital for a limited period of time, especially if they fell ill. If they lost their houses entirely, the hospital provided shelter, but the women were required to earn their keep by doing laundry, sewing, cleaning, or spinning.[50]

48) Alice Valentová – Jiří Aplt (ed.), *Hans Sachs. Aktovky* (Praha: 1964), 51.
49) Helmut Bräuer, *Zur Mentalität armer Leute in Obersachsen 1500 bis 1800* (Leipzig: 2008).
50) Kateřina Matasová, "Vdovy v báňských městech Krušnohoří na přelomu středověku a novověku," (diploma thesis, Jan Evangelista Purkyne University in Ústí nad Labem, 2009), 59–64; Petr Svobodný, "Die Spitäler in Böhmen und Mähren im Mittelalter und in der Frühen Neuzeit," in: Martin Scheutz – Andrea Sommerlechner – Herwig Weigl – Alfred Stefan Weiß (ed.), *Europäisches Spitalwesen. Institutionelle Fürsorge in Mittelalter und Frühen Neuzeit* (Wien – München: 2008), 351–380.

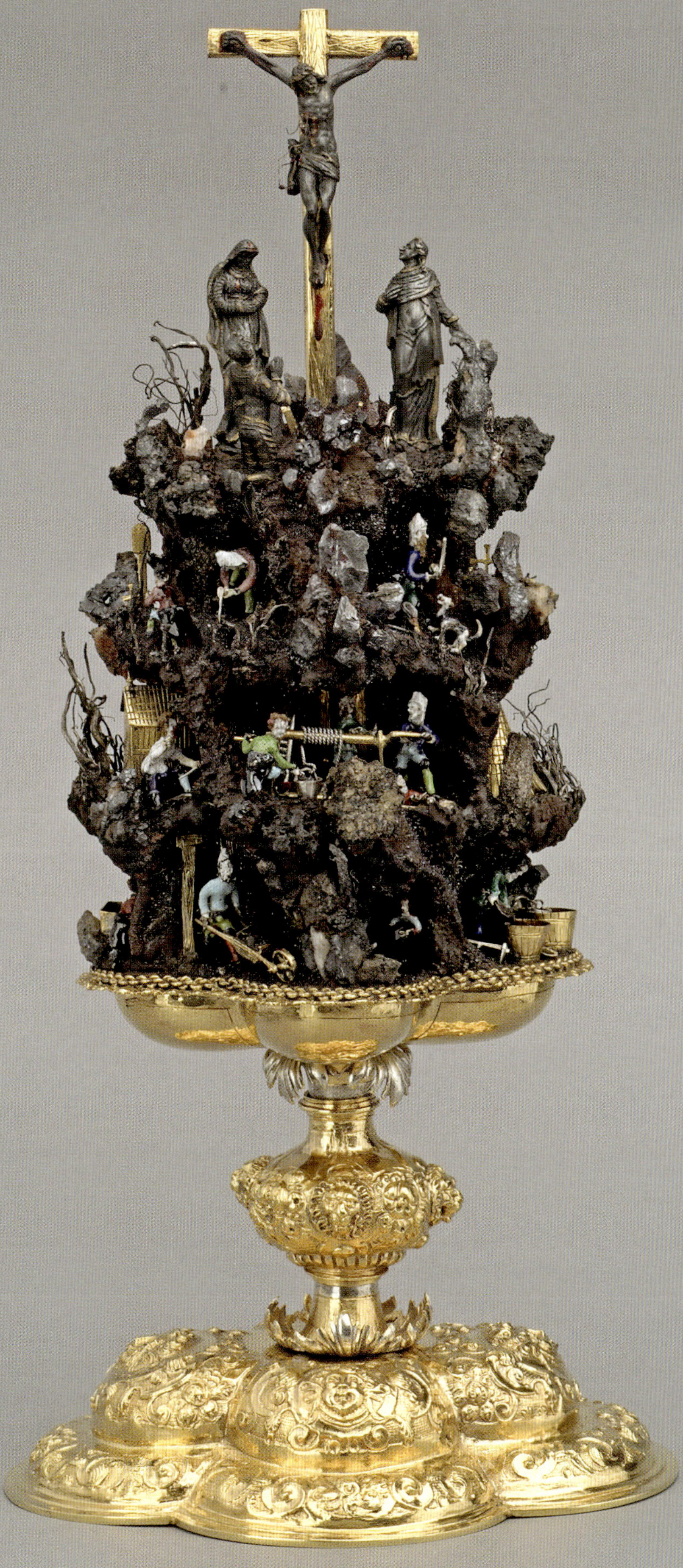

MINING GUILDS AND THEIR REPRESENTATION

Even though the Mining Code prohibited miners from associating in guilds, they found ways to bypass that regulation. Free, profession-specific associations were formed in the mining towns. For example, there were separate associations for miners and haulers, and for minters and coiners. It was customary for them to set up their own chapels with altars in churches, as in the Church of St. Barbara in Kutná Hora, which has separate chapels of mint masters, haulers and coiners. Elaborate illuminated graduals, i.e. liturgical songbooks, were acquired. The best known is the Kutná Hora Gradual (Kuttenberger Graduale), which was created around 1490 and includes a cover page with images of the mining profession and its activities. It is currently deposited in the Austrian National Library in Vienna. Magnificent liturgical vessels (monstrances and chalices) were also purchased. For guild festivals, these societies purchased expensive ritual chains and vessels, often decorated with designs associated with mining and ore processing. Examples include a richly decorated ceremonial necklace belonging to an unknown mining fraternity from Central Europe in the period between 1480 and 1520 (now in a private collection in Belgium), and a guild teapot from Goslar commissioned in 1477 by a rich mining entrepreneur by the name of János Thurzó (Goslar, Stadtmuseum). Objects of this kind were probably created by local artisans in Jáchymov, such as the goldsmith Conz Welcz, who made a miner's chalice with the stem decorated with mining motifs. Special mention should be made of the Esterhazy Pot from Banská Štiavnica, decorated with mining designs (1530, recrafted in 1630, currently in the Museum of Applied Arts, Budapest), and the Miners' Guild Horn from Wieliczka, Poland (1534, Cracow Saltworks Museum in Wieliczka). Wieliczka, where the horn originated, was the largest salt deposit in Central Europe and thus a major source of profit for the Kingdom of Poland.[51]

The handsteine (Lapides manuales)

A special form of mining industry representation were objects known as 'handsteine' (Lapides manuales, or 'hand stones') that were presented as gifts to important people. Most were in the possession of the Saxon electors, Emperor Charles V, and Emperor Rudolph II. The largest collection of handsteine is currently kept in the Kunsthistorisches Museum in Vienna. Their

51) Most of these rare artefacts were shown at the 'Europa Jagellonica 1386–1572' exhibition. Jiří Fajt (ed.), *Europa Jagellonica 1386–1572. Umění a kultura ve střední Evropě za vlády Jagellonců – katalog k výstavě* (Praha: 2012).

Fig. 18a Conz Welcz, design of a silver miner's cup from 1532. Reproduction ©Albertina, Wien.

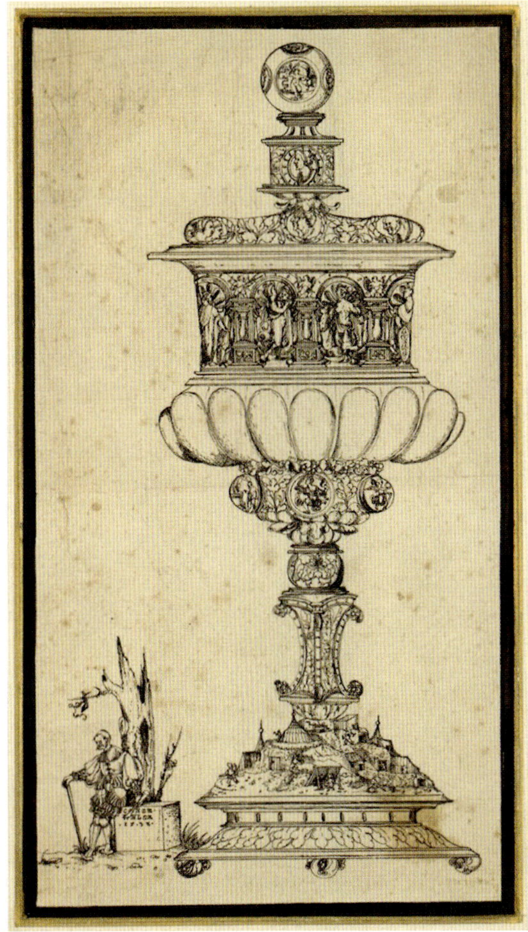

popularity peaked in the second half of the 16th century. A handstein was essentially a fist-sized peice of ore that was mined in a given mining region. It was mounted on a gilded stand and typically decorated with characters from the Bible and little figures of miners. The greatest number of handsteine were made in Jáchymov. They were designed by the best local goldsmiths and medallists including Conz Welcz and Caspar Ulich. In 1555, Conz Welcz crafted a silver ore handstein topped with a statuette of Caritas (now in the Kunsthistorisches Museum in Vienna). Welcz also created several Jáchymov medals and designs. The greatest number of Jáchymov handsteine were created by Caspar Ulich and his Jáchymov workshop. Ulich had learned his craft in the workshop of Conz Welcz.[52]

52) Walter Holzhausen, "Die Blütezeit bergmännischer Kunst," in: Heinrich Winkelmann (ed.), *Die Bergbau in der Kunst* (Essen: 1958), 113–248; Elisabeth Scheicher et al., *Die Kunstkammer. Kunsthistorisches Museum, Sammlungen Schloss Ambras* (Innsbruck: 1977); Peter Huber – Simone Huber, "St. Joachimsthal," *Lapis* 6/6 (1981), 19–26, 38–40; Rudolf Distelberger, "Gold und Silber, Edelsteine und Elfenbein," in: Ferdinand Seibt (ed.), *Renaissance in Böhmen* (München: 1985), 255–287; Peter Huber, "Die schönste Stuffe. Handsteine aus fünf Jahrhunderten, Gediegen Silber. Das Erz der Münzen, das Metall des Schmuckes, das Element mit dem Glanz. Das gediegene Silber und die Silbermineralien," *ExtraLapis* 8 (1995), 58–67; Peter Huber, "Faszination und Geschichte bergmännischer Handsteine," *Berichte der Geologischen Bundesanstalt* 41 (Wien: 1997), 99–104; Vera M. Hammer – Helene Hanzer – Petr Huber, "Der ‚Handstein' in der Mineralogischen Schausammlung des Naturhistorischen Museums Wien," *Der Anschnitt* 57/5–6 (2005), 200–206; Peter Huber, "Handsteine from Slovakia and Bohemia/Bergmännische Handsteine aus der Slowakei und Böhmen," *13. internationales Erbe-Symposium* (abstract, Banská Štiavnica, 15.–20. Juni 2015), 90–91, available at https://www.erbe-symposium.org.pdf.

← Fig. 18 Handsteine (Lapides manuales). Photography © Kunsthistorisches Museum Wien. →

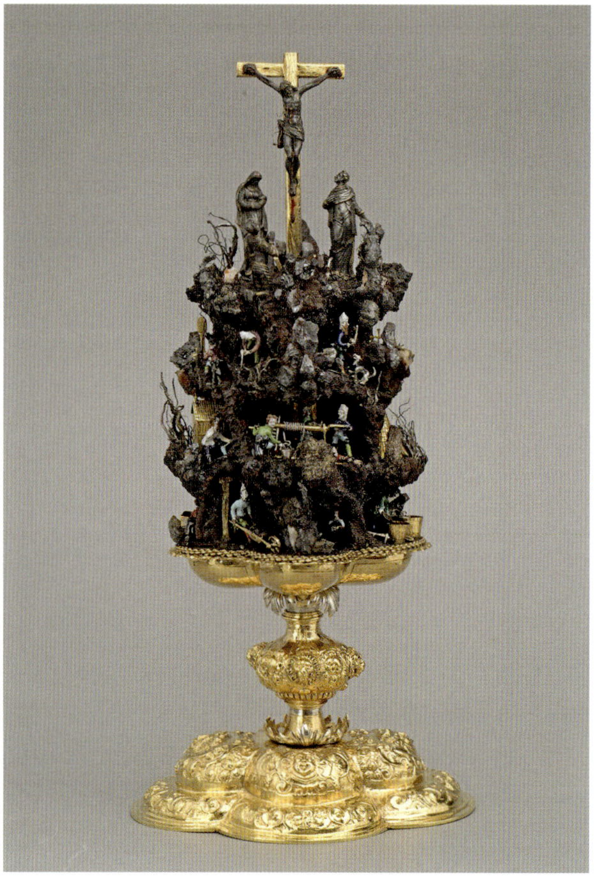

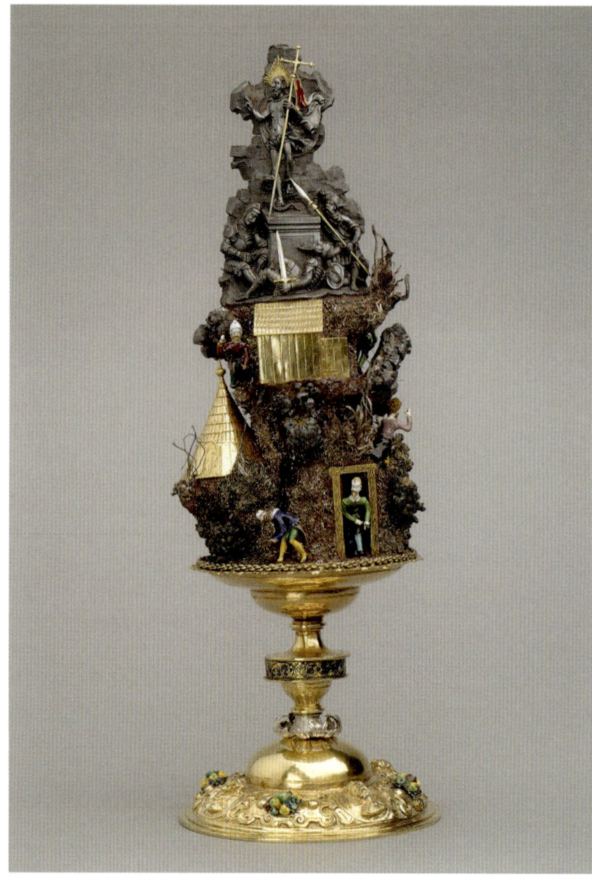

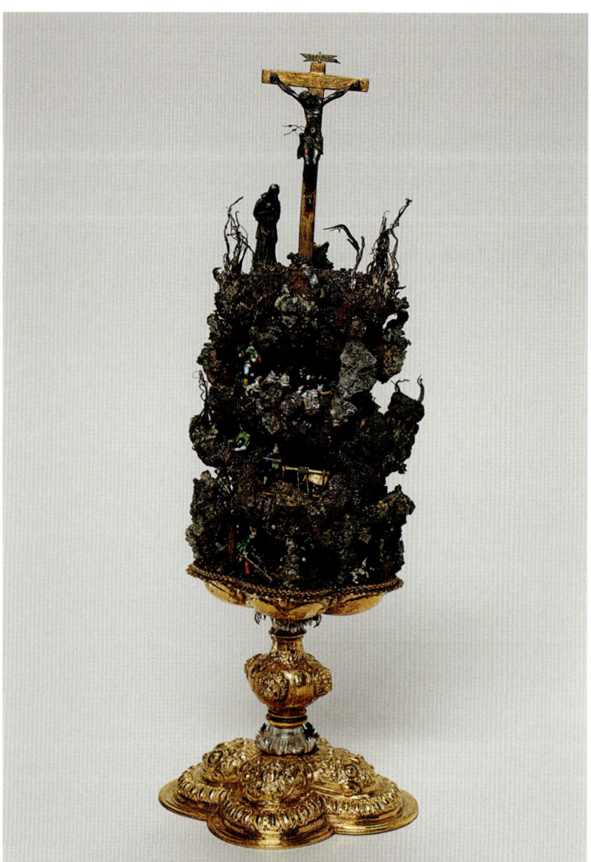

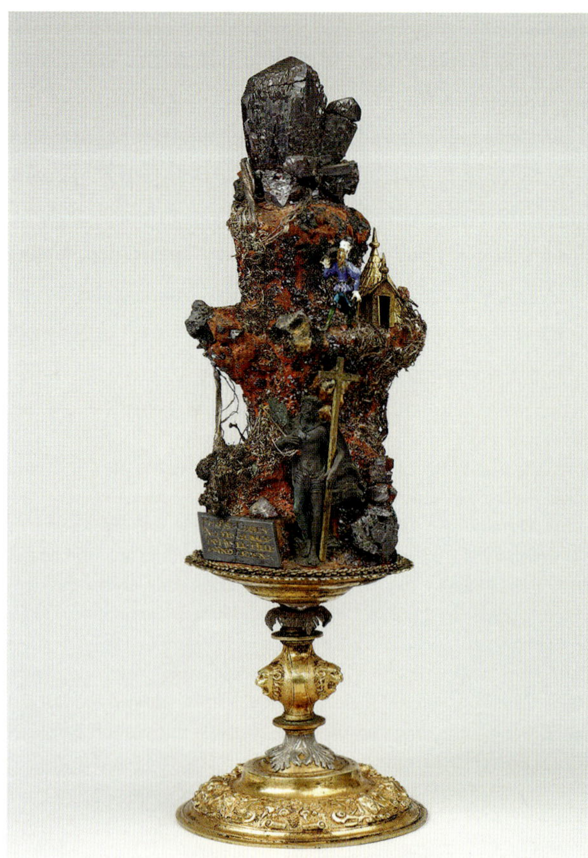

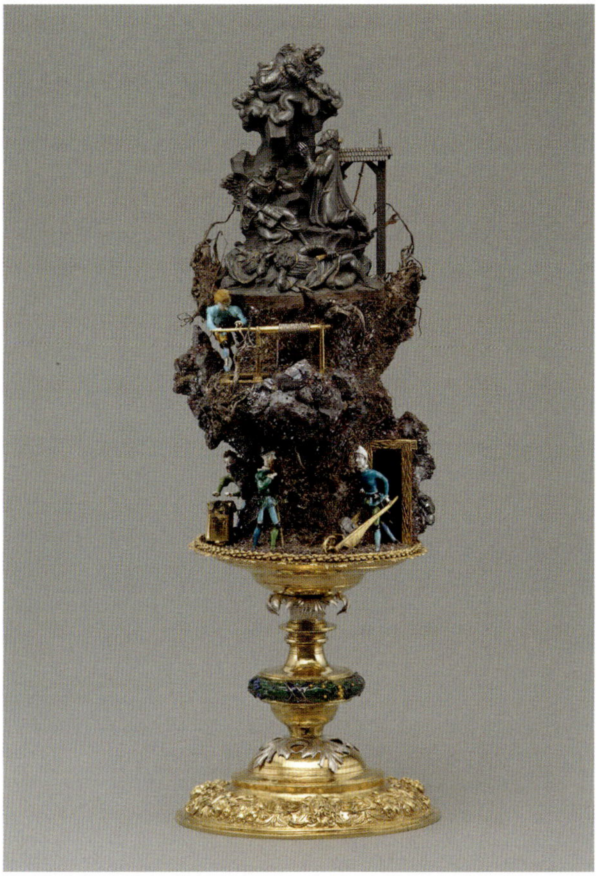
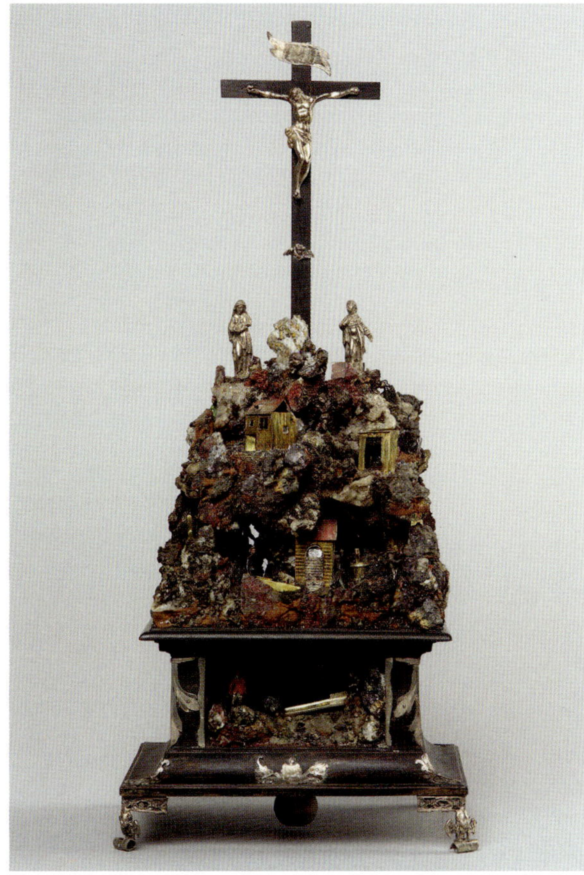
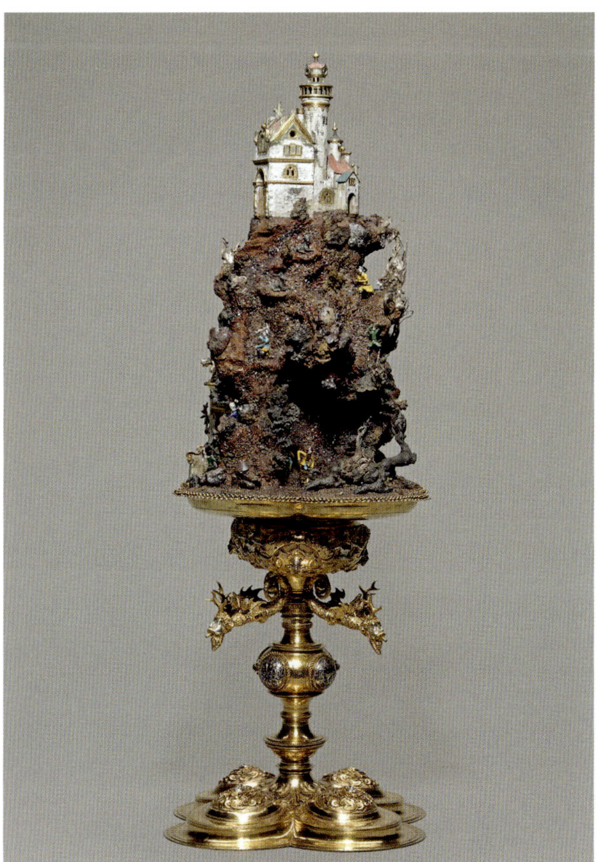
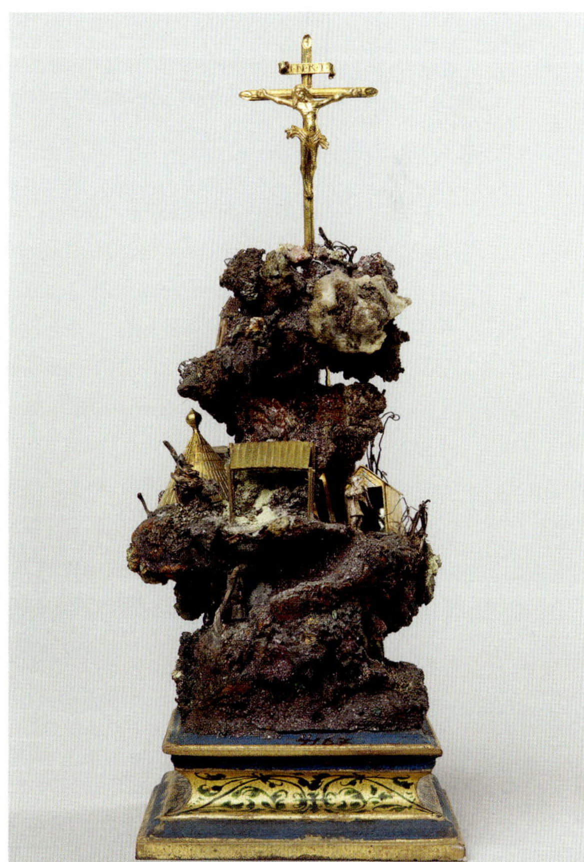

Jáchymov's minting and medal making were renowned. It was in the Jáchymov mint that the Schlick family minted the thaler silver coins (or talers, an abbreviation of *Joachimstaler*), each composed of 27.20 grams of pure silver.[53] The obverse side depicted a figure of St. Joachim and the heraldic shield of the Counts of Schlick, while the reverse represented the Bohemian lion. Coins worth a quarter or a half of a thaler were also minted. The Jáchymov minters were inspired by the Saxon Klappmünzentaler coin, which had the same weight and purity of metal (29.23 g, with the silver content of 27.41g). Unlike the Saxon coins, the Jáchymov coins had the year of issue marked on them (except for the trial mintage from the period between 1519 and 1520, which had no year mark). An important object of remembrance of the Schlick family's minting and medal making in Jáchymov is a Baroque coin chest of hammered silver, decorated with 44 Jáchymov thalers and commemmorative medals associated with the Schlicks. It was probably made in Augsburg in the workshop of the goldsmith Johann Andreas Thelot sometime between 1680 and 1690.[54]

The Schlick Family (Jáchymov) Jewellery Box (Fig. 19)
A silver coin box. The outer side is decorated with 44 Jáchymov and Planá thalers minted by the Counts of Schlick, which are set in silver-gilt frames. Some of them were added later. The bottom inside is decorated with a high relief of pomegranates, pears, and grapes. It is silverwork, by Johann Andreas Thelot, who lived and worked in Augsburg, and it comes with a proven origin. It was repunched in 1806. Silver purity: 875/1000, weight: 5721 g, height 23 cm, width 44 cm, depth 31 cm.

53) Petr Vorel – Lubomír Nemeškal, *Dějiny jáchymovské mincovny a katalog ražeb I. 1519/1520–1619* (Pardubice: 2010); Zuzana Holečková, "Šlikovské mince v období 1519/20–1528 a počátky mincovnictví v Jáchymově," in: Jan Klípa – Michaela Ottová (ed.), *Bez hranic. Umění v Krušnohoří mezi gotikou a renesancí* (Praha: 2015), 678–682.
54) Since 2016, the coin chest is deposited in the collections of the National Heritage Institute, State Chateau Sychrov, as a national cultural monument. It was loaned to the exhibition 'The Schlicks and Coin Minting' in Ostrov nad Ohří. More details available at: https://www.pamatkovykatalog.cz.

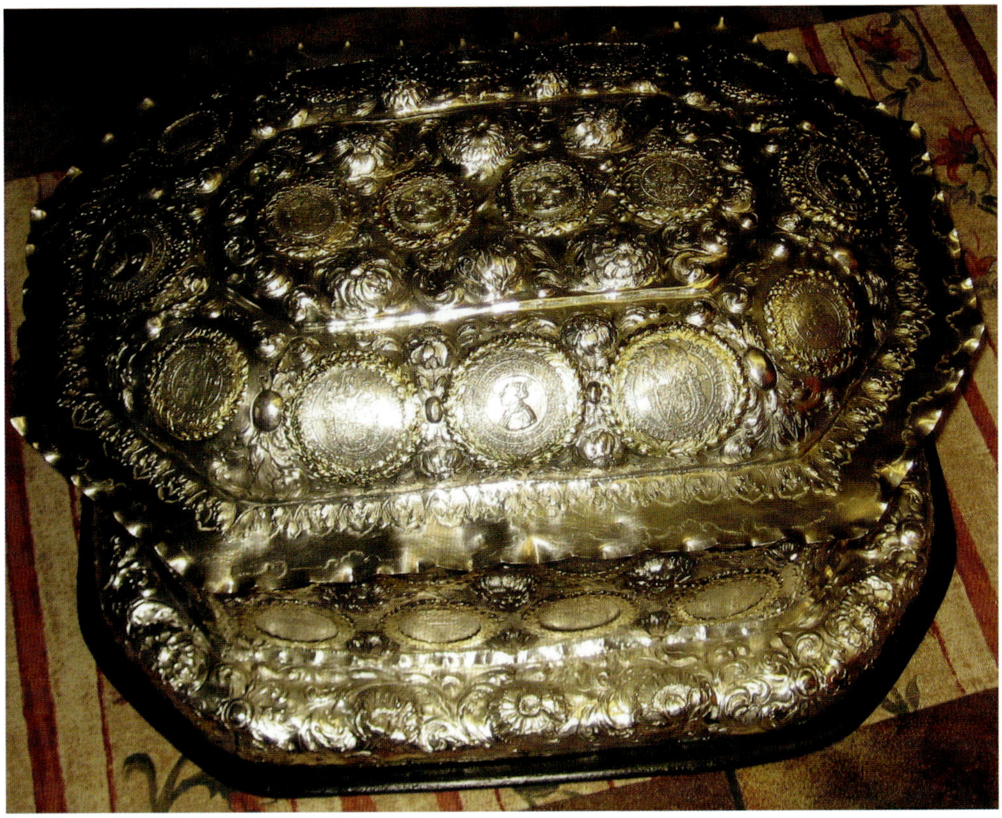

Fig. 19 Schlick (Jáchymov) jewellery box, Johann Andreas Thelot, 1680–1690.
Photograph © National Heritage Institute.

The Jáchymov Thaler (Joachimstaler) (Fig. 20)

This was a silver coin minted in Jáchymov from 1519 until 1528. It was modelled on Saxon coins of an equivalent weight and purity of metal (29.23 g, with 27.41 g of pure silver content). The Schlicks probably began minting coins as far back as 1519. In January 1520, they received permission from the Bohemian Diet to mint a coin 'the size of a larger grosz in the value of Rhineland gold coins, their halves and quarters.' From 1526, the Jáchymov thalers were also minted in another mint, probably located in Horní Slavkov. The Schlick coin minting was banned in 1528, only two years after the Habsburgs ascended the Bohemian throne. The obverse side depicted a figure of St. Joachim and the heraldic shield of the Counts of Schlick. It has an inscription on the rim that runs the length of the perimeter and reads 'Arma Dominorum Slickorum Stephani et Fratrum Comitum de Bassano' (The Coat of Arms of the Lords of Schlick, Stephan and His Brothers, Counts of Bassano), and an abbreviation of the name of St. Jáchym with the year. On the reverse side of the coin is a Bohemian lion and the inscription Louis the First King of Bohemia by God's Grace (LUDOVICUS-PRIM-D-GRACIA-REX-BOE). The monarch's name was subject to change.[55]

55) Josef Smolík, "Smlouva krále Ferdinanda I. s pány Šliky o hory a minci Jáchymovskou," *Památky archaeologické a místopisné* 20/5 (1903), 333–340; Martina Pospíšilová, "Narovnání o hory a kovy (1534)," in: Karel Schele – Jaromír Tauchen, *Encyklopedie českých právních dějin IV*. (Plzeň: 2016), 21–22; Petr Vorel, "Jáchymovské tolary z roku 1527 se

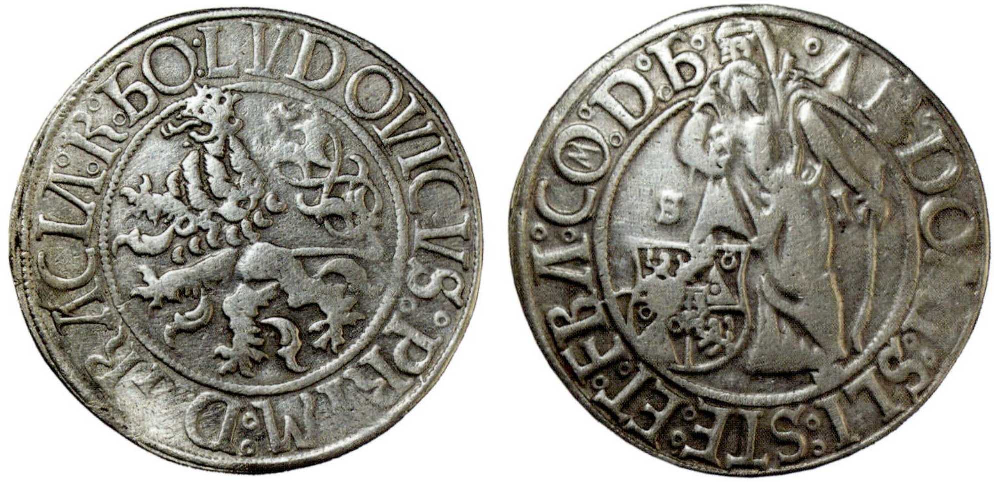

Fig. 20 Jáchymov thaler (Joachimstaler). Photograph by M. Vorel (2019).

The Jáchymov medals are of great artistic and historical value in the broader European context.[56] These were mainly medals with portraits of notable figures from the ranks of royals, electors, and the nobility. Medals depicting religious reformers (including Master Jan Hus and Martin Luther) are particularly noteworthy. Medals with various biblical themes were also common. [57] Particularly distinctive were the so-called plague thalers, with a typological image of a copper serpent on a pole on the reverse and the Crucifixion of Christ on the obverse.

Hieronymus Magdeburger, a medallist from Annaberg, is considered to be the founder of medal making in the Ore Mountains. Magdeburger was a contemporary of Christoph Füssel, a metal cutter from Kremnica (Kremnitz).[58] The most artistically valuable medals were created by the monogrammist CW, presumed to be the same person as the goldsmith Conz Welcz, who made handsteine and liturgical vessels, as mentioned above. In 1553 he made a chalice for the Jáchymov Church, commissioned by Margarethe von Hassenstein in 1548. His successor was Master CE, who worked closely with the Schlick family. Other local medal makers included Wolf Milicz, documented in Jáchymov in 1533, and his relative Nickel Milicz, a metal

jménem Jeronýma Šlika a jejich význam pro stanovení chronologie jáchymovských ražeb," *Numismatické listy* 68/1–2 (2013), 56–69.

56) Viktor Katz, *Die erzgebirgische Prägemedaille des XVI. Jahrhunderts* (Praha: 1932); Juliána Boublíková-Jáhnová, "Jáchymovské medaile. Významný fenomén evropského medailérství 16. století," in: *Jáchymovský smolinec a kovové radium*, *Studie z dějin hornictví* 40 (2011), 59–65; Juliána Boublíková-Jáhnová, "Bitevní a smuteční medaile jáchymovských řezáčů Conze Welcze a Nickela Milicze," *Numismatický sborník* 29/1 (2015), 60–69; Petr Schneider, "Krušnohorské medaile," in: Jan Klípa – Michaela Ottová (ed.), *Bez hranic. Umění v Krušnohoří mezi gotikou a renesancí* (Praha: 2015), 683–690.

57) Juliána Boublíková-Jáhnová, "Znamenité umění a mnoho krásných článků pravého náboženství. Jáchymovské biblické a Husovy medaile jako odraz luterství," *Dějiny a současnost* 39/9 (2017), 14–17.

58) Paul Adolf Bamberg, "Hieronymus Magdeburger, Peter Goldschmied und Jobst Leypold," *Berliner Münzblätter* 11/53 (1933), 129–138, 148–151; Paul Adolf Bamberg, "Die Münzmeister in Annaberg," *Deutsche Münzblätter* 60/62 (1940/42), 411–421; Barbara Balážová, "Das Erinnerungsmal für Christoph Füssl aus dem Jahr 1561 und andere Wiener Sepulkralkunstwerke für die Bürger der mittelslowakischen Bergbaustädte," *Epigraphica & Sepulcralia* 8 (2019), 85–102.

cutter and goldsmith who ran a large workshop in Jáchymov from 1540 until 1570. He worked from designs by Georg Pencz, Heinrich Aldegrever, Hans Holbein and Augustin Hirschvogel. In 1559, he donated a grisaille painting of the Risen Christ to St. Joachim's Church in Jáchymov. The workshop passed to his brother-in-law, Zacharias Kempf. Between 1541 and 1549, a monogrammist with the initials WS also made medals in Jáchymov, the best known being his medal with the portrait of Emperor Charles V.[59]

59) Viktor Katz, "Wolf Milicz, Nickel Milicz a Zachariáš Kempf. Příspěvek k dějinám jáchymovského medailérství 16. století," *Numismatický časopis* 2 (1926): 85–114; Juliána Boublíková-Jáhnová, "Počátky medailérství v Čechách. Jáchymovské portrétní medaile hrabat Šliků," *Historie* 57/1–2 (Sborník Národního muzea v Praze, Řada A, 2003): 1–44; Idem., "Jáchymovské medaile: významný fenomén evropského medailérství 16. století," *Studie z dějin hornictví* 40 (2011), 59–65; Idem., "Co se skrývá za jáchymovskou medailí s Davidem, Goliášem a Jonatanem? Medaile na přátelství od Wolfa Milicze podle grafik Hanse Sebalda Behama," *Časopis Společnosti přátel starožitností* 121/2 (2013), 94–101.

THE PATRON SAINTS AND PIETY OF MINERS

Mining had a strong religious component from the Middle Ages on. Just how valued mining was from time immemorial is illustrated, for example, by a passage in the Book of Job (28:1-11), where the human life journey is likened to a rich ore deposit. Jáchymov cantor and Lutheran priest Johannes Mathesius, brought the religious aspect of mining to absolute perfection in his sermons, published in Nuremberg in 1562 as *Bergpostill – Sarepta*.[60] (Fig. 21) This intermingling of life, faith, and profession bore artistic fruit too, in the form of a wide selection of excellent works of art in the mining towns. Examples include Hans Hesse's 'Miner's Altar' from 1522–1523 in St. Anne's Church in Annaberg-Buchholz, with mining scenes depicted on the central panel, wings, and base, (Fig. 22) and a panel painting by the same artist in the local Cemetery Church of St. Wolfgang, with the image of the patron saint and the 'Legend of Daniel' about the founding of the town and its mining origins (1515).[61] The plaque with the painting of St. Anne (a.k.a. Metercia) from 1513 in the Church of Our Lady in Rožnava (Rosenau) is also noteworthy.[62] Finally, mining scenes can also be found on the title page of the Kutná Hora Gradual from 1490 and the title page of the Kutná Hora Antiphonary from 1471.[63]

The piety of the miners, whether Catholic, Utraquist, or Protestant, was exemplary. When a mining settlement was established, a church was among the first buildings to be built. In most of the mining towns in the Ore Mountains, the churches were initially wooden and, unfortunately, little is known about their appearance as none of them have survived. Later, miners

60) Johannes Mathesius, *Sarepta oder Bergpostill Sampt der Jochimssthalischen kurtzen Chronicken I.–II.* (Praha: 1975); Jan Urban (ed.), *Johannes Mathesius, Hornická postila s krátkou jáchymovskou kronikou* (Praha: 1981); Jan Urban, "Johannes Mathesius und seine Sarepta/Johannes Mathesius a jeho Sarepta," in: *St. Joachimsthal in der Zeit Georgius Agricola. Zur Geschichte einer Bergstadt im 16. Jahrhundert / Jáchymov v době Georgia Agricoly. K dějinám horního města v 16. století* (Schneeberg – Karlovy Vary: 1994), 31–33, 80–81.

61) Ingo Sandner, *Hans Hesse. Ein Maler der Spätgotik in Sachsen* (Dresden: 1983); Jan Royt, "Malíř Hans Hesse a Roudnický oltář," in: *Hans Hesse. Pašijový cyklus z kostela Narození Panny Marie v Roudnici nad Labem, katalog výstavy* (Roudnice: 2011), 16–17; Idem., *Gotické deskové malířství v severozápadních a severních Čechách 1340–1550* (Praha: 2015), 75.

62) Štefan Batta, "Stredoveké baníctvo a hutníctvo na rožňavskej Matercii," in: *Zborník Banského múzea* 14 (Martin: 1989), 105–129; Štefan Batta, *Rožňavská Metercia* (Martin: 2001).

63) The gradual is now kept in the Österreichische Nationalbibliothek, Musiksammlung, the antiphonary is deposited at the National Library of the Czech Republic. For more information, see Josef Krása, "Knižní malířství," in: Jaromír Homolka et al., *Pozdně gotické umění v Čechách (1471–1526)* (Praha: 1978), 387–457; Jan Baťa (ed.), *Codex Kuttenbergensis / Kutnohorský kodex* (Praha: 2008).

Fig. 21 Jan Matheisus, Sarepta oder Bergpostill – title page, 1552–1562, Nuremberg – Leipzig. Reproduction © Münchener DigitalisierungsZentrum, Digitale Bibliothek.

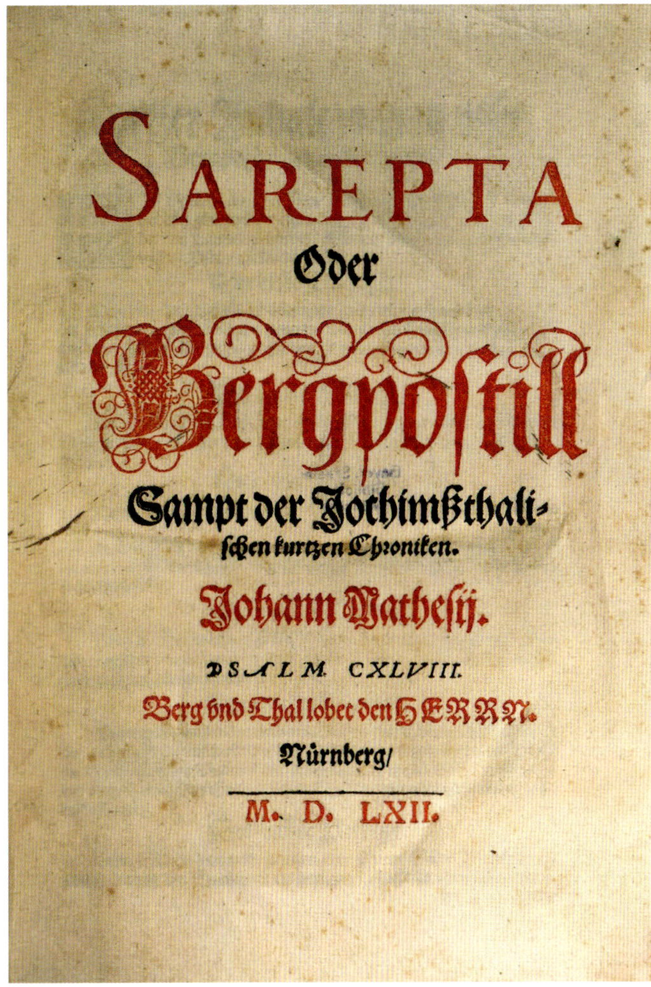

would build their own mining churches in the large mining towns. One of them was the famous Church of St. Barbara in Kutná Hora, a church dedicated to the patron saint of miners and the largest mining church in Europe.[64]

In Catholic and Utraquist mining towns, a distinctive cult of saints was forged to protect miners in their dangerous work.[65] Most mining shafts in the region were in fact dedicated to Christ, the Virgin Mary or one of the saints – a practice that was also perpetuated in the mining towns that embraced the Reformation, such as Jáchymov. Certainly the most popular saint in the mining towns was Saint Anne, the protector of families. Most mining towns in the Ore Mountains – including Annaberg, Krupka/Graupen, Boží Dar/Gottesgab, Jáchymov/Sankt Joachimsthal, and Horní Slavkov/Schlaggenwald – have a chapel dedicated to her, or at

64) Aleš Pospíšil, "Gotický plán chrámu sv. Barbory v Kutné Hoře ze sbírky vídeňské Akademie výtvarných umění (no. 16 841)," *Průzkumy památek* 12/1 (2005), 91–96; Pavel Kalina, *Benedikt Ried a počátky záalpské renesance* (Praha: 2009), 163–174.

65) Georg Schreiber, *Der Bergbau in Geschichte, Ethos und Sakralkultur. Wissenschaftliche Abhandlung nach* einem *Vortrag vor der Arbeitsgemeinschaft für Forschung des Landes Nordrhein-Westfalen* (1962); Jan Royt, "Hornická ikonografie, hagiografie a problematika konfesionalizace v horních městech střední Evropy v období středověku," in: Michaela Hrubá – Michaela Ottová – Jan Royt, *Ars Montana. Umělecký a kulturní transfer v otevřeném prostoru česko-saského Krušnohoří na prahu raného novověku* (Praha: 2016), 53–95.

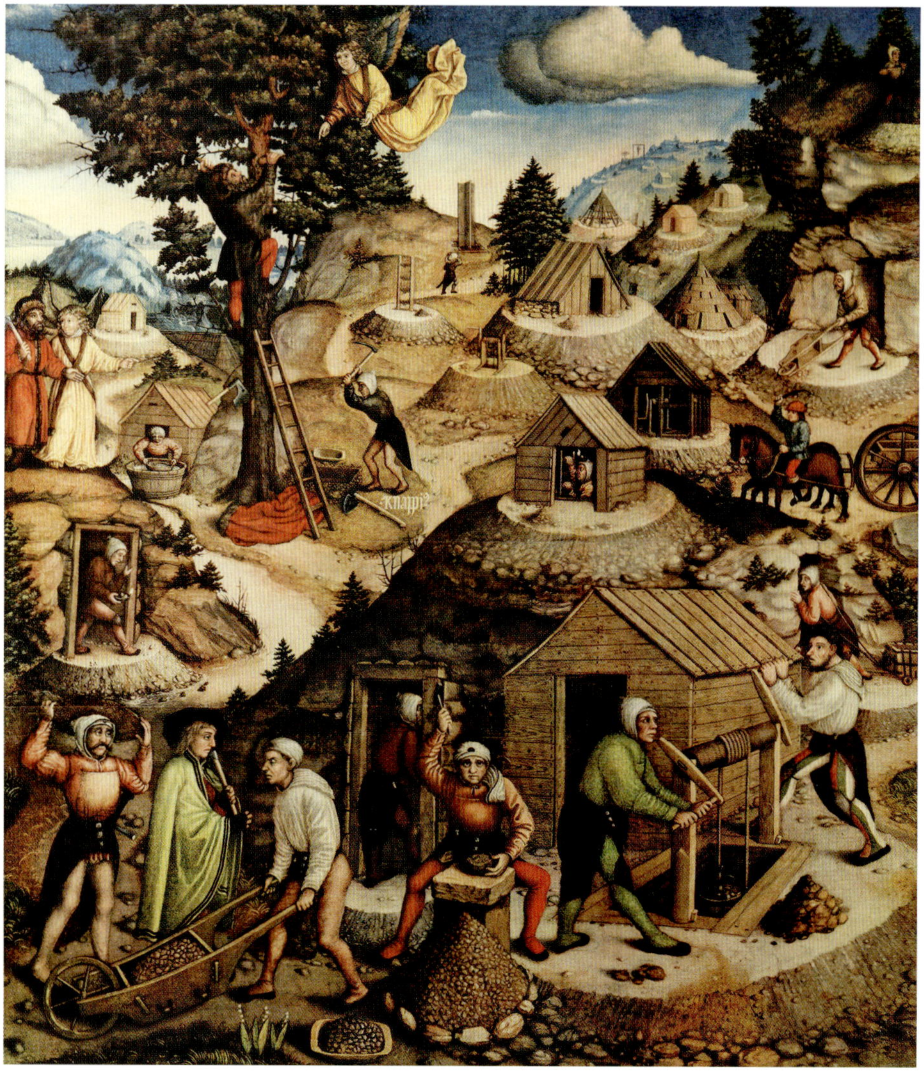

Fig. 22 Annaberg-Buchholz, Church of St. Anne, Miner's Altar – detail of the central part, Hans Hesse, 1522–1523. Photo by J. Royt (2019).

least a painting. (Fig. 23) Jáchymov was named after St. Anne's husband, St. Joachim, who also became its patron saint. Anne and Joachim appear alongside each other, for example, on the cover page of the Mining Code of Jáchymov, issued by the Lords of Schlick (Leipzig 1518). The earlier-mentioned panel painting of St. Anne from 1513 in the chapel of St. Anne in Rožňava, is a splendid example of the intermingling of the cult of St. Anne with the mining profession. It depicts St. Anne alongside the Virgin Mary and the Baby Jesus in the foreground, with the Old Testament theme of Nebuchadnezzar's dream as described by the prophet Daniel in the background. This story, with motifs of metal mining and the founding of mining settlements, was very popular with the mining town community. Hans Hesse depicted the legend in his altarpiece of St. Wolfgang in the cemetery church in Annaberg-Buchholz around 1515. The church in Annaberg, one of the most important mining towns in the Ore Mountains, is also dedicated to St. Anne and the town got its name from her.[66] The exceptional popularity of St. Anne in the

66) Ariane Grund, *Sankt Annen. Der Bergmannsdom in Annaberg-Bucholz* (Chemnitz: 2011). On the artistic representation in the upper towns in Saxony also: Ingo Sandner – Helmut Wilsdorf – Arndt Kiesewetter, *Spätgotische Tafelmalerei*

Fig. 23 Krupka, the cemetery church of St. Anne. Construction in 1516, completion in 1576. Painter Ludwig Richter 1836. Reproduction from the private collection of T. Šimková

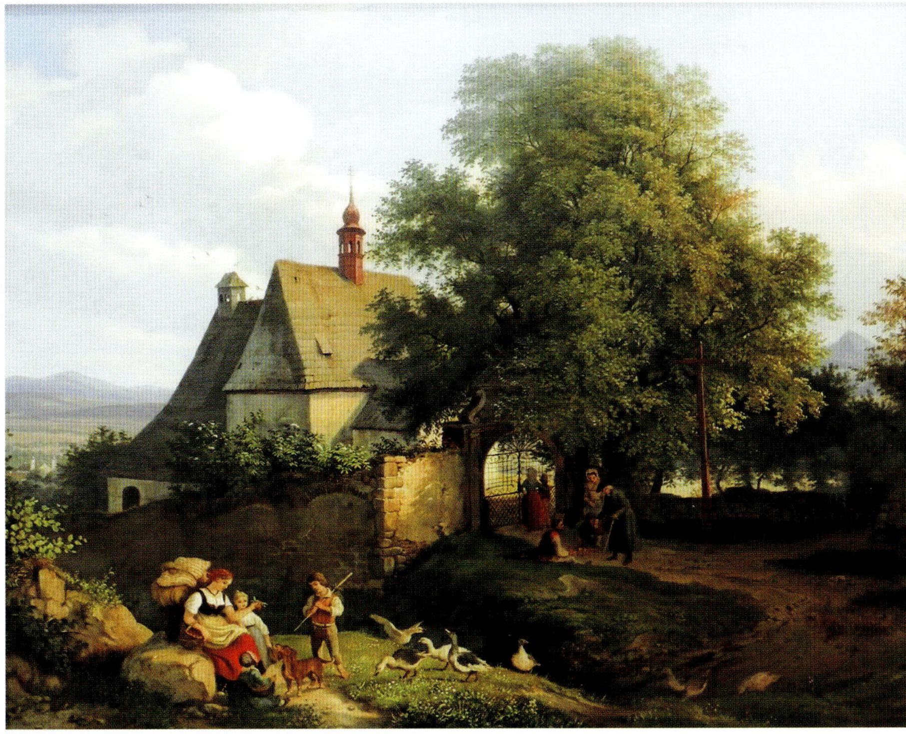

Ore Mountains is also illustrated by the fact that in addition to mining churches and chapels, mining facilities were named after her. The existence of the Midnight Vein of St. Anne (mentioned in 1524) and St. Rich Anne's Pit, is documented in the Jáchymov district in the 16th century. A silver-bearing adit and mine dedicated to St. Anne are also mentioned in the Černý Potok Valley. In the Slavkov Forest, mention is made in 1572 of the Vein of St. Anne near Pavlovice.[67]

Saint Barbara, the patron saint of miners, was also a popular saint in the mining towns. She was the patron saint of 'the good death,' who interceded for those dying without recourse to the sacraments. This was very important considering the risks that miners faced at every turn. Whole legions of saints were invoked for this purpose to ensure multiplied intercessions. They included the Ten Thousand Knights martyred on Mount Ararat and Saint Ursula's retinue of Martyred Virgin Handmaidens. A painting of St. Ursula can be found in the famous Upper Hungarian mining town of Banská Bystrica (Neusohl) and also in the nearby Poniky (Ponik), where gold, copper, and iron ore were mined in the Middle Ages.[68] Other popular intercessors were the Fourteen Holy Helpers who included Saint Barbara. Paintings of them can be found in Banská Bystrica (Neusohl), Abertamy (Abertham) in the Ore Mountains, and the Franciscan monastery in Kadaň (Kaaden).[69]

(Dresden – Basel: 1993); Alžběta Semrádová, "Kult sv. Anny v Čechách v období středověku a raného novověku (Katalog malířských děl)," (diploma thesis, Charles University, 2018); Hana Vorlová, "Svatá Anna Samotřetí v gotické plastice Českých zemí. Soupis a ikonografie," (diploma thesis, Palacký University Olomouc, 2002), 61. Includes a list of works pertinent to northwest Bohemia.

67) Jan Kořan, *Sláva a pád starého českého rudného hornictví* (Příbram: 1988), 111–114, 136–137.

68) Dušan Buran, *Studien zur Wandmalerei um 1400 in der Slowakei. Die Pfarrkirche St. Jakob in Leutschau und die Pfarrkirche St. Franziskus Seraphicus in Poniky* (Weimar: 2002).

69) Petr Hlaváček, *Nový Jeruzalém? Příběh františkánského kláštera Čtrnácti sv. Pomocníků v Kadani* (Kadaň: 2013); Petr Hlaváček – Milena Bílková, *Františkánské nebe v Kadani: renesanční příběh kláštera Čtrnácti sv. Pomocníků / Der Fran-*

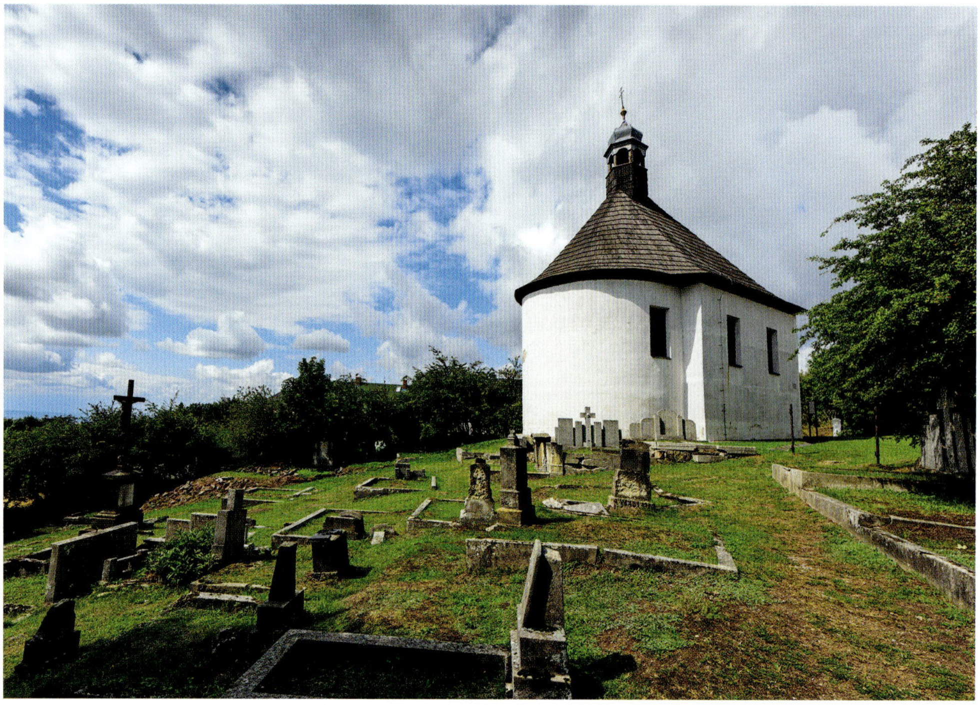

Fig. 24 Krupka – mining part of the town, St. Wolfgang's Chapel in Horní Krupka. Originally built in the 14th century, demolished in 1634 by the Swedes and rebuilt between 1692–1700 on the initiative of the owner of the estate, Vojtěch Václav Šternberk. Photograph by J. Peer (2019).

The mining community also venerated saints whose legends involved the windlass with wheels used as a torture instrument. One of them was Saint Erasmus, who was tortured by having his intestines wound around a windlass that resembled a miner's wheel. Another was Saint Catherine, whose body was woven into a complicated torture instrument with several wheel gears. This scene is depicted on the altarpiece triptych in Osek (Ossegg).

In Saxony, the patron saint of miners is St. Wolfgang, Bishop of Regensburg, who was typically depicted with a carpenter's axe pointed towards miners timbering a shaft. St. Wolfgang is depicted in the St. Wolfgang Altarpiece by Hans Hesse in St. Wolfgang's Cemetery Chapel in Annaberg-Buchholz; it shows the saint in a landscape, surrounded by mining motifs and a scene from the Legend of Daniel. The chapel in Horní Krupka (Obergraupen), which was built by miners in the 14th century, is also dedicated to St. Wolfgang. (Fig. 24) It was destroyed during the Thirty Years' War and rebuilt at the turn of the 17th and 18th centuries.[70] In the mining towns under Catholic or Utraquist royal administration, patrons of the nation were also venerated. Upper Hungary can serve as an example, where the legend of St. László (Ladislaus) is a common theme. A cycle about St. László can be seen in the church in Poniky (Ponik), and a painting depicting all the Hungarian provincial patron saints can be found in the chapel of St. Barbara in Banská Bystrica. In the Czech lands, the cult of the most important

ziskanerhimmel in Kadaň: Die Renaissancegeschichte des Klosters der Vierzehn heiligen Nothelfer (Kadaň: 2018); Bruno Pavol Viczencz, *Vznik úcty a modlitby ke čtrnácti svatým pomocníkům* (Praha: 2019).

70) For information on other monuments dedicated to St. Wolfgang in the region: Hana Pátková, "Bratrstva svatého Wolfganga v pozdně středověkých Čechách," in: *Za zdmi kláštera, cisterciáci v českých dějinách* (České Budějovice: 2010), 167–171; Vladěna Haragová, "Ikonografická rekonstrukce nástěnných maleb z kostela sv. Wolfganga v Doupově," *Památky západních Čech* 4 (2014), 20–35; Ludmila Novotná, "Fundátorka Anna Šliková, příspěvek k historii kostela sv. Wolfganga v Ostrohu," in: *Sborník muzea Karlovarského kraje* 18 (2010), 273–276.

Fig. 25 The coat of arms of Kutná Hora, incunabula of the Kutná Hora Bible. The municipal coat of arms of Kutná Hora with a crowned eagle and lion on a red-gold field bearing miners' hammers and a chalice, above which a crown floats. The coat of arms is held by shield-bearers in the form of two miners in hoods. Photo © Moravské zemské muzeum.

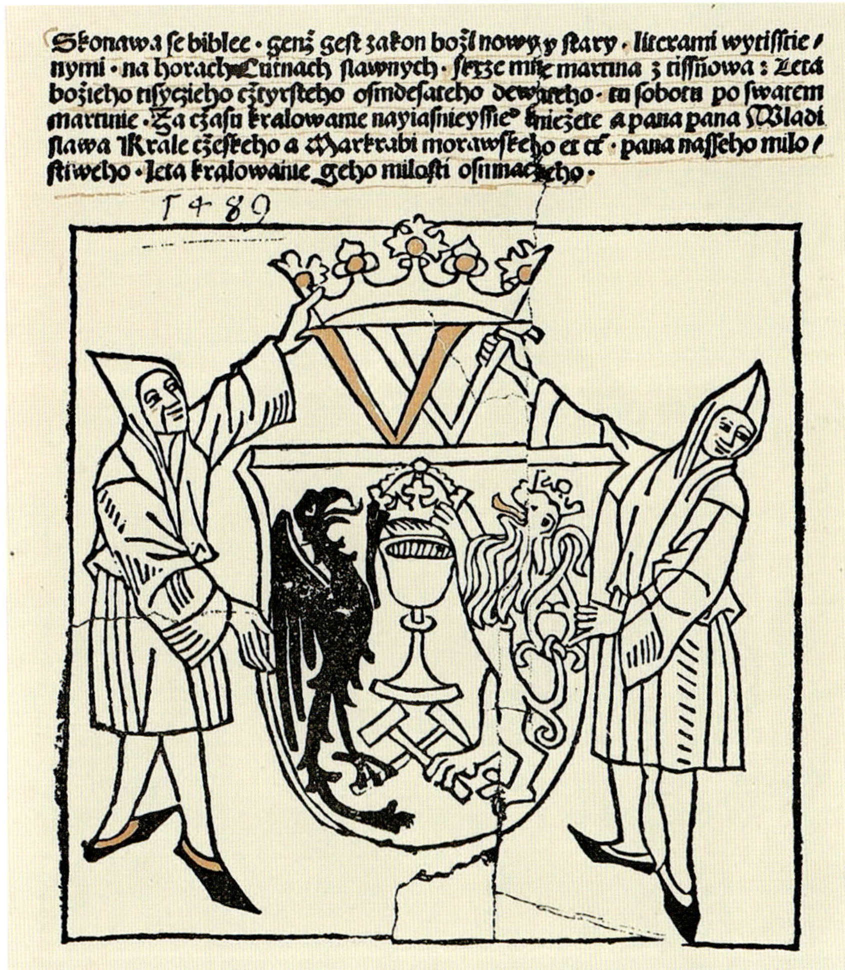

patron saint of the nation, St. Wenceslas, had the most tangible presence in the mining towns. A specific feature of Utraquist towns were altarpieces with the Last Supper of Christ depicted in the middle panel. An example can be found in the Church of St. Barbara in Kutná Hora (Kuttenberg). The chalice as a symbol of Utraquism is depicted in the Church of St. James in Kutná Hora and is also part of the town's coat of arms.[71] (Fig. 25) Motifs related to Jan Hus and the Utraquist tradition also appear in the Smíšek Gradual from Kutná Hora (Kuttenberg); they include an image of the martyrdom of Master Jan Hus and the execution of the parish priest Jan Chůdek and other Hussite priests by pushing them into the mining pits on 9 January 1420.[72] The Utraquists prayed to the Virgin Mary and to saints who, in contrast to Catholic piety, included Jan Hus and Jerome of Prague.

71) Oto Halama – Pavel Soukup, *Kalich jako symbol v prvním století utrakvismu* (Praha: 2016); Jan Royt, "Ikonografie Mistra Jana Husa v 15. až 18. století," in: *Hus na přelomu tisíciletí. Mezinárodní rozprava o českém reformátoru 15. století a o jeho recepci na prahu třetího milénia, Husitský Tábor, Supplementum* 1 (2001), 405–452; Jan Royt, "Utrakvistická ikonografie v Čechách 15. a první poloviny 16. století," in: Dalibor Prix (ed.), *Pro Arte. Sborník k poctě Ivo Hlobila* (Praha: 2002), 193–205.

72) Milada Studničková, "Úvodní iluminace Smíškovského graduálu jako klíč k interpretaci rukopisu," in: Dalibor Prix (ed.), *Pro arte, sborník k poctě Ivo Hlobila* (Praha: 2002), 183–189; Pavel Brodský, "Vyobrazení kutnohorských havířů v českých pozdně středověkých rukopisech," *Poznańskie Towarzystwo Przyjaciól Nauk* 106 (1989), 94–97.

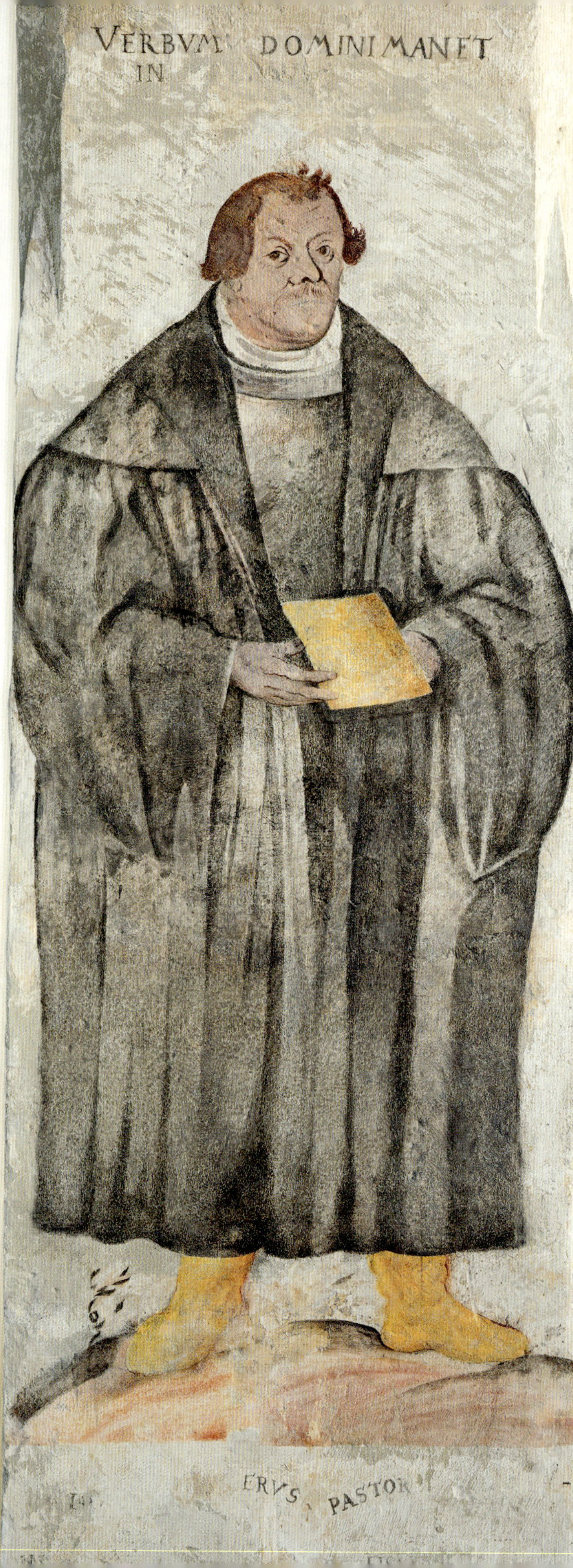

Fig. 26 Krupka, Church of St. Anne, painting on the epistle side of the nave triumphal arch depicting Martin Luther. Photograph by J. Peer (2019).

THE MINING TOWNS AFTER LUTHER'S THESES, AND CONFESSIONALISATION IN THE ORE MOUNTAINS

Changes in the religious landscape occurred in the mining towns after Martin Luther published his theses in 1517.[73] In the course of only three decades of the 16th century, religiosity was completely transformed and the predominantly German-speaking local population embraced Luther's reformation teachings. Lutheranism initially became widespread in northwest Bohemia and later spread to other areas, including mining towns in Upper Hungary.

Jáchymov can justifiably claim to be the most important intellectual centre of the Lutheran faith, even if the local community was diverse in terms of denomination, and staunch Lutherans as well as opponents of Luther or followers of the Catholic Church could be found here. This made Jáchymov attractive for theologians and scholars. Martin Luther himself paid a visit to the town, as did Justus Jonas in 1536, eminent reformer and professor at the University of Wittenberg, and later Georg Spalatin, personal secretary, spiritual advisor and court preacher to the Saxon Elector Frederick the Wise. Other visitors included the excellent theologian Philipp Melanchton (who came on the invitation of Johannes Mathesius), Thomas Müntzer, Balthasar Hubmaier, and Andreas Bodenstein von Karlstadt – the most radical Saxon reformer and a well-known iconoclast. In 1522, Karlstadt dedicated his defence of iconoclasm entitled 'Von Abtuhung der Bilder' to Count Wolfgang Schlick, whom Martin Luther also considered a friend. In doing so, he tried to win the Schlicks over to his radical views and inspire them to initiate a reformation in Jáchymov in the spirit of iconoclastic puritanism. But he failed in Jáchymov, just as he had previously failed in Wittenberg, from whence he had been driven by Luther. The founder of Jáchymov, Stephan Schlick, was approached by Martin Luther in 1522 as 'the most Christian layman,' to whom he explained the differences between the German and the Bohemian Reformations and his relationship to Hus. Count Schlick, who vacillated between Catholicism and the new Lutheran faith, was subsequently summoned before the Catholic Consistory in Prague on account of his contacts with the Lutherans. But Johannes Mathesius

73) Táňa Šimková, "Luterství v horních městech českého Krušnohoří – stručný nástin problematiky," in: Michaela Hrubá – Jan Royt, *Ars Montana. Umělecký a kulturní transfer v otevřeném prostoru česko-saského Krušnohoří na prahu raného novověku* (Praha: 2016), 241–250.

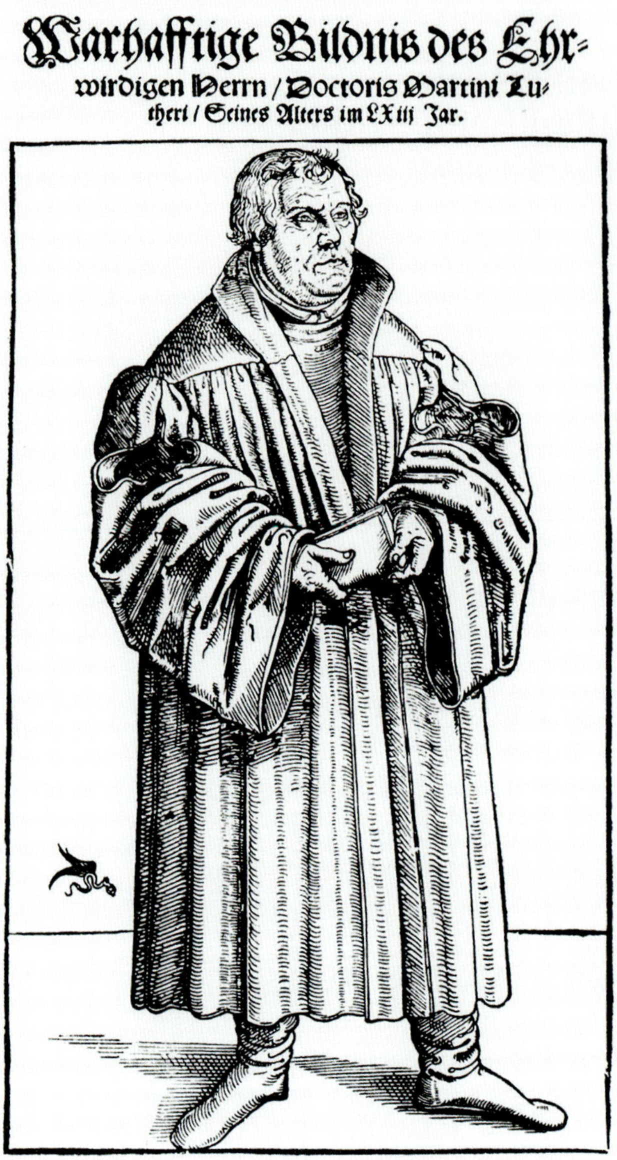

Fig. 27 Martin Luther – graphic art, probable model of a painting in the Church of St. Anne in Krupka, Lucas Cranach Sr. (Jr.?), woodcut. Reproduction from the private collection of J. Royt.

later made him the most important supporter of the Reformation in his sermons and texts and wrote in the same favourable spirit about the entire Schlick family.[74]

The Peace of Kadaň (Kaaden)

In 1534, a meeting between Catholic and Lutheran representatives took place in the royal town of Kadaň (Kaaden). It was presided over by King Ferdinand I and the Saxon Elector Johann Friedrich. The aim of the meeting was to establish an agreement that would allow for religious and political reconciliation, which was to include the formation of a Catholic-Lutheran alliance against the Calvinists and Anabaptists. The meeting was hosted by Albrecht Schlick,

74) Petr Hlaváček, "Luteránství jako skrytý fenomén českých duchovních a kulturních dějin," in: Jiří Just et al. (ed.), *Luteráni v českých zemích v proměnách století* (Praha: 2009), 18–21.

the royal governor of Kadaň, who also organised a symbolic feast of reconciliation in the garden of the Franciscan monastery. Historian Petr Hlaváček considers this event, documented in the Franciscan monastery chronicle, as evidence of the importance of the Schlick family in the religious and political life in the Bohemian-Saxon borderland and, by extention, the whole Kingdom of Bohemia.[75]

Confessionalisation was strongly reflected in the interior decoration of houses of worship.[76] In the older churches, the Gothic winged altarpieces and altars were often left behind by converted miners, but the veneration of saints had lost its importance since Luther rejected their role as intercessors.[77]

Martin Luther (1483–1546)

German priest and reformer, critic of the Catholic Church and founder of Protestantism, whose teachings forever changed the religious map of Europe. His most important work was the translation of the Bible into German, which was rapidly distributed throughout Germany thanks to the printing press, as were his sermons and other works. Luther's teachings soon spread from Saxony over to the Ore Mountains, where he found supporters among the German-speaking population, both among the nobility and the mining town populations. The painting of Martin Luther in the miners' church of St. Anne in Krupka (Graupen) testifies to that, which dates from the time when the church underwent a Renaissance reconstruction at the turn of the 16th and 17th centuries, and was modelled on prints of the reformer, which were widespread at the time. (Fig. 27)

Pillars of the Lutheran Faith

SOLA FIDE, SOLA GRATIA, SOLA SCRIPTURA, SOLA CHRISTUS / BY FAITH ALONE, BY GRACE ALONE, BY SCRIPTURE ALONE, BY CHRIST ALONE

Martin Luther gave believers the hope that they would be saved by faith alone and not by good deeds alone; that only God's grace can absolve man from sin and give him salvation; that the Scripture (the Bible) alone is the source of authority on correct Christian faith, and that the person and work of Jesus Christ is the foundation of the belief in the redemption of man.

From the 1530s onwards, newly built Lutheran churches conformed to the requirements later codified in the Augsburg Confession of Faith. Scripture alone (sola scriptura) and Faith alone (sola fide) became the fundamental pillars of Lutheranism. The seven Catholic sacraments were reduced to two (Baptism and the Eucharist). All this was reflected in the layout

75) Petr Hlaváček, "Kadaňský smír roku 1534 (Katolicko-luterský pokus o záchranu Jednoty Svaté říše římské)," in: *Lutheranus* 2007/2008, *Sborník Lutherovy společnosti* 2 (2008), 138–146.

76) Andrea K. Thurnwald, "Kirchenstuhl und Katechismus. Der Wandel von Liturgie und Sachkultur in Franken," in: Bauern Ritter, *Lutheranen* (Augsburg: 2017), 42–49; Táňa Šimková, *Hrad přepevný je Pánbůh náš. Saská luterská šlechta severozápadních Čech ve světle raně novověké sakrální architektury* (Ústí nad Labem: 2018), 52–54; Michaela Hrubá (ed.), *Sola Fide/Pouhou vírou. Luterská šlechta na Ústecku a Děčínsku a její kulturní dědictví* (Ústí nad Labem: 2019).

77) Jan Royt, "Horní město Jáchymov, reformace a umění," in: *Ústecký sborník historický* 2001, 351–359; Jan Royt, "The Mining Town of Jáchymov: Reformation and Art," in: *The Bohemian Reformation and Religious Practice* 5/2 (2005), 305–311.

of Lutheran churches. The altar, pulpit and baptismal font were highlighted. In Freiberg and Kraslice, the pulpit was supported by the figures of miners. The chapels built by mining guilds and wealthy miners disappeared, but the altars of mining guilds were kept in place, as we know from Annaberg (the miners' altar from 1522) and Annaberg-Buchholz (Hesse's miners' altar from 1522). The railing of the pulpit, decorated with symbols or figures of the Evangelists (or Church Fathers), were carried by the figures of Moses with the Tablets of the Law, Aaron the High Priest, or St. John the Baptist, thus evoking Luther's doctrine of Law and Grace. Lutheran baptismal fonts were richly decorated with reliefs of Christ receiving little children (*Let the little children come to me* – in polemic with the Anabaptists' refusal to baptise infants) or the waters of chastisement and forgiveness, corresponding to the prayer said at baptism. The stem of the baptismal font in Annaberg is decorated with figures of children dressed in miners' capes.[78]

In the new Lutheran churches there was only one altar with an altarpiece that was either painted or made of stone. Examples include the painted altarpieces by Lucas Cranach with the Lutheran theme of Law and Grace in Schneeberg and Jáchymov. Murals are rarely found in Lutheran churches. Instead, Biblical themes from both the Old and New Testaments often decorate the church gallery. These are either paintings or reliefs, the latter of which can be found in Annaberg, Most (Brüx), and Krupka (Graupen). The gallery of the now-nonexistent mining church in Kraslice (Graslitz) was decorated in a similar fashion. In Annaberg, in addition to religious themes, a remarkable cycle of the stages in the life of man and woman is depicted in the reliefs by Franz Mainburg. Depictions of Luther himself can also be found in Lutheran churches. An example is a mural in the church of St. Anne in Krupka (Graupen) that features the reformer's whole figure and which was inspired by an engraving by Lucas Cranach the Elder. Catholics also had their own churches in Lutheran towns. In Jáchymov, for example, they most likely used the cemetery church, which had an altarpiece with the theme of the Betrothal of St. Catherine painted by Lucas Cranach the Elder. It had been commissioned around 1519 by Heinrich Könneritz, Inspector of Mines, who remained Catholic. The confessional situation was very complex in Most (Brüx), where the local Church of the Assumption was used jointly by Catholics, Utraquists and Lutherans. Generally speaking, almost all the mining towns in the Ore Mountains converted to Lutheranism in the 16th century, although this did not safeguard them from religious conflict.[79]

In 1547, after the victory of Charles V over the Protestants at Mühlburg, the Bohemian King Ferdinand I supported the Catholic denomination in the country, but refrained from clamping down on Lutheranism in the mining towns, for reasons at least partially pragmatic, as the area was a guaranteed source of money.[80] In 1598, years before the Battle of White Mountain, miners from Výsluní (Sonnenberg) and Hora sv. Šebestiána (Sebastiansberg) relocated

78) Jan Royt, "Voda omilostňující a voda trestající: ikonografie luteránských křtitelnic v Čechách," in: *In puncto religionis: konfesní dimenze předbělohorské kultury Čech a Moravy* (Praha: 2013), 163–174.

79) Jan Royt, *Biblické příběhy na reliéfech Chrámu Nanebevzetí Panny Marie v Mostě* (Ústí nad Labem: 2011); Michaela Ottová – Jan Royt, *Kostel Nanebevzetí Panny Marie v Mostě v době konfesních změn (1517–1594)* (Ústí nad Labem: 2014).

80) Petr Vorel (ed.), *Stavovský odboj roku 1547. První krize habsburské monarchie* (Pardubice: 1999).

Fig. 28 Bohosudov, pilgrimage basilica of Our Lady of Sorrows. Giulio and Octavio Broggio, 1701–1706. Photograph by J. Peer (2019).

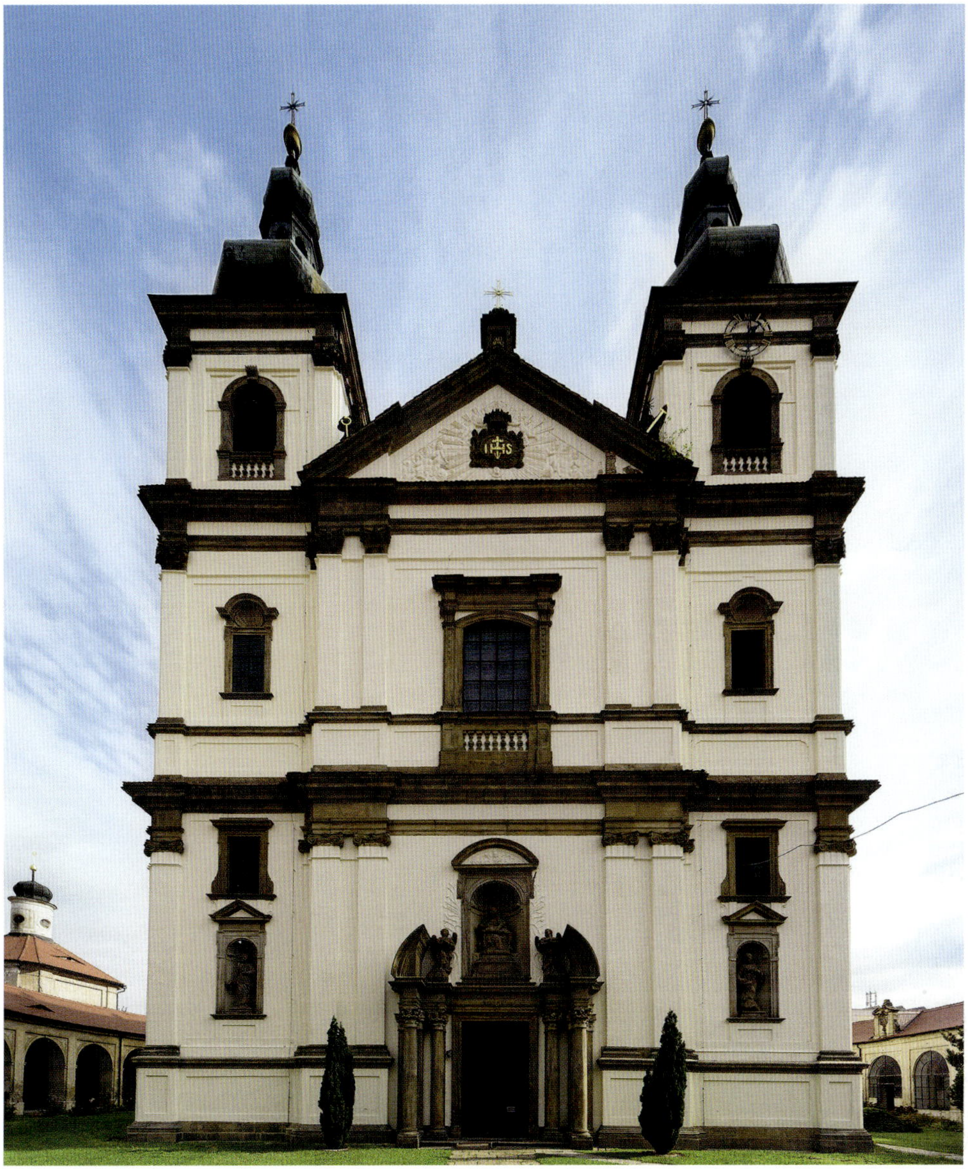

to Saxony due to the re-Catholicisation efforts of George Popel of Lobkowitz.[81] Disputes between the supporters of the Radical Reformation and its moderate followers took place in Jáchymov. The Letter of Majesty signed by Rudolf II in 1609 seemed to help achieve stability in the country, but after the victory of the Catholic camp in the Battle of White Mountain, non-Catholics had to either convert or leave the country. Interestingly, one of the impulses for the Estates' Revolt was the demolition of a church in the mining town of Hrob (Klostergrab) near Krupka (Graupen), which belonged to the Osek (Ossegg) Monastery. This was done at the behest of the Archbishop of Prague, Johann Lohelius.[82] In consideration of Johann Georg I,

81) Michaela Hrubá, "Jiří Popel z Lobkovic a prostředky rekatolizace na sklonku 16. století. (Příspěvek k dějinám rekatolizace v severozápadních Čechách)," in: *Ústecký sborník historický* 2000, 132–144.
82) Jan Kilián, *11. 12. 1617 – zboření kostela v Hrobu: na cestě k defenestraci* (Praha: 2007).

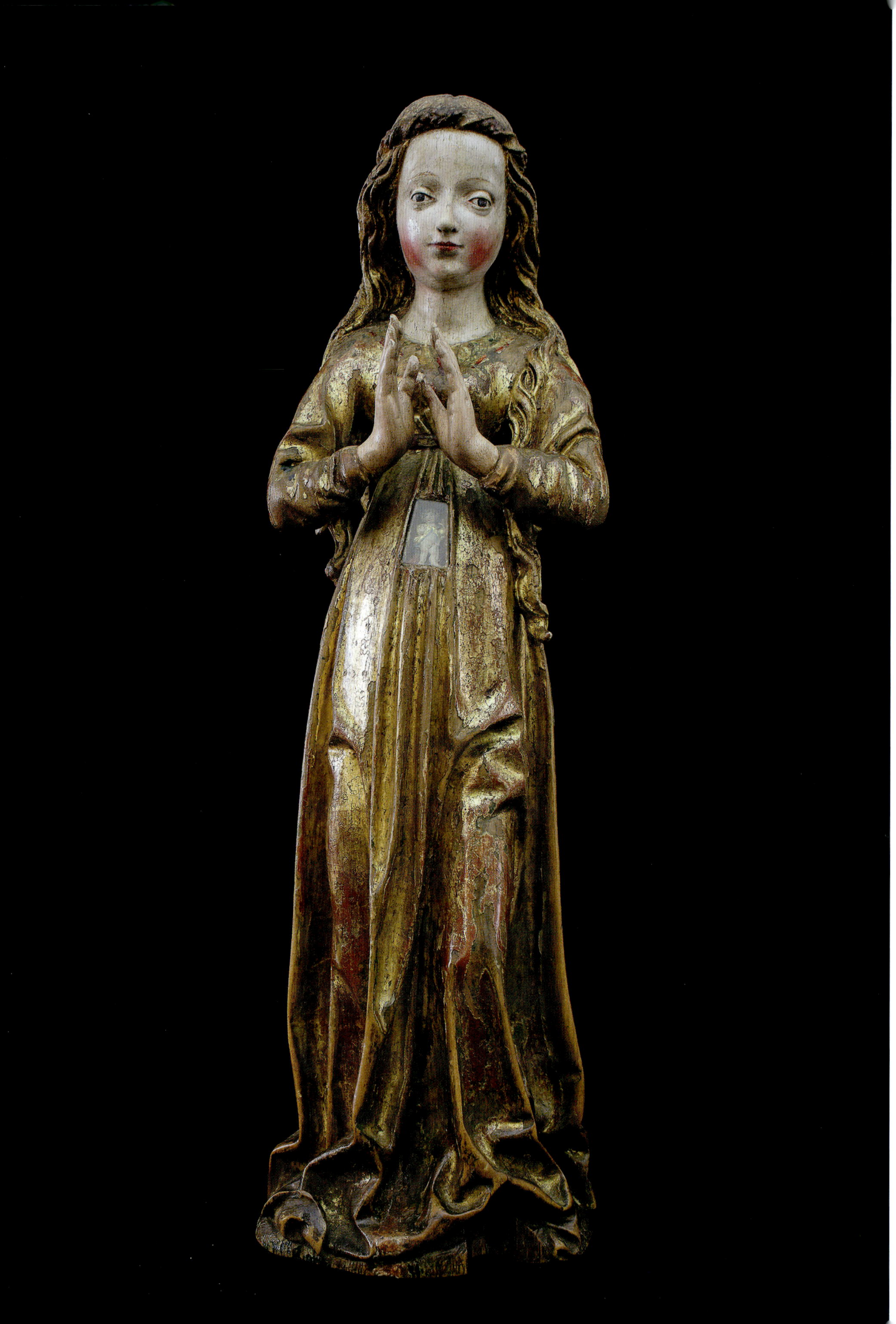

Elector of Saxony, who sided with Ferdinand II during the Estates' Revolt despite being a Lutheran himself, the treatment of non-Catholics in the mining towns was more lenient than in other parts of the country. Non-Catholics were still leaving some of the mining towns at the end of the Thirty Years' War.

It is hardly a coincidence that well before the Battle of White Mountain, Jesuits were invited to Chomutov (Komotau) by the aforementioned George Popel of Lobkowicz and founded a Jesuit college there. The local patres were entrusted with serving missions in the Ore Mountains mining towns, which were Lutheran.[83] In the 17th century, a tradition of pilgrimages to grace statues and paintings developed as part of the anti-Reformation struggle. The mediaeval tradition of Marian pilgrimages is documented in Bohosudov (Mariaschein) and Chlum Sv. Máří (Maria Kulm), which were the two most-visited pilgrimage sites.[84](Fig. 28) Pilgrims also travelled to the Church of St. James near Kraslice (Graslitz) and to the Church of Our Lady of Sorrows in Mariánské Radčice (Maria Ratschitz), two pilgrimage sites associated with the Cistercians.[85] Another such site was the Church of the Assumption of Our Lady in Horní Jiřetín (Ober Georgenthal), from which the route to neighbouring Saxony led via the local borough of Mariánské Údolí (Mariathal).[86] Perhaps the most notable mediaeval grace statue of Our Lady Expectant (Maria gravida) comes from the Pilgrimage Church of the Visitation of Our Lady in Květnov (Quinau), which was administered by the Jesuits of Chomutov (Komutau). Our Lady of Květnov (Quinau) was a very popular and revered intercessor for all women who longed for a child, and was rightfully hailed as the 'Queen of the Ore Mountains.'[87]

Our Lady Expectant of Květnov (Quinau) (Fig. 29)
This small statue of the bareheaded Virgin Mary, with a figure of the Child Jesus in a gesture of blessing placed in an opening in her stomach, has been venerated since the 16th century. There is a story linked to Květnov that tells of the miraculous discovery of the statue by a shepherd in 1342. It is more likely, however, that the statue was imported by Benes (Benesch Krabitz) of

83) Josef Koláček, "Kolej sv. Ignáce v Chomutově anno Domini 1591," in: *Památky, příroda, život. Vlastivědný čtvrtletník Chomutovska* 34/3 (2002), 1–15; Jiří Mikulec, "Jezuitská bratrstva v Chomutově," in: *Comotovia 2002* (Ústí nad Labem: 2003), 102–114; Jaroslav Pánek – Miloslav Polívka – Karin Warta, "Chomutovská divadelní hra z roku 1594: dramatický obraz náboženských, politických a národnostních rozporů v předbělohorské stavovské společnosti," in: *Comotovia 2002* (Ústí nad Labem: 2003), 31–78.

84) Jan Kvapil, "Severočeská pánev – Mariánská země? Překlad díla Atlas Marianus Wilhelma Gumppenberga do němčiny oseckým cisterciákem Augustinem Sartoriem," in: *Náboženské dějiny severních Čech* (Ústí nad Labem: 1999), 20–24; Jan Kvapil, "Augustinus Sartorius: Mariánský Atlas, Praha 1717 (koncepce barokního patriotismu vytvořená oseckými cisterciáky)," in: *Ústecký sborník historický* (2000), 145–166; Michaela Hoffmann, *Mariaschein – Bohosudov: ein Wallfahrtsort im Donröschenschlaf* (Brno: 2005); Iva Prošková, "Mariánská úcta v severozápadních Čechách: putování a zbožnost jako součást každodenního života barokních Čech," in: *Poohří* 5 (2015), 100–111; Šárka Radostová, "Socha trůnící Panny Marie Chlumské a její druhý život," in: *Ústecký sborník historický* 2004, 433–453.

85) Jan Royt, "Poutě a poutní místa v Čechách," in: *Cesty a cestování v životě společnosti/Reisen im Leben der Gesellschaft* (Ústí nad Labem: 1995), 309–314; Norbert Krutský, "Mariánské Radčice – poutní místo oseckých cisterciáků / Maria Radschitz – ein Wallfahrtsort der Ossegger Zisterzienser," in: *800 let kláštera Osek / 800 Jahre Kloster Ossegg* (Osek: 1996), 35–44.

86) Jan Royt, "Posvátná krajina severozápadních Čech," *Monumentorum Custos* 2017: 7–22; Iva Prošková, "Mariánská úcta v severozápadních Čechách: putování a zbožnost jako součást každodenního života barokních Čech," in: *Poohří* 5 (2015), 100–111.

87) Zdeněk Boháč, *Poutní místa v Čechách* (Praha: 1995,) 272–273.

← Fig. 29 Virgin Mary in Hope from Květnov, import, 1471. Photograph by J. Royt (2019).

Veitmile/Weitmühle, who acquired Květnov along with the entire Chomutov estate in 1471. As the Burgrave of Karlštejn, Chief Mintmaster of the Kingdom of Bohemia, and frequent envoy of Vladislaus II, he had many opportunities to visit the then famous pilgrimage site of Bogenberg near Straubing, where the statue of Maria Gravida was also venerated. The veneration of the Květnov statue may have been initiated by Beneš' wife Bonuše of Kamenná Hora (Anna von Steinberg), who bore her husband seven children.[88]

The counter-Reformation certainly played a role in the emergence of a strong cult of John of Nepomuk, martyr of the confessional secret, in the mining towns of the Ore Mountains. This may have been related to Nepomuk's popularity among the German-speaking Catholics as well as the population of neighbouring Bavaria. A local mining town without a statue of, or an altar dedicated to, John of Nepomuk would be hard to find.[89] Particularly in the Karlovy Vary (Karlsbad) and Cheb (Eger) regions, the motif of the Holy Trinity appears much more frequently on columns in towns and cities than it does in other parts of the country. This is probably for pastoral reasons, since the triune God was also worshipped by Lutherans.[90]

One of the most recent art-historical projects focusing on religious art and confessionalisation in Czech historical research has been *Umění české reformace* (The Art of the Czech Reformation), which also looked at the art of the Ore Mountains. As a key to the interpretation of the artworks, the authors used the confessional affiliation of the patrons who had commissioned them, with more emphasis on the central Utraquist part of the country and less on the Lutheran communities.[91] The findings on the basic classification of the artworks based on religious denomination were summarised and interpretive models were created. However, more detailed research in the Bohemian-Saxon border area shows that further verification and revision of those models will be necessary. Indeed, it is the Ore Mountains region and its development during the 'Silver Rush' that shows that religious denomination is a very important, but not the only, perspective from which to evaluate the richly structured and stratified body of visual arts in the Ore Mountains.[92]

88) Václav Šroněk, "Páni z Weitmile," in: Jaromír Homolka – Michaela Hrubá – Petr Hrubý – Michaela Ottová (ed.), *Gotické umění a jeho historické souvislosti II.*, in: *Ústecký sborník historický* 2003/1, 234–235.

89) Hans Pörnbacher, "Svatý Jan Nepomucký jako zemský patron Bavorska," in: *Svatý Jan Nepomucký 1393–1993* (Praha: 1993), 23–32; Jan Royt, "Ikonografie sv. Jana Nepomuckého," *Svatojanský sborník*, (Praha: 1994), 53–63.

90) Ivana Maxová – Vratislav Nejedlý – Zuzana Slížková – Pavel Zahradník, *Mariánské, trojiční a další světecké sloupy a pilíře v Karlovarském kraji* (Praha: 2004); Kateřina Adamcová – Zdenka Gláserová Lebedová – Viktor Kovařík – Vratislav Nejedlý – Pavel Zahradník, *Mariánské, trojiční a další světecké sloupy a pilíře v Ústeckém kraji* (Praha: 2012).

91) Kateřina Horníčková – Michal Šroněk (ed.), *Umění české reformace* (Praha: 2010).

92) Petr Hlaváček, "‚Prope Sudetos Montes' Hraniční oblasti Čech, Saska, Horní Lužice a Dolního Slezska jako jeden kulturní region (1520–1620)," in: Lenka Bobková – Jana Konvičná – Jana Wojtucka (ed.), *Společné a rozdílné. Česká koruna v životě a vědomí jejích obyvatel ve 14.–16. století. Korunní země v dějinách českého státu II.* (Praha: 2005), 423–434.

BETWEEN THE GOTHIC AND THE RENAISSANCE: IN SEARCH OF THE 'SAXON RENAISSANCE'

The specific character of the buildings and artistic monuments, the style and design of which places them between the Gothic and Renaissance movements, as well as the unique circumstances associated with the development of ore mining on the Bohemian-Saxon border, gave rise to the term 'Saxon Renaissance' It is chiefly used to refer to architecture from the time period concerned, but by implication it also describes other works of art that are part of the interior design. The term 'Saxon Renaissance' was coined by Václav Mencl in connection with the early Renaissance art of the 1630s, specifically in reference to a number of buildings built by the Schlick (Šlik) and Pernstein (Pernštejn) families in a wide geographic region of northwestern and eastern Bohemia.[93] But the first historians of art and culture to focus their interest on the Ore Mountains and more broadly the region of northwest Bohemia in the late mediaeval and early modern period were Walter Hentschell[94] and Josef Opitz,[95] both of whom published pioneering works on the subject. Art monuments from the Bohemian part of the Ore Mountains were also covered in the large synthetic projects entitled *A History of Czech Fine Arts*, *Late Gothic Art in Bohemia*, *Gothik in Böhmen* and *Renaissance in Böhmen,* and *Kunst der Renaissance und Manierismus in Böhmen.*[96] There is also a book by Eva Šamánková

93) Václav Mencl, *Tisíc a sto let české stavební tvorby* (Praha: 1957), 19–20.

94) Walter Hentschel, *Denkmale sächsischer Kunst. Die Verluste des zweiten Weltkrieges* (Berlin: 1973); Idem., *Dresdner Bildhauer des 16. und 17. Jahrhunderts* (Berlin – Böhlau: 1966); Walter Hentschel, *Bibliographie zur sächsischen Kunstgeschichte* (Berlin: 1960); Idem., *Peter Breuer. Eine spätgotische Bildschnitzerwerkstatt* (Dresden: 1951); Idem., *Meißner Bildhauer zwischen Spätgotik und Barock* (Meißen: 1934); Idem., "Cranach und seine Schule im Erzgebirge," in: *Glückauf!, Zeitschrift der Erzgebirgsvereins* 48 (1928), 43–48.

95) Josef Opitz, Alte Kunst der Bezirk Kaaden-Pressnitz. Eine kurze Übersicht, geordnet nach Orten, *Sonderabdruck aus der Heimatsbeilage der Kaadener Zeitung* (Kaaden: 1924); Idem., *Gotische Plastik des 14. und 15. Jahrhunderts in Böhmen I. Bezirk Kaaden* (Kaaden: 1924); Idem., *Gotische Malerei und Plastik Nordwestböhmens. Katalog der Ausstelung in Brüx – Komotau* (Brüx –
Komotau: 1928); Idem., *Die Galerie des Stiftes Osseg. Beschreibender Teil (Gemälde)* (Komotau: 1930); Idem., *Nordwestböhmen in der Kunst 1530–1680. Katalog der Ausstelung in Komotau* (Komotau: 1932).

96) Jaromír Homolka – Josef Krása – Václav Mencl – Jaroslav Pešina – Josef Petráň, *Pozdně gotické umění v Čechách (1471–1525)* (Praha: 1984); Karl M. Swoboda (ed.), *Gotik in Böhmen* (München: 1969); Jiřina Hořejší – Jarmila Krčálová, *Die Kunst der Renaissance und des Manierismus in Böhmen* (Prag: 1979); Ferdinand Seibt (Hsg.), *Renaissance in Böhmen* (München: 1985); *Dějiny českého výtvarného umění, Part I/2* (Praha: 1984); *Dějiny českého výtvarného umění, Part II/1* (Praha: 1989).

on the subject of Renaissance architecture.[97] However, these were overviews that were often not based on a detailed survey of monuments in the region and did not look for connections with works created on the Saxon side during the same time period. Nor did the works published in the Saxon part of the Ore Mountains usually consider the broader context of artistic development in northwest Bohemia.[98] Only a handful of smaller studies have touched on the common features between the art on the Bohemian and Saxon sides of the border.[99] Among the fundamental contributions to the history of workshop practice and painting in Saxony, which also included art imported to Bohemia, are the works of Ingo Sandner.[100] Most recently, the history of art in the Bohemian-Saxon border region in the most recent historical period has been the focus of works by Uwe Tresp.[101]

Although the characteristic features of the buildings, their period and style classification, and the formative impulses influencing the 'Saxon Renaissance' have been topics of interest for historians of architecture and art in Bohemia throughout the 20th century, a comprehensive study is yet to be done. They were summarised in Michaela Ramešová's unpublished work from 2013. This multi-layered work identifies the basic features of this architectural style and their origins. It also looks at the relationship between the periphery and the centre and its impact on the architecture of the Saxon Renaissance. However, the author mainly discusses the issue with respect to Prague as the centre in the context of Bohemia. Only in her final remarks does she rightly conclude that, rather than Prague, the developments in Bohemia should be viewed in relation to Saxony. In addition, she correctly assesses this centre-periphery relationship as equal and not hierarchical, in the sense that Saxony was the advanced centre and the Bohemian region the dependent periphery.[102]

Research on this issue, with a broader focus on the art-historical production in the border region between Bohemia and Saxony, was also done at the Department of History of the Faculty of Arts of J. E. Purkyně University. It was a joint study connected to several other projects that looked at the historical and cultural development of northwest Bohemia at the start of the early modern period.[103]

97) Eva Šamánková, *Architektura české renesance* (Praha: 1961).

98) Eduard Flechsig, *Sächsische Malerei und Bildnerei vom XIV. Jahrhundert bis zur Reformation, Bd. I–III* (Leipzig: 1908–12).

99) Wilhelm Junius, "Sächsich-böhmische Grenzkunst," in: Rudolf Wenisch (ed.), *Uhls Heimatbücher (Belderreihe)* (Kaaden: 1924); Wilhelm Junius, "Meister des thüringisch-sächsischen Cranach-Kreises," in: Georg Mentz (ed.), *Zeitschrift des Vereins für thüringische Geschichte und Altertumskunde, Neue Folge* 31 (Jena: 1935), 64–112.

100) Ingo Sandner (ed.), *Unsichtbare Meisterzeichnungen auf dem Malgrund. Cranach und seine Zeitgenossen. Wartburg-Stiftung Eisenach* (Regensburg: 1998); Ingo Sandner, *Spätgotische Tafelmalerei in Sachsen* (Dresden – Basel: 1993); Ingo Sander, *Hans Hesse – ein Maler der Spätgotik in Sachsen* (Dresden: 1983).

101) Uwe Tresp, "Erbeinung und Fehde zwischen Sachsen und Böhmen: Die Fehde des Jan von Lobkowitz auf Hassenstein gegen Albertiner (1493–1496)," in: Christine Reinle u. a. (ed.), *Zwischen adliger Handlungslogik und territorialer Verdichtung: Fehdeführung im spätmittelalterlichen römisch-deutschen Reich* (in print).

102) Michaela Ramešová, *Otázky saské renesance*, (diploma thesis, Charles University, 2012).

103) Michaela Ottová – Michaela Hrubá – Táňa Nejezchlebová (Šimková), "Kulturní transfer v česko-saském pohraničí v pozdním středověku a raném novověku (aktuální výzkum tzv. saské renesance v Čechách)," in: *Monumentorum Custos* (2011), 5–10.

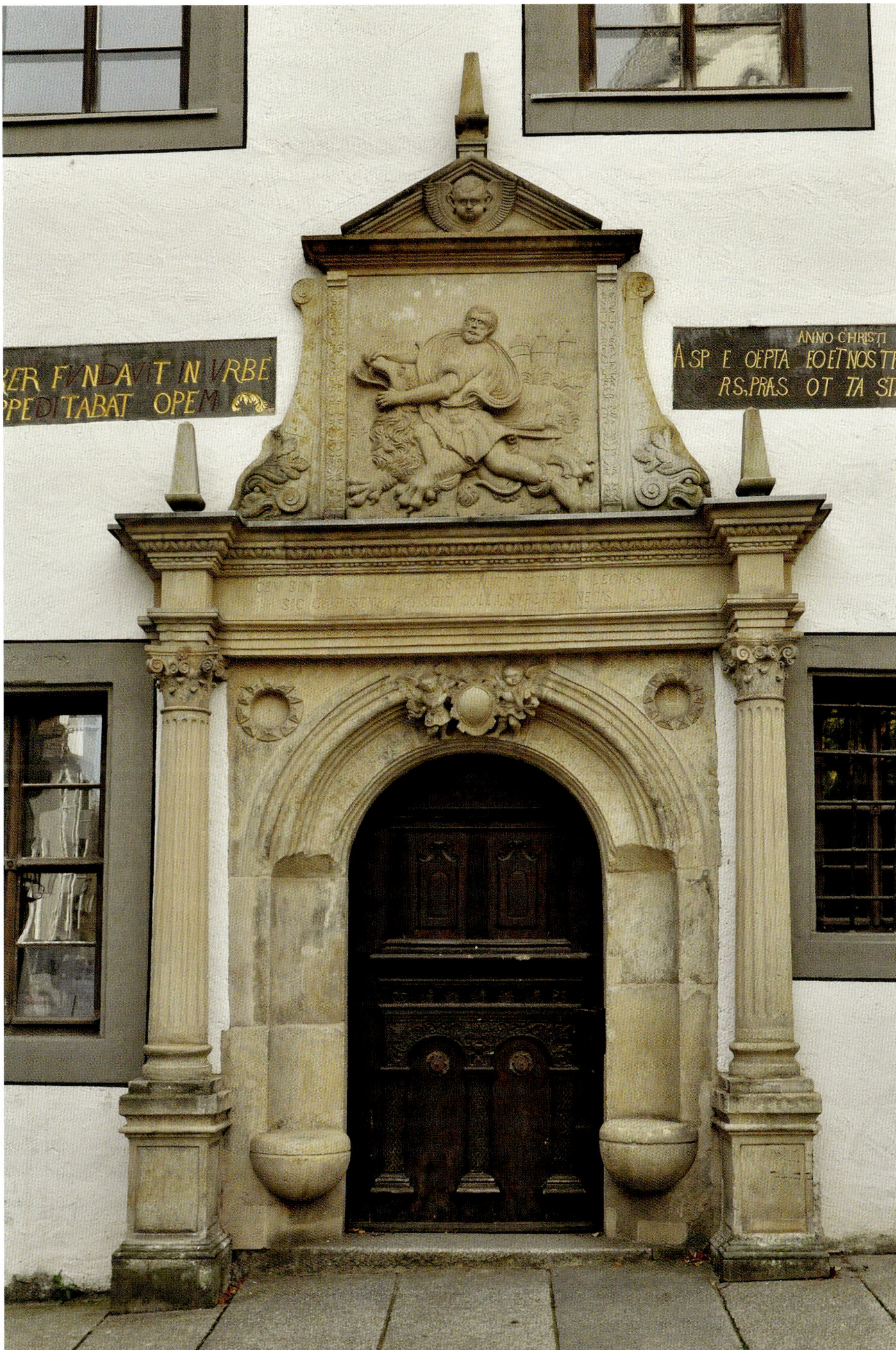

Fig. 30 Meissen, Brauhaus Meissen, Renaissance portal of the entrance to the former town brewery. Brewery built 1460, rebuilt 1569–1572 as a townhouse. Photo by T. Šimková (2016).

THE SAXON RENAISSANCE IN ARCHITECTURE

To identify the typical features and trace the development of the style known as the 'Saxon Renaissance,' we must first look at the Late Gothic architecture in Bohemia and Saxony. The two regions influenced each other and formed the basis of the architectural and artistic expression of a unique later style. Its most important characteristics were that it paraphrased the Gothic idiom and details and that it drew inspiration and resources from local artistic production. This gave rise to the distinctive look of architecture built between the turn of the 15th and 16th centuries and the 1720s.

The biggest impact on the cultural development of architecture in Bohemia was caused by the collapse of Peter Parler's workshop in the 15th century and the Hussite wars, which almost brought the country's cultural life to a halt. Major construction projects were suspended, and as a result architecture in Bohemia began to lose touch with European trends.[104] Although there were plenty of first-rate stonemasons working in Bohemia, they continued using traditional building methods after construction resumed during the reign of Vladislaus II.[105] Foreign master craftsmen were therefore called to Bohemia to work the biggest construction projects, bringing with them the practices and latest trends they knew from their workshops back home. This is how, for example, Master Erhard Bauer of Eichstatt, Bavaria, worked in Cheb (Eger) and turned down offers to work on royal construction projects in Prague,[106] and Master Hans Spiess of Frankfurt am Main worked on the construction of Prague Castle.[107] In the towns of northwest Bohemia, the proximity of the border fostered a very active exchange of Saxon craftsmen and allowed for a gradual introduction of the construction practices used by Arnold of Westphalia (Arnold von Westfalen) and his pupils. Northwest Bohemia was generally considered one of the first places where Late Gothic architecture of the Saxon type took root.

The area where Saxon craftsmen were able to work was limited due to a difficult political situation and deteriorating relations between the Prague royal court and the Wettins of Saxony. In the 1470s, the Wettins had become close allies with Matthias Corvinus, who had him-

104) Milada a Oldřich Radovi, *Kniha o sklípkových klenbách* (Praha: 1998), 53.

105) Pavel Kalina, *Benedikt Ried a počátky záalpské renesance* (Praha: 2009), 44, 45.

106) Pavel Vlček (ed.), *Encyklopedie architektů, stavitelů, zedníků a kameníků v Čechách* (Praha: 2004), 44–45.

107) Ibid., 612–613.

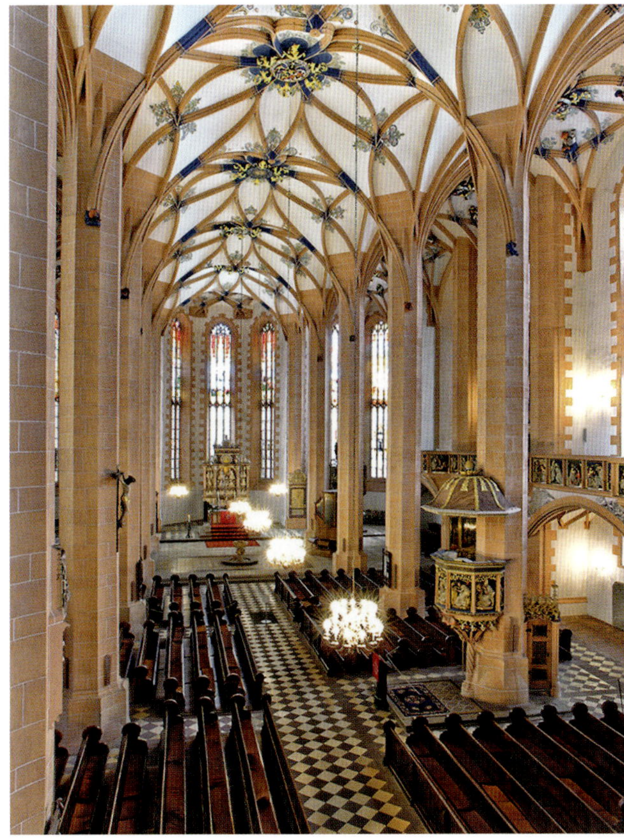

Fig. 31 Annaberg, Church of St. Anne, a three-naved church with circular vaults. Construction 1499–1525, from 1515 Jacob Heylmann of Schweinfurt as head of the ironworks. Photo by T. Šimková (2018).

self crowned King of Bohemia in 1471 against Vladislaus II and held Moravia, Silesia and Upper and Lower Lusatia.[108] It was in the neighbouring countries that, thanks to the close relations with Corvinus, the Saxon building style represented by the Wettin master builder Arnold of Westphalia was introduced.[109] Similarly, in some areas of northwest Bohemia that supported Corvinus, the most prominent nobles began to build in the Meissen style. In contrast, the situation prompted the royal court to refrain from hiring craftsmen from Saxony for the most important royal construction projects.

The situation changed after Corvinus' death, when relations between Saxony and the Kingdom of Bohemia were normalised. Nevertheless, two different artistic centres – Prague and northwest Bohemia – continued on their distinctive paths, each with somewhat different artistic leanings, while maintaining close ties with each other.

The Prague centre was undoubtedly characterised by the stonemasonry and architectural work of Benedikt Ried's workshop.[110] Ried's looping rib vault designs naturally influenced the work of his pupils and members of the workshop, who in turn influenced the style of architecture in the broader region, including northwest Bohemia with overlaps into Saxony, where the vaulting of St. Anne's Church in Annaberg serves as the best example.[111] (Fig. 31) The main

108) Milada a Oldřich Radovi, *Kniha o sklípkových klenbách*, 53.
109) Matthias Uwe Tresp, *Corvinus und die deutschen Fürsten: Das Beispiel der Wettiner*, in: http://renaissance.elte.hu.
110) Jan Białostocki, *The Art of the Renaissance in Eastern Europe. Hungary – Bohemia – Poland* (Oxford: 1976), 15.
111) Pavel Kalina, *Benedikt Ried*, 175–180.

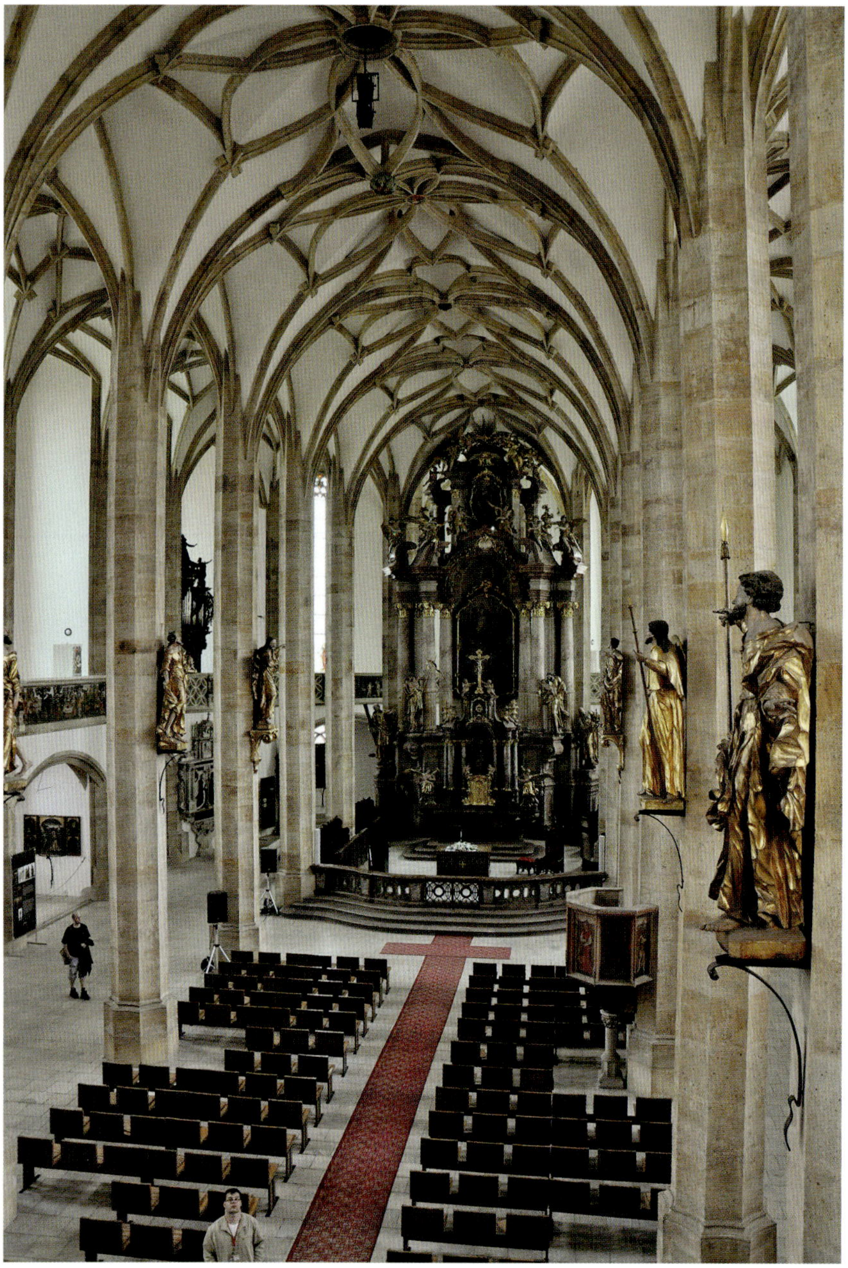

Fig. 32 Most, Church of the Assumption of the Virgin Mary, triple nave with circular vaults. Construction 1517–1602, 1517–1518 Jacob Heylmann of Schweinfurt, 1518–1531 George of Maulborn. Photo by T. Šimková (2012).

master builder assigned to design and build the vaulting of the church, was Ried's pupil Jacob Heylmann of Schweinfurt, who was later also involved in the construction of the Church of Our Lady in Most (Brüx).[112] (Fig. 32)

For the church in Annaberg, he designed a looping rib vault in the spirit of his training. According to Milada Radová, however, the Saxon masters were still firmly set in their traditional Gothic ways and were not impressed: '*...both in terms of construction techniques and artistic*

112) Karl Kühn – Josef Opitz, *Die Stadtpfarrkirche zu Brüx in Böhmen (1532)* (Brüx: 1932), 10; Heide Mannlová-Raková, *Kulturní památka Most: Děkanský kostel a jeho stavitelé* (Praha: 1989); Heide Mannlová, *Kostel Nanebevzetí Panny Marie v Mostě v dějinách československé pozdní gotiky* (Most: 1969).

Fig. 33 Louny, Church of St. Nicholas, triple nave with circular vaults with overlapping ribs. Construction 1517–1538, Benedikt Ried's ironwork. Photograph by T. Šimková (2019).

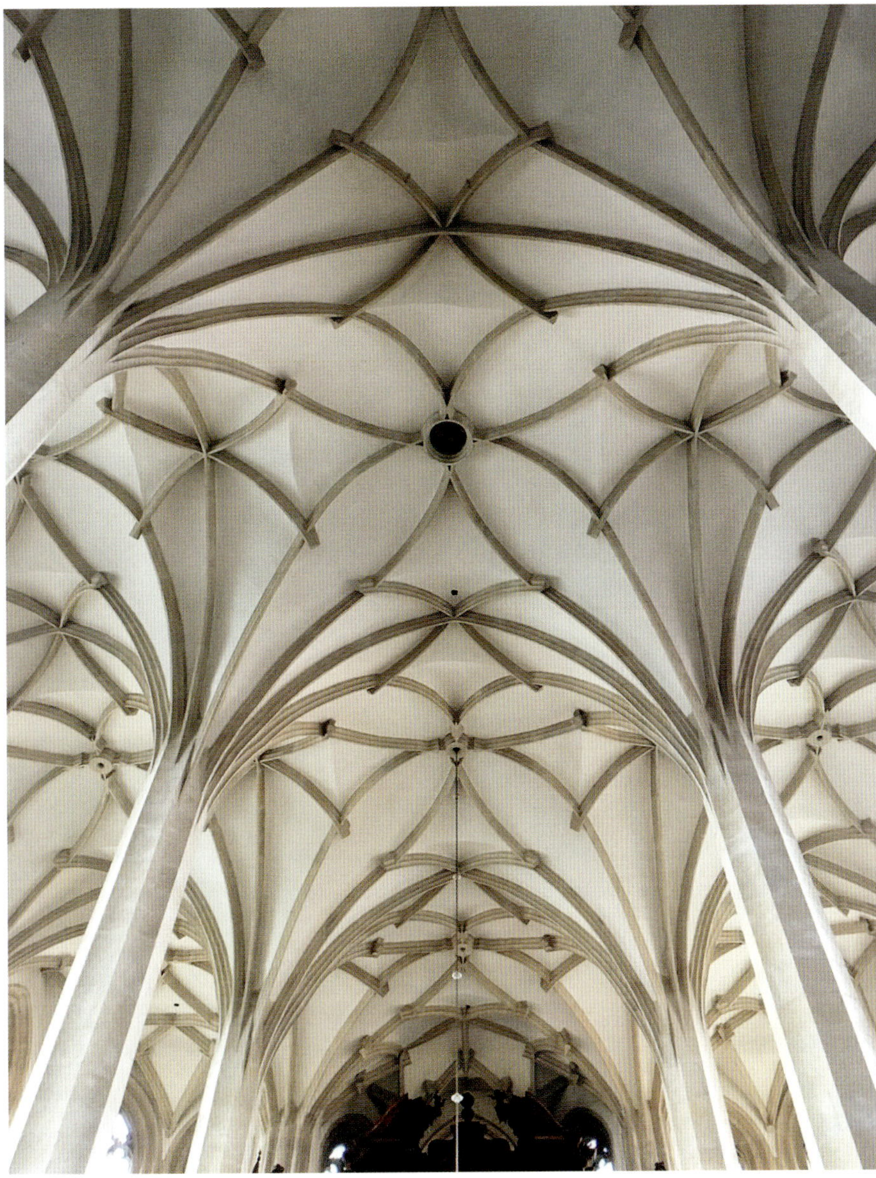

style, the new approach raised doubts, as it seemed too novel and artistically daring for the region of Saxony...' The concept was so unusual that a convention of stonemasons was called to Annaberg in 1518 to assess the design and implementation of the vault. Benedikt Ried presided over the assembly. The advanced construction solution, which was also submitted by Heylmann in his plans, was not appreciated. This ultimately led to the founding of a separate stonemason's lodge for Saxony, Bohemia, Lusatia and Silesia, which was independent of Magdeburg and could therefore develop autonomously in a direction set by Benedikt Ried and others.[113]

The independent stonemason's lodge opened as a result of the Anaberg convention enabled the free movement of stomasonry workers. In the following years, it also contributed significantly to cultural exchange, in the Ore Mountains in particular, and influenced the for-

113) Milada Radová, "Sjezd kameníků v Annabergu v roce 1518," in: *Architektura ČSSR* 4 (1967), 187.

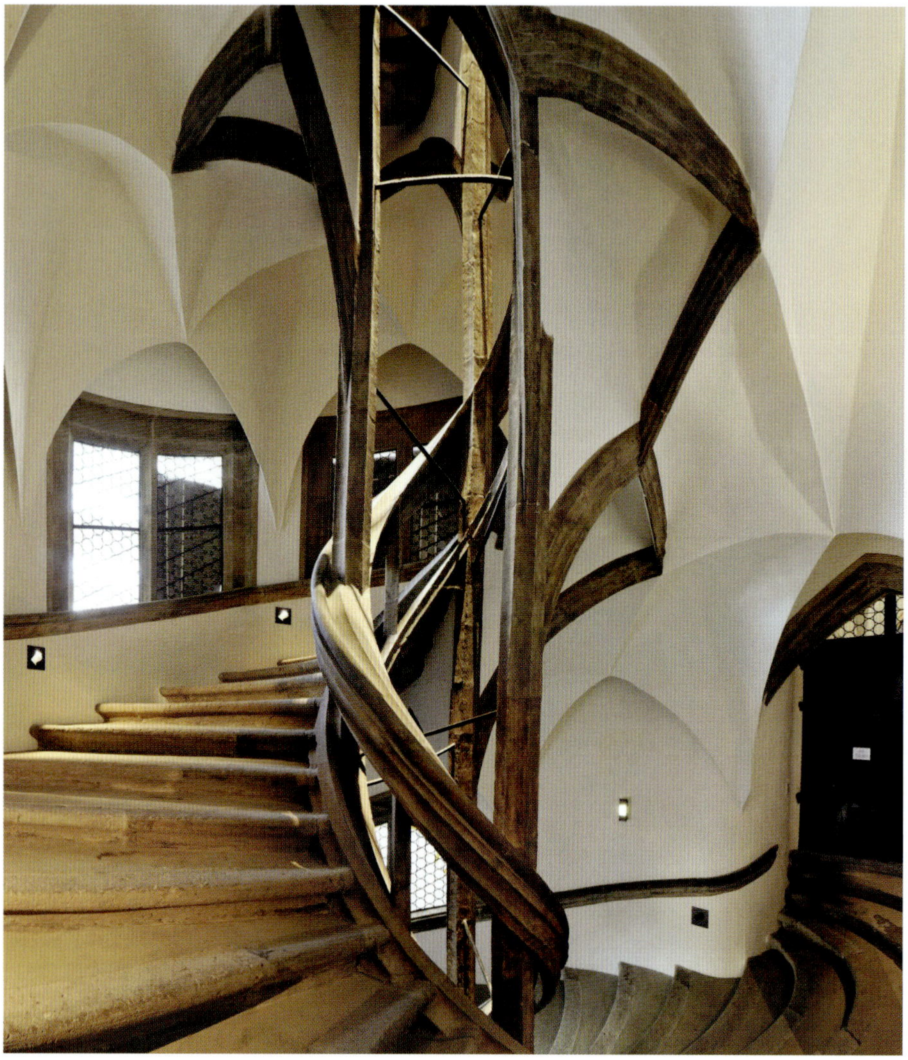

Fig. 34 Meissen, Albrechtsburg, the chamfered vault of the unusually designed spindle staircase of the castle. Construction 1471–1500, 1471–1482 by Arnold of Westphalia, 1482–1500 by Konrad Pflüger, 1521–1524 by Jacob Heylmann of Schweinfurt (alterations to the completed building).

mation of the Saxon Renaissance style. The Saxon environment also influenced a project undertaken by Benedikt Ried late in his career. This was the construction of St. Nicholas Church in Louny, which began in 1519 and has been evaluated by historian Václav Mencl as distinctly Saxon in style.[114] Mencl even went so far as to suggest that the church's design could have been influenced by the style of Arnold of Westphalia, since Ried had made a closer acquaintance with Arnold's pupils at the Annaberg Convention. Saxon influences can even be found in the church's spatial design, the origins of which can be traced to Schneeberg in Saxony. (Fig. 33)

Just as Ried's looping rib vault has come to characterise Late Gothic architecture in Bohemia, a trademark of the Late Gothic style in Saxony is undoubtedly the cell vault designed by Arnold of Westphalia. (Fig. 34) This master builder of the Wettin family pioneered a completely new style in Saxony that deliberately broke away from the Gothic building tradition of the region, and introduced brand new and unusual elements into the construction of buildings.

114) Pavel Kalina, *Benedikt Ried*, 200.

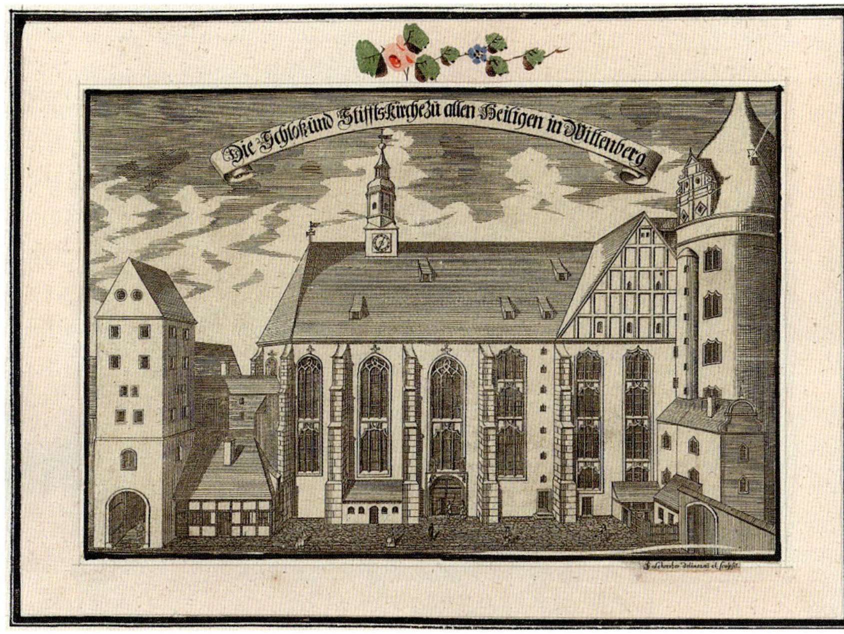

Fig. 35 Electoral residence with church in Wittenberg in an engraving from 1717. Reproduction © Deutsche Fotothek.

Arnold of Westphalia's style gained currency after his appointment as court builder to the Wettins in 1471, in whose service he remained until 1482.[115] In the early days of Arnold's career, Saxony underwent a significant economic, political and cultural upheaval, associated in particular with Ernest and Albrecht Wettin. The most distinctive period of the Westphalian style began on 4 June 1471, when Arnold was appointed master builder, with the mandate to oversee all the Wettins' construction projects.[116] This position meant he did not need to rely on any stonemason's lodge and could work independently and freely towards a new style. He actually used that new style in his very first project – the construction of the palace in Meissen, launched in 1471. Arnold of Westphalia's involvement marked a final farewell to the lingering decorative style of the Saxon Late Gothic of the 1570s. The work of Arnold of Westphalia was continued by his pupils. The most notable of them were Konrad Pflüger,[117] builder of the electoral residence of the Ernestine Wettins in Wittenberg and town builder in Görlitz (Fig. 35), and Hans Reynhart, who was active in Dresden and later worked for the Lords of Schönberg.

The way in which the Meissen style reached Bohemia was closely linked to the political and economic development within the country and to the relationship between Saxony and Bohemia. Northwest Bohemia kept very close ties with Albert (Albrecht) III, Duke of Saxony. This alliance started after the settlement of the dispute over the Bohemian-Saxon fiefs and was confirmed by Albert's marriage to Zdenka (Sidonie), the daughter of George of Poděbrady, King of Bohemia.[118] The close connection with Saxony is perhaps best illustrated by the un-

115) Milada a Oldřich Radovi, *Kniha o klenbách*, 17; Matthias Donath, "Herzog Albrecht der beherzte und die Bauten auf dem Meikßner Burgberg. Spätgotische Baukunst im ausgehenden 15. Jahrhundert," in: André Thieme (ed.), *Herzog Albrecht der Beherzte. Ein sächsischer Fürst im Reich und in Europa* (Weimar: 2002), 233–281.

116) Ibid., 29.

117) Pavel Vlček (ed.), *Encyklopedie architektů*, 320.

118) Franz Otto Stichart, *Galerie der sächsischen Fürstinnen. Biographische Skizzensämtlicher Ahnfrauen des kgl. Hauses Sachsen* (Leipzig: 1857), 194.

successful efforts to install Albert of Saxony on the Bohemian throne, supported by a group of noblemen led by Benes (Benesch Krabitz) of Veitmile/Weitmühl. Last but not least, the northwestern border region began to develop rapidly by following the Saxon models and after the introduction of mining with the participation of experts from Saxony.[119]

Because of the situation described above, the Meissen style was only adopted in the borderland where Bohemia was immediately adjacent to Saxony. In northwest Bohemia, the new architectural style was mainly championed by the strong Catholic nobility and the Franciscan Observant monasteries, which quickly adopted the rapidly developing style of Arnold of Westphalia. Northwest Bohemia's affinity for the neighbouring Saxony was motivated not only by family, property and political ties, but also by the noticeable absence of skilled local craftsmen and artists. This absence contrasted sharply with the nobility's newly-developed interest in replacing the conservative architectural production of the day with a new decorative style. For this reason, craftsmen from stonemasons' lodges in the wealthy mining and electoral towns in the Saxon Ore Mountains were hired by the nobility in northwest Bohemia, which is how the aforementioned style was imported there.

The oldest examples of the increasingly popular Meissen style are the ruins of the Doubravská hora (Dauersberg) Castle near Teplice (Teplitz). The castle was built around 1478 by Jan Ilburk of Vřesovice (Johann Illburg von Wresowitz, † 1485), who had an appointment at the royal court as servant to the queen dowager Johanna and Vladislaus II.[120] Only small remnants of the 1480s architecture have survived after multiple major reconstructions and renovations, but two window niches and a fragment of a bay window survive, which are topped with small cell vaults corresponding to designs known from Meissen buildings. This is clear evidence that the master builder of the castle near Teplice must have trained in Meissen.[121] Almost concurrently, construction activity began to pick up in Chomutov (Komotau), where Benes of Veitmile/Weitmühl, who was Chief Mintmaster of Bohemia and Burgrave of Karlštejn (Karlstein) Castle, decided to rebuild the former command post of the Teutonic Knights at St. Catherine's Church into a family residence. Construction began around 1483, and the vaults in the north hall and the central room of the commandery were probably completed by 1488.[122] (Fig. 36)

The vault shape and the three-layered helical groove in the section of the architectural elements are in keeping with Meissen Castle and once again speak of the builder's direct ties to a Meissen-based stonemason's lodge. It should be noted that the influence of Benes of Veitmile/Weitmühl's cultural and architectural taste was not limited to his private building projects.

119) Uwe Tresp, "Nachbarschaft zwischen Erbeinung und Hegemonienstreben: Die Wettiner und Böhmen 1471–1482," in: Miloš Řezník (Ed.), *Grenzraum und Transfer. Perpektiven der Geschichtswissenschaft in Sachsen und Tschechien* (Berlin: 2007), 33–67.

120) Tomáš Durdík, *Encyklopedie českých hradů* (Praha: 1998), 80; Jan Ilburk of Vřesovice was the grandson of a famous Hussite warrior. Jan Boukal, *Jakoubek z Vřesovic († 1462). Cesta chudého moravského rytíře k vládě nad severozápadními Čechami* (České Budějovice: 2016).

121) Milada a Oldřich Radovi, *Kniha o klenbách*, 63.

122) August Sedláček, *Hrady, zámky a tvrze království Českého XIV., Litoměřicko a Žatecko* (Praha: 1923), 317–322; Petr Macek, *Chomutov: stavebně historický průzkum historického jádra* (Praha: 1987).

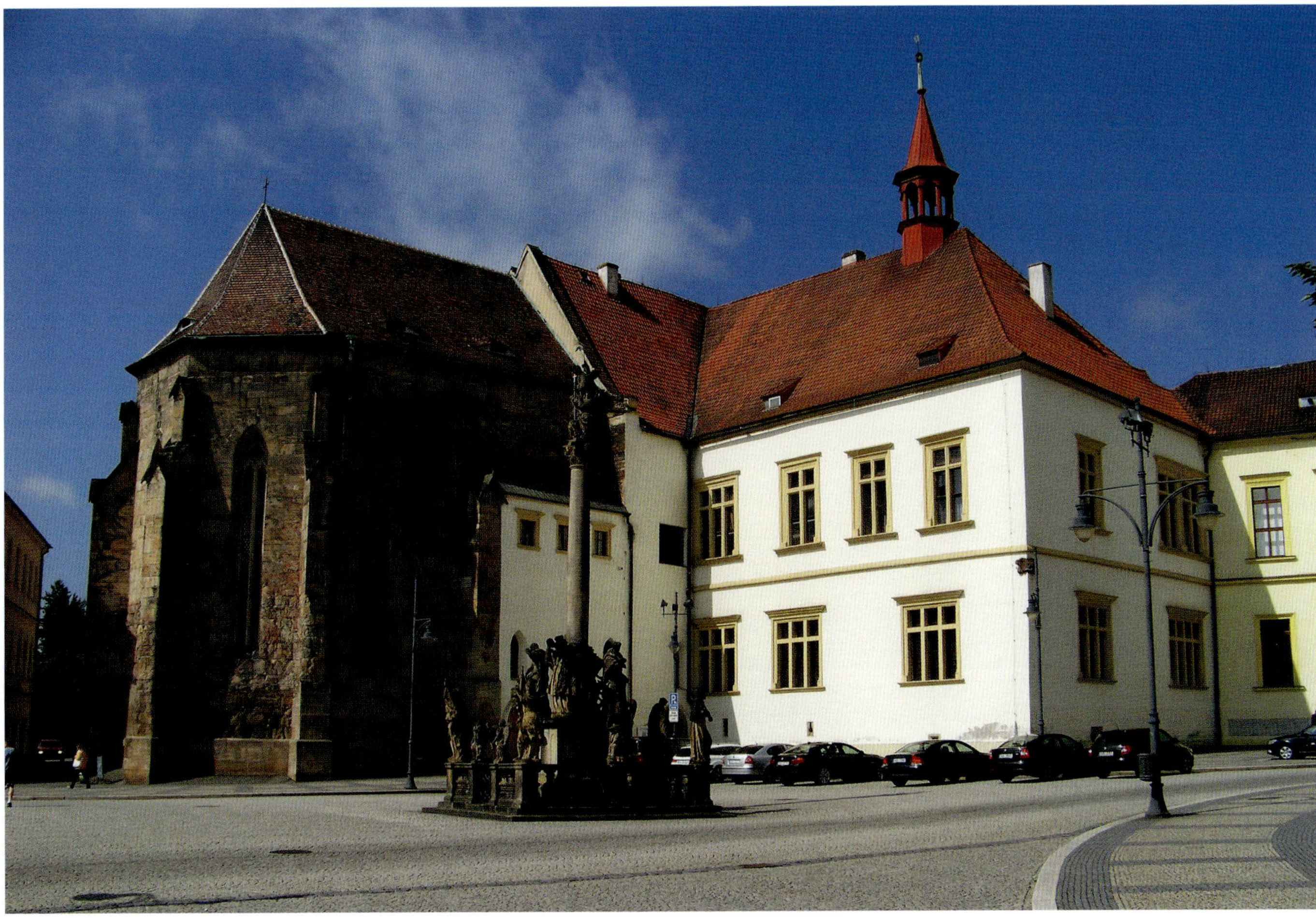

Fig. 36 Chomutov, castle with a church (former commandery of German knights). Reconstruction 1488–1540 for Beneš of Veitmile and Šebestián of Veitmile. Photo by T. Šimková (2014).

During his mandate as Burgrave of Karlštejn (1460–1469), he had the old burgrave's office at the castle rebuilt and completed in a relatively short time.[123] The reconstruction was executed by local craftsmen, who added some impressive details and striking vaults in the Meissen style. The construction activity was not limited to the castle, where the rooms of the Land Tables as well as the burgrave's office were topped with cell vaults, but included St. Palmacius' Church in the lower castle area, with a chancel that also has a cell vault.

In addition to the complex cell vaults, the Saxon Late Gothic style was also characterised by finer details and stonework and the layout of the buildings. Generally speaking, Late Gothic architecture tended towards significantly simplifying the traditionally decorative Gothic style by focusing on practicality and clarity over ornamentation, both in individual structures and the overall design. This was particularly evident in church buildings.[124] An illustrative example of this approach in Saxony is St. Anne's Church in Annaberg with its smooth, simple façade, undisturbed even by the outer wall supports. (Fig. 37)

123) Tomáš Durdík, *Encyklopedie hradů*, 131.

124) Ernst Ulmann (Hgs.), *Geschichte der deutschen Kunst 1470–1550. Architektur und Plastik* (Leipzig: 1984), 30.

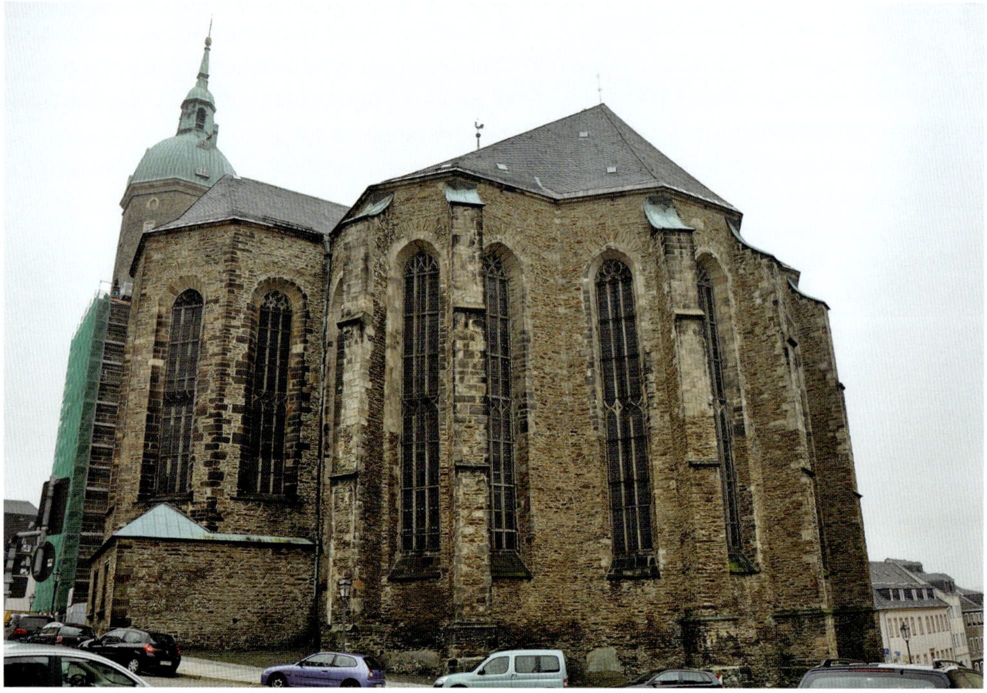

Fig. 37 Annaberg, Church of St. Anne, plain outer shell of the church. Construction 1499–1525, from 1515 Jacob Heylmann of Schweinfurt as head of the ironworks. Photo by T. Šimková (2011).

The first stage in the development of the architectural style in the Saxon-influenced mining towns began to undergo a transformation around the 1520s. At this time, à-la-mode Renaissance features were commonly used on both secular and ecclesiastical buildings, but their function was more as additional decoration while the body of the building had a Gothic appearance. It should be noted that such use of newly-adopted elements was not a sign of falling behind the times, but instead a common practice widespread in the broader region of Central Europe, where architectural impulses inspired by Italy came indirectly through the still prevalent and deeply-rooted Gothic building tradition.[125] The use of modified Renaissance elements by imitating models often only known in picture form should therefore be understood as a confident gesture of enriching the domestic building tradition, even if the result was often peculiar. But in the overall architectural concept and details, the Late-Gothic tradition continued strong: it was perpetuated in the works of the successors of Arnold of Westphalia and Benedikt Ried, who also left a mark in the Ore Mountain borderland and in both Upper and Lower Lusatia, either directly or through their stonemason's lodges.

This trend persisted until about the mid-16th century. From then on, a full-fledged Renaissance style slowly began to assert itself in domestic architecture, with new features combined with the local building tradition in a harmonious union.[126] Specifically when undergoing the Saxon Renaissance, the Saxon architectural tradition – which found its home in Bohemia as well, thanks to the presence of Saxon artists, builders and stonemasons – borrowed many elements from the Italian Renaissance style. These were mostly ornamental bands of diamonds, egg-shaped stones, pearls, and consoles, which were widely used, especially in the decoration

125) Táňa Šimková, *Hrad přepevný je Pánbůh náš* (Ústí nad Labem: 2018), 192.
126) Petr Macek, *Několik poznámek*, 35.

Fig. 38 Meissen, Kleinmarkt no. 10, detail of the late Renaissance decoration on the portal of the main entrance. Photo by T. Šimková (2012).

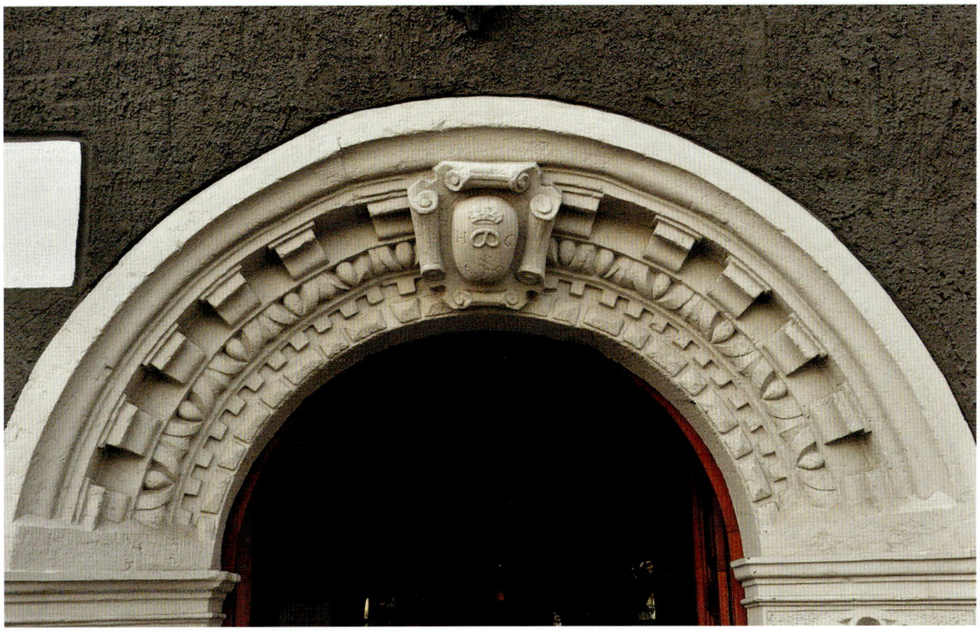

of portals and architectural details. (Fig. 38) These elements became so widespread and generalised in a wide range of building types that during the second half of the 16th century, they helped to bid farewell to the surviving Gothic tradition, which tended to custom-design each element in an original way. Instead, they fostered a movement towards the typification of architectural elements and features.[127]

The last and final stage in the development of the Saxon Renaissance style began sometime in the early 17th century. By that point, architecture was significantly influenced by the emerging Mannerism,[128] which manifested itself in fully embracing the principle of typification of individual elements that lent architecture a more restrained appearance. Another trademark of Mannerism was a deliberate deformation of the proportions, dimensions, and shape of the routinely-used Renaissance features. This stage did not last long, as the late phase of the 'Saxon Renaissance' was cut short by the Thirty Years' War, the exodus of the Protestant nobility from the Ore Mountains, and the onset of the Baroque era, which in the Bohemian part of the Ore Mountains was associated with re-Catholicisation.

127) Václav Mencl, "Vývoj okna v architektuře českého středověku," *Zprávy památkové péče* XX/ 6 (1960), 229.
128) Petr Macek, *Několik poznámek*, 35.

Fig. 39 Krupka, view from the castle on the historical centre of the town with the dominant parish church of the Assumption of the Virgin Mary. Photo by J. Peer (2019). ⟶

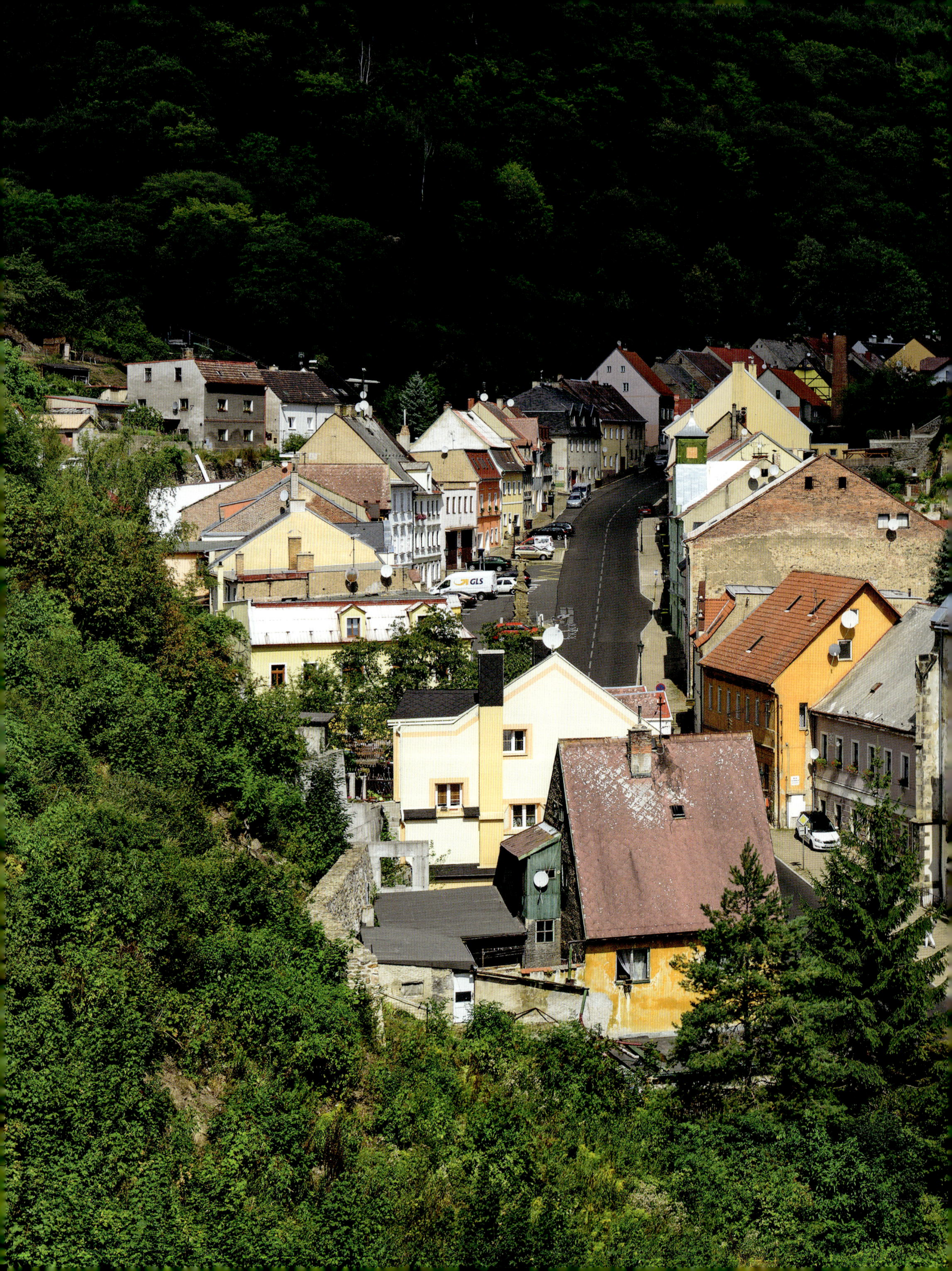

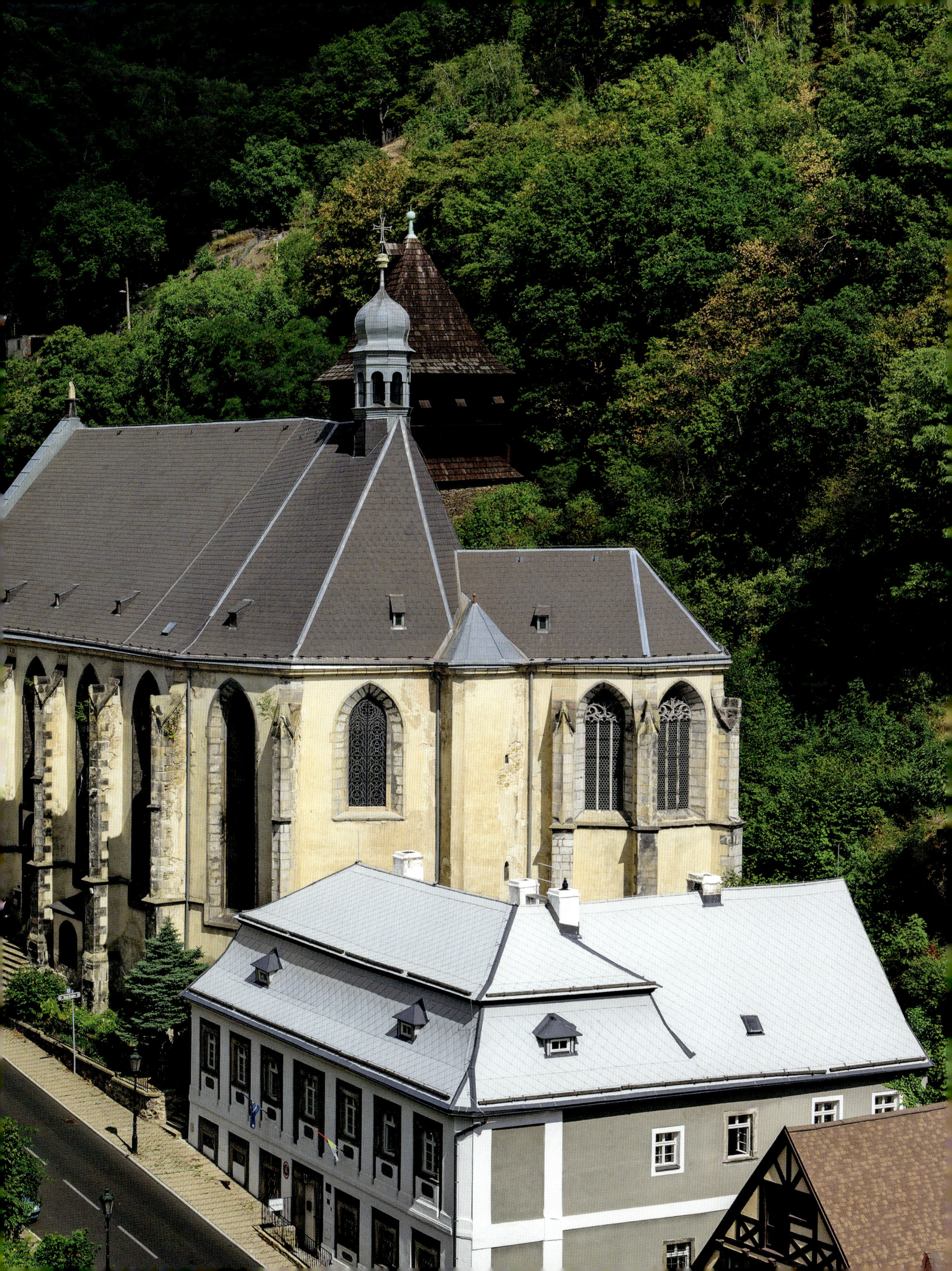

THE URBANISM AND ARCHITECTURE OF MINING TOWNS IN THE ORE MOUNTAINS

"...lies in the mountains, is inhospitable and very harsh."[129]

The appearance of the mining towns and villages in the Ore Mountains, which were often hastily built from the Middle Ages to the onset of the Early Modern Period, was dictated by the mountainous terrain but also by the specific conditions created by the mining industry. In terms of urban planning, there were two main types of mining town in the Ore Mountains: their design was determined both by the building methods and practices available at the time and, above all, by the often limited building space.

The first type, which arose from the time of the earliest settlement sites until the 16th century, were **unplanned towns**. Their design was shaped by the demands of the geographical terrain, with houses and plots of land built alongside a main road and adjacent streets.[130]

Within the relatively large group of unplanned towns, distinct typological subgroups were formed over time that differed from each other in terms of the road network, the shape of the main square and the placement of buildings on the plots. In northwest Bohemia, one town layout became especially common, typically in the hastily-founded, fast-developing settlements: **the unplanned town with a linear street layout**. Three subtypes exist within that category with respect to the mining towns: towns with little or no urban design, towns with a square created by the extension of a road, and towns with a regularly laid-out square.

An unplanned town with a linear street layout

This town type is characterised by the accretion of building plots alongside major roads and streams, where there was ample space favourable to building. The oldest row of development was

129) Jan Urban, "Zpráva Jana Jiřího Greiselia o studijní cestě do Jáchymova v r. 1670," in: *Historický sborník Karlovarska* 1 (1993), 9–17.

130) Lubomír Zeman, "Zástavba a urbanismus krušnohorských horních měst," in: *Sborník muzea Karlovarského kraje* 18 (2010), 43–94; Karel Kuča, "Krušnohorská města, jejich zakládání a urbanismus," in: Alžběta Kratochvílová (ed.), *Bohatství historického stavebního vývoje Krušnohoří* (Loket: 2011), 7–12. For more on the influence of Saxon urban planners and Renaissance theories on the layout of towns in the Ore Mountains, see: Jan Hanzlík, "Město a jeho koncept," in: Tomáš Karel – Alžběta Kratochvílová, *Proměny montánní krajiny. Historické sídelní a montánní struktury Krušnohoří* (Loket: 2013), 77–81.

thus typically located alongside transportation routes, with later buildings erected in subsequent rows, often cutting into the steep slopes on each side of the already built-up valley. Towns with multiple rows of buildings built over such a layout are not uncommon. One of the reasons this was possible was the way people made their living in the mining towns, where agriculture was so limited that it was not necessary to preserve any fields beyond the building sites. They were difficult to survey, given the shape and character of the terrain. Signs of urban design can thus be detected especially in the location of the most important town buildings, such as churches, manor houses and burgher houses, which usually occupied the most prominent plots.

A great example of a town without a central square is **Krupka** (Graupen),[131] which is also one of the oldest mining towns in the eastern Ore Mountain region. In addition to tin, copper ore was mined in Krupka, and later also tungsten and molybdenum. The oldest record of the town's existence dates back to 1305. It is a document issued by King Wenceslas II, in which he approved the claim by Zvěst of Trmice to inherit the Krupá Mountain.[132]

The legend about the origin of Krupka

In his *Bohemian Chronicle* of 1541, Wenceslaus Hajek of Libočany connected the discovery of tin in Krupka with Princess Libuše, who supposedly had a prophetic vision: 'I see a rugged mountain, very rich in tin and lead.' As for tin, Hájek connected its discovery in the region with a man named Vladek, who apparently found a metal rod in the woods and presented a part of it to Queen Judith (1135–1174) in Teplice.[133]

The mining settlement, including the castle district above the entrance to a major road, coalesced as far back as the 13th century, and the oldest town buildings were probably already constructed at that time.[134] It could have been preceded by an even older original settlement in the vicinity of St. Procopius' Church near the road leading from Teplice to Bohosudov.[135] The original mining settlement of Kirchlice (Kirchlitz) by the Liščí potok (i.e., 'Fox Brook') was located near this church. St. Procopius was also venerated as the patron saint of miners. According to tradition, the church bell used to summon the miners for their shift and also announced the end of the shift.

Similarly to Kašperské Hory, where the earliest mines were located near the Church of St. Nicholas and then in the 15th century the extraction site was moved to a new location several miles further, the mining site in Krupka also changed locations at one point; it was moved to the valley, where another mining settlement had existed since the 13th century with the Church of the Assumption, near an important trade route to Saxony. Krupka (Graupen) is

131) Hermann Halwich, *Geschichte der Bergstadt Graupen* (Prag: 1868); Emanuel Poche et al., *Umělecké památky Čech II.* (Praha: 1978), 151–152; Jan Klípa – Michaela Ottová (eds.), *Bez Hranic. Umění v Krušnohoří mezi gotikou a renesancí* (Praha: 2015), 650–662.

132) August Sedláček, *Hrady, zámky a tvrze království českého, Part XIV* (Praha: 1923), 354.

133) Jan Linka (ed.), *Václav Hájek z Libočan, Kronika česká* (Praha: 2013), 63, 447.

134) Karel Kuča, *Města a městečka v Čechách, na Moravě a ve Slezsku, Part III Kolí–Mi* (Praha: 2002), 229.

135) Michal Urban et al., *Horní města Krušných hor. Ústecký kraj* (Sokolov: 2015), 77.

mentioned as a town in 1330 in the charter of John of Bohemia, whereby it was pledged to the nobleman Thimo von Colditz. Thimo had close ties with John of Bohemia, who had originally built Krupka Castle.[136] This marked the beginning of a defining era in the town's history: during the 174-year tenure of the Colditz family of the nobility, the most important buildings in the town were built and the shape of its historical core was formed. The Colditzes considered Krupka to be their main place of residence in Bohemia, where they could use their mining experience gained in the mines they operated around Colditz itself. The silver mined in Colditz could apparently be directly exploited thanks to the privilege of minting coins. This right was granted by Louis IV, King of the Romans, to the brothers Thimo the Elder and Henry in 1318 by means of a document confirming them in their imperial fiefs.[137] Thimo V of Colditz granted the town a number of privileges, including the brewing right, the salt trading right, and the weekly and annual market right. King Vladislav II of Bohemia and Hungary elevated Krupka to the status of a subject town with the Grant of Arms dated 13 January 1478. The town received the right to bear a coat of arms, the right to seal documents with the royal red wax, and the right to appoint a town council and a mayor.[138]

During the tenure of the Lords of Colditz, the so-called Krupka Mining Order was formed in 1482,[139] in which the excavation and maintenance of the Dürnholz (locally Duršlovka) drainage adit is mentioned. The adit was 1.5 km long and extended to the foot of Komáří vížka (Mückentürmchen) hill.

The Dürnholz Drainage Adit of Krupka

The beginnings of mining in the adit date back to the turn of the 1460s and 1470s. The entrance to the now inaccessible adit lies about 30 metres below the Starý Martin adit in Krupka. The full and precise route of the adit is only known from reconstructions, which have been done using depictions of known parts of the adit in J. Zechel's 1704 map, and scant data from written sources and maps. It took until the mid-16th century to drive the total length of 1,500 metres and build the entrance under Komáří vížka.

At the beginning of the 16th century Krupka came into the possession of the powerful Albrecht II Lord Liebsteinský of Kolowrat (†1510), who was an influential advisor to Vladislaus II, in addition to being the Burgrave of Karlštejn, the Royal Hofmeister and the Highest Chancellor of the Kingdom of Bohemia. He greatly admired the grace statue of the Virgin Mary that was found, according to legend, in the vicinity of Krupka. He founded a pilgrimage church

136) Michaela Hrubá, "Historie Krušnohoří mezi středověkem a raným novověkem," in: Michaela Hrubá et al., *Ars Montana. Umělecký transfer v otevřeném prostoru česko-saského Krušnohoří na prahu raného novověku* (Praha – Ústí nad Labem: 2016), 22. For ore on the noble family of Colditz, see Kurt Truöl, *Die Herren von Colditz und Ihre Herrschaft* (Leisnig: 1927); Denko Čumlivski, *První dvě generace rodu pánů z Koldic usedlé v Čechách a jejich činnost: Těma (I.) z Koldic 1303 až Těma (II.) z Koldic 1383* (diploma thesis, Charles University, 1974).

137) Tobiáš Jirsík, "Česká větev rodů pánů z Koldic na dvoře Lucemburků" (bachelor thesis, Charles University, 2015), 35.

138) Karel Kuča, *Města a městečka III.*, 226.

139) Jiří Majer, *Rudné hornictví v Čechách, na Moravě a ve Slezsku* (Praha: 2004), 92; Ladislav Jangl, *Vývoj dolování v lokalitě Krupka. Ložiska cínových rud v Krušných horách 5* (Kutná Hora: 1970).

there above an older church and obtained indulgences for pilgrims in Rome. The pilgrimage church was consecrated after his death in 1515.[140]

The next owner of the Krupka estate was the highest scribe of the Bohemian Kingdom, Volf of Vřesovice (Wolf von Wrzessowitz, †1569). His mother was buried in Krupka in 1518 under a magnificent figural tombstone.[141] In 1576, the town came under the ownership of Emperor Rudolf II, who gave it to his brother Matthias. From his hands it passed to Adam of Sternberg – to the chagrin of Krupka burghers, who would have liked to make it a royal town. In 1710, the Sternbergs sold the castle to the Lords of Clary-Aldringen of Teplice, who owned it until 1918. [142]

The historical town was built up over time alongside a spine road ascending up to what today is Bohosudov, through the bottom of a sharply-cut valley running towards the border. The town probably grew too rapidly to allow for a central square to be laid out and the role of a square is fulfilled today by a gentle widening in one section of the main road. The road is flanked by small plots of land, 10-20 metres wide, with terraced houses overlooking the road; these houses represent the oldest and most attractive part of the surviving historical buildings of Krupka. Other buildings, situated along the side streets and in the second, more sparsely developed line running horizontally across the valley slopes, are mostly of a later origin.

The historic centre was enclosed by two town gates: the upper gate, known as Míšeňská (Meissen gate), and the lower gate called Drážďanská (Dresden gate). The gates and the castle, exposed on the western slope of the valley, represented the town's only fortification. At the same time, they constituted the town's construction boundary, which was only crossed early in the 16th century, when St. Anne's Church was founded outside its limits. However, the church's location outside the town centre was not chosen due to a lack of building space but rather for hygienic reasons, as it was intended as a cemetery church.

The seat of the municipal government was the town hall, which changed its appearance several times. The first mention in historical sources of the town's main church, the Church of the Assumption, comes from 1331. Its location on a generously sized plot facing the castle across the way clearly indicates the elite position of the building within the town, which also fulfilled a strongly symbolic-demonstrative role. The importance of the building is further supported by how the site was treated in later years, when it was extended by a rather laborious excavation and consolidation of the steeply rising slope behind the church when plans were made to expand and rebuild the church in the late 15th century. [143]

The building plot of the Hospital Church of the Holy Spirit at the southernmost end of the town development, near the now defunct town gate dating back to 1440, was similarly

140) Jaroslav Macek, *950 let litoměřické kapituly* (Kostelní Vydří: 1997), 240.

141) More on the tombstone of Sabina Satanéřová of Drahonice, the wife of Vilém of Vřesovice (†1531): Jan Klípa – Michaela Ottová, *Bez hranic*, 599; Zuzana Křenková, "Pohřebiště pánů z Vřesovic v zaniklém klášteře františkánů observantů v Krupce," in: *Zprávy a studie Regionálního muzea v Teplicích* 29 (2012), 109–114.

142) August Sedláček, *Hrady, zámky, tvrze XIV.*, 362; Hermann Hallwich, *Geschichte der Bergstadt Graupen in Böhmen* (Prag: 1868).

143) Táňa Šimková, "Stavební vývoj kostela Nanebevzetí Panny Marie v Krupce," in: *Monumentorum Custos 2014* (Ústí nad Labem: 2015), 41–42.

adapted.[144] The building plot for the church was probably adjusted before construction began so that the building could be built at all. We can therefore assume that the small built-up centre of Krupka was already almost full and the narrow, cramped plot was chosen for the construction of a small church out of necessity. But we cannot rule out the option that hygiene concerns played a key role: since its foundation, the church had adjoined a small hospital, and its location as far away from the residential houses as possible to avoid infection would have been a logical choice.

Other unplanned towns with no urban design or adaptation include the smaller mining towns of **Luby** (Schönbach) and **Jindřichovice** (Heinrichsgrün)**,** both established in the early 14th century. They did not originate as mining towns, although mining activity later became a key factor in drawing attention to their locations and played a role in their subsequent development. While Luby, like Krupka, is an unplanned town without a demarcated central square, Jindřichovice does show an urban design, even if it was added later in its development.

The origins of the mining town of **Jindřichovice** date back to the 13th century, when it was mentioned in a document by Pope Gregory X from 1273 as the property of the Cistercian monastery in Teplá. In 1340, Jindřichovice and the tin mines nearby (in Přebuz) were bought by Petr Plik, the owner of Nejdek, who played a leading role in the development of mining and ore processing in Nejdek. The Church of St. Martin was also built at that time.[145]

Tin, silver and lead ores were found near Jindřichovice. In 1434, chancellor Kaspar Schlick was awarded Jindřichovice by Emperor Sigismund for his merits.[146] The Schlicks built a castle there and tried to take advantage of the rich ore deposits in the area. In 1537, Jindřichovice was promoted to a mining town and at the request of Viktorin Schlick, King Ferdinand I gave the town permission to come under the jurisdiction of Loket. A town hall is documented in Jindřichovice in 1518. Like other mining towns, Jindřichovice had a school, which was opened in 1592.[147]

Initially, the Schlicks in Jindřichovice lived in a fortress, which they converted to a Renaissance chateau. Later it was substantially rebuilt by the Nostitz family in 1672. (Fig. 40) The only trace left by the Schlicks' ownership of the chateau is a stone relief with a depiction of St. George placed by the entrance. In 1627 the Schlicks had to sell Jindřichovice and Sokolov to Otto Nosticz. The town was then in the possession of the Nosticz family until 1945.[148] (Fig. 41)

The Erfurt Trade Route

The Bohemian basin faced specific challenges with regard to long-distance trade routes. The border was mainly defined by mountains covered with impenetrable forest, which caused difficulties in connecting Bohemia to the main international roads. Access to Bohemia was provided by passes cut out in the border forest, which were protected by guardhouses, stockades, and later castles.

144) Táňa Šimková, *Standardní nedestruktivní stavebně-historický průzkum: Krupka (Ústecký kraj, okres Teplice): kostel sv. Ducha* (No. 4273/5-2645) (Ústí nad Labem: NPÚ ÚOP v Ústí nad Labem, 2016, Sbírka stavebně-historických průzkumů, sign. 1828/A).

145) Pavel Trnka, "Diplomatika a správa kláštera Teplá ve druhé polovině 15. století" (PhD diss., Charles University, 2016), 258 and notes.

146) August Sedláček, *Hrady, zámky a tvrze české, Part XIII.* (Praha: 1937), 170.

147) Karel Kuča, *Města a městečka v Čechách, na Moravě a ve Slezsku. Part II H–Kole* (Praha: 1997), 703.

148) Karel Kuča, *Města a městečka, Part II*, 703–704.

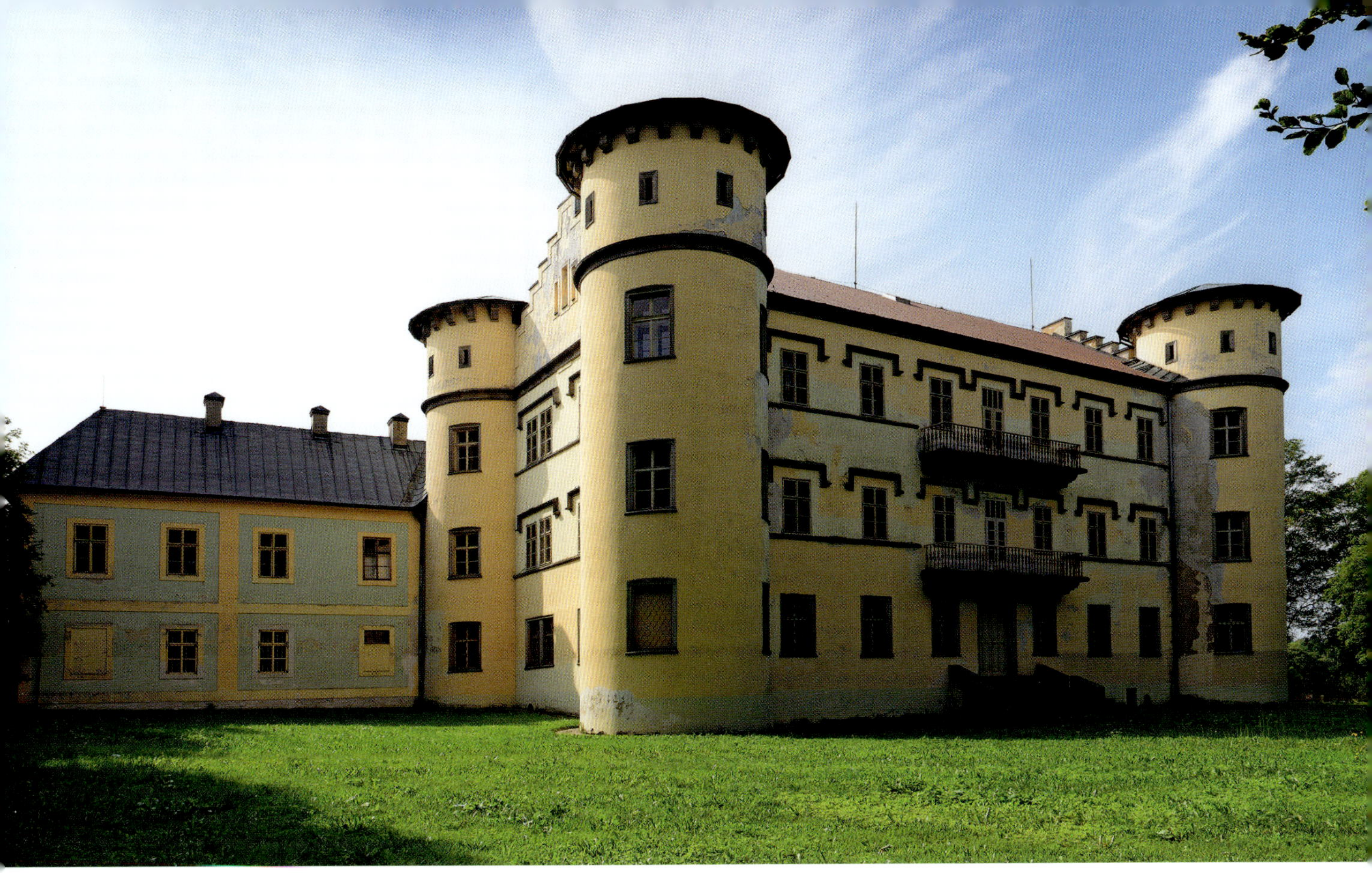

Fig. 40 Jindřichovice, chateau, general view from the north of the complex in the form after the major reconstruction in 1672. Fortress 1572 – Victorin Schlick, reconstruction 1672 – Johann Hartwig von Nostitz. Photo by J. Peer (2019).

From the passes, long-distance roads passed through Prague to the northern border and on to the sea. For the region of the Ore Mountains, an important route was the 'Via Magna' that led from Prague westwards into the empire via Rakovník and Sedlec nad Ohří, where it branched off. The first branch connected the kingdom with Bamberg, while the second, also known as the Erfurt, Sedlec, or Osek branch, provided a connection with Erfurt and Halle.[149]

Jindřichovice took advantage of its favourable location on the highway to Erfurt as early as around 1273,[150] which also determined the housing development, which was highly irregular and scattered. In the 1520s, the prominent locations above the narrow valley with the road were occupied by Viktorin Schlick's fortress, replaced by the Schlicks' castle built in a slightly different position at the end of the 16th century,[151] and St. Martin's Church on the opposite hill. Immediately lining the road were mostly half-timbered town buildings.

149) Ivan Vávra, "Osecká cesta – hrobská cesta," in: *Historická geografie* 20 (1982), 187–201; Eva Černá – Tomáš Velímský, "Česko-saské kontakty a problematika středověkých cest přes Krušné hory a Děčínské stěny," in: Kristina Kaiserová (ed.), *Čechy a Sasko v proměnách dějin* (Ústí nad Labem: 1993), 359–370; Zbyněk Sviták, *Úvod do historické topografie českých zemí* (Brno: 2014), 102.

150) Lubomír Zeman, *Zástavba a urbanismus*, 59.

151) Pavel Vlček, *Ilustrovaná encyklopedie českých zámků* (Praha: 2001), 288.

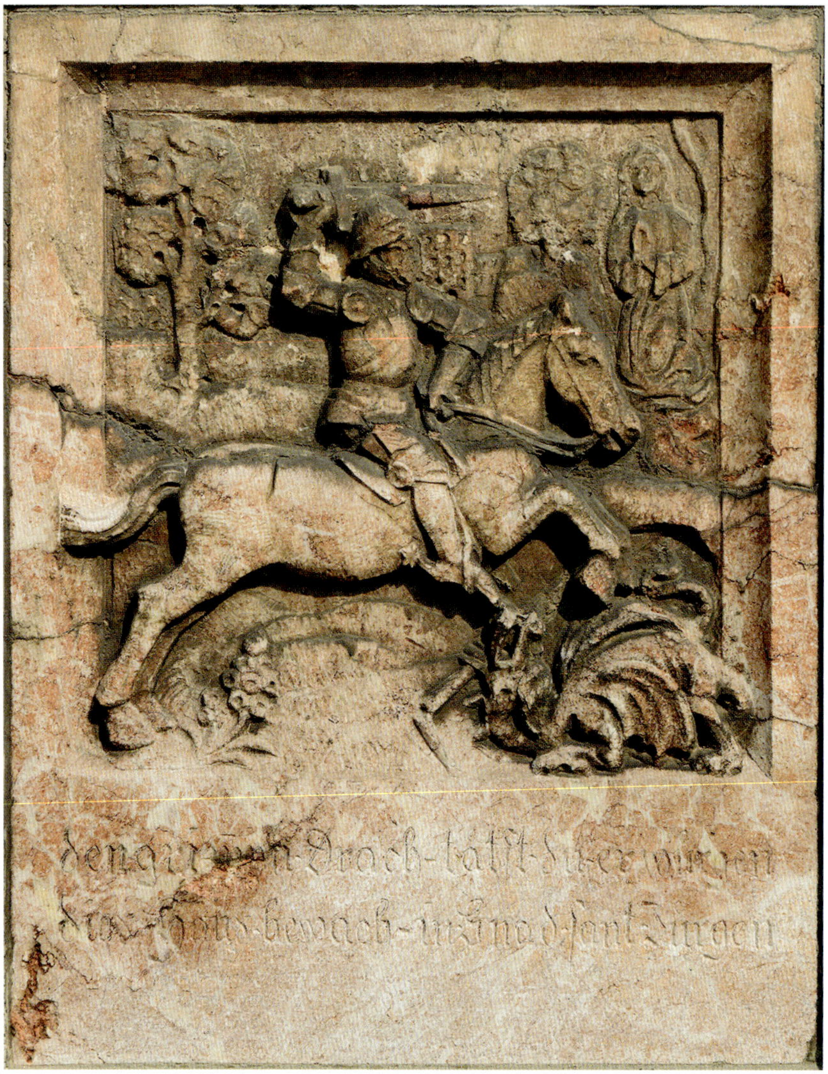

Fig. 41 Jindřichovice, chateau, relief with St. George from the original Renaissance chateau. Photo by J. Peer (2019).

After 1523, the area under the castle was extended along the road to include a rather modest public square, the western end of which was occupied by the magistrate's house and later the town hall. As mining activity ramped up and the population grew during the 16th century, so did the pressure for housing development. Whereas in Krupka, houses built later were arranged in a second line running parallel behind the first row of houses, Jindřichovice had no room for such a solution, as the space along the highway was very limited. Instead, new buildings filled the gaps between the existing houses, and the previously demarcated square was built up at the end of the 16th century.[152]

Kraslice (Graslitz) was situated on the same trade route as Jindřichovice. The first mention of the town of Kraslice comes from around 1352.[153] The area of the so-called Lubský

152) The houses along the road leading up to the castle were built later, during the Baroque and Classical periods. Lubomír Zeman, *Zástavba a urbanismus*, 60.
153) Petr Jančárek, *Města českého Krušnohoří v předbělohorské době. Příspěvek ke studiu jejich sociální struktury* (Praha: 1971), 37.

újezd (Schönbacher Ländchen) was probably settled as far back as the 12th century as part of the colonisation efforts of the Cistercian Abbey of Waldsassen. The building of the town was preceded by the construction of a guard castle called Hausberg (also, Neuenhaus) overlooking the trade route, and the town of Greslas was created by merging several smaller settlements in the outer castle area in the mid-14th century. Přemysl Otakar II (Ottokar II of Bohemia) granted the castle, including the outer castle area and the mines in Kraslice, as a fief to Henry of Plauen, and Kraslice remained a crown fief until 1577. The Lords of Plauen started an intensive mining campaign for silver, lead, and tin in the area around Kraslice. In the 14th century the settlement grew so much, due to mining activities that on 15 August 1370 Charles IV made it a town with the same priviliges as those enjoyed by Loket.[154]

In the 15th century, Kraslice changed hands several times. A major change in ownership, which influenced the intensity of the mining business, occurred in 1527, when Kraslice was acquired by Jeroným (Hieronymus) Schlick.[155] The discovery of new deposits triggered an influx of miners and prospectors, especially from Saxony. In 1541, Kraslice became a free mining town and passed into the hands of the Šumburk (Schönburg) family in 1575.[156] Before long, the local population converted to Lutheranism and the town became one of the centres of the Lutheran faith in the western part of the Ore Mountains.

The booming mining activity made Kraslice one of the most populous towns in Bohemia before the Thirty Years' War, a fact which also influenced its appearance.[157] The urban design was dictated by the layout of the terrain and the importance of access to water for the mining business. There were mostly half-timbered houses with small adjoining gardens, whose gabled front façades overlooked the main road, which was significantly widened in the centre of the housing area into an irregular public square. In contrast to Jindřichovice, subsequent residential development in Kraslice sprawled along the Svatava River and Stříbrný (Silver) stream, where additional building space was available. As a result, the public square area remained undeveloped, except for the original wooden church, which was replaced at the beginning of the 17th century by the representative hall-type Church of Corpus Christi, inspired by Saxon architecture.[158] At the period of the town's peak prosperity, additional mining settlements cropped up around it, including Bublava (Schwaderbach), Hraničná (Markhausen), Sklená (Glasberg), Smolná (Pechbach), Tisová (Eibenberg), and Zelená Hora (Grünberg).

Mining activity in the area declined in the early 17th century and most local miners left for Saxony after the Battle of White Mountain. Copper mining and processing persisted, as is evident from two remarkable paintings from the Nostitz picture gallery in the castle in Jindřichov (now in the National Technical Museum in Prague) with the motif of mining and processing

154) Tomáš Durdík, *Encyklopedie českých hradů* (Praha: 2005), 293; August Sedláček, *Hrady, zámky, tvrze XIII.*, 179–180; Lubomír Zeman, *Zástavba a urbanismus*, 47.

155) August Sedláček, *Hrady, zámky, tvrze XIII.*, 180.

156) Walter Schlesinger, *Die Landesherrschaft der Herren von Schönburg. Eine Studie zur Geschichte des Staates in Deutschland* (Münster – Köln: 1954).

157) Petr Jančárek, "Sociální struktura báňského města Kraslic na konci předbělohorského období", in: *Minulostí Západočeského kraje* 28 (1992), 127–174.

158) Vladimír Prokop – Lukáš Smola, *Sokolovsko: umění, památky a umělci do roku 1945* (Sokolov: 2014), 328–337; Alfred Riedl, *Zur Geschichte der Kirchen in Graslitz* (Dettingen am Main: 1967).

copper ore in Kraslice. The paintings were commissioned between 1630 and 1631 by an unknown mining entrepreneur in Kraslice.[159]

It is also interesting to note that the well-known humanist Paulus Niavis set the events of his famous text about mining in the Ore Mountains, *Iudicium Iovis* (The Judgment of Jupiter, 1495), in the Kraslice region.[160] The title page of the book has illustrations in the background of what are most probably actual places in Kraslice: Hausberg and Glassberg with the Chapel of St. Adalbert.

Paulus Niavis – Schneevogel (1460–1517) (Fig. 42)

Paulus Niavis, born Paul Schneevogel, was a German humanist, educator and writer. He was born in 1460 in Cheb (Eger), and educated in Plauen, Ingolstadt and Leipzig. After graduation he worked as a teacher and head of the city schools in Halle and Chemnitz. From 1490 he held civil service positions in Zittau and Bautzen, where he served as a councillor until his death in 1517. He contributed significantly to the reform of Latin Lutheran education with his works on didactics based on examples from everyday school life and on engaging students in dialogue about the material being taught. In addition, he wrote the first literary text about mining in the Ore Mountains, *Iudicium Iovis*, in 1495.[161]

The town of **Nejdek** (Neudek) was built in the same way, with the long-distance road also leading under a watchtower. A section of the road was expanded to form a public square. The square in Nejdek is noticeably elongated, with buildings lining its sides.[162] In Nejdek, which is situated in the valley of the Rolava (Rohlau) River, tin has been mined since the 14th century. The beginnings of mining in the area are associated with the Plicks of Plickenstein, who owned a castle above Nejdek, founded by Konrad Plick in the mid-13th century and serving to protect the road from Chodov to Saxony.[163] The mining settlement under the castle was probably built after the mid-13th century and relied for supplies on the towns of Suchá (Thierbach) and Heřmanov, although neither of them is mentioned in sources before 1341.[164] Peter Plick of Plickenstein, who received the castle as a fief from John of Bohemia, also founded the local Church of St. Martin, built between 1341 and 1364.[165] Nejdek was owned by the Plicks until

159) Vladimír Prokop – Lukáš Smola, *Sokolovsko,* 241–242.

160) Idem.

161) Rudolf Wolkan, *Böhmens Antheil an der deutschen Litteratur des XVI. Jahrhunderts 3* (Praha: 1894), 159; Paul Krenkel (ed.), "Paulus Niavis, Iudicium Iovis oder Das Gericht der Götter über den Bergbau: ein literarisches Dokument aus der Frühzeit des deutschen Bergbaus," *Freiberger Forschungshefte* 3 (Berlín: 1953); Joachim Knape – Ursula Kocher, "Niavis, Paul," in: *Neue Deutsche Biographie* 19 (Berlín: 1999), 195; Gerhard Weng, "Paul Schneevogels (Paulus Niavis') Beziehungen zum Bergbau," in: Friedrich Naumann (ed.), *Sasko-české vztahy v 16. století* (Chemnitz: 2001). Available at: https://www-user.tu-chemnitz.de.

162) Karel Kuča, *Krušnohorská města*, 7. More on the history of Nejdek: Josef Pilz, *Dějiny města Nejdku do roku 1923*. 1st edition 1911. Czech translation by Miroslav Holeček, Ingeborg Kosťová (Nejdek: 2003).

163) August Sedláček, *Hrady, zámky, tvrze XIII.* (Praha: 1937), 181.

164) These villages continued to be part of the Nejdek estate. See Květoslava Haubertová – Gustav Hofman – Ladislav Lešnický, *Soupis západočeských urbářů* (Plzeň: 1993), 100.

165) Emanuel Poche et al., *Umělecké památky Čech II.* (Praha: 1978), 458–459.

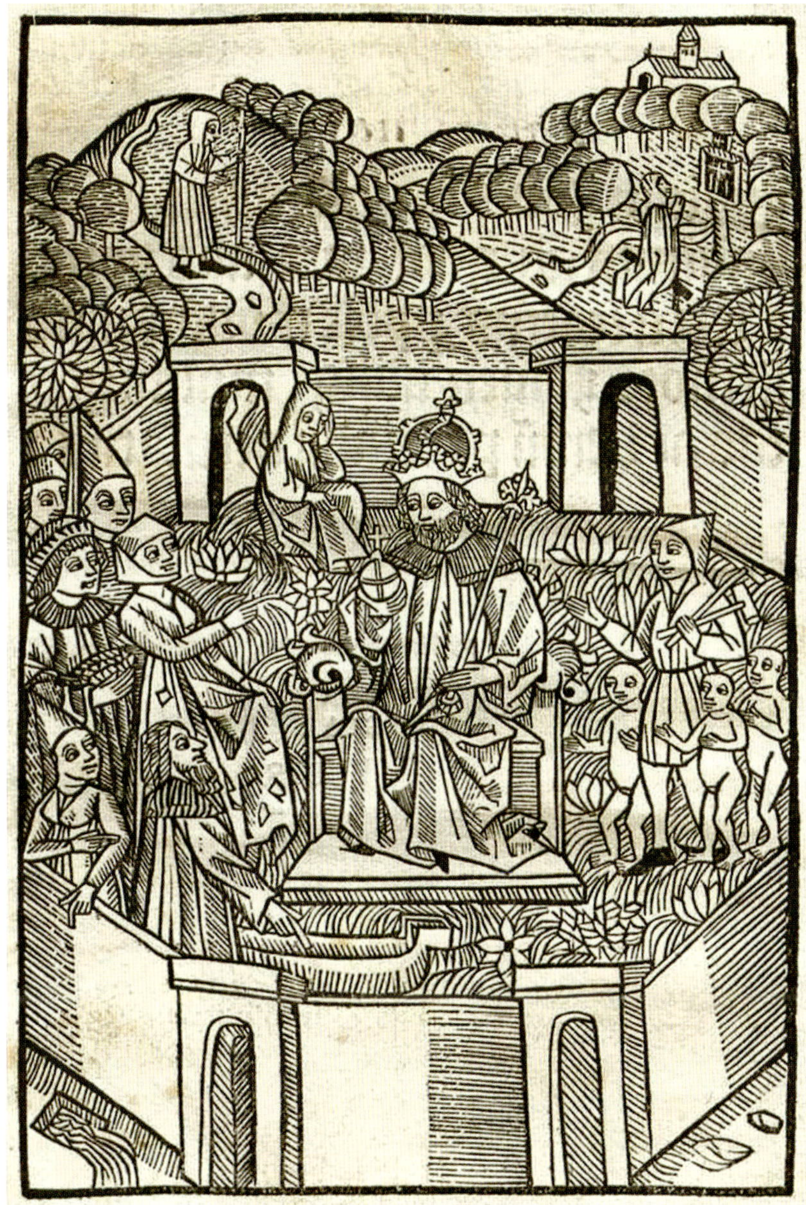

Fig. 42 Paulus Niavis – Schneevogel, *Iudicum Iovis*, title page of a treatise with engraving, origin 1495, Czech title Jupiter's Judgement. One of the motifs of the treatise is, among other things, the trial and subsequent judgment of Jupiter in the dispute between the miners and the gods. Photo © Bayerische Staatsbibliothek.

the end of the 14th century. After that point, ownership changed multiple times until 1446, when Hannes Henninger von Seeberg sold it to the Schlicks.[166] The Schlicks' tenure of Nejdek, between 1446 and 1602 was the golden age of tin mining in the area. In addition to tin ore, hematite was also mined here, from which iron was extracted. The Schlicks also supported the development of the town and built a Renaissance chateau. In 1602, they sold Nejdek to Fridrich Colonna of Fels, who in turn sold it to Herman Czernin of Chudenice in 1632, and after the mid-17th century, the town passed to the Hartigs.[167]

166) Rudolf Schreiber, *Der Elbogner Kreis und seine Enklaven nach dem dreissigjahrigen Kriege* (Prag: 1935), 182–183. For more on the acquisition, see Michal Novotný, "Šlikové. Majetková struktura panství a společenské postavení rodu do roku 1487" (diploma thesis, Charles University, 2007), 130–131.
167) August Sedláček, *Hrady, zámky, tvrze XIII.* (Praha: 1937), 181.

The most advanced type of unplanned towns were those in which urban development took place around a regularly laid-out central square. Of the oldest towns in the Ore Mountains, Hrob (Klostergrab) and Hroznětín (Lichtenstadt) belong in this category.[168] Both towns feature a generously-sized, rectangular square, surrounded by representative buildings adjacent to each other, with individual blocks lining the street that runs through the square.

In both cases the church building stands free in the open space of the square. In **Hroznětín** it is accompanied by small irregular buildings of the younger settlement horizon. The town's structure also shows the original layout of the ploughed area, which is connected to the older buildings of the town, probably dating back to its oldest historical period, when the Premonstratensians of Teplá controlled it as a strategic settlement centre on the important trade route to Erfurt.[169] The original urban design, dating back to the 13th century, was characterised by the rudiments of a rectangular pattern of streets running from a spacious trapezoidal square. But this design was later overlaid by a spontaneous housing development, which started in the 16th century when the Schlicks owned the estate, and continued in response to the dynamic mining activity in the vicinity of the town in later years. Hroznětín had been held by the Schlicks since the 1430s.[170] After 1500, an important Jewish ghetto with its own synagogue developed on the north bank of the Bystřice (Wistritz) River.[171]

The types of urban design seen of the mining towns described above were logically maintained in the two following settlement waves during the 16th century. Unplanned towns with a linear street layout continued to be the predominant type, but a distinctly rural layout similar to the *Waldhufendorf* (forest village) soon prevailed within the group of newly-founded towns. This clearly illustrates the fact that, although the newly founded mining settlements were quickly granted town status in response to their promotion of mining, structurally they were hardly different from typical mountain villages, which grew spontaneously and over a very short period of time.

The 'Waldhufendorf' forest village

In the High Middle Ages, valley villages were typically founded in mountain areas and foothills. They are characterised by buildings being located higher up from a watercourse or central road, very often on natural or man-made terraces. Buildings located closer to the stream in the valley were usually built at later stages of development. Typically, there is no central square, although in some cases a square was added afterwards during subsequent urban development.[172]

To a certain degree, this is the case with **Jáchymov** (Sankt Joachimsthal), which is indisputably the most renowned mining town in the Ore Mountains. (Fig. 43) It was founded by

168) Michal B. Soukup, *Středověké Duchcovsko* (Duchcov: 2009).

169) Lubomír Zeman, *Zástavba a urbanismus*, 49.

170) Michal Novotný, *Šlikové*, 131.

171) Jiří Fiedler, *Židovské památky v Čechách a na Moravě* (Praha: 1992), 84; Lubomír Zeman, *Zástavba a urbanismus*, 51; Blanka Rozkošná – Pavel Jakubec, *Židovské památky Čech: historie a památky židovského osídlení Čech* (Brno: 2004), 158.

172) Jiří Škabrada, *Lidové stavby. Architektura českého venkova* (Praha: 1999), 60–61.

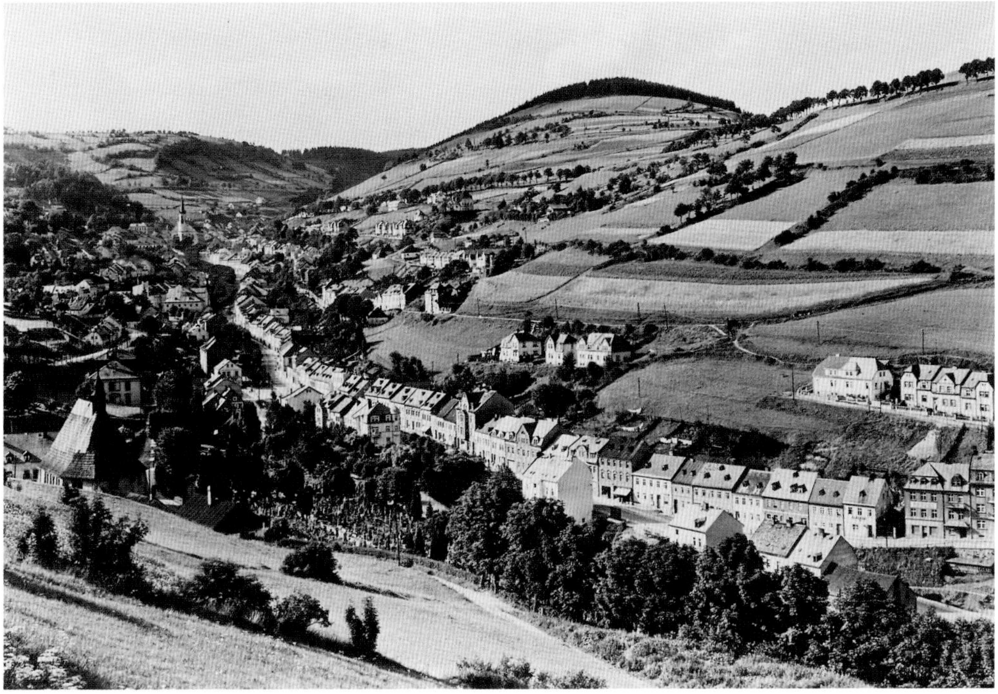

Fig. 43 Jáchymov, general view of the town on a postcard from 1935. Photograph from the private collection of T. Šimková.

the Schlicks in 1516, when first mention was made of Konradsgrün, a settlement with only a handful of houses and a mill.[173] Since 1437, the valley had been owned by the Schlick family, who had received it from Emperor Sigismund. The commencement of mining in the area is associated with Kaspar Bach and Hans Oeser, two miners who started digging the first adit called Nálezná (also known as the Adit of the Three Kings) in 1512.[174] When money started to run out, Stephan Schlick, based in Ostrov nad Ohří (Schlackenwerth), took over the financing of the prospecting works. Count Schlick invited mining experts Kaspar Mergenthal and Egidius Bauerlein from Saxony to the valley in 1516, to assess the profitability of ore veins in the area. Count Schlick, who became the main organiser of the mining activity, founded a mining association, to which he also invited Johann Pflug von Rabenstein and other noblemen and mining entrepreneurs from Saxony. Once the excellent quality of the silver ore and the suitability of the site for mining were confirmed, Heinrich von Könneritz was called in, under whose guidance the miners struck a rich silver vein. This was the beginning of the Jáchymov silver rush. At the request of Count Schlick, the local settlement was renamed Joachimsthal (St. Joachim's Valley / Jáchymov). In 1516, there were five mines in the area but their number grew in the following years, as did the population, which was dominated by miners from Saxony.

173) Heribert Sturm – Anton Müller, *St. Joachimstahl* (St. Joachimstahl: 1930); Stanislav Burachovič, *Jáchymov v zrcadle času. Stručné dějiny prvních radonových lázní světa* (Karlovy Vary: 2007); Andrea Huczmanová, "Jáchymov – jeden z fenoménů českého království. Sonda do poměrů města 16. století" (diploma thesis, Charles University, 2013).
174) Karl Knopf, *Die Wunderstadt St. Joachimsthal* (Leipzig: 1909), 11.

Heinrich von Könneritz (1483–1551)

Heinrich von Könneritz came from a noble family in Thuringia, which had settled in Saxony at the end of the 15th century. A close associate of Stephan Schlick, he was the Inspector of Mines and Mint Master in Jáchymov. At the same time he was a mining entrepreneur and co-owner of the mines. He is also credited with co-authorship of the Jáchymov Mining Code of 1518. In addition, he is believed have written a chronicle in which he recorded the early days of mining in Konradsgrün, of which only fragments are known from later chronicles. He held the office of the Mint Master until 1528, when the Schlicks had to return the minting rights to the monarch. Also known is his connection with Georg Agricola, who benefited from von Könneritz's expertise in writing his 'Bermannussive de re metallicadialogus.' In 1545, von Könneritz left Jáchymov for the court of the Saxon Elector Johann Friedrich. The altar in the Church of All Saints depicting the mystical betrothal of St. Catherine, which comes from Cranach's workshop, commemorates this important figure associated with the most important period of Jáchymov.[175]

Stephan Schlick, Count of Passaun and Weißkirchen (1487–1526)

His great uncle was Kaspar I Schlick (†1449), a man with a meteoric career, who became Imperial Chancellor in the service of Sigismund of Luxembourg and was promoted to the rank of Count in 1433. He was granted extensive properties near Cheb (Eger) and Loket (Elbogen), which were later inherited and shared among various branches of the family. Stephan's father Kaspar II Schlick (†1505) obtained the estate of Ostrov nad Ohří (Schlackenwerth), which included Jáchymov. He had five sons by his wife Elisabeth of Gutenstein. One of the sons, Stephan, was a capable entrepreneur and mining organiser. His wealth, education and diplomacy brought him into the circles of the court of Louis II, which led to a star-crossed decision: He joined the campaign against the Turks, who were threatening Hungary. He died alongside the king in the fateful Battle of Mohács on August 29, 1526. His brothers erected an epitaph with his image by the western entrance to St. Joachim's Church in Jáchymov. It includes a Latin verse that reads: 'His piety, love for the king, and famous bravery robbed him of his fatherland, wife and government.'[176]

The city grew rapidly. The Jáchymov Chronicle tells about the first parish priest, Georg Beck, and about the foundation of All Saints' Church, which later became a hospital church.[177] A school is also mentioned, whose cantor was Benedikt Kenuffler.[178] Soon the town also had its own administration, headed by Nickel Halthendorf as the first chief magistrate. Above the valley with the growing mining agglomeration, Stephan Schlick built Šlikův hrádek (Freudenstein Castle) with its dominant tower.[179] (Fig. 44)

175) Jan Klípa – Michaela Ottová, *Bez hranic*, 672–674.

176) Jan Klípa – Michaela Ottová, *Bez hranic*, 670; Richard Schmidt, *Soupis památek historických a uměleckých v Království českém XL. Politický okres Jáchymovský* (Praha: 1913), 36–37.

177) Richard Schmidt, *Soupis památek historických a uměleckých*, 563–565.

178) An important source for learning about the town's history is a chronicle written by the Dean of Jáchymov, Gregor Lindner: *Paměti z dějin města Jáchymova*, which describes events from 1515 until 1600. The manuscript is deposited in the State District Archives Karlovy Vary, Jáchymov collection; the text is available in digital form at http://www.portafontium.eu.

179) Tomáš Durdík, *Ilustrovaná encyklopedie českých hradů – Dodatky* (Praha: 2002), 23–25; Richard Schmidt, *Soupis*

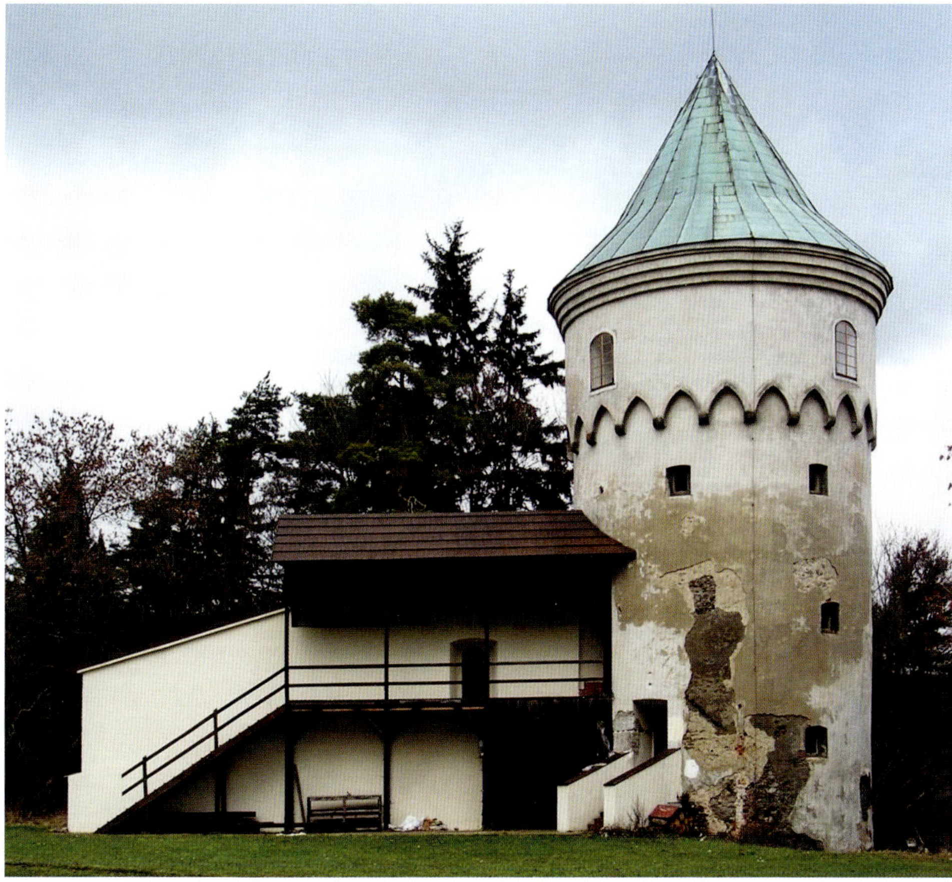

Fig. 44 Jáchymov, Freudenstein Castle above Jáchymov, general view of the relics of the building. Construction 1516–1517 – Stefan Schlick, building design by Jan Münnich, alternative name Schlick's Castle. In 1525 it was burnt down and after subsequent restoration it served as the residence of the royal mining governors. Photo by T. Šimková (2019).

In 1519, the first experimental minting of Jáchymov thalers took place at Freudenstein, which was probably related to the request of the Schlicks for the right to mint coins. The Schlick family obtained the minting privilege from the Land Diet in 1520. At that time, 200 mines were already operating in Jáchymov, employing around a thousand miners. The town's population grew rapidly to 5,000. On January 6, 1520, King Vladislaus II promoted Jáchymov to the status of a free royal mining town and granted it a coat of arms.[180] (Fig. 45)

In the same year, Magister Silvius Egranus, a native of Cheb (Eger) and a follower of Erasmus of Rotterdam, was appointed priest.[181] From the early 1520s, the town was divided into four districts. Each had its own local government that also maintaned public order in the town, where, according to sources, gambling, drinking parties and prostitution were rampant. Despite efforts to maintain order and protect the health of the miners, the plague broke out in the town in 1521 and not even the local nobility, including the Schlick family, were spared.

památek historických a uměleckých, 78–81.

180) Anton Müller, *Kurze Geschichte der freien Bergstadt St. Joachimstal* (Joachimstal: 1926), 6. Drawing on older literature and translations of German editions of the Jáchymov chronicles, this book offers a popular account of the history of Jáchymov: Josef Sudovský – Vladimír Horák, *Kronika horního města Jáchymova a jeho hornictví v kontextu dějin zemí České koruny* (Ústí nad Labem: 2009), For details on the town's early days, see esp. 30–40.

181) Karlheinz Blaschke, "Egranus, Johannes Sylvius," in: *Neue Deutsche Biographie* 4 (Berlín: 1959), 341–342.

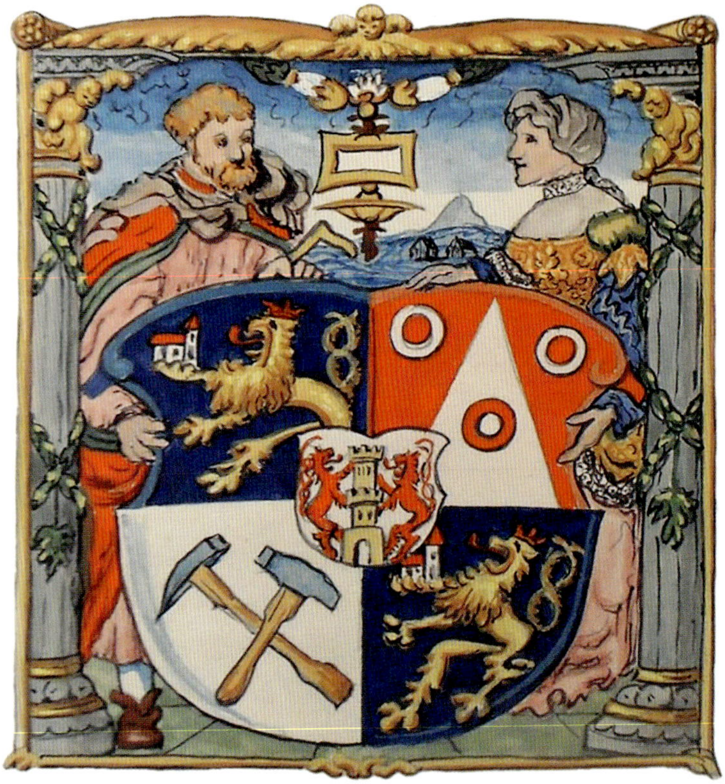

Fig. 45 The town coat of arms of Jáchymov in the version from 1520. Reproduced from the book Knopf, K. Die Wunderstadt St. Joachimsthal. Weipert 1914.

How life was organised in the town

In the richly populated Jáchymov, law and order had to be ensured. A set of specific rules therefore served to regulate people's behaviour. This is a unique collection of documents that testify to maintaining discipline in an early modern town. The following documents, among others, were introduced over time for the residents of Jáchymov, which included: Forestry Regulations (1526), Hospital and Municipal Treasury Regulations (1531), Gamekeeper Regulations (1538), Building Regulations (1538), Fire Protection Regulations (1539, 1555, 1787), Regulations for Tailors (1539), Regulations for Blacksmiths' Journeymen (1540), Regulations for Weighers (1542), Dance Regulations (1543), Regulations for Master Brewers (1545), and Regulations for Shoemakers' Journeymen (1546). Standard guilds were also set up for individual professions (such as blacksmiths, locksmiths, and pewterers). Another important document of life in the town is the Church Order, published by the brothers Hieronymus and Vavřinec (Lorenz) Schlick in 1538, and another by Johann Mathesius in 1551.[182]

By 1525, the population of Jáchymov had grown to about 10,000. The large numbers of miners, influenced by reports about peasant revolts in Germany, demanded better work

182) Ludmila Kubátová, *Statuta horního města Jáchymova z roku 1526* (Praha: 2012); Josef Hrdlička – Jiří Just – Petr Zemek (ed.), "Evangelické církevní řády pro šlechtická panství v Čechách a na Moravě 1520–1620," in: *Prameny k českým dějinám 16.–18. století.* Řada B, sv. VIII (České Budějovice: 2017), 123–124, 125–138.

conditions, which brought about a rebellion in the town. Nearly 3,000 miners rose against the town's administration and the Schlicks, and ransacked the town hall and Freudenstein Castle. A compromise solution was eventually reached and the Schlicks published an addendum to the Mining Order, which adjusted the responsibilities and powers of the mining officials. A new town statute also came into force.[183]

When Stephan Schlick, the owner of the estate, was killed in the Battle of Mohács in 1526, his brother Jeroným took over the town. Like other towns, Jáchymov improved its fortifications in response to the Turkish threat. Bastions were built in the south and north end to protect the town.[184] The town's population at the time was around 15,000. The newly elected king, Ferdinand I, confirmed all of Jáchymov's privileges, but it was his intention to limit the power of the Schlicks. In 1528, the family lost its right to mint Jáchymov thalers and to sell and export silver freely. From the very beginning, the business activities of the Schlicks were associated with the Fugger, Welser and Nützel merchant companies based in Nuremberg.[185] From this point on, mining in Jáchymov and the local mint was under royal control. The expansion of the city, typical of the first period under the ownership of the Schlicks, was now curbed, although mining activity was reaching its peak.[186] In 1533, 134 ore veins were discovered, 614 mines and 13 large smelting sites were in operation, and about 8,000 miners worked in the mines. It is estimated that the population at that time increased to more than 18,000, making Jáchymov the most populous Bohemian town after Prague.[187]

The conflict between the king and the Schlicks escalated in the mid-1540s. In September 1545, the Schlicks were forced to surrender all mines and their yields, Freudenstein Castle, and other holdings including Jáchymov, which fell under royal administration. Supervision of the mines was entrusted to Bohuslav Felix of Lobkowitz and Hassenstein and Christoph of Gendorf. The Schlicks were left with only the income from the fiefs, the so-called 'tithe', and they were allowed to mint coins (1- and 2-thaler coins) at their estate in Planá by Mariánské Lázně (Marienbad).[188] The symbols of the Schlicks were removed from the town's coat of arms in 1546, by order of the king. (Fig. 46) In the second half of the 16th century, mining slowly decreased. The gradual decline of the town is evident from a 1613 report, which states that – after and outbreak of the plague in that year – only 529 people lived in the town, 'not counting servants and children.'[189]

The rapid development of the town is reflected in its urban layout. In response to the discovery of rich silver ore deposits in the area and the continually increasing mining activity, houses were built spontaneously and hastily without a solid urban plan. The result was a rather chaotic housing development along the main road running along the bottom of the rising Já-

183) Karl Knopf, *Die Wunderstadt St. Joachimsthal*, 24.

184) Richard Schmidt, *Soupis památek historických a uměleckých*, 32.

185) Josef Janáček, "Die Fugger und Joachimstahl," in: *Historica* 6 (1963), 109–144.

186) Karl Knopf, *Die Wunderstadt St. Joachimsthal*, 30.

187) Ibid., 14.

188) Ibid., 31; Josef Smolík, "Smlouva krále Ferdinanda I. s pány Šliky o hory a minci Jáchymovskou," in: *Památky archeologické a místopisné* 20/5 (1903), 333–340; Martina Pospíšilová, "Narovnání o hory a kovy (1534)," in: Karel Schelle – Jaromír Tauchen, *Encyklopedie českých právních dějin IV.* (Plzeň: 2016), 21–22.

189) Josef Sudovský – Vladimír Horák, *Kronika horního města Jáchymova*, 90.

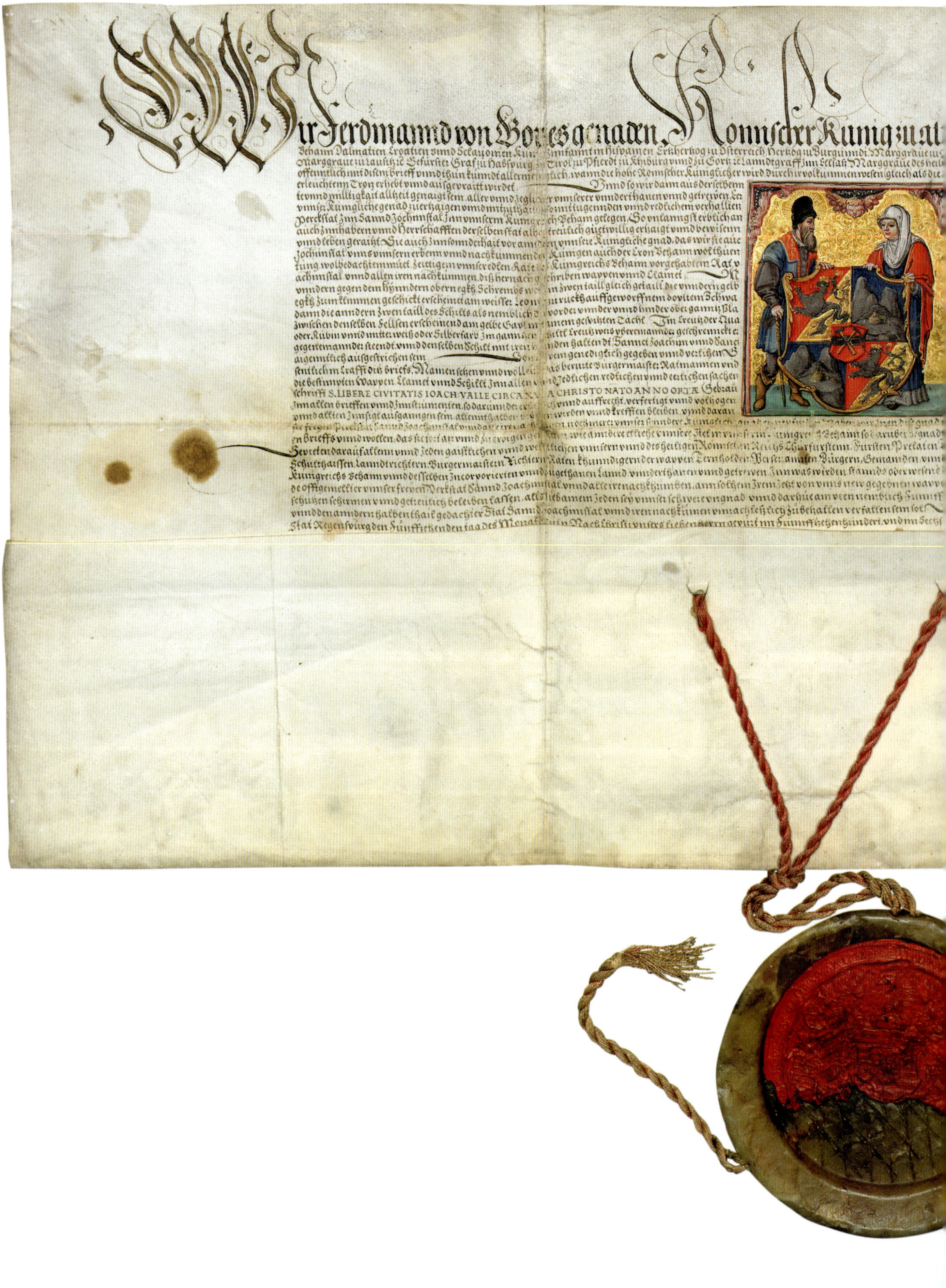

Wir Ferdinand von Gotes genaden, Romischer Kunig zu all[illegible]
Beham Dalmatien Croatien vnnd Sclavonien Kun[illegible] Infannt in Hispanien Ertzherzog zu Osterreich, Herzog zu Burgundi, Marggraue zu [illegible]
Marggraue zu Laußitz ꝛc. Gefürster Graf zu Habspurg [illegible] Tirol zu Pfierdt zu Kiburg vnnd zu Gortz ꝛc. Lanndtgraff Im Elsaß, Marggraue des heil[illegible]
offenntlich mit disem brieff vnnd thun kundt allermen[illegible]glich, wann die hohe Romischer Kuniglicher wird durch ir volkummen wesen gleich als die [illegible]
erleuchtenn Tron erhebt vnnd ausgebraitt wirdet. Vnnd so wir dann aus derselbenn
[illegible]tevnnd milltigkait allhzeit genaigt sein, aller vnnd yegli[illegible]r vnnserer vnnderthanen vnnd getrewen [illegible]
vnnser Kunigliche genad zuertzaigen vnnd mitzuthail[illegible] [illegible]ntlugennden vnnd redlichem verhallten
Perckstat Inn Sannd Jochimstal, Inn vnnserm Kunigr[illegible]ch Beham gelegen, So vnlanngst erblich an
auch Innhabern vnnd Herrschafften derselben stat all[illegible] treulich guetwillig erzaigt vnnd bewisenn
vnnd leben geraicht, Sie auch Innsonnderhait vor ann[illegible]ern vnnsere Kunigliche gnad, das wir sie auc[illegible]
Jochimstal vnns vnnsern erbenn vnnd nachkummen de[illegible] Kunigen auch der Cron Beham wol thuen
tung, wolbedachtemmuet, zeittigem vnnser edlen Rate [illegible] Kunigreichs Beham vorgehabtem Rat, v[illegible]
achimstal vnnd allen iren nachkummen, diß hernach g[illegible]schriben wappen vnnd Clainet [illegible]
vnndern gegen dem hynndern obern egkh, Schrembs w[illegible] in zwen taill gleich getailt die vnndern gelb
egkh zum klimmen geschickt erscheinet am weisser Leon [illegible] zu ruckh auffgeworffnem dopltem Schwa[illegible]
dann die anndern zwen taill des Schilts als nemblich d[illegible] vorder vnnder vnnd hinder ober gantz Bla[illegible]
zwischen denselben Fellsen erscheinend am gelbe Gar[illegible] [illegible]nnen gesvihten Tachl Im Creutz der Qua[illegible]
oder Rubin vnnd mitten weiß oder Silberfarb Im gann[illegible] [illegible] Creutzweis vbereinannder geschrenckt ꝛc.
gegeneinannder steendt, vnnd denselben Schilt mit iren [illegible] [illegible]nden halten dt, Sannct Joachim vnnd Sanc[illegible]
aigenntlich ausgestrichen sein — Sein[illegible] [illegible]vem genedigklich gegeben vnnd verlihen [illegible]
sentlich in crafft dits briefs. Namen setzen vnnd woll[illegible] [illegible]as berurte Burgermaister Ratmannen vnd
die bestimbten Wappen Clainet vnnd Schillt Inn allen [illegible] Jedlichen redlichen vnnd eerlichen sachen
schrifft S. LIBERE CIVITATIS IOACH: VALLE CIRCA X[illegible] A CHRISTO NATO ANNO ORTÆ Gebrau[illegible]
Inn allen brieffen vnnd Innstrumenten, so darinn der [illegible] [illegible] vnnd aufrecht, verfertigt vnnd volzogen
vnnd allten Innsigl ausgangen sein, allennthalben [illegible] [illegible] werden vnnd krefften bleiben, vnnd daran
[illegible]
[illegible]en brieffs vnnd wollen, das sie [illegible] an vnnd zu ewigen [illegible] wie anndere etliche vnnsere Stet in vnnserm [illegible] Kunigreich Behaim [illegible] begnad[illegible]
Sevreten darauf allenn vnnd yeden gaistlichen vnnd we[illegible]ltlichen vnnsern vnnd des heiligen Romischen Reichs Churfurstenn, Fursten, Prelaten [illegible]
Schulthaissen, Lanndtrichtern, Burgermaistern, Richtern, Raten, Khunndigern der wappen, Ernholden, Persevannten, Burgern, Gemainden vnn[illegible]
Kunigreichs Beham vnnd desselben Incorporierten vnnd [illegible]ugethanen Lannd vnnderthanen vnnd getrewen, Inn was wirden stannds oder wesens [illegible]
de offtgemellter vnnser freyen Perckstat Sannd Joachimstal, vnnd alle ire nachkhumben, ann solhem Irem jetzt von vnns new gegebnen wapp[illegible]
schutzen schirmen vnnd getreulich beleiben lassen, als liebe ainem yeden sey vnnser schwere vngnad vnnd darzue ainer peen nemblich Funff[illegible]
vnnd den anndern halben thail gedachter Stat Sannd Joachimstal vnnd iren nachkumen vnnachleßlich zubezallen verfallen sein sol. [illegible]
Stat Regenspurg den Funffzehenden tag des Monat[illegible] [illegible] Nach Christi vnsers lieben Herrn geburt im Funffzehenhundert, vnd im Sechs[illegible]

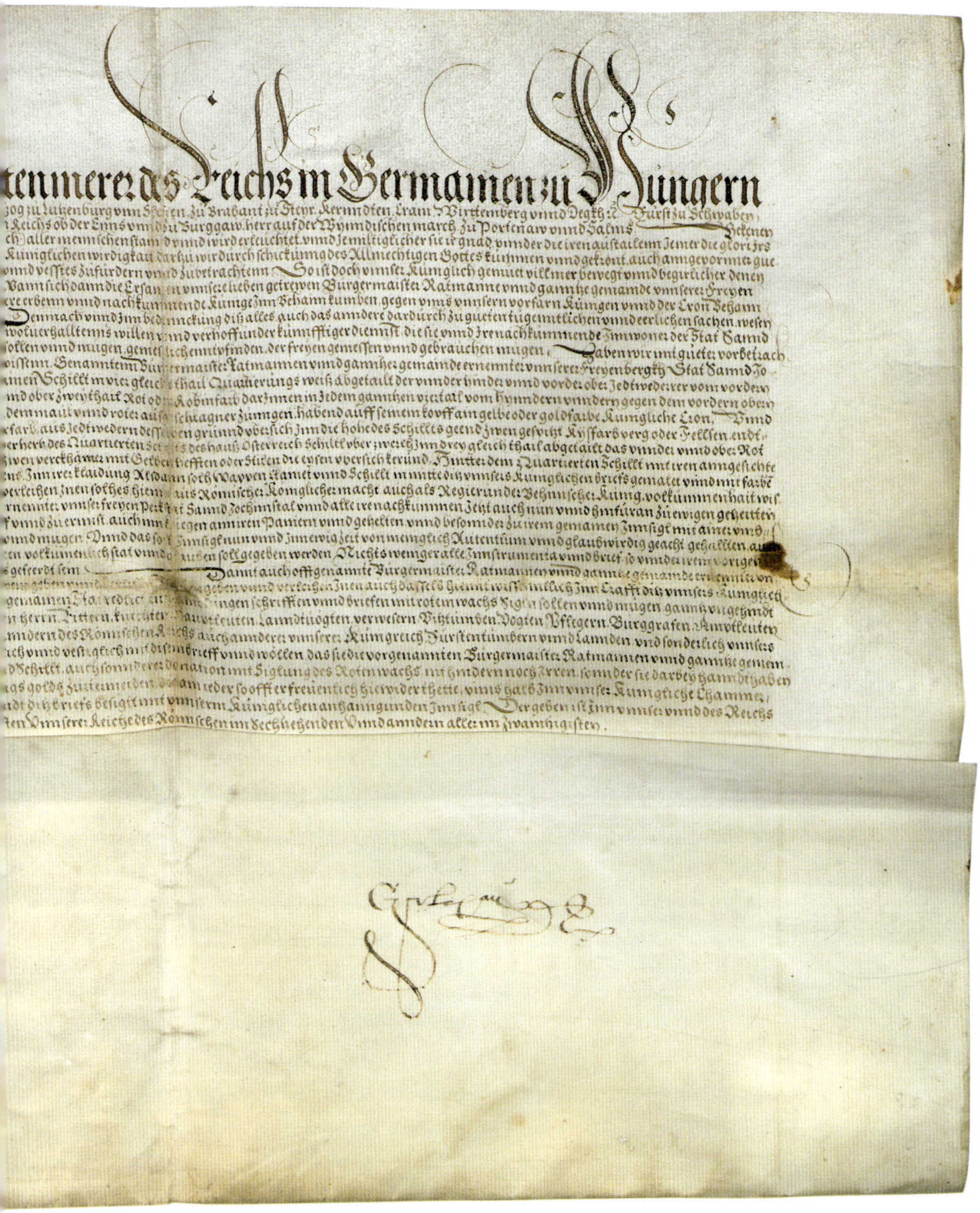

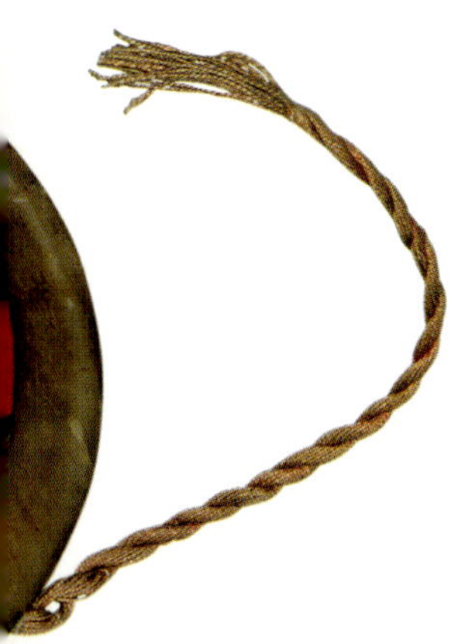

Fig. 46 Charter issued in Regensburg on 15 February 1546 by Ferdinand I of Habsburg to the royal mining town of Jáchymov. The king confirms all the existing privileges and grants a new municipal coat of arms and the right to seal with red wax. The 70 x 36–34.3 cm document is written in German, has a partially damaged royal seal attached and is an archival cultural monument. The coat of arms of the town consists of a shield divided into four fields. The first and fourth fields are red and golden with a silver two-tailed lion walking, the second and third fields have a mine shaft with a miner's house between the rocks. In the centre of the shield is a shield in Austrian colours with two crossed mining hammers. The shield is held by St. Joachim and St. Anne. Reproduction © SOkA Karlovy Vary.

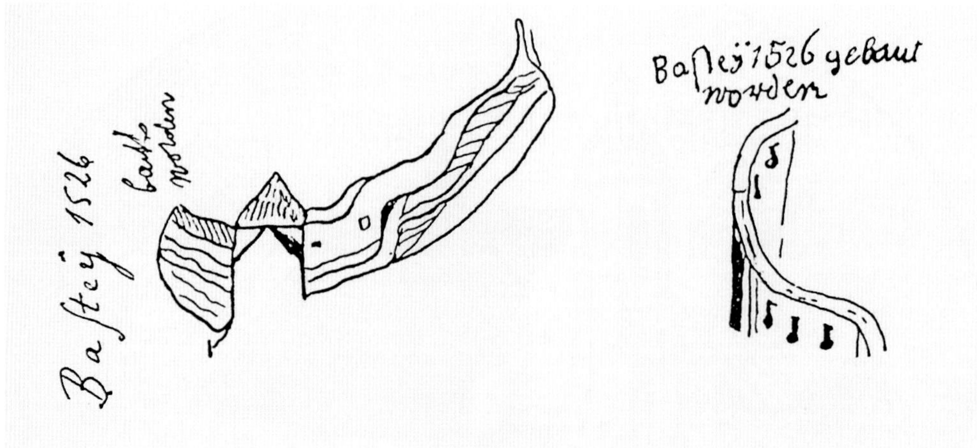

Fig. 47 The appearance of the town bastions in Jáchymov on the old mining map. Reproduction from Schmidt, R., Soupis památek historických a uměleckých v politickém okresu Jáchymovském. Praha 1913.

chymov valley. Its relatively steep slopes held the town in a protective embrace, so no special fortification works were undertaken.[190]

Partial fortification of the built-up area happened much later, in 1526, when the upper and lower ends of the valley were closed off by bastions. (Fig. 47) According to the illustrations on old mining maps, the bastions had defensive towers with town gates, complemented by high walls with shooting galleries, which closed up the valley.[191] The bastions essentially defined the town's perimeter. However, because of the fire hazard, smelting sites with auxiliary facilities were set up below the lower bastion, so essentially outside the built-up area, thus extending beyond the town's limits and into the adjacent valleys.[192]

The delineated area of the town was soon filled with the houses of the rapidly growing population. As a result, new rows of houses were added behind the main residential line. To achieve this objective, the steep slopes of the Ore Mountains in Jáchymov were flattened into terraces to allow for the construction of houses. The housing density is clearly illustrated by the steep increase in population between 1516 and 1533, when it rose from 1,050 to 18,000.[193] The natural centre of the town's oldest built-up area was the so-called Chlebný trh (Brotmarkt, or Bread Market), today's Na Slovanech Square, where the old half-timbered town hall once stood and where the wooden chapel of St. Anne was built in 1517 and rebuilt as a brick chapel after a fire in 1642. (Fig. 48)

It was not until around 1520 that the town underwent urban modernisation, along with a new housing development in the northern part of the town around the Church of St. Joa-

190) Freudenstein Castle, built by the Schlicks in 1517, served more as a family residence and mining administration centre than as a defensive object. Richard Schmidt, *Soupis památek historických a uměleckých*, 32.

191) Both towers were demolished in 1835 during the construction of a new road through the town centre; Richard Schmidt, *Soupis památek historických a uměleckých*, 32.

192) Petr Jančárek, *Města*, 48.

193) Petr Jančárek, *Města*, 49; Lubomír Zeman, *Zástavba a urbanismus*, 51.

Fig. 48 Jáchymov, Chapel of St. Anne, general view from the north. Built in 1517 – wooden chapel, rebuilt after a fire in 1642 as a brick chapel. Photograph by J. Peer (2019).

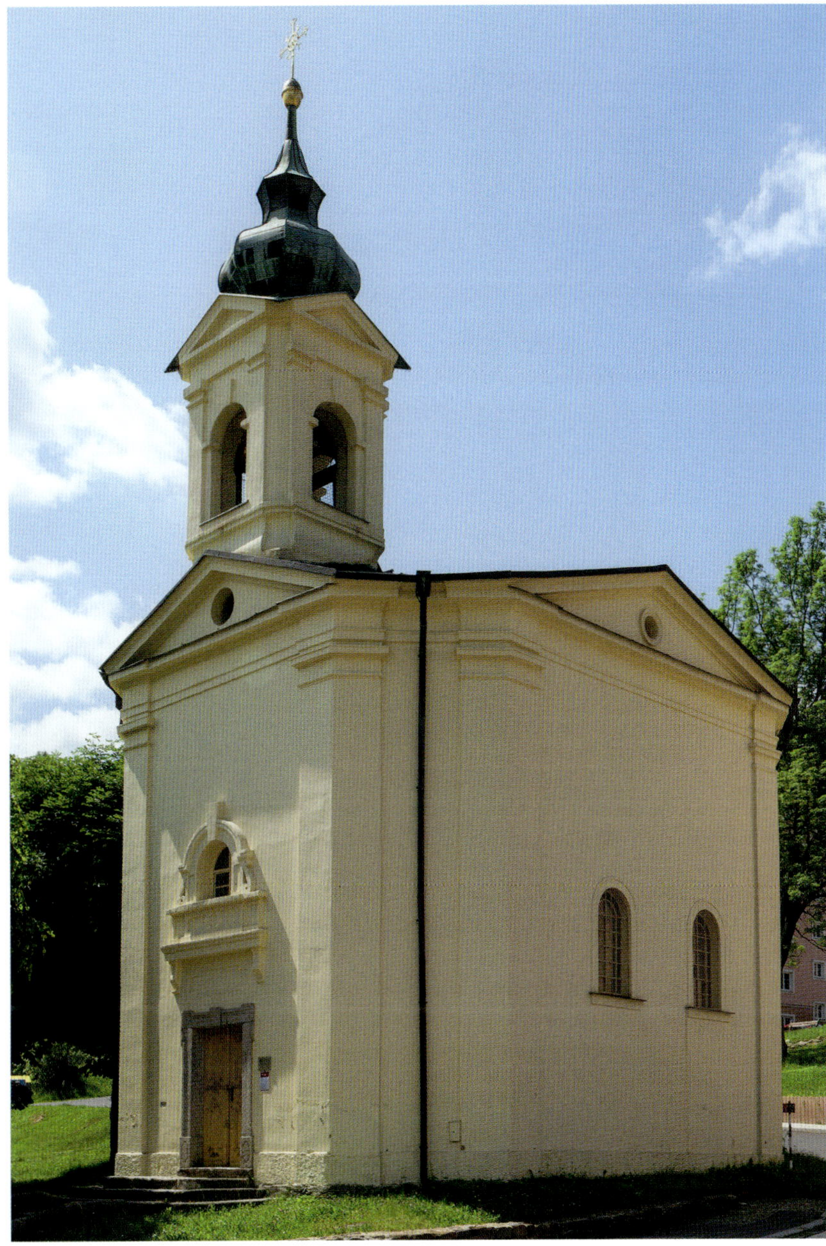

chim. A new square was laid out and subsequently surrounded by representative stone houses,[194] which were probably in sharp contrast to the existing, predominantly half-timbered architecture.[195] An example of a Renaissance house in Jáchymov is No. 143, which reputedly belonged to Heinrich von Könneritz, the Inspector of Mines, and served as his official resi-

194) Lubomír Zeman, "Stavební vývoj města Jáchymova," in: *Jáchymov. Architektonická perla Krušnohoří* (Loket: 2009), 7–18.
195) Lubomír Zeman, *Zástavba a urbanismus*, 51–53; Richard Schmidt, *Soupis památek historických a uměleckých*, 30, 99; Milena Hauserová, "Prostorové uspořádání jáchymovských domů," in: *Jáchymov. Architektonická perla Krušnohoří* (Loket: 2009), 46–47; Lubomír Zeman – Alžběta Kratochvílová, "Dispozice a uspořádání městských domů v Jáchymově," in: Michaela Hrubá – Michaela Ottová – Jan Royt (ed.), *Ars Montana*, 93–305.

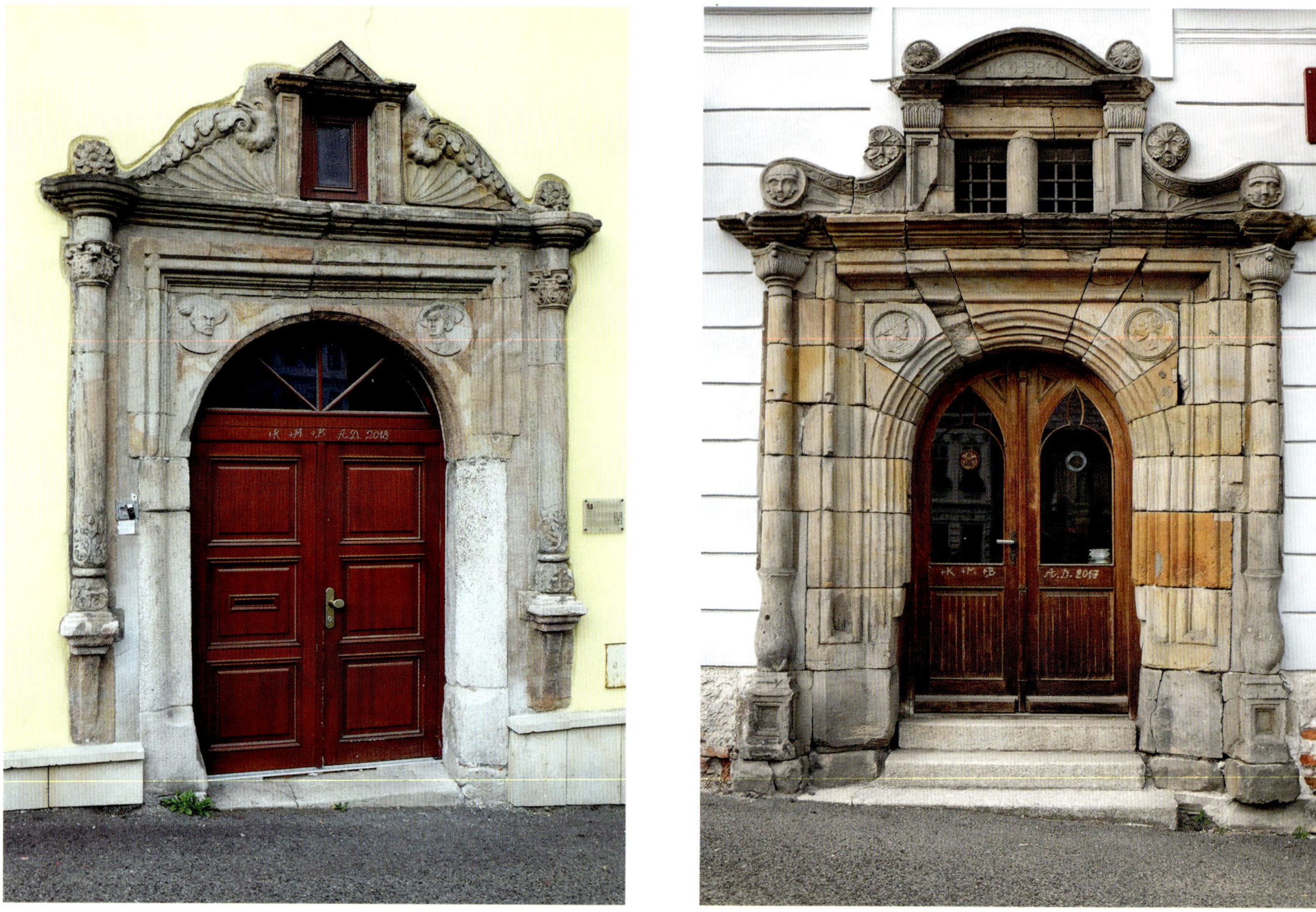

Fig. 49a, b Jáchymov, portals of town houses with characteristic Renaissance decoration and arrangement. Photos by T. Šimková (2019).

dence. A large number of similar Renaissance houses have survived to this day, some of which were later rebuilt, while others still boast Renaissance portals, often flanked by seats. The magnificence of the portals and stone lining testifies to the wealth of those who built these houses. They clearly used the services of first-rate stonemasons who also worked for the Schlicks or on the construction of the town church. (Fig. 49) Among them was Georg von Bamberg.[196] Renaissance houses made of stone also stood in the vicinity of the Jáchymovský Brook, but only their cellars, now filled in, have been preserved. Some of these houses disappeared in 1544 by order of Count Schlick – perhaps the first attempt at a controlled redevelopment of the built-up area in Jáchymov.

The town's wealth was reflected in extensive housing development during the Renaissance. A new royal mint was built on the new square (today's Hornické náměstí / Miners' Square) between 1533 and 1536, replacing the original Schlick mint where the Jáchymov thalers were minted from 1520. (Fig. 50)

196) Emanuel Poche et al., *UPČ 1*, 563–565; Gabriela Lebocová – Alžběta Kratochvílová, "Portály jáchymovských domů," in: *Jáchymov. Architektonická perla Krušnohoří* (Loket: 2009), 48–56.

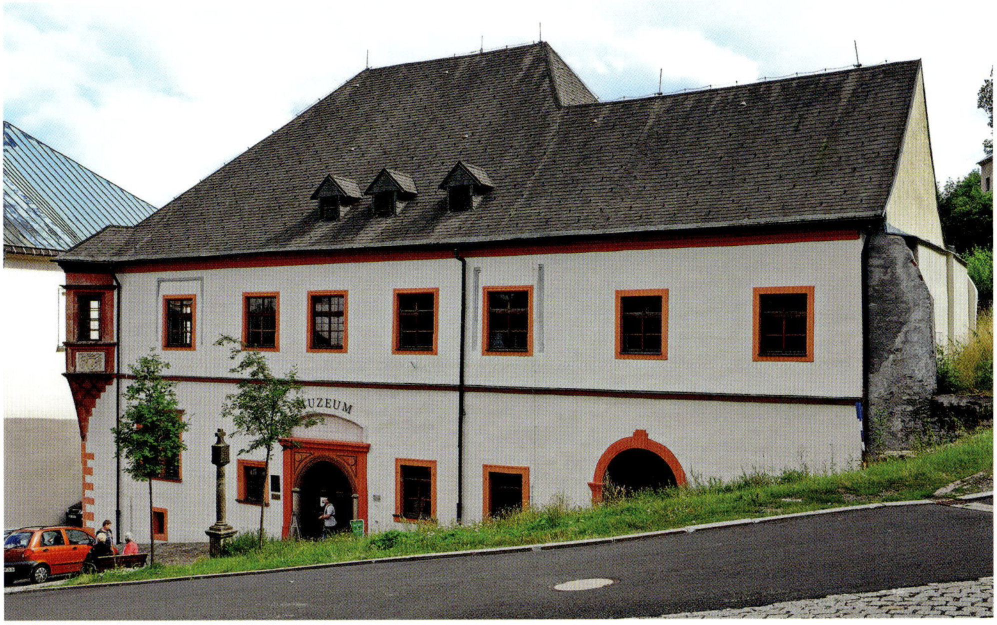

Fig. 50 Jáchymov, Royal Mint, general view from the north-east. Founded in 1520 by rebuilding the town house of Kunz Eirolt under Stephan Schlick, rebuilt 1532–1536. Photo by T. Šimková (2019).

In 1535, the town council bought the house of Lorenz Schlick, where the famous Latin school was established. Between 1540 and 1544, a new Renaissance town hall was built on the foundation of a splendid Renaissance house of Jerome Schlick, which the town council bought for 2,000 gold coins. (Fig. 51)

Between 1534 and 1540, a church dedicated to St. Joachim was also built, which became the main church of the town. In 1539, it received a clock on its tower, and in 1542 a new bell was installed. The church has not survived, however, as it was completely destroyed by fire in 1873. In 1533, the construction of All Saints' Church and a new hospital was also completed. The hospital no longer exists, but the church has retained its original character despite later modifications. It is the oldest half-timbered religious building in the western Ore Mountains.[197]

The prosperity of Jáchymov was recognised by many notable personalities who visited the town. In 1532 George, Duke of Saxony (†1539), who was a member of the Order of the Golden Fleece and a faithful Catholic despite the growing popularity of the Lutheran faith, spent the night here. Two years later, King Ferdinand I visited the town and expressed his interest in the construction of a mint and spoke highly of Mathesius' Latin library. In 1542, at the invitation of Johann Mathesius, Martin Luther briefly visited the town and complimented Jáchymov, noting that it was founded to praise God: '*Sicutacciditym Joachymstal und Annaberg. Ita Euangelion promanabit in easgentes, quaeni hilfueranteciam omnibus damnatibusillud…*'[198] He spoke positively about the founder of the town, Stephan Schlick as a man who lived by the true Word of God: '*…und das Joachimsthal eben ein Ort ist (des mancherley Volkshaben), da sienis-*

197) Jan Klípa – Michaela Ottová (ed.), *Bez hranic*, 677.
198) Martin Luther, "Vorlesung über Jesaja und Hohenlied, In Esaiamprophetam d. Doc. Martini Lutheri Enarraciones, Anno Domini 1527, Caput LIIII," in: *D. Martin Luthers Werke. Kritische Ausgabe (Weimarer Ausgabe), Abt. 1, Band 31/2* (Weimar: 1914), 443.

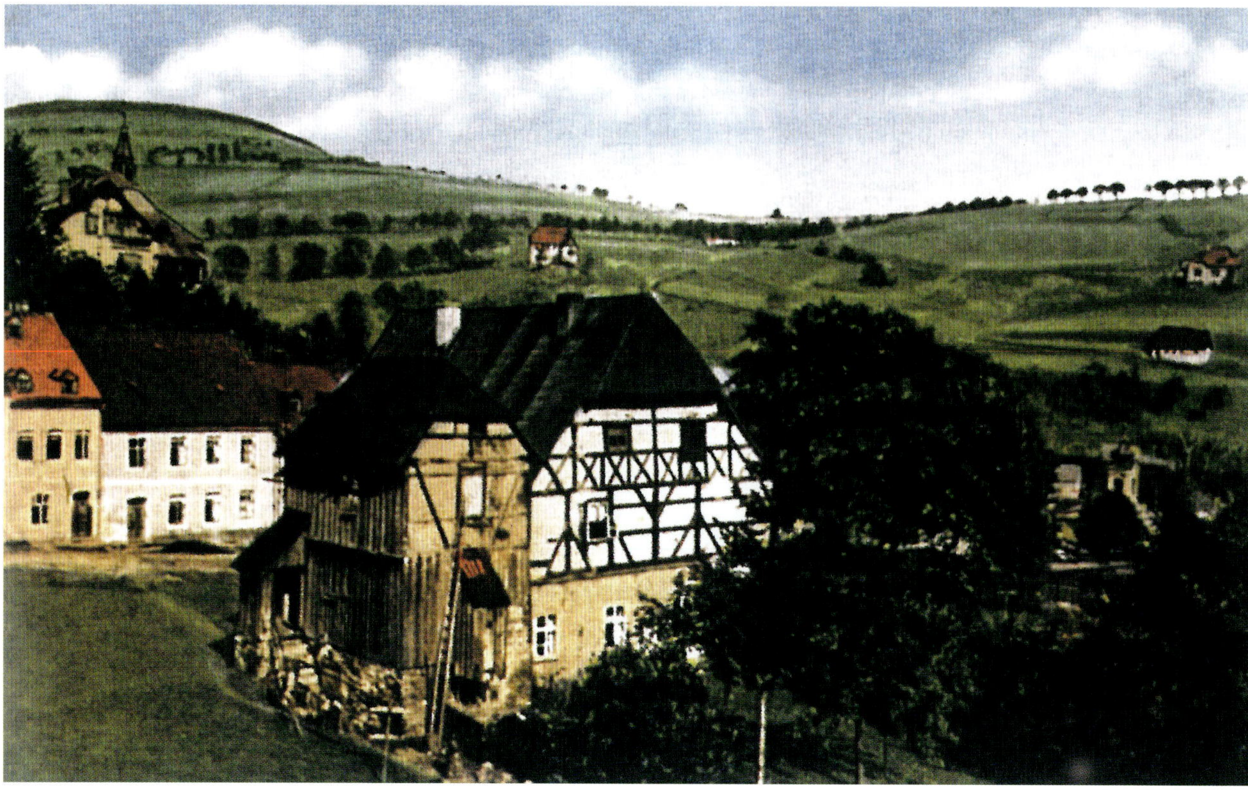

Fig. 51 Jáchymov, old half-timbered town hall. The old town hall stood on the so-called Chlebný Market, today's Slovany, near the Chapel of St. Anne. The house served as a town hall between 1520–1531, was converted for habitation in 1544, and was demolished in 1946. Reproduction from the book Hloušek, J., Jáchymov – Joachimsthal I. Jáchymov 2016.

ten und hecken können, E. G. wollten dem löblichen Exempel nach des berühmten Herrn Stephan Schlicks, E. G. edelsgeblüts, fest ob dem reinem Wort Gotteshalten.'[199]

After the foundation of Jáchymov, there was a significant increase in the founding of mining towns, which continued beyond the middle of the 16th century. Unplanned towns with a linear street layout continued to be the most common type, although most of these towns assumed the character of forest villages. This corresponded to the fact that although – by virtue of their assigned privileges and mining orders – the new settlements were technically towns, they in fact retained the feel of villages, in terms of their size, character, and type of housing development, characterised by houses built loosely along the main road that was followed by long, demarcated fields of cultivated land.

These 'village towns' include **Vejprty** (Weipert), **Pernink** (Bärringen), **Přebuz** (Frühbuß), **Kovářská** (Schmiedeberg) and **Abertamy** (Abertham).

The town of **Vejprty** (Weipert) was founded in the border region between Saxony and Bohemia.[200] A mining settlement, which later grew into a town, was built without overall

199) A letter by Martin Luther to Counts Hieronymus and Lorenz Schlick, written in Wittenberg on 9 October 1532, in: Martin Luther, *Briefwechsel 6, 1531–1533, Weimarer Ausgabe, Briefe 6*, No. 1965 (Weimar: 1935).

200) Carl G. Schmidl – Michal Luft, *Geschichte der Stadt Weipert* (Komotau: 1890); Emanuel Poche et al., *UPČ 4*, 184–185; Zdena Binterová, *Historie Vejprt* (Chomutov: 2007).

planning along the trade route from Bohemia to Annaberg in Saxony, with freestanding houses built along the valley floor and without a distinct town centre. The character of the original mining town was obscured in the second half of the 19th century by industrial buildings and splendid tenement houses in the centre of the town. Perhaps the earliest mention of mining in Vejprty comes from the early 15th century, when the Weiberg family from Meissen founded a hammer mill for processing iron ore called Weiberg. In 1506, Bohuslav Felix of Lobkowitz and Hassenstein passed the already inactive mill to Hans Schneider. Around 1550, a silver rush broke out in Vejprty when a rich vein was struck under the roots of a fallen fir tree. This area fell under the jurisdiction of the Inspector of Mines for Přísečnice, who had a very deep adit called 'Sv. Jan na poušti' (St. John in the Desert) driven into the earth. The village of Nové Zvolání (New Convocation) was established near the adit. The mining town received a boost when Emperor Rudolf II, by his charter of 3 January 1607 allowed miners and craftsmen settled in the town to practise their trade and manage their property freely, and also when in 1609, Rudolf II issued his Letter of Majesty, granting religous tolerance in the country, as the majority of the population of Vejprty professed Lutheranism. In 1617, Emperor Matthian promoted Vejprty to a royal mining town with the right to bear a coat of arms and use a seal. During the Thirty Years' War, the town was raided by marauding Swedish armies led by General Banner, and after the Renewed Land Ordinance was promulgated in 1628, some of the town's residents left for the other side of the border.

Mining resumed in the 1690s. An ironworks owner from Wisenthal in Saxony started mining silver ore in the area, with royal support (which included exemption from military tax and relief from contribution debts and tax debts). In 1713, during the reign of Emperor Charles VI, ten mines were documented in Vejprty and nine in Nové Zvolání. The flooding of mine shafts became a major technological problem, and the cost of draining them so high that the mines became unprofitable and were abandoned. Mining operations were briefly resurrected in the last third of the 18th century by Count Kolowrat, President of the Chamber of Court. Miners from the mining towns in Upper Hungary, who knew how to pump water out of the mines, were called in. The Antoni Zache mine was reopened, but after some time became unprofitable as well. The majority of the population made a living by bobbin lace making, which spread to the Ore Mountains in 1561 on the initiative of Barbara Uttmann of Annaberg,[201] and found its way to Vejprty in 1693. In the 18th and 19th centuries, the town was also known for the production of rifles and weaved ribbons.[202] In the valley of the Bílá Bystřice (Weiße Wistritz) River, high in the mountains (900 metres above sea level), the mining settlement of **Pernink** (Bärringen) was founded, which was also elevated to the status of a royal mining town during the silver rush in the Ore Mountains.[203] On 19 November 1532, King Ferdinand I granted the Pernink town rights at the request of Count Heinrich Schlick. In 1545, all the Schlick mines were confiscated by King Ferdinand I. Between 1552 and 1553, Heinrich Schlick sold the

201) Hans Burkhardt, *Annaberger Barbara-Uthmann-Büchlein. Ausgewählte Abhandlungen zum Thema Barbara Uthmann* (Annaberg: 1999); Jürgen Stabe (ed.), *Barbara Uthman in Annaberg* (Annaberg – Bucholtz: 2002); Joachim Mehnert, *Barbara Uthmann: Eine ungewöhnliche Frau* (Taucha: 2005).

202) For more details on the subject: Miroslav Slanina, *Puškařství ve Vejprtech* (Chomutov: 2015).

203) Emanuel Poche et al., *UPČ 3*, 9; Michal Urban, *Horní města Krušných hor: Karlovarský kraj* (Sokolov: 2014), 274-291.

Ostrov estate to his cousin Joachim Schlick, who confirmed all the privileges to Pernink on 2 October 1559. Historical sources tell us that there were dozens of shafts in the town and its surroundings during that period. Some of them were dedicated to the Virgin Mary and other saints, such as St. Wenceslas, St. James and St. Anthony, as was customary in mining towns. In 1623, the Ostrov estate, with its 54 shafts and adits was acquired by Julius Henry, Duke of Saxe-Lauenburg of the House of Ascania, who settled in Bohemia shortly before Uprising of the Estates in 1618.

Henry built a splendid family residence in Ostrov nad Ohří (Schlackenwerth) and thus became one of the most important aristocratic figures to shape the new Baroque identity of the Ore Mountains. However, he was no longer able to rely on the profits from mining, as it was no longer economically viable.[204] Like most other towns in the Ore Mountains, Pernink was a linear town, with houses lined up along the Bílá Bystřice River and alongside the road from Hroznětín (Lichtenstadt) and Ostrov to Schwarzenberg in Saxony. Even before the middle of the 16th century, the houses were added without a precise plan, and the small plots of land belonging to the houses indicate that, due to the altitude and other concerns, farming was not part of the plan.

The origin of the mining town of **Přebuz** (Frühbuss), which is located on both sides of the river Rolava (Rohlau), which flows near the border with Saxony, was initiated by the Schlicks.[205] Tin (cassiterite) had been panned and later mined in the area since the Middle Ages. The earliest mention of a panning site is from 1340. Přebuz was promoted to a mining town in 1553 and three years later a Mining Order was issued for the miners. Unfortunately, the local ore deposits were soon depleted, and in the 1580s mining activity languished. Mining was resumed in the second half of the 17th century, when the estate was owned by Johann Hartwig Nostitz. The mining office was reopened in 1677, but at the beginning of the 18th century, the mines were closed. The mining settlement, located high up in the mountains without an easy access, stretched across both banks of the Rolava River. It was a linear village, with similarly sized plots arranged perpendicularly to the riverbed, which formed the axis of the settlement. A church was then built on a small hill called Kirchenberg.

Kovářská (Schmiedeberg), in the Černá Voda (Schwarzwasser) valley, was founded on the road to Přísečnice in a place where iron ore had probably been processed since the 13th century. It is documented in the sources on the Přísečnice (Preßnitz) estate owned by the Schlicks around 1535, and is also mentioned in 16th-century land registers compiled by the Schlicks, and in documents about the forced sale of the Přísečnice estate to Ferdinand I.[206] In 1555, the monarch granted the estate to Bohuslav Felix of Hassenstein and Lobkowicz, the leader of the Lutheran nobility in the region, who was based in Chomutov (Komotau) and held extensive estates in the Ore Mountains. From 1548 he was the Inspector of the Mines in Jáchy-

204) Michal Vokurka, "Sasko-lauenburští vévodové jako příklad aristokracie v Čechách 17. století," in: *Bohemiae Occidentalis historica* 3/2 (2017), 5–29; Jaroslav Fiala, "Vzestup a pád města Ostrova v 17. století a útěk jeho obyvatel před vrchností," in: *Historický sborník Karlovarska* 6 (1998), 53–65.

205) Emanuel Poche et al., *UPČ 3*, 165; Petr Rojík, *Historie cínového dobývání v západním Krušnohoří* (Sokolov: 2000), 49–88; Vladimír Prokop – Lukáš Smola, *Sokolovsko*, 588–596.

206) Jaroslav Kloub, "Šlikovský urbář panství Přísečnice z roku 1533," *Comotovia 2013* (Chomutov: 2014), 5–16.

mov and from 1576 the highest chamberlain of the province. In 1555, he granted the manor to Bohuslav Felix of Hassenstein and Lobkowicz, the leader of the Lutheran nobility of the region from Chomutov. The latter had extensive property in the Ore Mountains region. From 1548, he was a mountain captain in Jáchymov and from 1576 he was an *Oberstlandkämmerer* (High Chamberlain).[207] He got permission from Rudolf II to process all iron ore slags on the Přísečnice estate. In 1579, he had an iron ore mill with a furnace built near the old road leading from Přísečnice to Jáchymov in Kovářská. The hammer mill was run by Hans Kraus of Jöhnstadt, an experienced ironworker. However, his name was associated with the illegal export of iron to Saxony and with the felling of trees, which had been forbidden by order of Rudolf II.[208]

Mining acitivity and the founding of new towns brought settlement to the highest elevations of the Ore Mountains. Among the mining towns built at the highest altitudes was **Abertamy** (Abertham).[209] The earliest record of the settlement on the Schlick estate is from 1529, when Mathesius mentioned it in his *Jáchymov Chronicle*. Fifty years later, Abertamy, where a register of married couples had been kept since 1544, was promoted to a royal mining town with the right to bear a coat of arms. The town's wealth came from silver and tin. From the point of view of urban planning, the town was built in a very chaotic manner; the only axis was the road, which gave the town an elongated plan running from east to west. The layout shows that the site was founded in a rather impulsive fashion, with houses clustered together with minimal land around them, which shows that for geaographical and other reasons, farming was not intended. The decline of the silver mines occurred before the Thirty Years' War. Tin, which was used to make utensils and various objects to be used in a church setting (baptismal fonts, holy water stoups, candlesticks, etc.), was mined here until the 19th century. An interesting case is **Loučná** (Böhmisch Wiesenthal), founded in 1527 on the border with Saxony. While on the Bohemian side, the settlement has a village character, the Saxon part of Loučná (now Oberwiesenthal) was built according to strict Renaissance rules over a regular square grid layout with streets laid out at right angles.

In addition to the unplanned towns with no significant urban design, the biggest wave of mining settlements produced towns with demarcated central squares. Some of the towns founded in the preceding wave also represented this type. There are only three towns with demarcated central squares in this group, which makes it the smallest group: **Měděnec** (Kupferberg), **Mikulov** (Niklasberg) and **Místo** (Platz).

Of particular note among them is **Mědenec**, founded around 1520 by the Lords of Vitzthum at a site with rich copper and silver deposits.[210] The first documented reports of mining in the area are from 1449, but the remains of two furnaces that have been found north of

207) Petr Hrubý, "Vývoj pozemkové držby Bohuslava Felixe Hasištejnského z Lobkowicz," in: *Vlastivědný sborník Kralupska* 5/1–2 (1998), 32–50.

208) Jaroslav Kloub, "Vývoj kovářské do poloviny 17. století," *Comotovia 2015* (Chomutov: 2016), 107–131.

209) Emanuel Poche et al., *UPČ 1*, 23; J. Rödig – Eduard Porkert, *Abertham u. seine Schule* (Abertamy: 1938); Adolf Schug, *Heimatbuch Landkreis Neudek* (Augsburg-Göggingen: 1978), 243–245; Michal Urban – Helmut Albrecht, *Hornické památky Montanregionu Krušné hory / Erzgebirge* (Jáchymov: 2014), 36–47.

210) Ladislav Bílek – Ladislav Jangl – Jan Urban, *Dějiny hornictví na Chomutovsku* (Chomutov: 1976), 33–34; Emanuel Poche et al., *UPČ 2*, 364; Zdena Binterová, *Od Hory sv. Šebestiána po Krásnou Lípu* (Chomutov: 2000), 93; Michal Urban, *Horní města – Ústecký kraj*, 50–181.

the village indicate that mining had already begun there in the early 13th century. In 1544, the town was divided between two owners: one part belonged to the Hauenstein estate of Heinrich von Schlick, while the other was still owned by the Vitzthums, whose administration was located in Měděnec.

In 1568, Měděnec passed into the hands of Ursula von Vitzthum. Kaspar von Vitzthum asked Emperor Rudolf II to promote Měděnec to a mining town. The emperor answered his request in 1588, on condition that that town would follow the Jáchymov Mining Code. Kaspar, in order to maintain the high status of the town, allowed the residents to cut meat together and have a baker's shop, to hold weekly markets, to brew and serve beer, to build a municipal spa and a salt chamber, and to move and handle property freely. These privileges in the Vitzthum part of Měděnec were confirmed in 1605 by Christoph Taubenreuther, the mint master of Jáchymov and imperial major, who acquired the estate in 1597. These rights of the Fictum district were confirmed in 1605 by the new owner, who in 1597 became the Jáchymov mintmaster and imperial major, Christopher of Taubenreuth. However, he ordered that the townspeople must only buy manorial malt and were allowed to brew no more than seven batches of beer a year. When he died, his widow Ursula, née Zettelberg, sold her share to Heinrich von Schlick in 1628. From then on, the whole town belonged to the Hauenstein estate until 1663.[211]

The urban plan of Měděnec is very interesting in terms of the layout of the buildings and public spaces. The maps of the Stabile Cadastre show a regular, rectangular main square with sides of almost identical length. The square has a church and is surrounded by blocks of houses with adjacent plots of land that are separated by perpendicular side streets. Although the subsequent housing development was never fully completed, the surviving fragment shows that this was the basis of an urban design used at the time, which featured a regularly laid out rectangular street network with blocks of houses. Měděnec is thus one of the earliest examples of a Renaissance town with an urban plan on the Bohemian side of the Ore Mountains, a type that continued to be used and developed especially in the second half of the 16th century.[212]

Místo (Platz) is a similar case to Měděnec. This small town in the valley of the Prunéřov (Brunnersdorf) stream was founded in 1549 under the Lobkowicz castle of Hasištejn (Hassenstein), which protected the old road that passed across the Ore Mountain ridge to Saxony. An original plan to build a Renaissance-type town over a regular grid layout is a clearly discernible, with a centre occupied by a large, almost square-shaped piazza, with a church and with streets running from it. However, only a fragment of what could have been remains. Mining for silver and other ores was not very advanced in the area, which may have curbed further development.[213]

The examples of Měděnec and Místo usher in one last type of mining towns in the Ore Mountains, established in the 16th century. These towns represent the most advanced urban

211) Zdena Binterová, *Od Vejprt po Měděnec* (Chomutov: 1999), 93–102; Michal Urban et al., *Horní města – Ústecký kraj*, 154–155.

212) Karel Kuča, *Krušnohorská města*, 9.

213) Lubomír Zeman, *Zástavba a urbanismus*, 87; Michal Urban et al., *Horní města – Ústecký kraj*, 210; Zdena Binterová, *Místo* (Chomutov: 2001).

solution of the cluster of towns presented here: **towns laid out on a grid plan.** Their regular pattern with a precisely demarcated main square and a harmonious distribution of public buildings is in stark contrast to the unplanned layout with linear housing development, typical of the earliest mining towns. This difference accurately reflects the fact that it was during the Renaissance, in contrast to the Gothic era, that the first generally-accepted doctrine of urban planning and construction was introduced.

The grid urban plan

The geometric layout of Renaissance towns with its strictly defined pattern was based on the theoretical treatises of the time. In these, street blocks of buildings were deemed more important than the individual buildings that formed the constituent parts of the urban organism. The grid plan, or gridiron, was also inspired by the Ancient Roman military camps with spine roads and straight side streets intersecting at right angles. The result was a chequerboard pattern of 'fields,' which were subsequently filled with blocks of buildings. A significant role in the search for the ideal Renaissance city was also played by the change in war tactics, in which firearms and artillery began to prevail; it is no coincidence that the first places to be built over a grid urban layout were military strongholds.[214]

In the Ore Mountains, the grid plan of Renaissance towns first appeared on the Saxon side. **Marienberg**, founded on a rich silver ore deposit in 1521, is a particularly good example. The walled-in historic core is still clearly discernible in the midst of the buildings constructed in later periods. In its centre is a large, almost square-shaped public square, around which the houses are arranged in a regular grid pattern of blocks separated by a network of streets. Somewhat surprising perhaps is the location of St. Mary's Church, which stands neither on the square nor in the main row of buildings that demarcate it, but further back in the eastern corner. This location was probably chosen out of necessity, as the building was constructed between 1558 and 1564, when the main row of buildings forming the square's perimeter had probably already been built.[215]

The oldest gridiron towns in the Bohemian part of the Ore Mountains were built as a result of direct Saxon influence, specifically in the area of what is today the northern end of Karlovy Vary (Karlsbad), which used to be located in Saxony before the border was redrawn in 1547. This is how **Horní Blatná** (Bergstadt Platten) was built in 1532, followed by **Boží Dar** (Gottesgab) a year later. Thanks to detailed historic sources, a description of the process by which these two towns were founded and laid out has been preserved. The first step involved finding a suitable location, ideally situated on a plateau. After laying out a rectangular square, all the plots of land were measured, specifically 199 plots in Horní Blatná and 600 in Boží Dar. The whole town was laid out in this way, although it was never completely built up due to later historical development.[216] The appearance of the buildings depended on the prosperity

214) Jiří Hrůza, *Svět měst* (Praha: 2014), 274.
215) Jan Hanzlík, "Město a jeho koncept," in: Tomáš Karel – Alžběta Kratochvílová (ed.), *Proměny montánní krajiny. Historické sídelní a montánní struktury Krušnohoří* (Loket: 2013), 77–81.
216) Lubomír Zeman, *Zástavba a urbanismus*, 69, 72.

of the mines. Particularly sophisticated and affluent architecture can be found in Horní Blatná, which by the end of the 16th century became one of the most important mining towns in the Ore Mountains.

Horní Blatná is undoubtedly one of the best-preserved towns in the Ore Mountains, and fully deserves its status as an urban monument zone. The oldest mention of a settlement in the area is from 1518, but the tradition of tin panning and mining in today's Horní Blatná goes back to to the 14th century. In 1532, on the initiative of the Saxon Duke Johann Friedrich, a mining town was founded near the iron and tin ore mines. Its origin is recorded in the old city chronicles, which also mention the construction of certain houses and ore processing mills.[217] Miners were brought in, mostly from Schneeberg. Along with Boží Dar, these were the last mining towns to be established in the western part of the Ore Mountains.[218]

The Saxon possession of Horní Blatná and Boží Dar

The rich tin deposits around Horní Blatná and Boží Dar included locations around the Černá Brook (Schwarzbach), the Blatenský Brook (Breitenbach, a.k.a. Široký Brook) and Kozí Brook (Ziegenbach). In the early 16th century, these sites were located in the southern end of the Schwarzenberg mining district, which was part of the Schwarzenberg estate that belonged to the Duchy of Saxony. It took until 1547 for the border to be redrawn and for the manor, including the town, to come under the Kingdom of Bohemia, based on an agreement between Ferdinand I and Moritz, Duke (and later Elector) of Saxony. There was, however, a continuing dispute over the territory, which was finally settled in 1556 in Schneeberg, where an agreement was reached that determined the exact borders between Saxony and Bohemia. The borderline between the two countries was enforced by boundary markers. [219]

The town was established on a greenfield site by laying out the pattern and then building houses in the predetermined plots of the grid plan. The demarcated street blocks were gradually filled with brick houses built in a mixture of Gothic and Renaissance styles, and their surviving fragments bear marks of the Saxon Renaissance architectural style. A Lutheran school, a hospital, a parish and a monumental church were constructed. The plots of land probably filled up quite slowly, as only one house is mentioned by sources to have existed in 1534, surrounded by otherwise empty plots. By 1537, the town already had 97 houses, but twenty of them remained empty due to the high turnover of miners.[220]

In 1546, Horní Blatná and Boží Dar were occupied by the army of King Ferdinand I, led by Felix Bohuslav of Lobkowicz. Based on a secret agreement between Moritz of Saxony and King Ferdinand I, Horní Blatná became part of Bohemia. A year later, it was promoted to a royal mining town. At the end of the 16th century, it had a population of about 2,000. The example

217) Nikola Růžičková, "Město a jeho hornictví – Prameny k hornické činnosti ve vybraných knihách Horní Blatné a Krupky," in: *Krušné hory v centru zájmu montánní archeologie* (Dresden: 2018), 111–117.
218) Emanuel Poche et al., *UPČ 1*, 402; Karel Kuča, *Města a městečka, Part II*, 146–148.
219) Jaroslav Fiala, "Stará česko-saská hranice mezi Jáchymovem a Božím Darem," in: *Historický sborník Karlovarska* 5 (1997), 32–50.
220) Petr Cais, *Archiv města Horní Blatná 1535–1945 (1954) – Inventář* (Karlovy Vary: 2006), 4–5.

of Horní Blatná shows the fate of the mining towns after the enactment of the Renewed Land Ordinance (1627), which allowed only the Catholic denomination in the Czech lands. Miners of Lutheran faith left the mining towns in substantial numbers and went to Saxony. The last miners left Horní Blatná in 1653 and 1654, and in Saxony they founded a new mining town not far from the border, naming it Johanngeorgenstadt after the Saxon Elector Johann Georg I of Saxony.[221] The re-Catholicisation of the town was accompanied by a widespread dissemination of the cult of St. John of Nepomuk, whose statue was erected on a pillar in front of the church even before this important baroque saint was canonised.[222]

Closely connected with the town of Horní Blatná is the mining settlement of **Potůčky** (Breitenbach), located right on the border with Saxony. Like Horní Blatná, Potůčky belonged to the Saxon Elector until 1546 and subsequently passed to the Kingdom of Bohemia, on the basis of an agreement between Moritz of Saxony and Ferdinand I. Locally found ores of silver, tin, cobalt and iron aroused the interest of miners. The earliest mention of mining in the area is from 1532. At the time, there were seven stamp mills on the Blatenský Brook, which were part of the mines of Horní Blatná. The core of the settlement consisted of houses built near the iron mill, which was constructed by the Blatná townspeople in 1570. A note about the existence of a cobalt mill comes from the same year, and a silver smelting site is documented in 1615. The existence of Potůčky as a municipality started in 1654, when miners and smelters began to build their homes alongside the Černý Brook (Schwarzbach) and Hraniční Brook (Grenzbach). The town was referred to as Breitenbach for the first time in 1723, by the chronicler Engeeschal of Johanngeorgenstadt in Saxony.[223]

The mining town of **Boží Dar** (Gottessgab, literally 'Gift from God') is one of the highest settlements in Bohemia.[224] Legend has it that the town was named by its founder, the Saxon Elector Johann Friedrich. When invited to sit on a stool made of solid silver from the mines of Boží Dar, he is believed to have said: *'Diese sedle Metall das ist euer Brot, das ist eine Gabe Gottes. / This precious metal is your bread, it is the gift of God.'* (Fig.52)

The territory where the town was founded was covered by an impenetrable border forest, and the precise demarcation of the border was subject to disputes. The conflict escalated at the turn of the 15th and 16th centuries, when the first tin and silver pebbles were found in the area. Soon after that, a miner by the name of Hans Chramm, who worked for Kleinhempel, the wealthy hammer man, discovered a rich vein of silver ore at the western foot of Mount Fichtelberg. The Saxon Elector, Johann Friedrich, who acquired the estate in 1533, subsequently granted the community the freedom to mine. In the same year, the boundaries of the future town were laid out and 600 building plots were measured for future settlers. The Saxon tenure lasted until 1547, when the town passed to the Bohemian king.

221) Vítězslav Bartoš, "Přínos českých horníků emigrujících do Saska roku 1654, speciálně do Johanngeorgenstadtu," in: *Studie z dějin hornictví* 34 (2006), 98–102; *Nový velký ilustrovaný slovník naučný IX.* (Praha: 1930), 119. A similar case study was published by Ivana Ebelová, who followed the foundation of a new town beyond the Saxon border for miners from Cínovec: Ivana Ebelová, "Die Böhmischen Exulanten aus Zinnwald. Ein Beitrag zur Gründung von Neu-Georgenfeld in Sachsen," in: *Neues Archiv für sächsische Geschichte* 89 (2018), 309–323.

222) Karel Kuča – Lubomír Zeman, *Památky Karlovarského kraje* (Karlovy Vary: 2006), 221.

223) Petr Cais, *Archiv města Horní Blatná*, 6.

224) Poche et al., *UPČ 1*, 114.

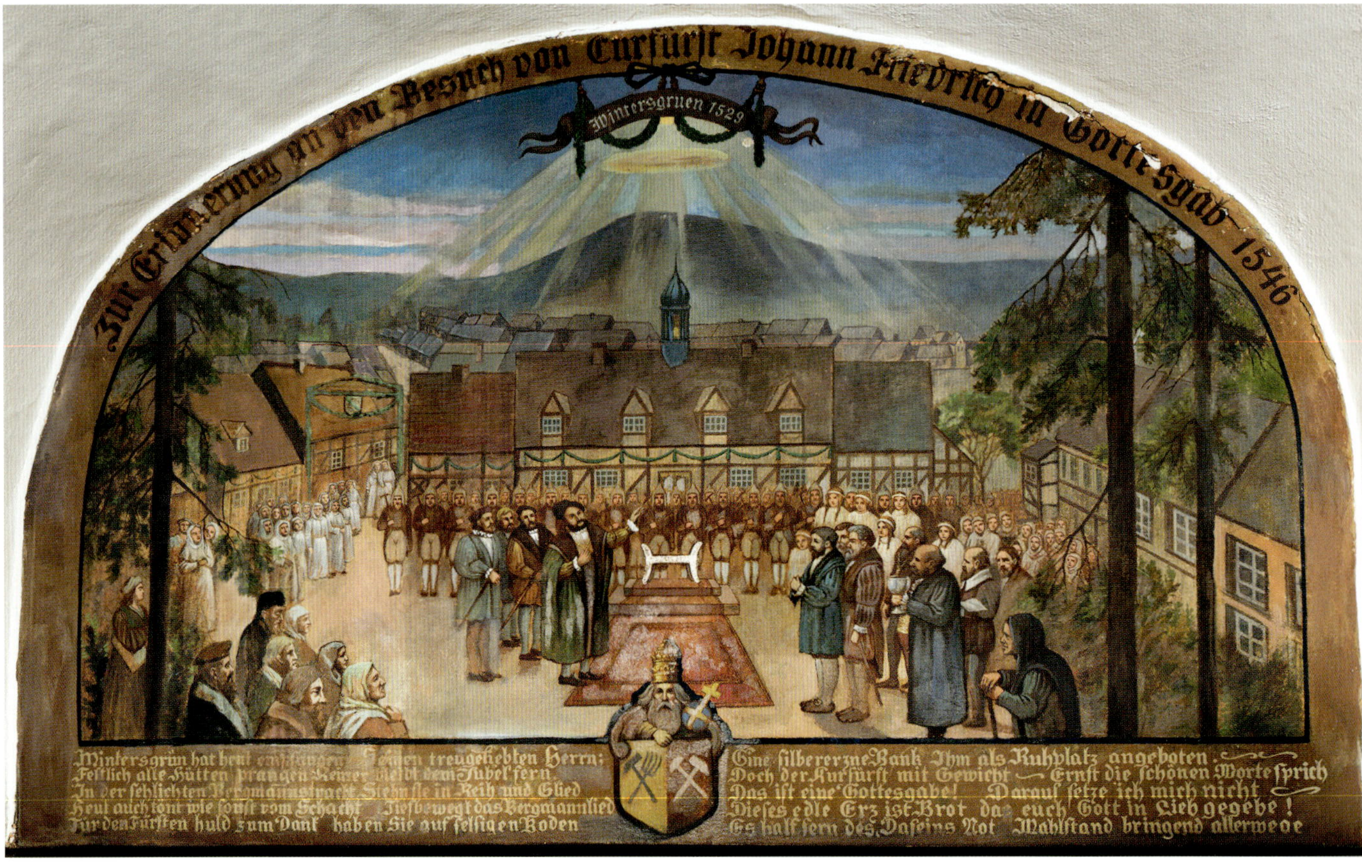

Fig. 52 Boží Dar, Hotel Zelený dům, mural depicting the legend of the founding of the town. Photograph by J. Peer (2019).

After its foundation in 1533, the town began to grow, but it had to wait until 1546 before it received its free mining town privileges, including the right to elect a town council of 12 councillors headed by a chief magistrate. The town was also granted the right to hold a trial, the right to trade, and the right to hold a weekly market every Friday and an annual market on the feast of St. Nicholas. The Emperor confirmed the town's privileges in 1608, probably with the intention of supporting the suffering mining industry.

The town's 16th century layout is still discernible today. Boží Dar is one of the earliest examples of a Renaissance mining town on the Bohemian side of the Ore Mountains. The grid plan is used here, although it is slightly rotated to respect the course of the stream and the path alongside it, which used to be an important road running from west to east. The basis was a regular square, with a pair of streets connected to each of its corners. A town hall and a church, which was originally made of wood, were the town's landmarks. The building that is today the Zelený dům hotel is one of the oldest inns in the Ore Mountains. (Fig. 53) It has a mural that commemorates a visit by Martin Luther. (Fig. 54) Sadly, only a handful of monuments from the extensive Renaissance urban development have been preserved, as most were destroyed in the devastating fire of 1808.[225]

225) Stanislav Burachovič, *Boží Dar/Gottesgab* (Boží Dar: 2001).

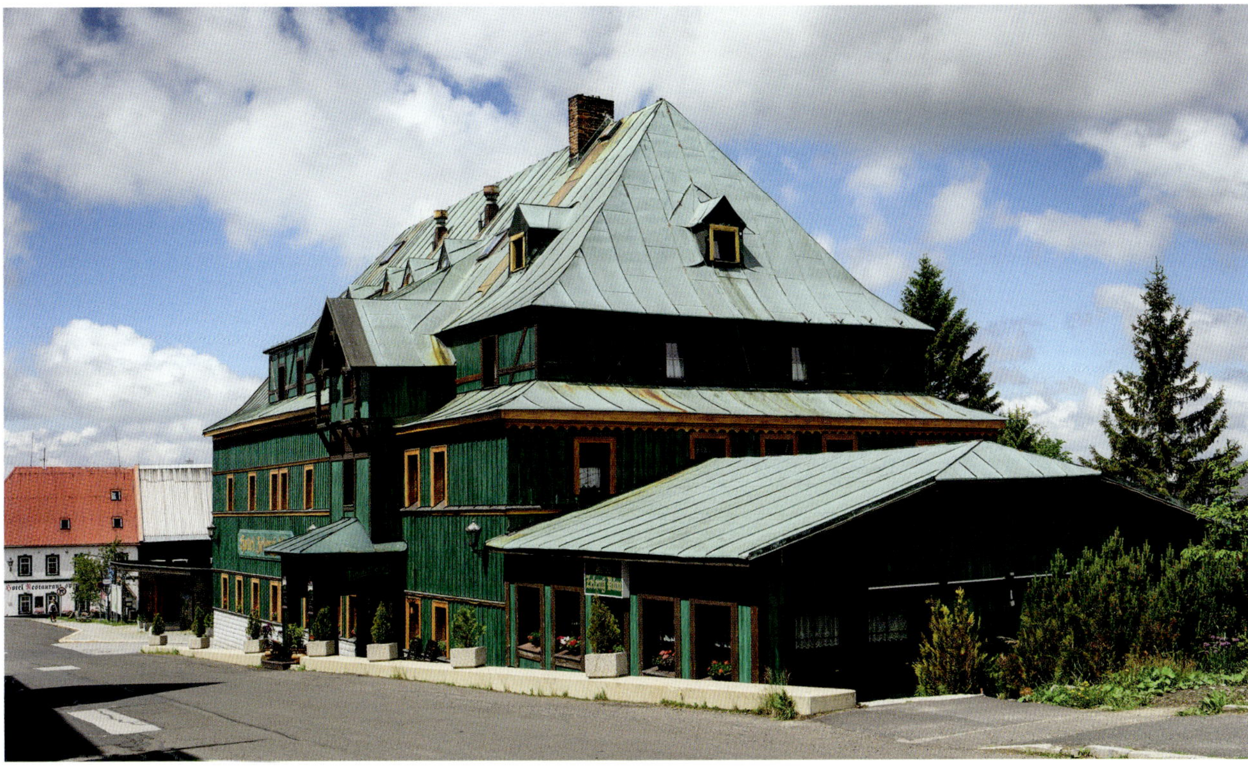

Fig. 53 Boží Dar, Hotel Zelený dům, general view from the east. Original inn built 1542, rebuilt 1917.
Photo by J. Peer (2019).

Gridiron towns continued to be built in the second half of the 16th century. In 1558, during the last phase of new mining town development in the Ore Mountains, three towns were founded: **Hora Sv. Šebestiána** (Sebastiansberg), **Hora Sv. Kateřiny** (Katharinaberg) and the especially noteworthy **Výsluní** (Sonneberg).[226]

Hora Sv. Šebestiána was probably founded by the owner of the Chomutov (Komutau) estate, Šebestián of Weitmile, who founded a church dedicated to St. Sebastian. The importance of the new settlement was accentuated by the fact that a trade route from Chomutov to Marienberg in Saxony, founded in 1521, ran through the area. By 1549, Hora Sv. Šebestiána must have become a town, because a document issued in that year mentions the chief magistrate, the town council, and a mining entrepreneur by the name of Paul Kocha, who admitted to owing 1,400 thalers to investors from Krakow and Wroclaw. Based on information from the Chomutov land register, we know that in 1560 the town was divided into four districts, in which the bergmeister ensured compliance with the Jáchymov Mining Code. In fact, the Schlicks had applied a similar division scheme in Jáchymov, as it was easier to govern and maintain order in smaller areas. This was therefore a proven method of town governance, which continued to thrive under the tenure of the next owner, Bohuslav Felix of Lobkowicz and Hassenstein.[227] Hora Sv. Šebestiána is mentioned as a town in 1562, when Bohuslav Felix,

226) Jaroslav Bílek – Ladislav Jangl – Jan Urban, *Dějiny hornictví na Chomutovsku* (Chomutov: 1976), 35–36; Emanuel Poche et al., *UPČ 4* (Praha: 1976), 292; Zdena Binterová, *Od Hory sv. Šebestiána po Krásnou Lípu* (Chomutov: 2000), 37–67; Michal Urban a kol., *Horní města Krušných Hor – Ústecký kraj*, 304–305.
227) Vlastimil Růžek, "Dějiny obce Hora Svatého Šebestiána," in: Památky, příroda, život 10/2 (1978), 43–45; Petr

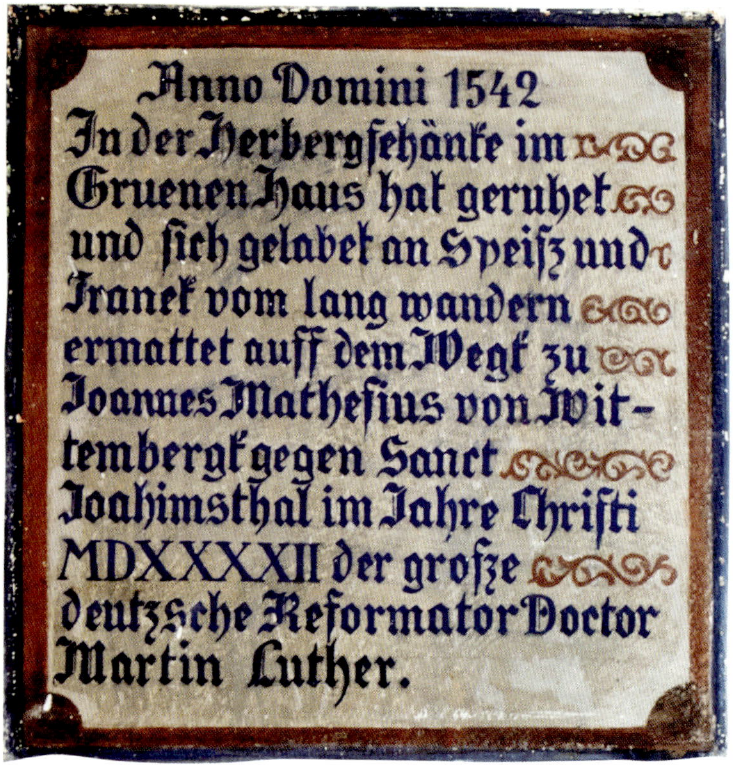

Fig. 54 Boží Dar, Hotel Zelený dům, memorial plaque commemorating Martin Luther's stay in Boží Dar. Photo by J. Peer (2019).

who was of the Lutheran faith, granted the growing village many privileges including the right to use a seal, the free movement of burghers, the right to hold trials, the right to hold weekly and two annual markets, the right to trade in beer and wine and, finally yet importantly, mining rights. In 1589, Bohuslav Felix's son, Waldemar, traded Výsluní and the entire Chomutov estate for Mladá Boleslav with Jiří Popel of Lobkowicz. Popel, who had the reputation of a less-than-tolerant Catholic, embarked on a re-Catholicisation campaign in Výsluní, which drove many miners to Saxony. Their departure may have curbed the urban development of a town that had been so magnificently designed.[228] After Popel's political fall, the town passed to Emperor Rudolf II. Later on, Emperor Matthias gave it permission to bear a coat of arms, and in 1617, after buying itself out of servitude for 849 threescore of groschen, Výsluní was promoted by Matthias to a royal mining town. Between 1644 and 1647, attempts were made to renew mining activity and an adit by the name of Jonáš was opened. Other active mines included Sv. Anthony, St. Erasmus and the Holy Trinity mines. Around the mid-18th century, more mines were opened: Požehnání Boží (Lord's Blessing), Milostivá ruka Páně (The Merciful Hand of the Lord) and Sv. Juda Tadeáš (St. Jude Thaddeus). From 1803 until 1849,

Rak, "Městské lokace Šebestiána z Weitmile," in: *Ústecký sborník historický* 2014/1–2, 7–28; Petr Hrubý, "Vývoj pozemkové držby Bohuslava Felixe Hasištejnského z Lobkowicz," in: *Vlastivědný sborník Kralupska* 5/1–2 (1998): 32–50.

228) Petr Hrubý, "Bohuslav Felix Hasištejnský z Lobkovic. (Rodinné a majetkové zázemí luteránského předáka v předbělohorských Čechách)," in: *Ústecký sborník historický* 2000, 98–131; Michaela Hrubá (Neudertová), "Jiří Popel z Lobkovic a prostředky rekatolizace na sklonku 16. století. (Příspěvek k dějinám rekatolizace v severozápadních Čechách)," in: *Ústecký sborník historický* 2000, 132–144.

hematite was mined in the mine of St. Wenceslas, located betweem Sobětice (Sobietitz) and Výsluní.[229]

Šebestián z Veitmile (Sebastian von Weitmühl) was also present at the origin of the mining town of **Hora Sv. Kateřiny** (Katharinaberg), which also lies on the ridge of the Ore Mountains.[230] It is very likely that a settlement was founded there in 1350, but the earliest report of the town's existence is from 1480. In 1528, on Šebestián's initiative, the community was promoted to a free mining town, where silver and especially copper ores were mined. A mine with a particularly rich vein was dedicated to St. Nicholas. However, the local deposits were not as rich as had been estimated, and the town remained rather small. Nonetheless, in 1597, its mining town privileges were confirmed by Rudolf II. The original mining settlement had accumulated around the Kateřinský Brook in the valley and had the appearance of a forest village with a linear layout. The newly established town was situated on the hill called Růžový vrch (Stadtberg). Even though the original intention was to use a regular grid town plan, the local terrain reuired a modification. A narrow, rectangular public square was situated on the narrow ridge of the hill, with only two streets running from it. A church was then built on the hill above the square. The plot of land on which it stands indicates that its construction had been planned all along since the town was first laid out. Hora sv. Kateřiny, where no major changes were made to the historical architecture until the 20th century, is an exceptional example of a town in which two phases of a mining town development are reflected, and where two distinct urban designs of a mining town were used.[231]

Of particular note in **Výsluní** is the town's layout, in which a lot of thought went into finding the right location for the church. Unlike in Horní Blatná, where a massive church took up a part of the public space on the square, or Boží Dar, where in a manner similar to Marienberg the church was relegated to the depths of the residential area, the church in Výsluní was conceived as a visual landmark, visible through an alley running along the main axis of the square.[232]

Another town with a trace of the Schlick family that was laid out on a regular ground plan, is **Oloví** (Bleistadt). It is situated on a plateau above the valley of the river Svatava.[233] At the instigation of the Schlicks of Jáchymov, lead began to be mined here, which was used as an additive in melting silver and had previously been brought in large quantities from England. The area where Oloví is situated was already populated in the early mediaeval period: around 1200, one of the oldest castles called Hartenberg was built as a royal border castle on a promontory above the Svatava Valley. It was owned by the Hartenberg ministerial family, which hailed from Cheb (Eger). In cooperation with the monastery in Waldsassen, the family colonised the region and carried out prospecting activities. Mining was already carried out in the area at the turn of the 13th and 14th centuries, as we know that the owner of Hartenberg,

229) Karel Kuča, *Města a městečka v Čechách, na Moravě a ve Slezsku, Part VIII. V–Ž and appendices* (Praha: 2011), 459–462.

230) Emanuel Poche et al., *UPČ 1*, 397–398.

231) Michal Urban, *Tři studie k hornické a kulturní krajině českého Krušnohoří s výchozími body Krupka, Hora Svaté Kateřiny, Jáchymov* (Most: 2011); Petr Jančárek, *Hornictví v Hoře sv. Kateřiny za feudalismu* (Teplice: 1980).

232) Jiří Hrůza, *Svět měst*, 298; Karel Kuča, "Poznámky ke kompozici ortogonálních městských lokací v Čechách," in: *Archaeologica historica* 20 (1995), 119–121.

233) Emanuel Poche et al., *UPČ 2*, 529.

whose name was Tut, donated part of the local mines near Hartenberg to his monastery in Waldsassen in 1314.[234] The town was founded by the Schlicks in 1519, and in the same year a mining code was issued for local miners, and Stephan Schlick granted town rights to the local residents in 1523.

The first book of mining records was kept as far back as 1524. It tells of the poor condition of the 28 local mines and the little interest of the current owners in mining. The Schlick family held Oloví until 1547, when the Hartenberg estate was confiscated because of their participation in the revolt against Ferdinand I, and in 1551 it was granted to the Lords of Plavno (Plauen). As the new owners showed little interest in mining, the royal treasury did not receive the much-anticipated funds. For this reason, in 1561, Ferdinand I separated Oloví from the Hartenberg estate and placed it in the jurisdiction of the Jáchymov mining governor's office. By a deed from 2 June 1561, he promoted Oloví to a royal mining town and granted it the privilege of mining ores, especially lead, which until then belonged to the owners of the Hartenberg estate. The privileges were subsequently extended on 16 January 1558, and again in 1580 and 1597 under Emperor Rudolf II. Lead ore mining continued in the succeeding centuries, and Oloví had its rights and privileges confirmed by all the subsequent rulers. Unfortunately, the city was very often affected by fires. A particularly devastating one happened in 1700, when the town hall burned down, and with it the entire archive of the town.

The regular urban layout was maintained chiefly by a large rectangular public square, with a Lutheran church in the centre and another free-standing building next to it, which was the mining office. The houses on the square had at least one upper floor and they were half-timbered, with the ground floor fully timbered. Unfortunately, none of them has been preserved. The most magnificent building on the square used to be the half-timbered town hall with an upper floor, which was demolished in 1882. In parts of the city farther from the square, the regular urban layout of the streets was followed more loosely.[235]

234) August Sedláček, *Hrady, zámky a tvrze království Českého, Part XIII* (Praha: 1905), 167.
235) Lois Eißner, *Bleistadt, einst königlich freie Bergstadt 1523–1973* (Schwandorf: 1973), available at https://gpecher.de.tl (cit. 17. 8. 2020). Václav Kotěšovec, *Pohledy do historie měst a obcí Kraslicka* (Praha: 2011), 154–155; Vladimír Prokop – Lukáš Smola, *Sokolovsko*, 578–581.

FAITH AND PIETY IN MINING TOWNS IN THE CONTEXT OF RELIGIOUS MONUMENTS

'We Praise You, Lord. We Worship You, Lord…'[236]

The churches represent an important set of monuments that attest to the wealth of the mining towns in the Bohemian Ore Mountains and their advanced culture. In addition, churches were a crucial component of the lives of the miners and all the townspeople, for whom their faith provided a fundamental foundation for facing life's challenges, as well as a source of security. The religious buildings which are preserved, and their interior decoration and furnishings, are also an important testimony to the cultural tradition and status of the mining towns. Many of the sacred buildings that evolved in the beginning of the early modern period reflect the transformation of Late Saxon Gothic into the Renaissance architecture within the same cultural context. A great number of them bear clear marks and features – untouched by subsequent reconstructions – of the respective architectural styles at particular stages of their development. It is therefore possible even today to get a fairly accurate idea of the staying power of the Gothic visual aesthetics, which persisted in sacred architecture in various forms until the early 17th century when it was replaced by the Baroque style as part of the re-Catholicisation process. The religious buildings, their furnishings and decoration also bear witness to the specific kind of faith and piety of the mining community, which was present in the mining towns of the Ore Mountains and represents an indispensable component of the cultural heritage of the region, as well as being a unique ingedient of the Renaissance in the Czech Lands.

For the purposes of our introduction to the developments outlined above, the mining town of **Krupka** (Graupen) seems an ideal case in point. It has a collection of churches that testify to the historical development of the town, from its beginnings to the threshold of the 17th century. The oldest religious building, which was certainly part of the town's origins even if it is located outside of the historic centre, is the **Church of St. Procopius**, now overlooking the road from Teplice to Bohosudov.[237] (Fig. 55) Due to a fire in 1939, only a fragment survives

236) Hana Volná – Ondřej Macek (ed.), Martin Luther, "Tři symboly neboli vyznání křesťanské víry," in: *Je jeden jediný kopec… Výbor z díla II.* (Praha: 2010), 90.

237) The church was founded at the old mining settlement of Kirchlice, see Ludomír Kocourek – Květoslava Kocourková – Karel Vilím – Jindřich Körschner, *Krupka z cínu zrozená* (Teplice: 2005); Táňa Šimková, *Stavebně-historické zaměření kostela sv. Prokopa v Krupce*, manuscript (Ústí nad Labem: 2012).

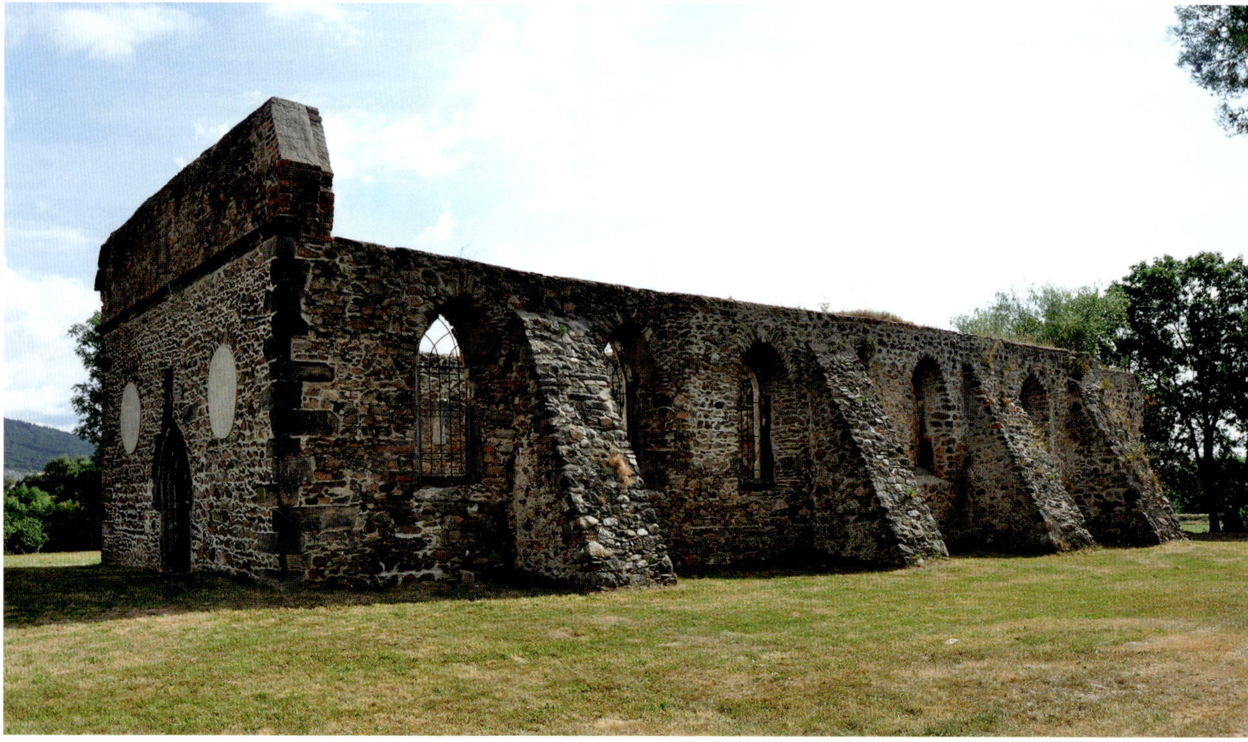

Fig. 55 Krupka, Church of St. Procopius, general view from the east. Construction in the 13th century, rebuilt in the early 15th century, part of the triple nave added in the early 16th century. Alterations 1643–1677, ruins after fire in 1939. Photo by T. Šimková (2022).

today of this church that, according to older literature was likely founded in the 13th century, although recent research suggests that this dating has not been reliably documented. The church was certainly there before 1331, the year in which it is mentioned in sources as a parish church for Kirchlice, a town that preceded Krupka. An Early-Gothic polygonal chancel with a shortened, square-shaped nave has been preserved from the oldest construction phase. In the next construction phase, a star vault with six points was created. Its appearance, combined with the remnants of tracery in the pointed windows, points to its origin at the beginning of the 15th century. However, especially with regard to the profile of the portal with interlaced rods in the northern façade of the nave, the vaults are more commonly considered to have been built in the Late Gothic period at the turn of the 15th and 16th centuries. Assuming this was the case, the nave was extended westwards at or around the same time to include another square-shaped section. Its internal layout was divided into three naves separated by central piers, supporting a line of cross vaults. This alteration can probably be linked to the year 1507 when, as we learn from the dedicatory inscription, construction was completed, thanks to the patriciate of Krupka.[238]

After the foundation of Krupka around 1330, the main settlement activity moved to what is now the historic centre. As the town developed and flourished, the need certainly arose

238) Hermann Hallwich, *Geschichte der Bergstadt Graupen*, 88, 108; Jan Klípa – Michaela Ottová (ed.), *Bez Hranic. Umění v Krušnohoří mezi gotikou a renesancí* (Praha: 2015), 661.

for a suitable church that would serve the growing population. Although the existence of the **parish church of the Assumption** is recorded in 1352 for the first time,[239] it can be assumed to have been built earlier, perhaps around 1330 when John of Bohemia granted Krupka as a fief to Thimo of Colditz.[240] This would also correspond to the fact that, in 1331, the older church of St. Procopius at the original mining settlement below Krupka ceased to serve as a parish church.[241]

Thus the first sacred building in Krupka was built under the castle before the mid-14th century. It was situated on a narrow plot of land cut into a steep slope, forming a visual counterpoint to the castle. Since the church was oriented in a way that would ensure the chancel faced east, the view of a relatively large section of a polygonal elongated chancel, now used as an oratory with a sacristy, is blocked by the later-built church building. As a result, there is no clear view of the fragment of the older church from the main road, and the whole building can only be viewed from the interior, or to some extent from the castle. A now defunct nave of an unknown appearance was attached to the chancel; we know that it was no more than 20 metres long due to the dimensions of the construction plot.

The chancel also used to look different. First, it was not divided into a ground floor with a sacristy and a top floor with an oratory, but instead was conceived as a very airy space filled with light. This was ensured by tall arched windows that reached down to the floor and were completed with stone seats at floor level, which probably served as choir pews during mass. The windows were very probably decorated with tracery, but their exact appearance is unknown because they were replaced by the current windows in the late 15th century. The chancel vault of the older church also dates from this reconstruction. Remnants of the older vaults with sharp arches and probably stone ribs can now only be veiwed from the roof truss, where they look like scars in the unplastered masonry. The truss of both the older and the current church was entered through a small stone turret, preserved in the southeast corner of the chancel. In the older church, it was entered through a portal that has since been bricked up, which was probably decorated with an elaborate frame in the form of a saddle-shaped portal, which was moved to the sacristy during subsequent reconstructions. It is very likely that this entrance to the turret was covered by a splendid and elaborately crafted wrought-iron door, decorated with coats of arms with a two-tailed lion.

A bell bearing the name of Jesus was cast for the church in 1403, but it is not clear whether it was hung in the church tower or in a separate bell tower, because the first record of the existence of a bell tower at the parish church of Krupka comes from a time shortly before 1479, when it is mentioned in reference to a fire in the town.[242] The fire was probably also the reason behind the extensive reconstruction of the older church, or rather the construction of a new

239) Václav Vladivoj Tomek (ed.), *Registra decimarum papalium* (Praha: 1873), 79.

240) Emanuel Poche et al., *UPČ 2*, 152–153; Táňa Šimková, "Stavební vývoj kostela Nanebevzetí Panny Marie v Krupce," in: *Monumentorum Custos* 2014, 31–48; Luboš Lancinger – Jan Leibl – Táňa Šimková, *Standartní nedestruktivní stavebně-historický průzkum: Krupka, kostel Nanebevzetí Panny Marie* (*Ústí nad Labem: NPÚ ÚOP* v Ústí nad Labem, 2014), coll. SHP a NZ, sign. 1739/A, 3.

241) Michal Urban et al., *Horní města – Ústecký kraj*, 113.

242) Hermann Hallwich, *Geschichte der Bergstadt Graupen*, 49; Luboš Lancinger – Jan Leibl – Táňa Šimková, *Kostel Nanebevzetí Panny Marie v Krupce*, 3.

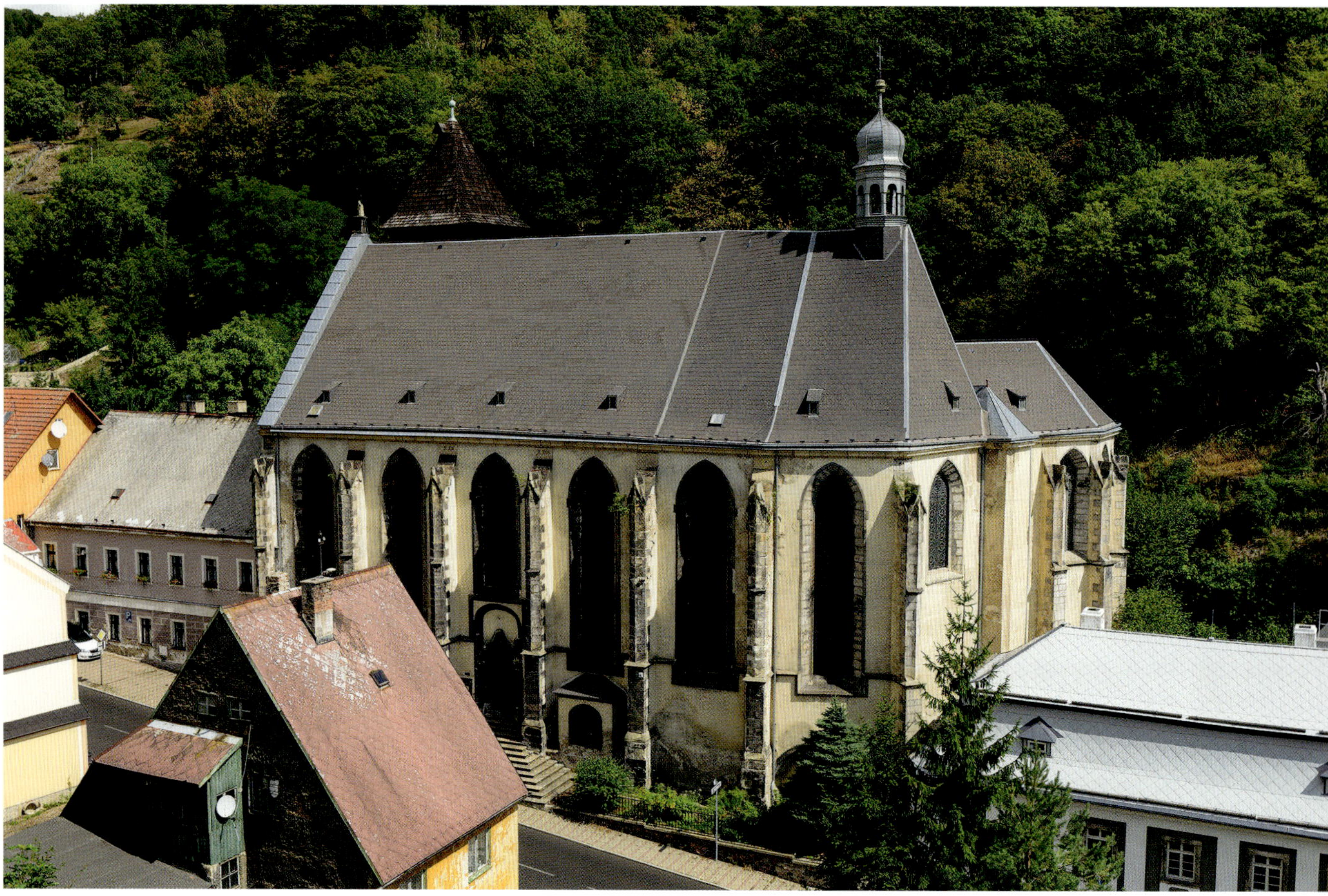

Fig. 56 Krupka, Church of the Assumption of the Virgin Mary, general view of the southern facade of the church. Construction around 1330, general reconstruction of the church to its present form 1484–1486 – the author of the building probably Conrad Pflüger. Photo by J. Peer (2019).

parish church in Krupka. We know from the report of Hermann Hallwich, who described the fire as devastating for the whole town, that the row of buildings reaching from the lower gate all the way to the castle, including the town church, burned to the ground, destroying the bell tower that had recently been completed.[243] The acute need for a new parish church provided an opportunity to build a representative church in a style that was in line with the contemporary trends of the Saxon Late Gothic.

Construction began soon after the fire in 1479. Records from 1484 mention the excavation of the foundations for the new church and bell tower. But even before that, Tiem of Colditz, who owned Krupka, hired the Saxon master stonemason Konrad Pflüger to design and build the church.[244] Pflüger was the leading Saxon stonemason of his time, who had trained in the workshop of Arnold of Westphalia and worked at the Wettin court, in Lausitz, and the Saxon borderland. His involvement determined the final apperarance of the new church, which be-

243) Hermann Hallwich, *Geschichte der Bergstadt Graupen*, 51.

244) Mentioned in the contract as *Meister Kunz Steinmetz*. Milada & Oldřich Radovi, *Kniha o sklípkových klenbách* (Praha: 1988), 66; Luboš Lancinger – Jan Leibl – Táňa Šimková, *Kostel Nanebevzetí Panny Marie v Krupce*, 5.

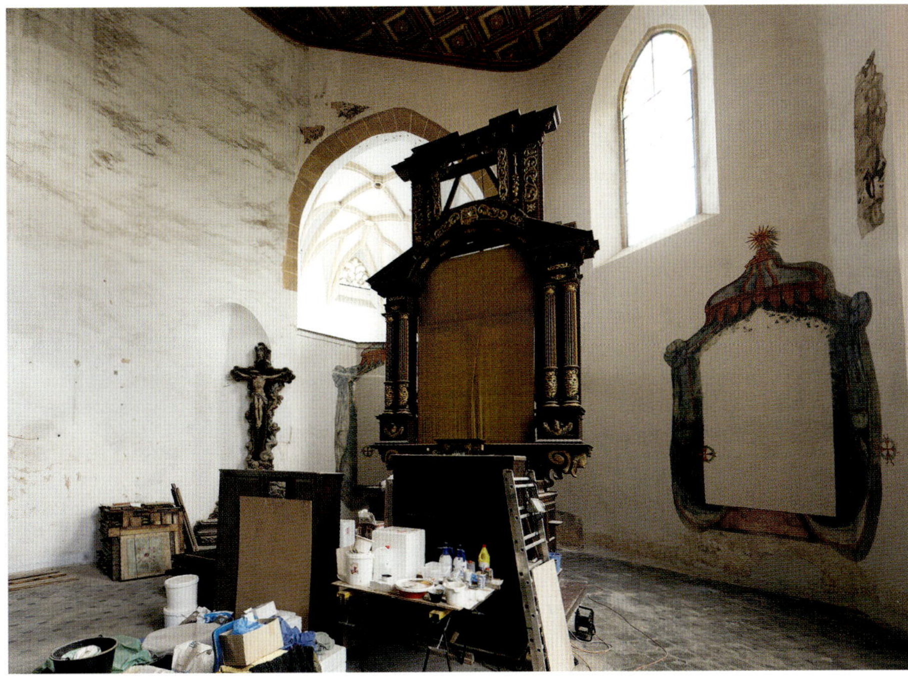

Fig. 57 Krupka, Church of the Assumption of the Virgin Mary, view into the presbytery towards the sacristy created from the presbytery of the older church. Photo by J. Peer (2019).

came one of the examples of Saxon Late Gothic. The construction of the church proceeded apace and by 1486 the new church was completed and consecrated.[245] (Fig. 56)

A spacious single-nave church with a rectangular nave and a wide polygonal chancel was built on the old church plot, which had been enlarged and reinforced. The sheer mass of the building required a change in orientation, and the new church was built in the north-south direction and attached to what remained of the older church with the side of its chancel. (Fig. 57) This feature necessitated the construction of a brick archway under the new church chancel, which served as a passageway connecting the rear end of the plot with the bell tower. Extensive blocks of carefully-chiseled sandstone are still noticeable in the masonry of the corridor and are probably the remains of the earlier church building.

The masonry was strengthened by buttresses, whose sharp, tapered top parts were the first references to the Gothic building tradition of Saxony, for which pointy elements and profiles, as well as austere decoration, are characteristic.[246] A direct homage to the Saxon Gothic style is the appearance of the main portal in the shape of a donkey's back and decorated with the broken rods of the lateral pillars that ascend from ornate sills and plinths. The surviving fragments also indicate that the portal used to have rich polychromatic decoration. This is a characteristic decorative feature of Late Saxon Gothic, introduced by Arnold of Westphalia, which occurrs in the Late Gothic architecture of Saxony and the broader region of northwestern and northern Bohemia.[247]

The interior of this spacious church building, which resembled the hall churches popular in Saxony in terms of its shape, brightness, and size, was marked by a notably austere use of

245) Luboš Lancinger – Jan Leibl – Táňa Šimková, *Kostel Nanebevzetí Panny Marie v Krupce*, 39.

246) Milada a Oldřich Radovi, *Kniha o sklípkových klenbách*, 31.

247) These decorative elements were occasionally used in other churches, incl. Česká Lípa, Benešov nad Ploučnicí, Jedlka, Louny, and Most.

decorative stone elements. Apart from the main portal, stone decoration was probably limited to the tracery in the arched windows of the nave and chancel. While they did not survive, we know they existed from the later traceries in the windows of the older chancel, which adjoined the new church as a side chapel. To unify it visually with the new church, its buttresses were remodelled and a continuous window cornice put in. The height of the older chancel was adjusted, which created a space on its ground floor that was probably used as a strongbox. A similar space can be found, for example, in the Church of St. Nicholas in Kašperské Hory (Bergreichenstein).

New vaults were constructed, as the old ones had probably been damaged in the fire. The ribs of the new vaults seem to grow straight out of the masonry and are decorated with broken edges – another example of a Saxon Late Gothic feature in this church. In contrast to the older church, the new church got a flat ceiling, but the buttresses supporting the outer walls

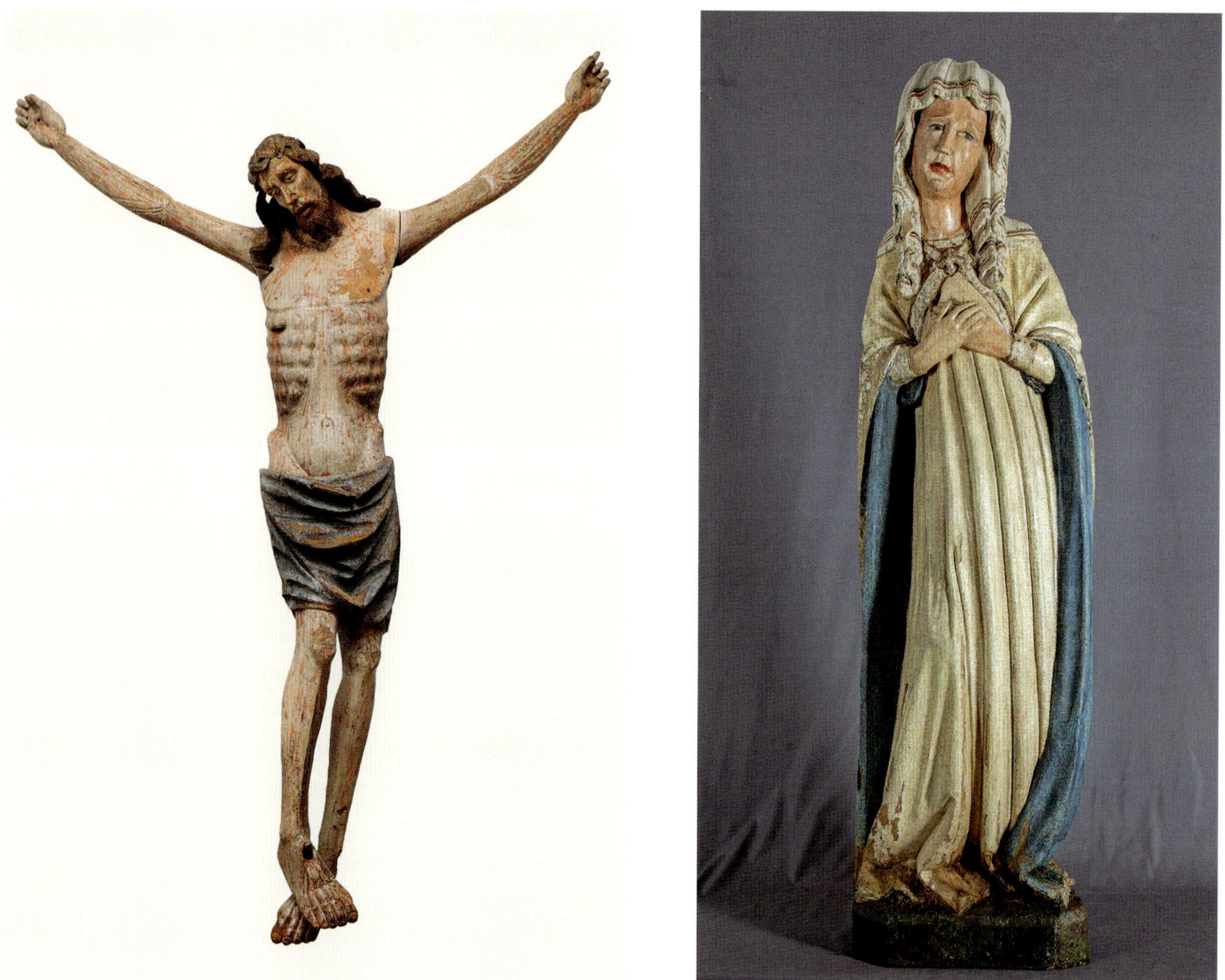

Fig. 58 Christ Crucified and Our Lady of Sorrows from Krupka. Master of Týn Calvary – circle, northwest Bohemia, 1436. Photo © Diocese of Litoměřice.

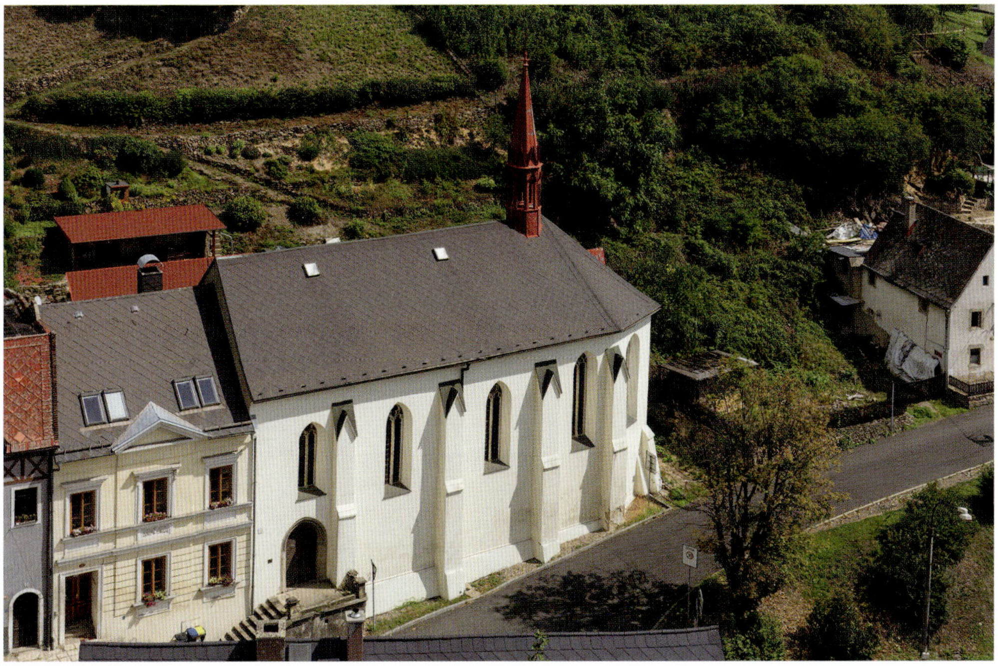

Fig. 59 Krupka, Church of the Holy Spirit, general view of the southern façade of the church from the castle. Probably built 1444–1445, rebuilt after a fire in 1556. Photograph by J. Peer (2019).

indicate the intention to build vaults. Thus decorative features mainly comprised of altarpieces and statues, as well as simple linear wall paintings framing the windows.[248]

The most remarkable features of the church are the holy stairs from 1733, located directly opposite the church entrance. They are an imitatation of the holy stairs in Rome, known as Scala Sancta Sanctorum, which are said to have come directly from Pilate's Palace in Jerusalem. The church was regothicised in 1911.

The monumental Corpus of the Crucified Christ and the statue of the Virgin Mary of Sorrows that are currently kept in the depository of the Litoměřice Bishopric came originally from this church. The statues used to be part of the Calvary in the triumphal arch of the church, which included the figure of St. John the Evangelist, now lost. The statues were carved around 1436 by an artist associated with the workshop of the Master of the Týn Calvary.[249] (Fig. 58)

The parish church of the Assumption was not the only sacral building found in Krupka at the end of the 15th century. Another church, the **Hospital Church of the Holy Spirit**, was built at a time when the western façade of the old Church of the Assumption still stood overlooking the road. The hospital church was probably constructed between 1444 and 1454.

248) Václav Potůček – Jiří Černohorský, *Orientační malířský restaurátorský průzkum omítkových vrstev v interiéru kostela Nanebevzetí Panny Marie v Krupce*; *Restaurátorský průzkum a návrh na restaurování vitrajového prosklení oken kostela Nanebevzetí P. Marie v Krupce* (Dubí u Teplic: NPÚ ÚOP v Ústí nad Labem, 2002), Sbírka restaurátorských zpráv, sign. 1948/R.

249) Jan Klípa – Michaela Ottová (ed.), *Bez Hranic*, 656–657; Milena Bartlová, *Mistr týnské kalvárie. Český sochař doby husitské* (Praha: 2004), 64; Michaela Ottová, *Sochařství 15. století v severních a severozápadních Čechách* (Praha: 2004), 74–79.

Many design details confirm that assumption, although the literature usually gives 1556 as the year of its origin, after a major fire in the town. (Fig. 59) The hospital was financed by foundations set up by rich miners and ore processing entrepreneurs, such as Jeschke of Colditz.

In terms of its appearance, the church corresponds in most details and structures to the still valid principles of the High Gothic style of the first half of the 15th century. An irregular, simple, single-nave church with a polygonal chancel was built on a cramped plot typical of Krupka, and the nave was probably connected to the wooden hospital building, which left even less room for the church. On the west side, the space for development was significantly lim-

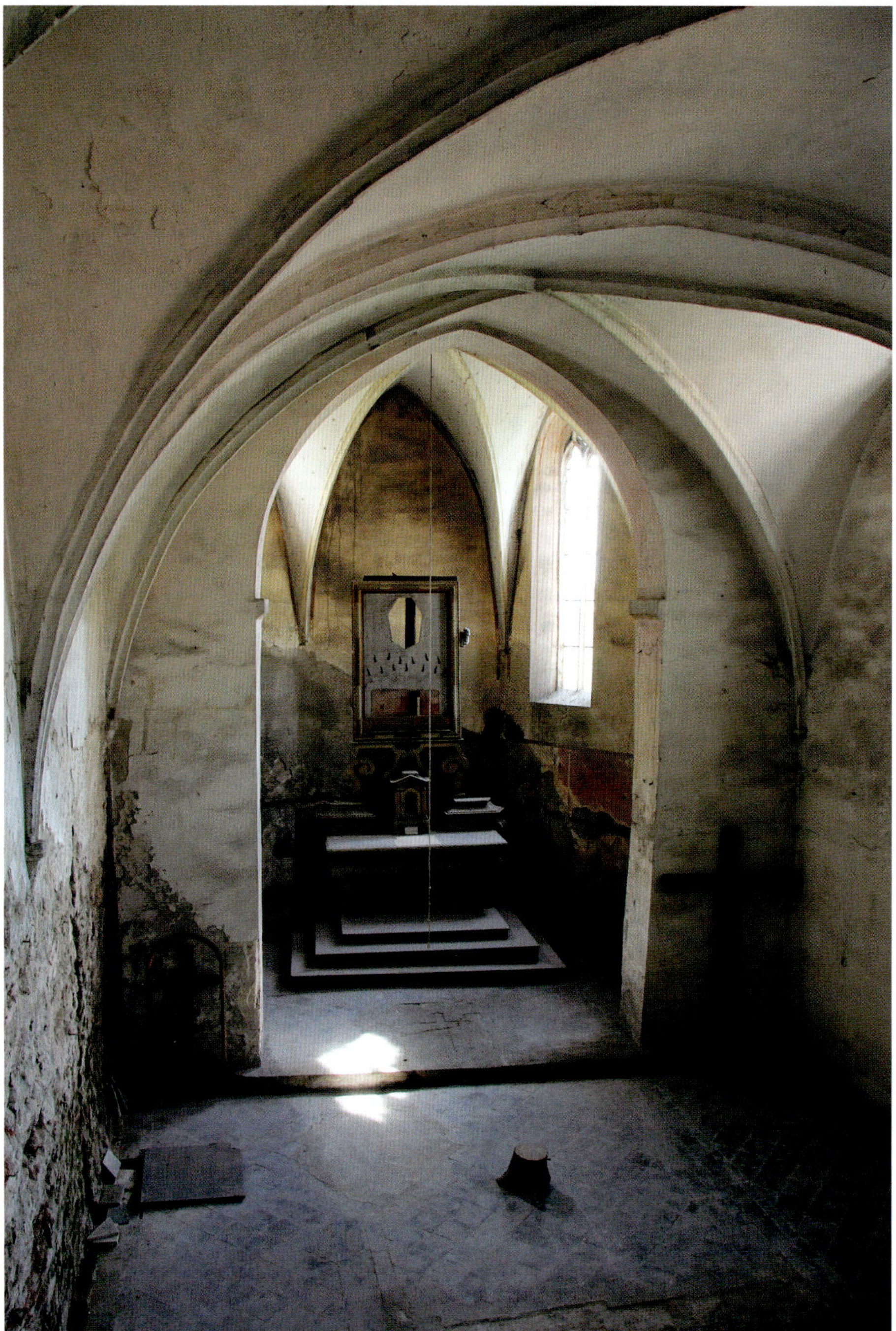

Fig. 60 Krupka, Church of the Holy Spirit, general view of the interior from the west. Photo by T. Šimková (2016).

ited by the older town gate, demolished in 1851.[250] The simple appearance of the church was probably based on the fact that it was only intended to serve the needs of the town hospital.

During its construction, the Church of the Holy Spirit received a number of stone details, mainly in the window openings. The patterns of the tracery are mostly simple and include quatrefoils, raindrops, and trefoil arches, in keeping with the trends in stonemasonry of the High Gothic after 1420, when the appearance of the architecture veered away from rich and dynamic patterns à la Parler and back to the simplicity of the Early Gothic.[251] The dark red polychromy of the masonry material of the mullions and is also quite Gothic in style. Some remnats of it are preserved in the windows of the nave.

After the exterior walls had been completed, cross-ribbed vaults on consoles were built in the interior. (Fig. 60) In the nave, the vault had the length of three vault fields with intervault ribs, while in the chancel, the length was reduced to a single field of a six-part pointed arch vault. The most interesting thing about the vault is that its details tell us about how it was constructed. The disproportion between the angle of the corner consoles and the end parts of the ribs that rest on them, indicates that outer walls were built first along with the consoles, and only then were the vaults put in as the most challenging component of the project, both financially and technologically. In fact, there is not just one but two types of console in the Church of the Holy Spirit, which differ in terms of length but not in terms of shape. Such a variety of otherwise identical elements can probably be ascribed to the work of different stonemasons, although they were made in the same set.

Like the window traceries and mullions, the vault ribs and consoles were polychromed with a white lime coat as a base layer. The stone elements of the vault were painted grey. The colour scale included two shades of grey, with pale grey on the ribs and the foregrounded consoles, and dark red or black on the receding parts of the consoles. The goal of using of two contrasting colour shades and their distribution on the foregrounded versus receding architectural elements was probably to achieve a stronger effect of light and shadow refraction, which was the main aesthetic tool used by post-Classical and Late Gothic style to emphasise linearity.

The renovation of the church after the fire in 1556, reported in historical documents and accentuated in the literature to date, is not noticeable in the appearance of the church today. It can be assumed that the fire to which reference is made affected mainly the roof trusses. However, we have no evidence for this assumption, as the current truss is modern and dates back to the reconstruction of the church that took place at the turn of the 19th and 20th centuries.

The interior decoration probably included a relief with the depiction of the Descent of the Holy Spirit, made between 1430 and 1440, which is now on display in the Church of the Assumption in Most (Brüx). The relief was originally part of a Gothic altar, later incorporated into a Baroque altar, of which only a part survives. The design of the relief, which can be linked to the workshop of the Master of the Týn Calvary, as well as the monumental statues of the Crucified Christ and Virgin Mary of Sorrows from the parish church, was consistent with

250) Dobroslav Líbal – Marie Heroutová, *Krupka. Stavebně historický průzkum objektů* (Praha: NPÚ ÚOP v Ústí nad Labem, 1978), s. p., Sbírka SHP & NZ, sign. 515/A.
251) Václav Mencl, "Vývoj okna v architektuře českého středověku," in: *Zprávy památkové péče* 20/6, 224.

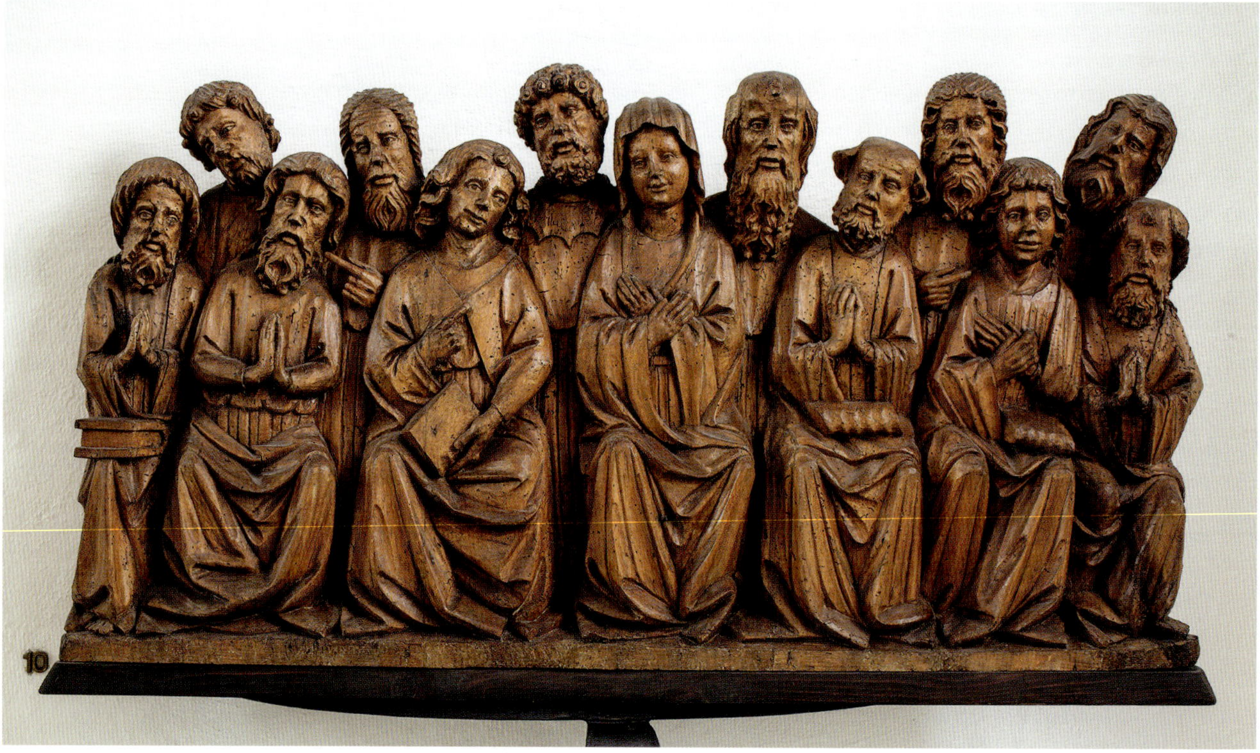

Fig. 61 Descent of the Holy Spirit from Krupka. Master of Týn Calvary – circle, northwest Bohemia, 1430–1340. Photo © Diocese of Litomerice.

the dedication of the church, common for hospital churches, as the sick hoped to be cured through the Holy Spirit.[252] (Fig. 61)

Early-Renaissance sacred architecture in Krupka is thus represented chiefly by the **Church of St. Anne**. (Fig. 62) It was constructed over a long period of time, from 1509 to 1609, due to the parlous financial state of the town council that decided to build it. During the first stages of construction, the church was rarely used, and regular liturgical services only began to be held after a renovation in the late 16th century by Krupka's Lutheran community.

The Church of St. Anne has an unusual layout consisting of a massive polygonal chancel adjoining a distinctive transept. The reason for this floor plan is not clear today. The most probable explanation is that the original intention was to build a much larger church, possibly on a Latin cross plan, but the project remained unfinished for financial reasons. Even the construction of the core of the church around 1510 encountered difficulties.

The design of the church, built at the beginning of the 16th century, followed the continuing Gothic tradition, including a polygonal chancel, which was probably built as a separate space, prepared for the addition of a nave later on. After the perimeter wall of the chancel had been built up to the level of the cornice, the space was probably closed off on the western side by a temporary wall, so it could be used for liturgical purposes without being disturbed by

252) Jan Klípa – Michaela Ottová (ed.), *Bez Hranic*, 659; Michaela Ottová, *Sochařství 15. století v severních a severozápadních Čechách*, 70–73.

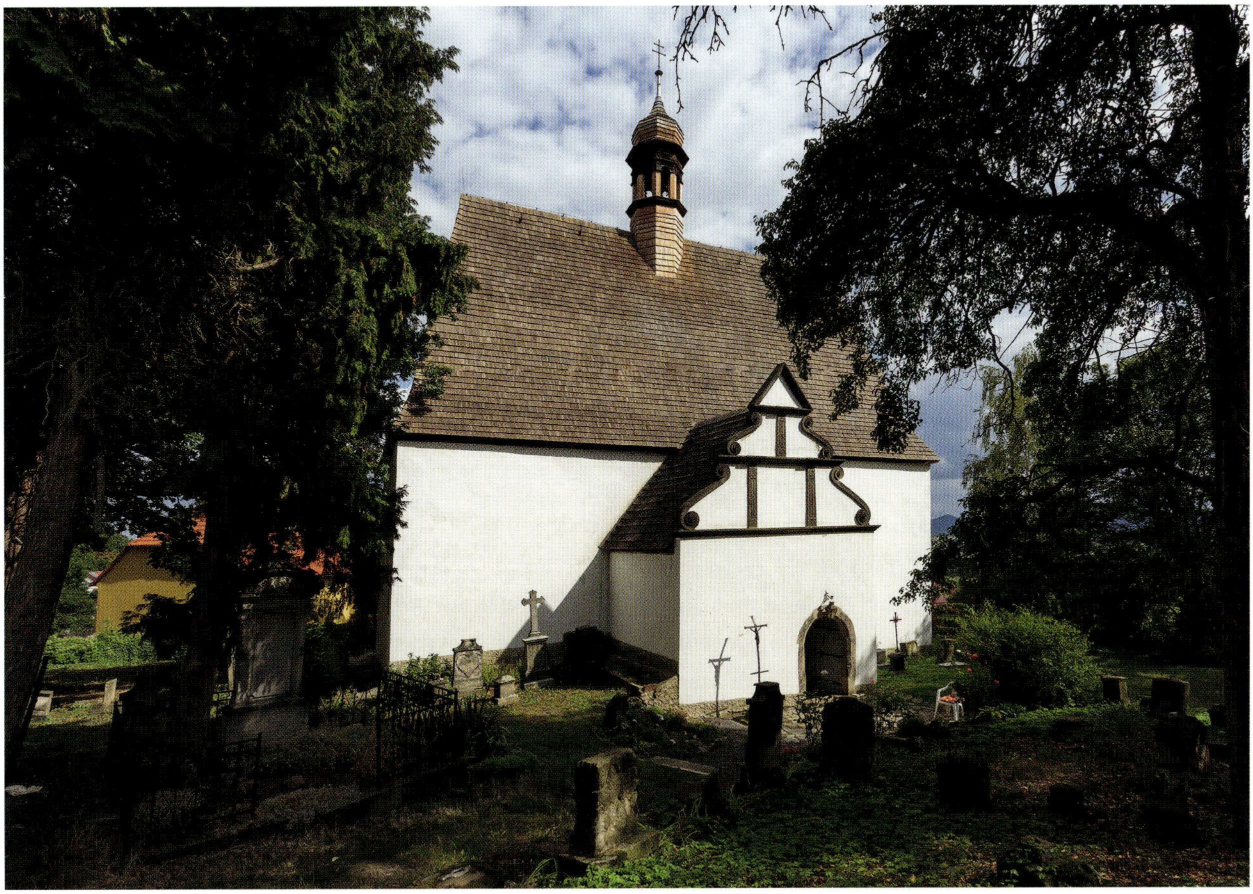

Fig. 62 Krupka, Church of St. Anne, general view from the west. Photo by J. Peer (2019).

the ongoing contruction of the nave. This was fairly common practice in mediaeval and early Renaissance construction.[253] In the case of St. Anne's Church, this hypothesis is supported by clues in the roof truss of the chancel: according to dendrochronological dating, the chancel was covered with a roof immediately after the completion of its masonry, just after the end of the winter of 1509/1510.

The furnishing of the chancel, with its simplified linear window tracery made of stone, can certainly be dated back to the first phase of construction. Like the roof trusses, its appearance bears witness to the transitional period in which the Gothic style was still strongly present, yet new trends were emerging in art and design that undermined the older Gothic convention and aesthetics, and which were typical of the period after 1510.[254]

253) The practice of closing off an unfinished building with a temporary wall, behind which the finished parts of the church could continue to serve their normal purpose, was common in Bohemia, particularly in the most renowned churches including St. Barbara's Church in Kutná Hora (Kuttenberg), where a temporary wall was put in around 1558 when the finances ran short. Another example is St. Vitus' Cathedral. The elite status of these buildings in the Kingdom of Bohemia is supported by many historical written sources. Thus, there is sufficient evidence of the procedures used in their construction, quite apart from the in situ evidence. This is, however, not the case with St. Anne's Church in Krupka. For a detailed discussion of this issue, see e.g. Various authors, *Kutná Hora* (Praha: 2000).
254) Václav Mencl, *Vývoj okna*, 228–229.

In the Ore Mountain region, the Late Gothic style became popular in window tracery around 1510, when the 'noses' in the trefoil arches were slowly phased out, as in the window arch tracery in the south side of the chancel of St. Anne's Church. Another Late Gothic feature was the strong individualism in rendering the tracery lines. While continuing the tradition of Benedikt Ried, as in the use of the curved, flame-like shapes in the windows of the apse, their patterns no longer followed the prescriptive Gothic norms. The tracery in Krupka, in view of its early origins around 1509, represents a very advanced example of the emerging trend, which appeared later in a fully developed form in, for example, the window tracery of the Chruch of the Assumption in Most (Brüx).[255] In the second phase of the first construction stage, a rectangular transept was added to the narrow chancel.

A tree-ring dating analysis of the truss indicates that the transept was completed around 1510/1511, like the chancel. Its construction can therefore be considered the second phase of one construction stage. Timber felled in the winter seasons of 1509/10 and 1510/11 was subsequently used in the construction of a separate nave truss. It was connected to the roof of the presbytery in concept, not in fact. The two trusses were only connected later when new structural elements were inserted as part of putting in a new roof over the completed church building.

Similarly, as in the chancel, the construction of the nave included putting in stonework details, such as the window tracery in the southern façade and the portal of the main entrance in the western façade of the nave. The window tracery shares some features with the tracery in the chancel, which puts their origin in the Late Gothic period when the style of Benedikt Ried was dying out. The simplified profile of the main portal also dates it back to the beginning of the 16th century. It is dominated by two distinctive bars and a set of concave and bell-shaped mouldings, as well as the absence of overlapping bars at the tip of the arch. These features correspond to the period after 1510, when stonemasons typically moved away from the elaborate morphology of Gothic portals, and the rich Late Gothic tradition continued only as a reverberation.[256]

The construction of the core of the church was completed in the early 16th century, once the transept was finished. It was, however, only a temporary solution, not consistent with the original plan, as written sources refer to the church as temporary or unfinished. Given the current appearance of the church, this could mean that the church was useful for practical purposes in the life of the community, but did not meet the reuirements of of a fully-fledged church bulding. The premature termination of the construction may have been due to money running out, a fact of which written sources make no secret.

Both historical documents and material evidence place the second construction phase at a much later time, around 1609. From the preceding long period of the 16th century, no further construction changes are indicated, either in written documents or in the building itself. Only in 1577 is a tenuous mention made in sources of the first Lutheran Mass. Some scholars put the origin of a unique mural on the inside of the triumphal arch, which probably depicts

255) Václav Mencl, *Vývoj okna*, 229.
256) Václav Mencl, "Vývoj středověkého portálu v českých zemích," in: *Zprávy památkové péče* XX No. 4 (1960), 153.

Fig. 63 Krupka, Church of St. Anne, general view of the interior with a wooden painted chancel. ⟶
Photo by J. Peer (2019).

Martin Luther, at the same period. But it should be noted that based on iconographic and stylistic analysis by various authors, the estimated time of origin ranges over a long period between the 1570s and the early 17th century. The artist who painted Luther was clearly inspired by the engraving by Lucas Cranach the Elder.

The next construction stage that has been reliably documented is the enlargement of the church in 1609. A wooden organ loft was built into the transept in the same year. (Fig. 63) Compared to its current appearance, the loft was originally supported by no more than a pair of carved columns. The long west part of the loft was anchored quite casually in the masonry of the nave, which necessitated a later addition of multiple tie rods and anchors that left scars and imprints in the masonry.

According to the coat of arms, the now-extinct high altar was commissioned by Nikel Gühre and created probably by the sculptor Franz Ditrich of Freiberg. The organ loft was decorated with striking paintings on wooden panels with motifs from the Old Testament, starting with the Fall of Man and ending with the erection of the brazen serpent in the desert. The scenes are modeled on drawings. The painted decoration was initiated by Daniel Frank and financial support for the individual panels came from various mining workers' guilds, as is evident from the emblems underneath each panel. (Fig. 64)

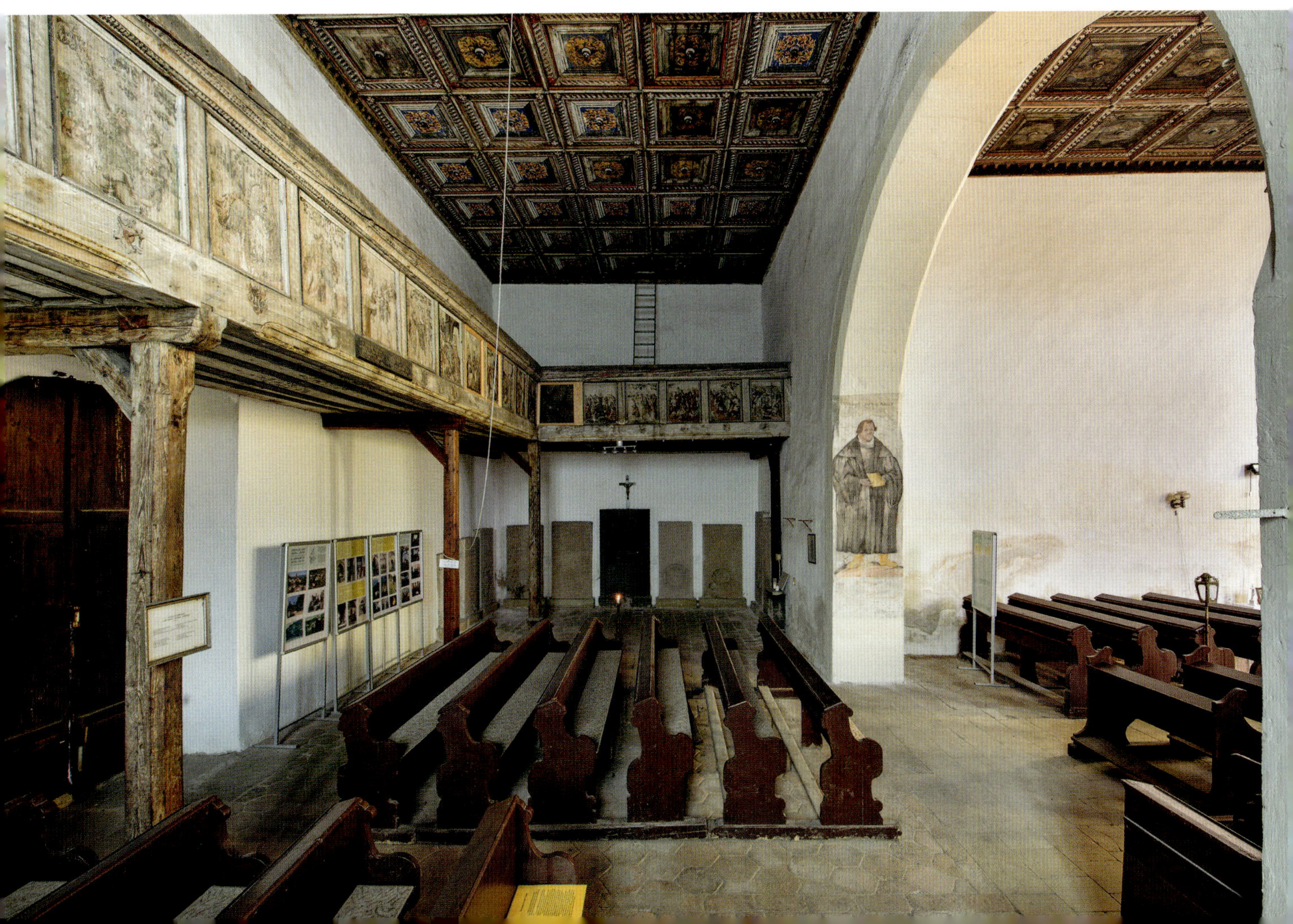

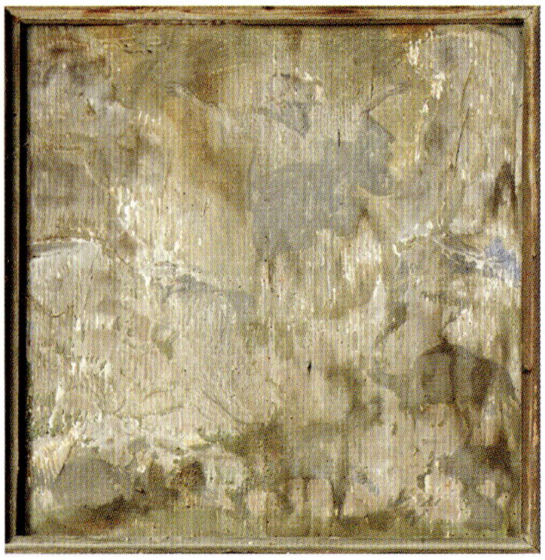
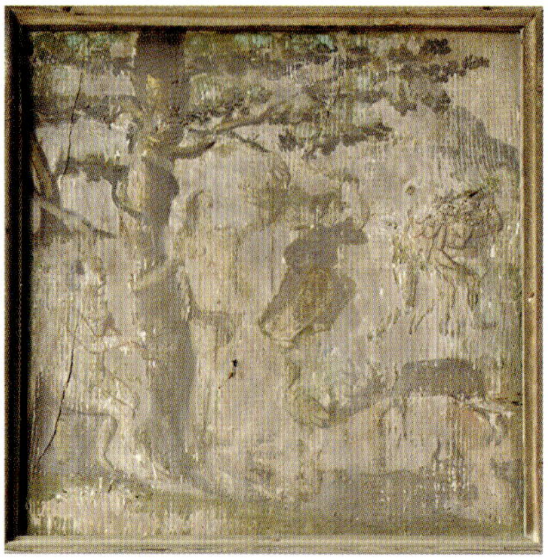
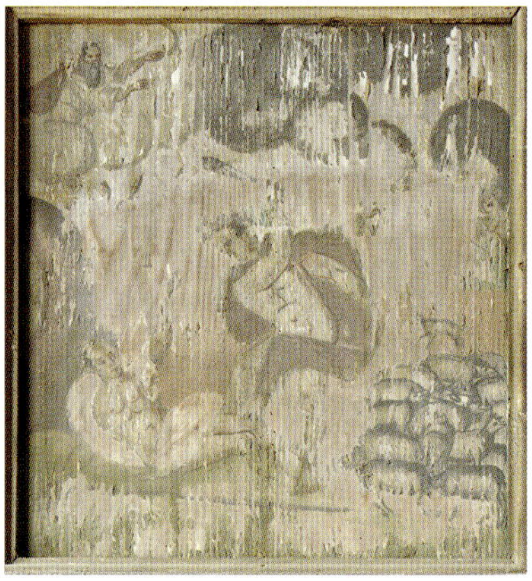
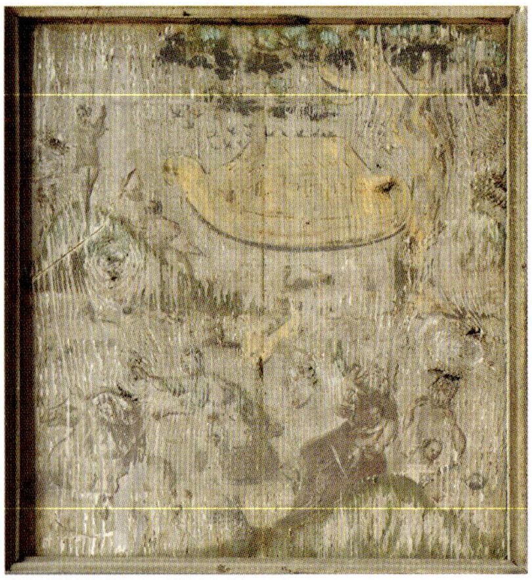
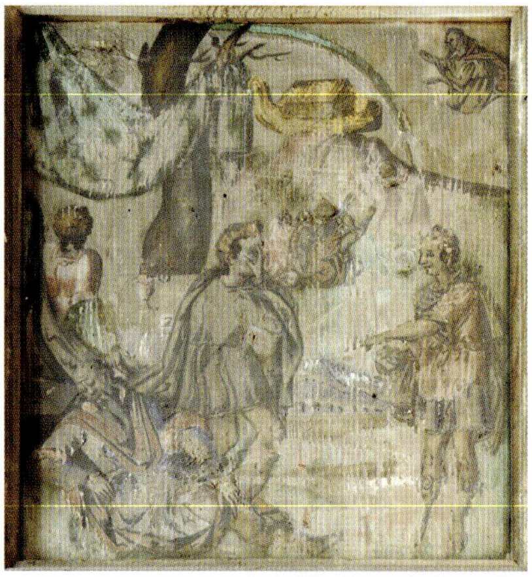
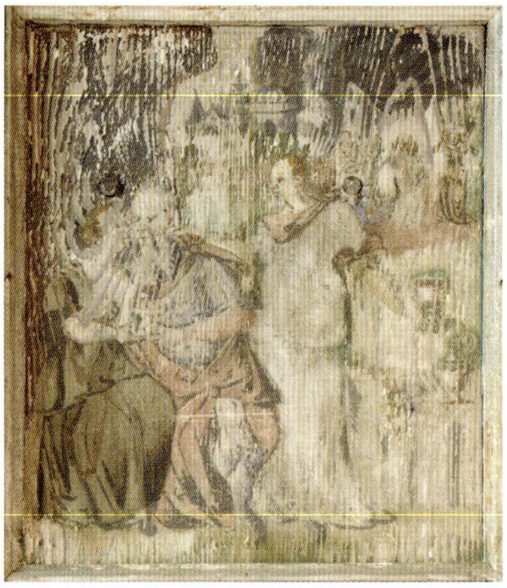
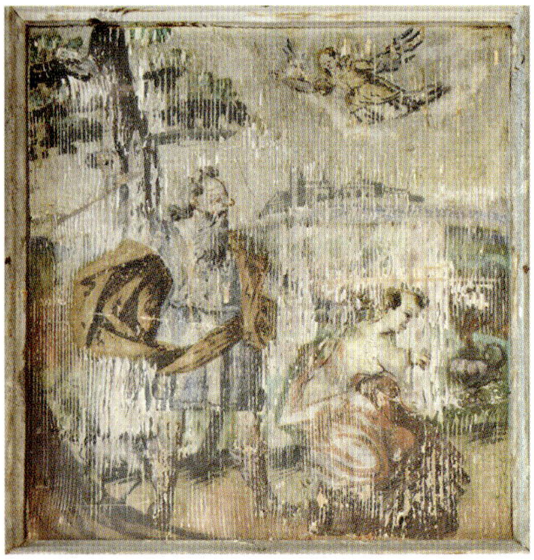
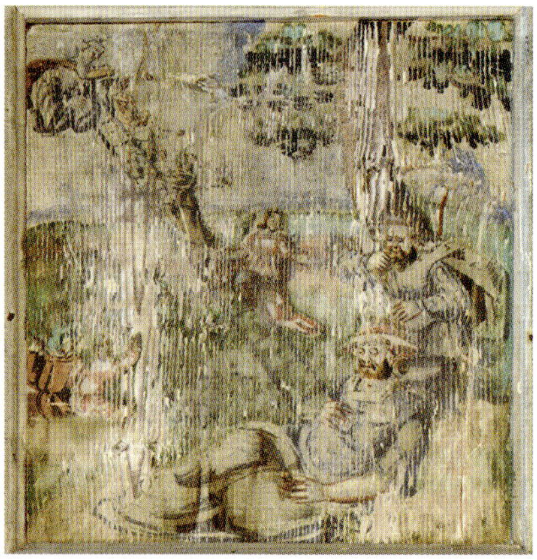
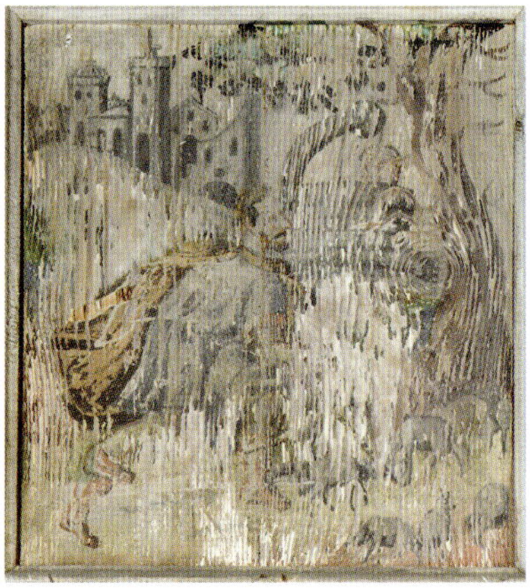
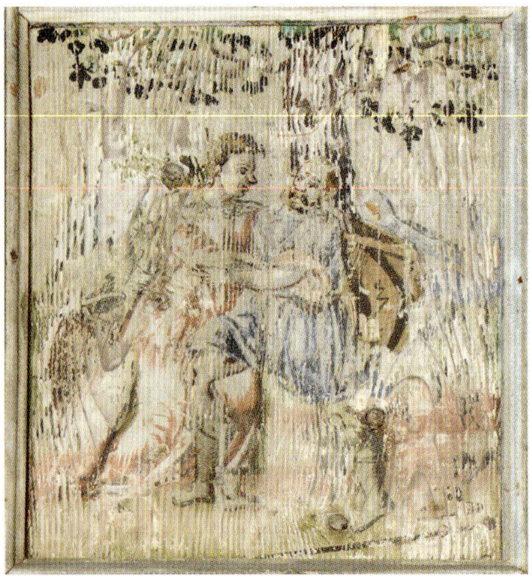
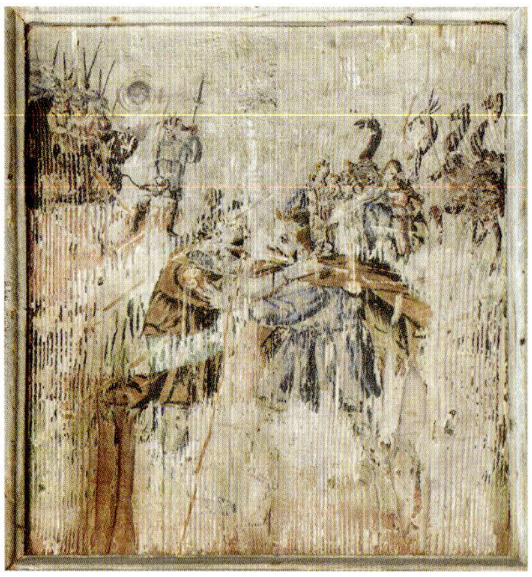
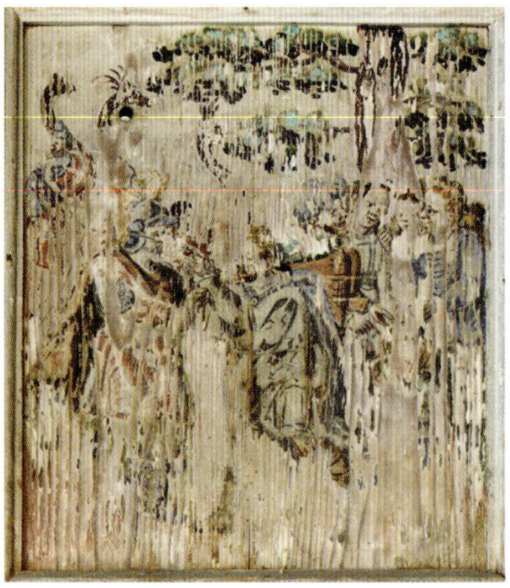

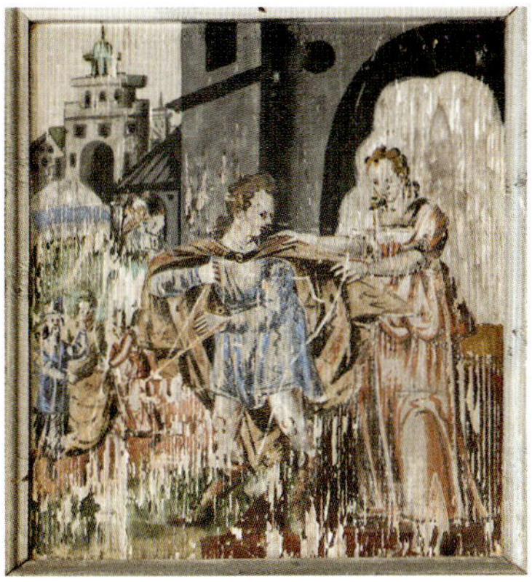
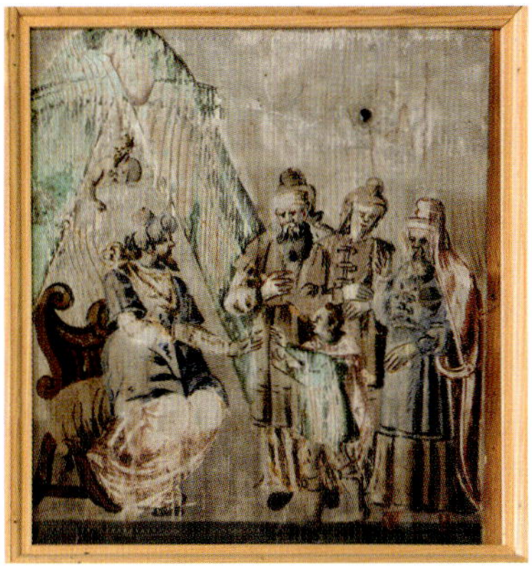
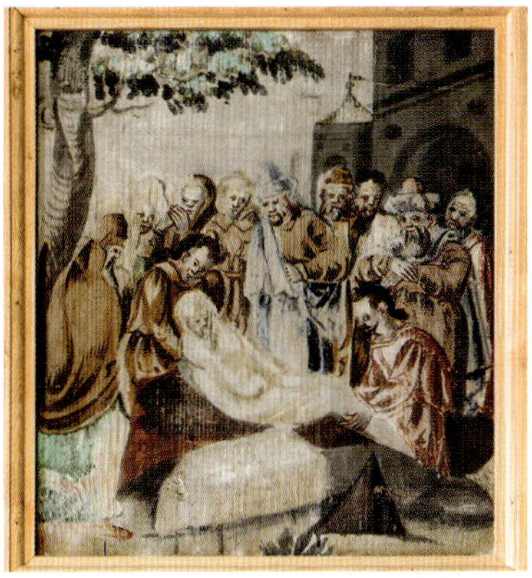
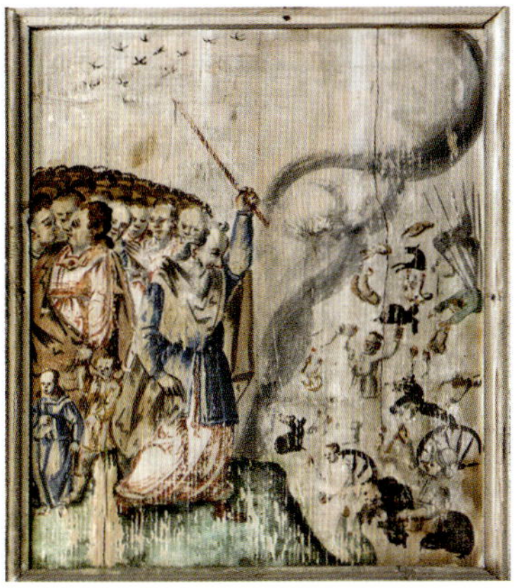
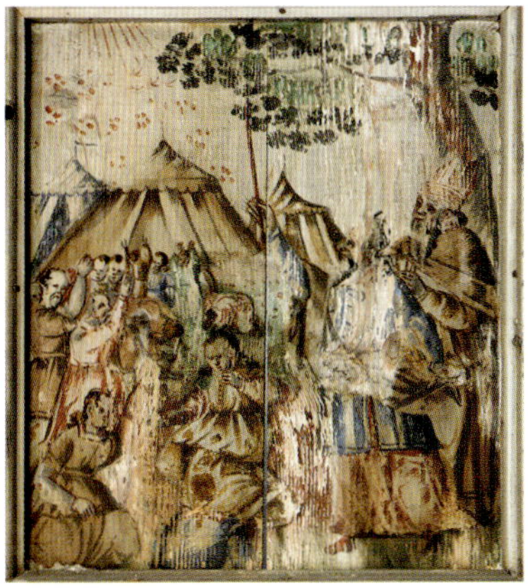
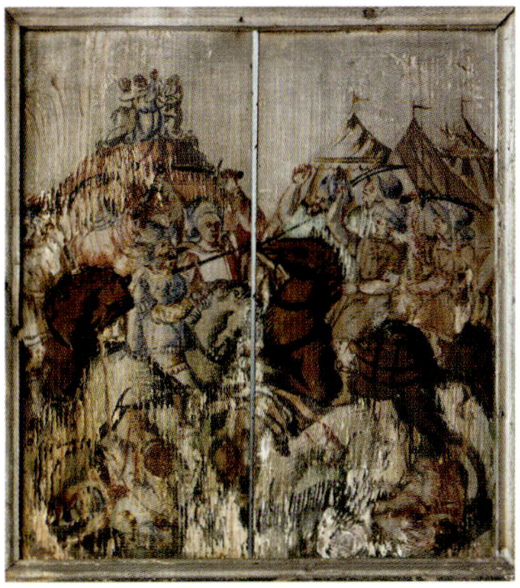
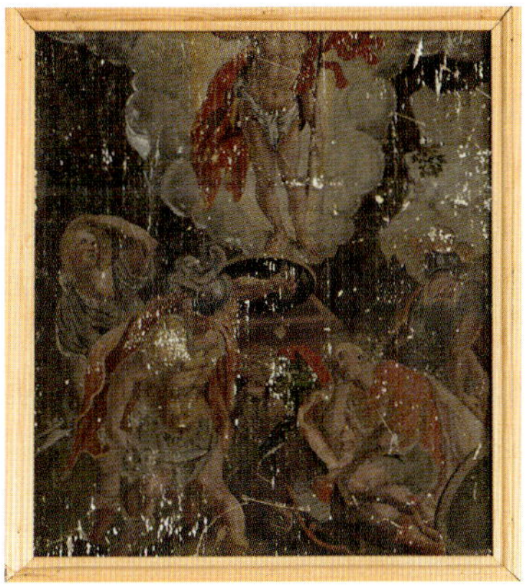
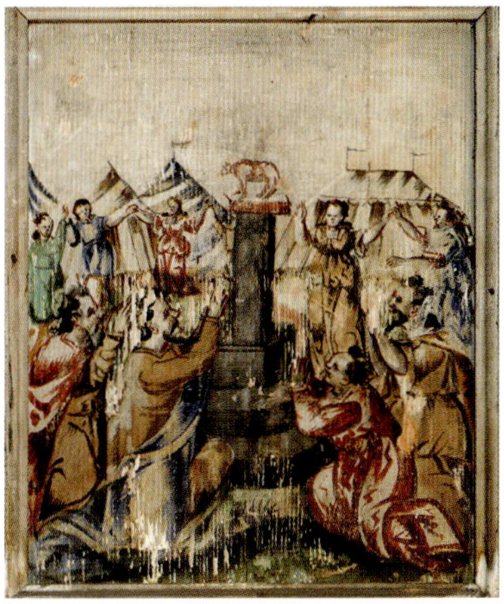
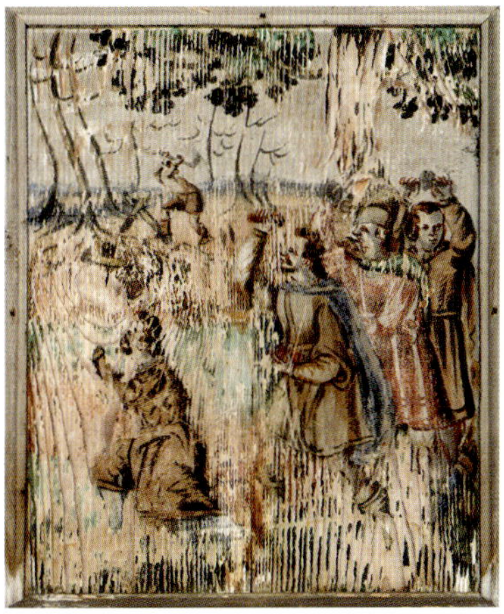
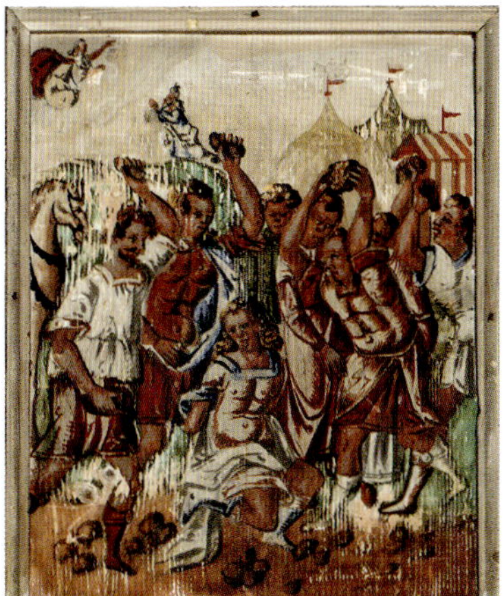
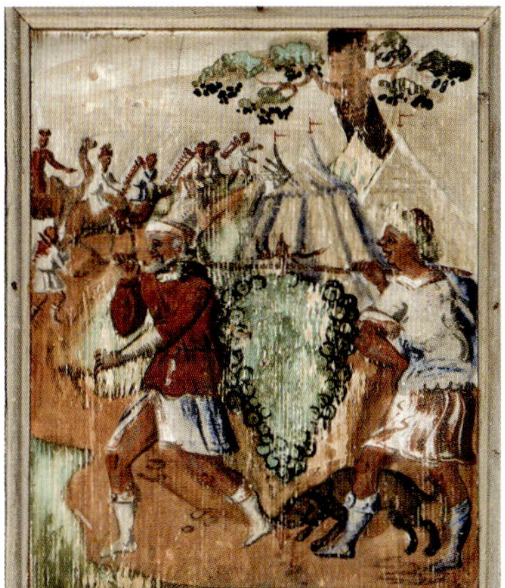
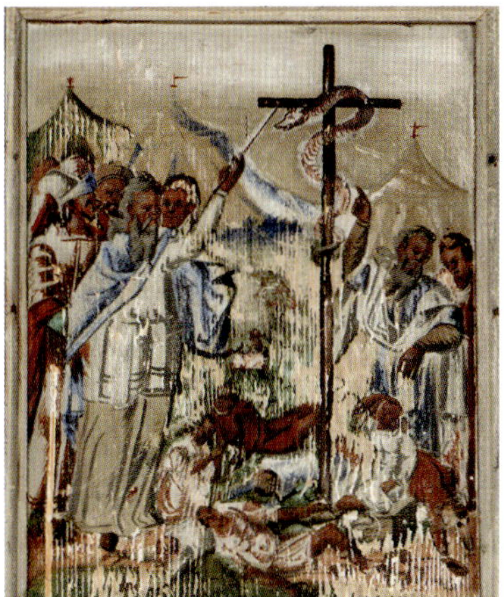

The addition of the organ loft shows that Lutheranism had taken a firm hold in the town, and increasing the capacity of a church in this manner used to be common in the Protestant community. The Lutheran faith of the congregation is also reflected in the motif of the decoration of the parapet, which is strongly Christocentric. The addition can also be seen as a distinct expression of bourgeois self-presentation, manifested by the painted guild emblems under the panels in the organ loft. It can be assumed that these are the emblems of the individual patrons of the building. The visual presentation of the bourgeoisie is a typical sign of emancipated urban society at the turn of the 16th and 17th centuries. In Krupka it made itself known at the end of the 15th century with the construction of the town church of the Assumption of the Virgin Mary, which was not funded by the nobility, but through the town's endowment.

The installation of the organ loft – the dating of which we know from historical sources as well as from a plaque on the front of the west gallery – required more alterations in the nave. First of all, an opening was made for an entrance to the organ loft at the level of the western wall. There, a rectangular portal with undulating vaulting attachments in the shape of leaves was inserted. Surprisingly, the ornamental side of the portal faces the nave and not the antechamber. On the other hand, it seems logical that the superior church space was given precedence in terms of the aesthetic impact, both ritually and artistically, over the auxiliary space of the antechamber. The western external wall of the nave was probably also refurbished. Two vaulted niches were put in at the level of the organ loft, but it is unclear whether these were used as storage or as seats to increase the comfort of the churchgoers, or if windows had originally been put in (and later bricked up) to add light to the interior of the otherwise somewhat dark loft, where the only source of light was a window in the southern wall of the nave.

An access staircase made of stone was added to the new entrance to the organ loft, leading from a newly-constructed square-shaped antechamber that partially covered the older nave entrance. Also, the building of the antechamber involved putting in stonework elements that date the construction back to the late stage of the Saxon Renaissance at the beginning of the 17th century.

One of those elements is a simple entrance portal with a bevelled arch which rests on the columns, with its undulating vaulting extensions in the shape of leaves. The square window

⟵ Fig. 64 Krupka, Church of St. Anne, chancel decoration.
1. Creation of man, 2. Original sin, 3. Cain and Abel, 4. Noah's ark, 5. The covenant between the Lord and Noah, 6. Noah drunk with his daughters, 7. Abraham's sacrifice, 8. Jacob's ladder, 9. Jacob and Rachel meeting at the well, 10. Jacob's wrestling with the angel, 11. Reconciliation of Jacob and Esau, 12. Jacob presents Esau with gifts, 13. Joseph of Egypt and Putipharca, 14. Joseph of Egypt interprets Pharaoh's dreams, 15. Burial of Jacob, 16. Crossing the Red Sea, 17. The gathering of the manna, 18. The Israelites are victorious over Amalek. Moses, Aaron and Hur on the hilltop, 19. Resurrection of Christ (originally perhaps Moses takes the tablets of the law from the Lord), 20. Jews worship the golden calf, 21. Moses breaks the tablets of the law and punishes the idolaters, 22. The stoning of Moses' follower Hur, who tried to prevent the worship of the golden calf, 23. Caleb and Joshua bringing grapes from the land of Canaan, 24 Moses and the brazen serpent in the Jewish camp.
On the chancel there is a German inscription from 1609: 'Jahr die Gottes Ackrgebarect war / Des gluch diese Kirche wie man sieht / wiederrenoviert und zugericht / So doch wol über hundert Jahr / Ubgebaut und wüstgestanden war /Gott geb Kirchenvätern und alle fromm Christen / Die mich des angenom. / Vor ihr Unkost und Arbeit / Nach diesem die ewig Seeligkeit. Amen.'
Photo by J. Peer (2019).

in the southern wall of the antechamber has the same ornamentation. The softly undulating vaulting extensions are a characteristic feature of the stonework details of Saxon Renaissance architecture. Thus, at least the reconstruction of the church can be reliably placed in the category of these buildings.

This is demonstrated by the appearance of the gable of the antechamber, made of masonry and featuring stonework details, even though its current look comes from the early 20th century. From older photographs taken prior to this renovation it is clear that even in its authentic earlier form, the triangular gable was equipped with stone cornices and vertical columns that partitioned it into several fields. It is unclear whether or not there used to be voluted mouldings on the side of it, because the edge of the gable in the photographs is blocked by the gable roof of the antechamber. But it is quite possible, especially considering the fact that, there are voluted mouldings on the cemetery gate, which was built at around the same time. (Fig. 65)

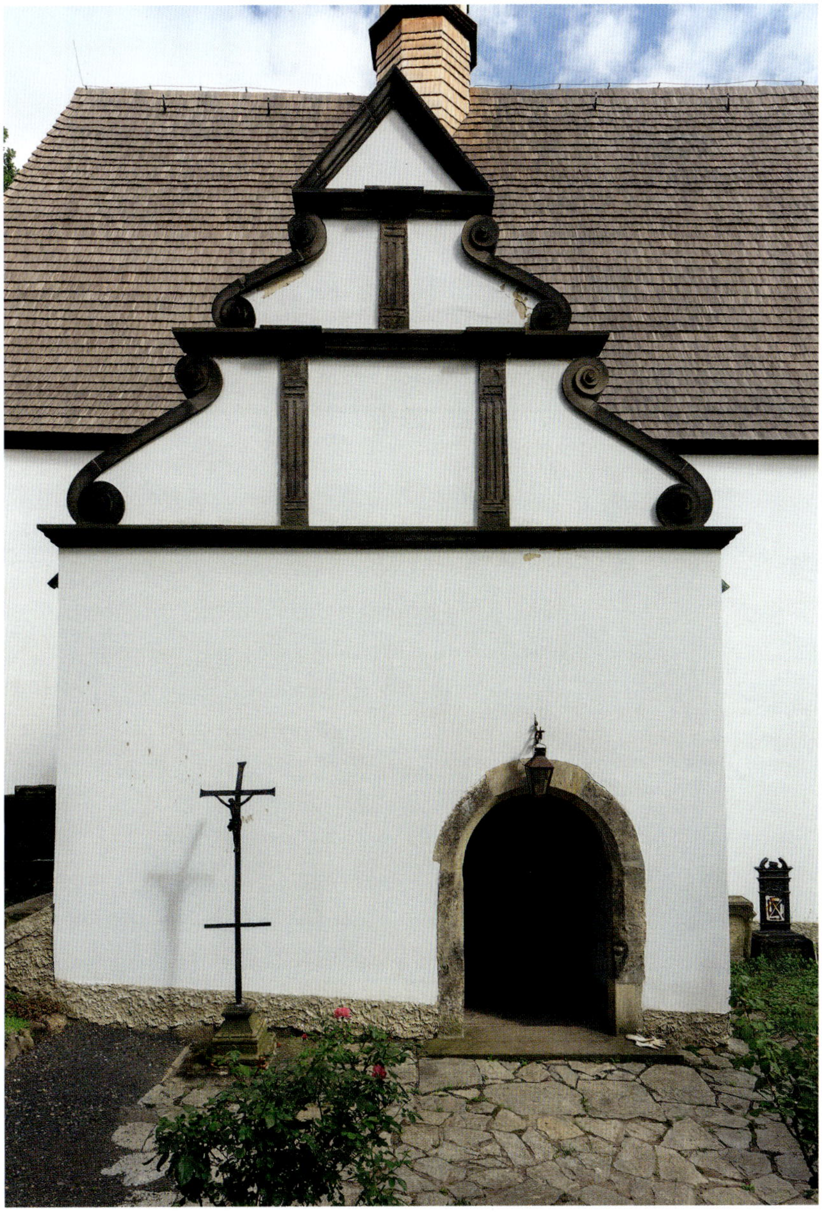

Fig. 65 Krupka, Church of St. Anne, gable of the narthex with original Renaissance stone elements. Photo by J. Peer (2019).

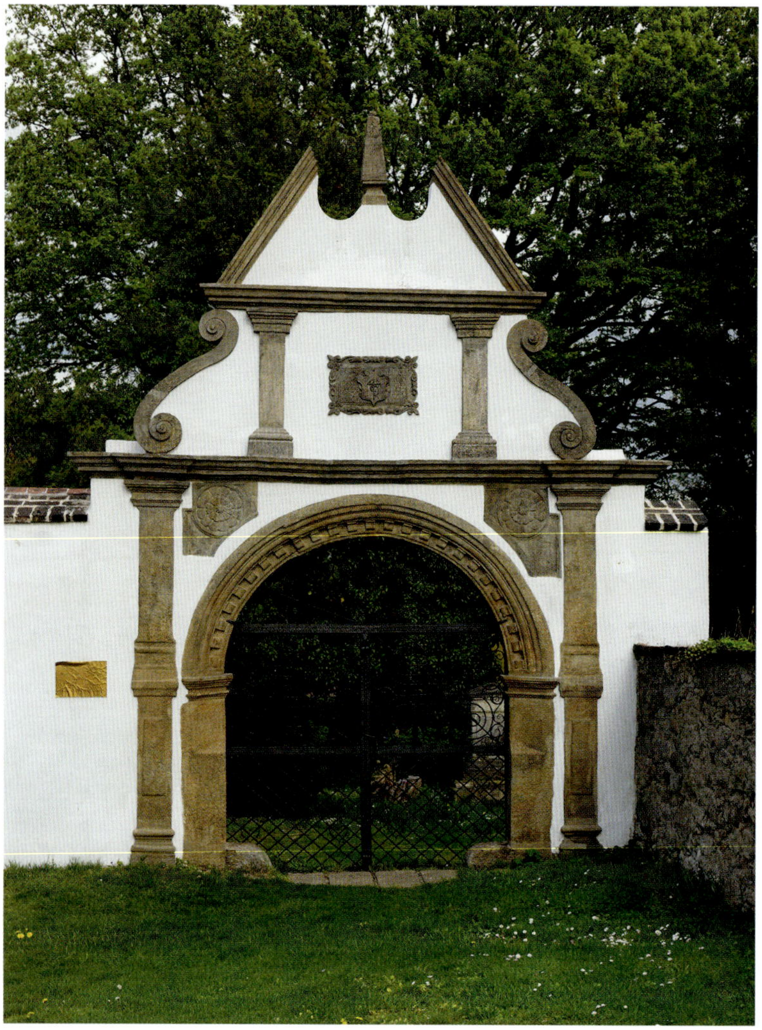

Fig. 66 Krupka, Church of St. Anne, entrance gate to the cemetery grounds. Construction in 1615 on the initiative of the townsman Georg Klippel, the wrought-iron grill was made in Dresden in 1619. Photo by J. Peer (2019).

A cemetery was established near the church sometime around 1609, as revealed by the stone elements in the enclosure wall, which are decorated with studded ornamentation.

The installation of the organ loft and the addition of the antechamber probably inaugurated a more extensive reconstruction of the church and the church grounds. In 1609, a cemetery was established by the church, enclosed at its northern border by a stone wall with a blind arcade on stone cut columns. The capitals of the columns are decorated with a low-relief studded motif. This element can also be seen as a characteristic feature of Late-Renaissance Saxon architecture. However, somewhat surprising is the use of ornamentation in such a utilitarian structure as a cemetery wall was, which demonstrates that it was meant to be viewed from the cemetery grounds.

In 1615, a Renaissance cemetery gate was built at the expense of Georg Klippel, as we learn from the inscription and the coat of arms on the stone plaque set in its gable. (Fig. 66) Klippel also financed the magnificent Renaissance grille, which was inaugurated in 1618. He also commissioned the plaque with the motif of Joseph of Egypt and Potiphar's wife on the organ loft, as his coat of arms indicates. The gate, in contrast to the rest of the church, is more Mannerist in appearance, chiefly due to the broken triangular pediment with an obelisk on the top.

This element is more characteristic of the Mannerist and Early Baroque styles, and in this time period was more typically seen in the architectural context of Prague. The fact that it was used in Krupka demonstrates once again that the borderland of the Ore Mountains was oriented towards Saxony, whose advanced construction and architectural models and elements had influenced it since at least Gothic times. However, other features of the gate, including the voluted lower part of the gable, the stone roses in the spandrels and the design of the portal of the gate's clear opening still reference the form and details of Saxon Renaissance architecture, which makes it an example of a transitional type of structure that stands on the border between the Renaissance and Mannerism. In 1618, the gate received an elaborate wrought-iron grille, which is fully Renaissance in style.

We know that a painted ceiling was also added in this construction phase in 1613. Originally, the ceiling was composed of painted panels with simple circular floral motifs that had knobs in the centres. The same pattern was later used in the parish Church of the Assumption. It is impossible to determine how the panels were attached to the ceiling, as the original ceiling was replaced by the current one in the second half of the 20th century. However, it does not seem likely that a traditional coffered ceiling was put in. It is more probable that the painted panels were nailed into the simple bottom part of a lath or beam ceiling. The signature of Daniel Frank, who either designed or financed the making of the ceiling, survives on the reverse of one of the ceiling panels.

Although the Church of St. Anne in Krupka was used by Lutherans in the late 16th century, it had originally been built as a Catholic church. The construction of exclusively Lutheran churches in the region was rare in that period, for several reasons. First of all, as was the case in Krupka, Lutherans mostly used older Catholic churches that were transferred to the use of the Lutherans simply by changing their status. The second reason, and probably the more serious one, was the fact that the construction of Protestant churches was actively obstructed by church and royal authorities, and they were basically illegal. Isolated examples of such churches therefore appear either in locations where the bearers of the Lutheran faith were originally Saxon nobles, or in mining towns, which enjoyed a number of perks and exemptions because they were indispensable to the country's economic welfare.[257]

The capital of mining towns in the Ore Mountains was **Jáchymov,** and its principal **Church of St. Joachim and St. Anne** was undoubtedly the most notable ecclesiastical building in the area. (Fig. 67) It was built between 1534 and 1540 and was the first Lutheran church in Bohemia. Thanks to an abundance of written records of Jáchymov under the Schlick family and the attention the building has received from architectural and art historians, a lot of interesting and often unique information about the church has been accummulated.

While the designer of the church is unknown, we do know that Hans Kopp and Johann Münnich were the executive builders, Wolf Müller of Ostrov (Schlackewerth) was the master carpenter, and master stonemason Georg of Bamberg was in charge of the stonemasonry

257) On the issue of building Lutheran churches in northwest Bohemia, see: Táňa Šimková, *Hrad přepevný je Pánbůh náš. Saská luterská šlechta severozápadních Čech ve světle raně novověké sakrální architektury* (Ústí nad Labem: 2018).

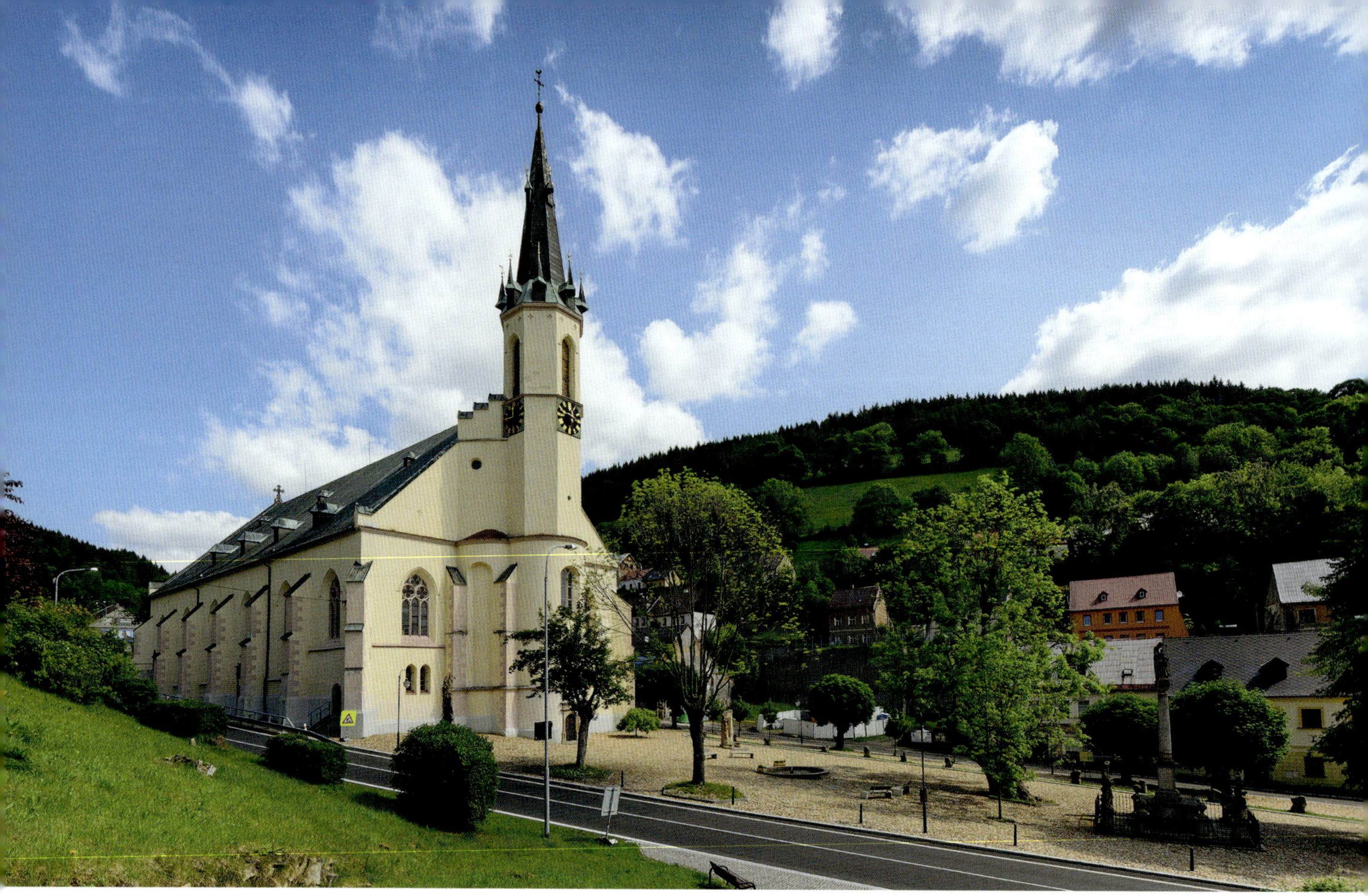

Fig. 67 Jáchymov, Church of St. Joachim and St. Anne, general view from the south-west. Construction of the church 1534–1540, the present appearance is based on the reconstruction after the fire in 1873. Photo by J. Peer (2019).

work.[258] The church was meant to represent the founding noble family of Schlick, who had a tomb built in the church and occupied part of the gallery, a fact which they marked with their coat of arms. In addition, the church is a monumental memorial to Stephan Schlick, who was killed in the Battle of Mohács in 1526 – a fact that is commemorated in the antechamber. The Jáchymov church is undoubtedly the largest sacral building built by the Lutherans on Bohemian territory in the 16th century. It reflected the wealth of the town as well as the generosity of the patrons of the arts. The church was primarily intended to represent the Schlick noble family, who were the founders of the town.[259]

258) Milena Hauserová, "Kostel sv. Jáchyma v Jáchymově. Architektura skromného výrazu nebo torzo velkého konceptu?" in: Michaela Hrubá – Michaela Ottová – Jan Royt (ed.), *Ars Montana*, 271–291; Lubomír Zeman – Alžběta Kratochvílová, "Kostel sv. Jáchyma v Jáchymově. První luteránský kostel v Čechách a jeho přestavba Josefem Mockerem," in: *Svorník* 10/2012, 190.

259) Richard Schmidt, *Soupis památek historických a uměleckých*, 45–68; Emanuel Poche et al., *UPČ I*, 564–565; Jan Royt, "Horní město Jáchymov, reformace a umění," in: *Gotické umění a jeho souvislosti I.*, *Ústecký sborník historický 2001*, 351–359; Jiří Fajt, "Na paměť statečného a zbožného Štěpána Schlicka (+1526), zakladatele Jáchymova. Monogramista I. P. a dvorská reprezentace za Ludvíka Jagellonského krále uherského a českého," in: *Doba jagellonská v zemích české koruny (1471–1526)* (Praha: 2003), 133–151; Milena Hauserová, "Kostel sv. Jáchyma v Jáchymově. Architektura

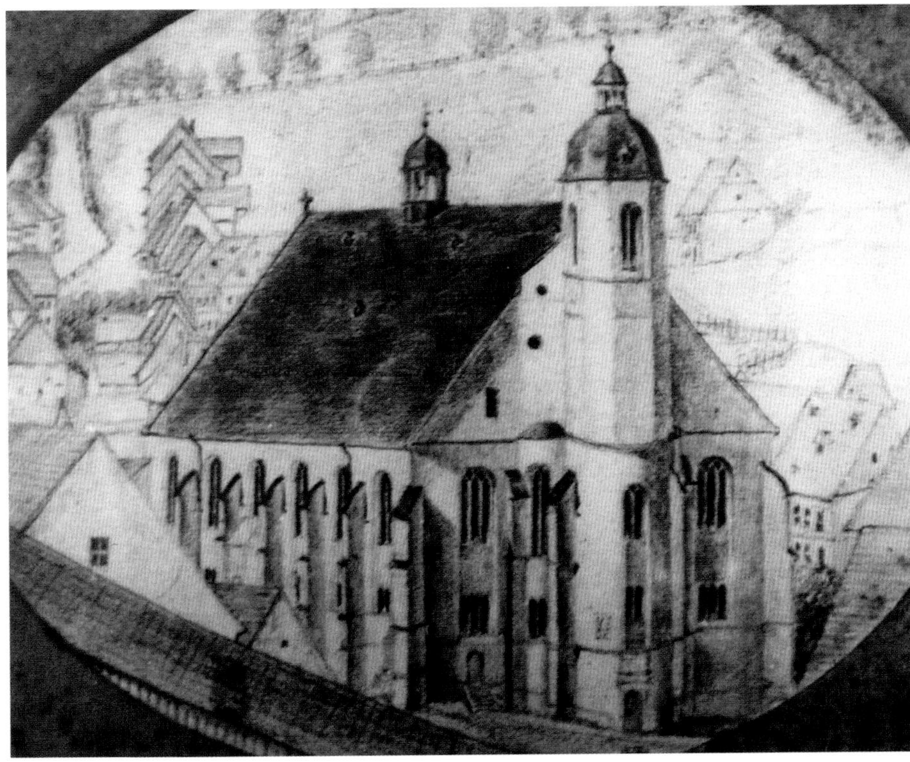

Fig. 68 Jáchymov, Church of St. Joachim and St. Anne in the depiction before the fire in 1873. Reproduction from the book Schmidt, R., Soupis památek historických a uměleckých v politickém okresu Jáchymovském. Praha 1913.

The first mass was celebrated in the church on St. Catherine's Day on 25 November 1537, at a time when the windows and gable walls had not yet been completed.[260] Once again, this demonstrates the fact that the construction of a church did not have to be completely finished before services could be held in it, as can be assumed in the case of the Church of St. Anne in Krupka. The edifice in Jáchymov was conceived as a hall church with three naves, a design based on layouts commonly used in Saxon Gothic churches, which were built chiefly for the puprose of preaching in Saxon towns. In appearance, it closely resembles the churches in Most, Annaberg, Schneeberg or Marienberg in Saxony. The tower on the main façade of the original Jáchymov church, the appearance of which is known from the drawings and plans made before the fire in the late 19th century, also looked similar to the towers on the Saxon churches. (Fig. 68) It was constructed, in keeping with the popular Renaissance design, as a polygonal structure on a circular foundation. This tower type, which became particularly common in the Ore Mountains in the late 16th century, was also used, for example, in the the completion of the Church of St. Lawrence in Horní Blatná. As this was a Reformation building, the chancel was not emphasised. In 1564, ten polygonal wooden columns without a tectonic function were placed in a unified space that had been lined with galleries around the entire perimeter. The columns were later decorated during the Baroque period. The windows were altered beyond recongition during a renovation in 1873. A total of 16 new main windows were complemented by Gothic-like ledges and topped by compressed pointed arches with tracery of two quatre-

skromného výrazu nebo torzo velkého konceptu?" in: Michaela Hrubá – Michaela Ottová – Jan Royt (ed.), *Ars Montana*, 271–291.

260) Lubomír Zeman – Alžběta Kratochvílová, *Kostel sv. Jáchyma*, 190.

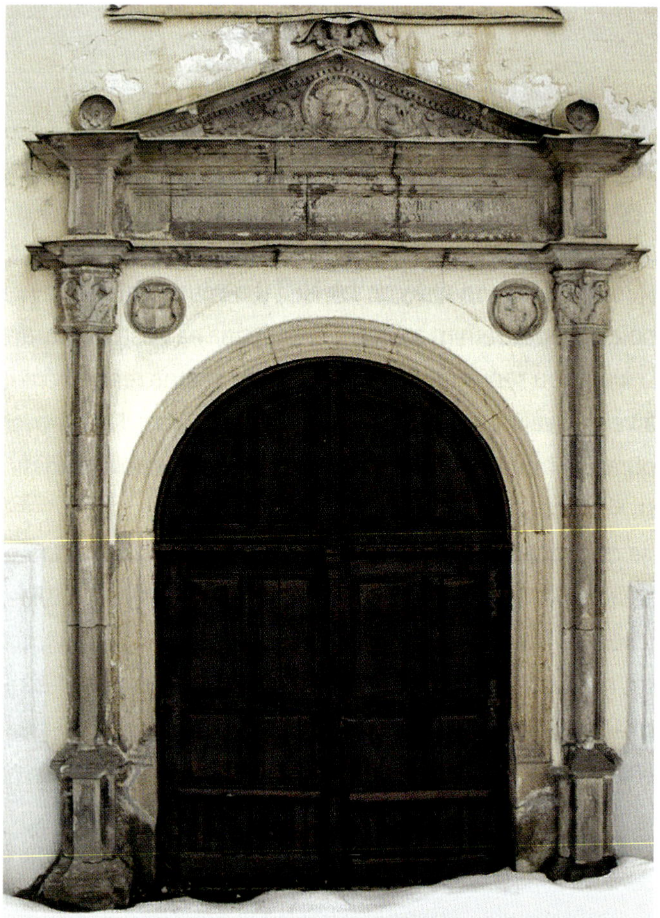

Fig. 69 Jáchymov, Church of St. Joachim and St. Anne, western portal to the church called Hornický with Schlick motifs. Photo © National Heritage Institute.

foils and one trefoil. The original windows were rectangular, each with a semicircular top and two stone mullions. The mullions used to be simply interlaced under the arch to resemble tracery, similar to the windows of the tower, which have been preserved. Originally, because the space under the galleries needed more light, there were 16 smaller, three-part windows under the large windows. They were bricked up during the renovation of 1873, since the new galleries were not put in after the old ones had been destroyed in the fire. Also preserved from the original 16th century building is a plinth ledge that runs the length of the church's perimeter and, where the terrain requires it, it is raised at right angles to the level necessary.

The dimensions of the church were probably dictated by the need to ensure capacity for the ever-growing population of the town and the surrounding area, which in its heyday reached an almost unbelievable number of five thousand.[261] According to the latest research, the monumental church with three naves was meant to be vaulted, but the vaults were never built. Instead, between 1564 and 1573, a set of massive wooden pillars were erected with the intention of supporting a presumably painted coffered ceiling. While the construction was under way, mining activity in Jáchymov began to decline. It probably also became clear that

261) Milena Hauserová, "Luteránský kostel," in: Tomáš Karel – Alžběta Kratochvílová (ed.), *Proměny montánní krajiny. Historické sídelná a montánní struktury Krušnohoří* (Loket: 2013), 87–89.

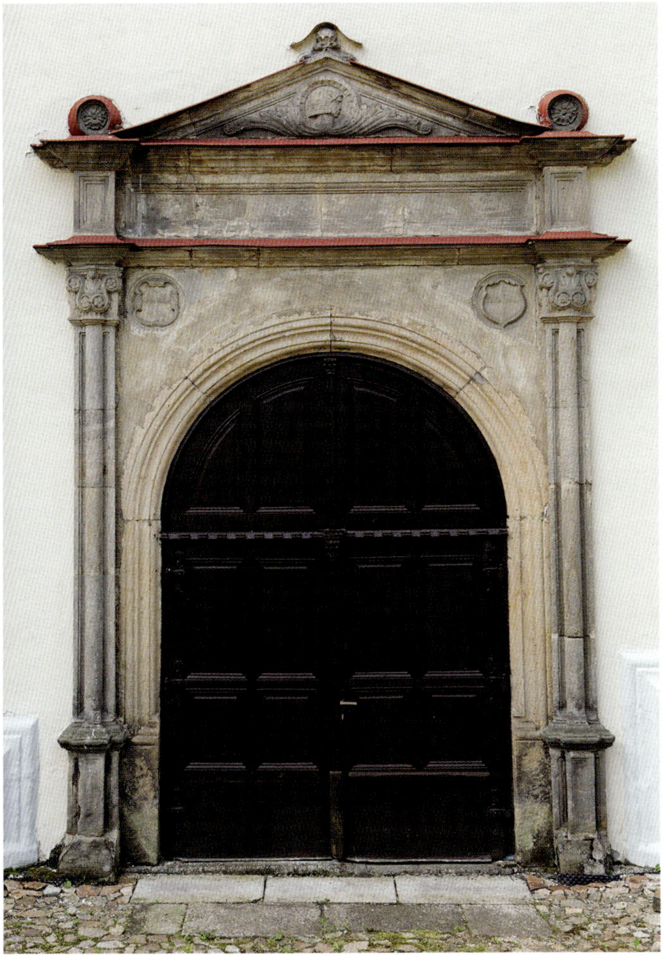

Fig. 70 Jáchymov, Church of St. Joachim and St. Anne, northern portal to the church. Photograph by J. Peer (2019).

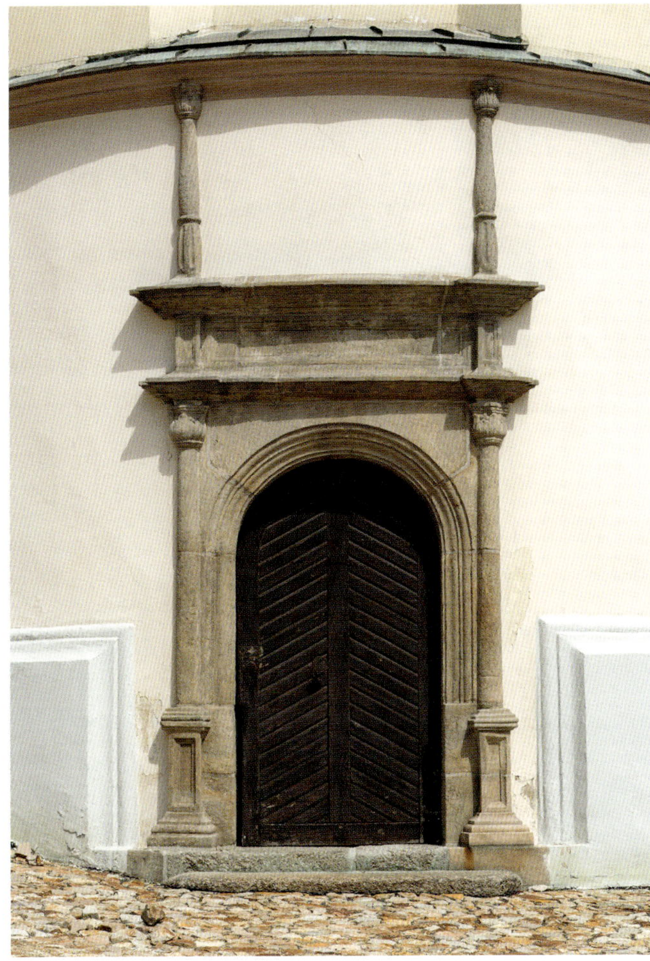

Fig. 71 Jáchymov, Church of St. Joachim and St. Anne, portal to the sacristy of the church. Photograph by J. Peer (2019).

a hall church with three naves and a ribbed vault might be too complicated, considering the small width of the perimeter walls, and the original concept was abandoned. A design featuring a flat-roofed ceiling was more within the town's budget, since its mining activity and thus also its economic prosperity were starting to wane.[262]

The church has three portals. The main portal is on the north side, while the side portals are in the east and west façades. The most splendid is the portal on the western façade, called the miners' portal, which faces towards the Svornost (Unity) shaft that used to be a symbol of the wealth of Jáchymov and the Schlick family. (Fig. 69) The portal is the work of Georg of Bamberg and consists of a pair of columns with capitals decorated with the dolphin motifs, which is a reference to Christ in the spirit of the early Christian tradition. A frieze is placed

262) Milena Hauserová, "Luteránský kostel," in: Tomáš Karel – Alžběta Kratochvílová (ed.), *Proměny montánní krajiny. Historické sídelná a montánní struktury Krušnohoří* (Loket: 2013), 86. Lindner's Chronicle of Jáchymov explicitly states that the original intention was to build a vaulted ceiling, but the masonry was too fragile to support it, and flat ceilings were built instead. Lubomír Zeman – Alžběta Kratochvílová, *Kostel sv. Jáchyma*, 190.

on the columns, with a plaque that bears a memorial inscription in Latin composed in 1536 by the humanist Johann Neff: *'HVNC PIETAS REGISQVE FAVOR ATQVE INCLITA VIRTVS ORBARVNT / VITA CONIVGE ET IMPERIO D(OMINVS) STEPHANVS SCHLICK COMES ZG AN(NO) 1526 AESTIS 40.'* The portal is topped with a triangular pediment with a medallion in the likeness of Stephan Schlick, inspired by his portrait on a medal by Oldřich Gebhart or David Ederlein. Schlick's face, turned to the left, is characterised by a short beard. He is wearing a flat hat with a wide brim and his hair is covered with a calotte. The sides of the medallion bear his cornucopia fused with a curved swirl, from the mouth of which a dolphin emerges. The circular medallions in the spandrels of the portal have empty escutcheons that probably originally bore the painted coats of arms of Stephan Schlick and his wife, Margaretha von Rabenstein. It is clear from the decorations that the portal is really an epitaph of the deceased founder of the town, Stephan Schlick.

The same escutcheons adorn the other two portals. The triangular escutcheon of both the north and east portals displays a medallion with the portrait of a beardless soldier in profile, wearing a helmet with a raised visor. (Fig. 70) There is also a small, semicircular portal, with the original frame preserved around the door to the sacristy in the western wall, right by the southern corner. At the top of the arch, the emblem of the Schlicks' Bossano estate is carved in an escutcheon that unfolds from above.[263] (Fig. 71)

The church interior was articulated with galleries and had rich Renaissance and Baroque furnishings, most of which were destroyed in the fire of 1873, which also destroyed the interior as well as the truss and a large part of the perimeter walls.[264]

Perhaps the most significant monument was the large panelled altarpiece, commissioned in 1545 in the Wittemberg workshop of Lucas Cranach the Younger by Hieronymus and Lorenz Schlick in honour of the founder of the town, Stephan Schlick. According to reports of its appearance we can assume it was inspired by the Reformation ideas of Martin Luther.[265] We know it from the description and outline drawn by the Jáchymov priest Lindner in *Liber memorabilis*. (Fig. 72)

The retable was conceived as a polyptych with a central panel, fixed and movable wings, a retable and a predella. The central panel bore a depiction of the Crucifixion with Christ on the cross between the thieves and multiple onlookers. Apparently, there were also Jewish scholars berating the Saviour. In the middle distance of the painting is a depiction of Christ's journey to Calvary. On the inner side of the left movable wing was a painting of Christ's Resurrection, and the right wing had the image of Christ praying on the Mount of Olives. The outer side of the left wing was decorated with the figure of Moses with the tablets of the law in his hand, personifying the time of the Law, while the outer side of the right wing was dominated by Jesus as

263) Jan Klípa – Michaela Ottová (ed.), *Bez Hranic*, 670; Jiří Fajt, *Na paměť statečného a zbožného Štěpána Schlicka (†1526), zakladatele Jáchymova*, 146; Pavel Kašpar – Vladimír Horák, *Schlikové a dobývání stříbra* (Praha: 2009), 32.
264); Jan Royt, "Jáchymov, reformace a umění," in: *Gotické umění a jeho historické souvislosti I. Ústecký sborník historický* 2001 (Ústí nad Labem: 2002), 351–359.
265) Jan Royt, *Gotické deskové malířství v severozápadních Čechách* (Praha: 2015), 57–60.

Fig. 72 Jáchymov, Church of St. Joachim and St. Anne, drawing of Cranach's burnt altar. Reproduction from the book by Schmidt, R., Soupis památek historických a uměleckých v politickém okresu Jáchymovském. Praha 1913.

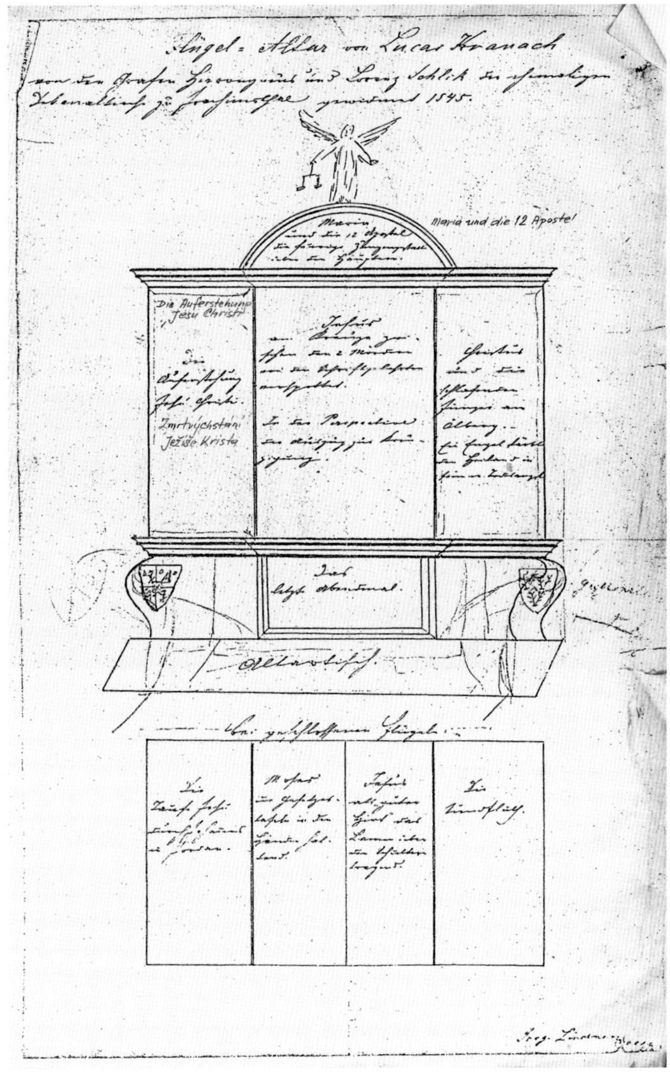

the Good Shepherd with lambs, representing the time of God's grace and man's justification by faith. On the left fixed wing was the Baptism of Christ in the river Jordan, where water serves as the element that cleanses man from sin. On the right fixed wing was the deluge, where water acts as the element that punishes sinners. In the segmental attachment of the central panel, the Descent of the Holy Spirit was depicted. At the top of the retable was a statue of the Archangel Michael weighing the souls – a symbol of the Last Judgment. The predella with the motif of the Last Supper had an intriguing iconography. Besides the apostles, representatives of the Reformation including Martin Luther, the Saxon Elector Frederick the Wise and even the painter Lucas Cranach the Elder and his son, sat down to the sacred feast. In the right corner of the predella was Cranach's signature in the form of a winged dragon. The reverse side of the free-standing altar also had painted decoration. According to the description, it depicted God the Father with the following inscriptions: *'Ich glaube in Gott Vater, allmechtigen Scheppfer Himmels und der Erden,'* and *'Decret unicenoe Synodi / contra Cikoma Caus hub. / Centant. Ao 787/ Jus: ipsa: Nam Deus est quod imago docet. Sed non Deus: / Hancvideas sed mentecolasquodcernis in ipsa, ars moriendi'* – referring to the last things of man, the Last Judgment with the Kingdom

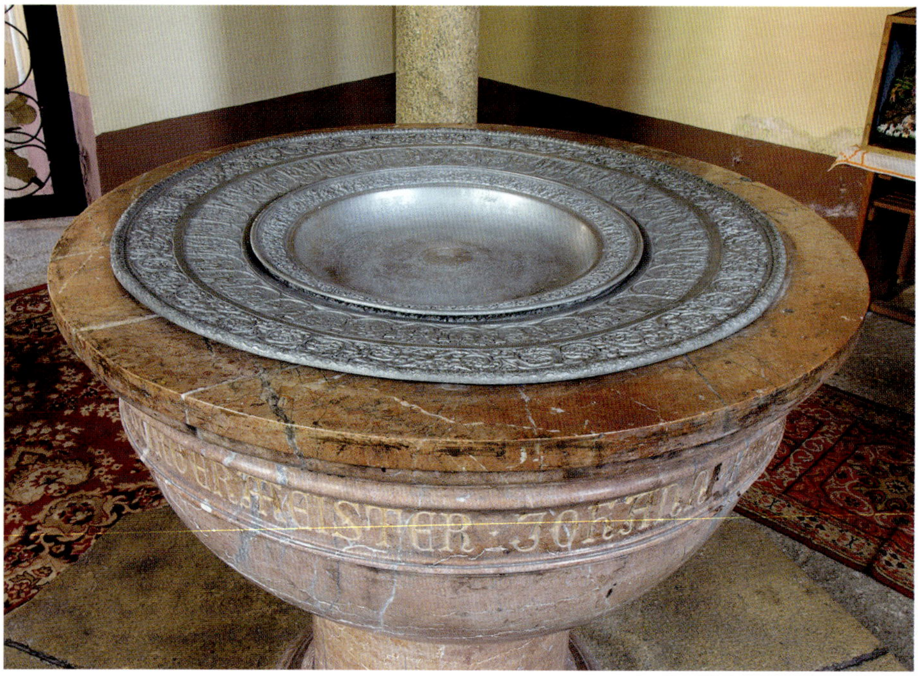

Fig. 73 Jáchymov, Church of St. Joachim and St. Anne, silver wreath of the original baptismal font, Hans Wildt, 1575. Photo © National Heritage Institute.

of Heaven, and interestingly also various episodes from the life of the miners in Jáchymov. There was also a depiction of the founder of Jáchymov, Count Stephan Schlick. We can get an idea of what the burnt altar in Jáchymov looked like from the existing Cranach altar in the parish church of St. Wolfgang, in the Saxon mining town of Schneeberg. [266]

According to Boehm's description, there used to be eight Renaissance epitaphs in the church. Three of them supposedly had paintings by Albrecht Dürer, which is possible given the wealth of Jáchymov's mining entrepreneurs.[267] Other valuable furnishings were also destroyed, including a silver pulpit supported by the figure of a miner. It is interesting to note that in the Lutheran church, burgher and mine investor Andreas Selttenreich, had a Tomb of the Lord built from silver ore in 1559 and, a year later, a wealthy burgher named Nickel Militz purchased a silver statue depicting the 'Ascension of the Lord,' presumably Christ Triumphant. The body of Christ on the altar of the Holy Cross was also made of silver. According to a report from 1863, the fire in the church was so intense that the silver from the melted relics flowed all the way to the Royal Mint across the street.

Of the original Renaissance furnishings of St. Joachim's Church, a panel painting of St. Christopher, modelled on a drawing by Lucas Cranach the Elder, was almost miraculously preserved. It is currently kept in the Museum in Karlovy Vary. According to the description of the Jáchymov Dean A. P. Boehm, the painting used to hang on the Epistle side of the church. Later it was moved to the Hospital (Cemetery) Church of All Saints.[268] Also preserved was

266) Heinrich Magirius, *Schneeberg, St. Wolfgang* (Passau: 1996), 18–25; Heinrich Magirius – Christian Kelm – Martin Eisbein – Martin Mühlfriedel – Lucas Mühlfriedel, "Der Cranachaltar in der St. Wolfgangskirche zu Schneeberg," in: *Zeitschrift für Kunsttechnologie und Konservierung* 6 (1992), 298–314.

267) Anton Boehm, *Gedächtnis Beitrag über die k. freye Bergstadt Joachimstahl, 1. Teil 1525–1699*, 297–304.

268) Jan Klípa – Michaela Ottová (ed.), *Bez Hranic*, 675; Magdaléna Hamsíková, *Recepce díla Lucase Cranacha st. v malířství první poloviny 16. století v Čechách* (PhD diss., Charles University, 2011), 273–275.

a Renaissance baptismal wreath made of cast tin, which is now mounted on a new baptismal font. (Fig. 73) It is a remarkable work decorated with ornamental and figural reliefs, which was cast in 1575 by the Jáchymov tinsmith, bell-maker and blacksmith Hans Wildt. It was probably commissioned by Hans Roth, a wealthy burgher of Jáchymov, as his coat of arms with the initials HR and the date of 1575 indicate.

The outer bands of the wreath are covered with geometric patterns, and palm leaf and acanthus ornaments. The central part is composed of two smooth panels divided into 35 fields by arcades with baluster columns, in which seven scenes from the Passion are repeated five times: Christ on the Mount of Olives, The Arrest of Christ, Jesus before Caiaphas, Christ Crowned with Thorns, Pilate Washing his Hands, Christ Carrying the Cross, Calvary. The outer smooth edge of the wreath bears the emblem of Jáchymov and the master signature of Hans Wildt: a bell and the initials 'H W.' (Fig. 74)

Two bays of a Renaissance grille railing, which was built in the early 17th century around the baptismal font in the south corner by the old sacristy, are also part of the original furnishings.

The Church of St. Joachim was meant to serve as the Schlick family mausoleum. Sadly, the 1541 tombstone (damaged in a church fire) of Lorenz Schlick's first wife, Katherine of Wartenberk, has not been preserved. The figure of the deceased used to be surrounded by eight circular medallions with portraits bearing the names Joannes, Veronice, Catharina, Adam, Christoph, Susanna, Stephan and Eleonora. The tombstone bore the inscription: '*Dum gravidod ub iumtent aret coporepartum, Inclytacum foetuproh. Caharinaperit. Obiit VII. Kalenda May Anno Domini M. D. XLI.*' Of the entire tombstone, set into the sacristy wall, only a sandstone portrait medallion survives. It is 0.33 metres in diameter and contains a relief of a boy's head and the inscription STEFAN (Stephan Schlick). (Fig. 75)

Other Renaissance tombstones have been preserved in the interior of the church. A much damaged sandstone tombstone from 1575, measuring 1.80 x 0.75 metres, is situated in the pavement under the organ loft. However, the upper left half of the stone is broken off, and

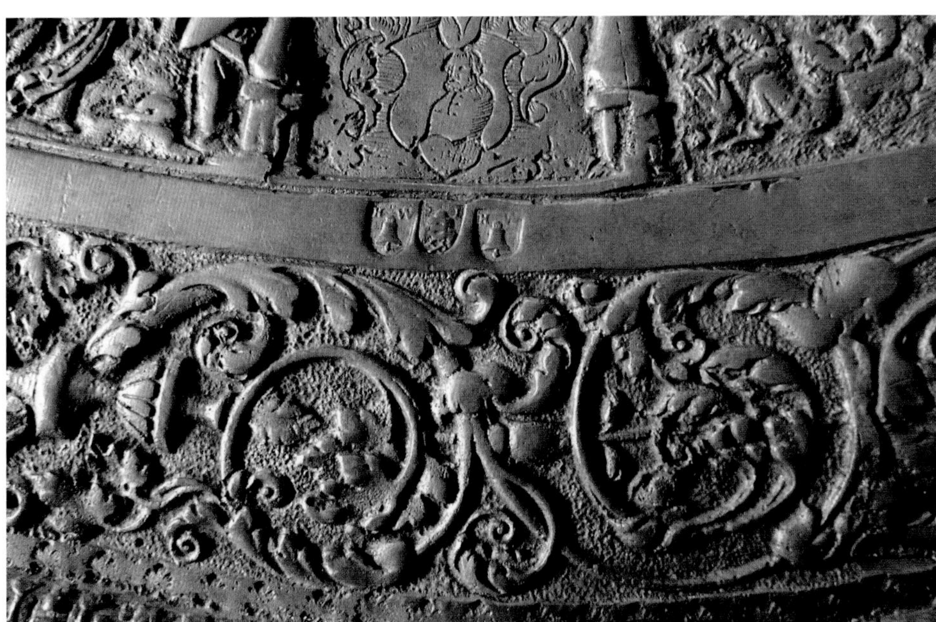

Fig. 74 Jáchymov, Church of St. Joachim and St. Anne, detail of the decoration of the silver wreath of the original baptismal font. Photograph by J. Royt (2019).

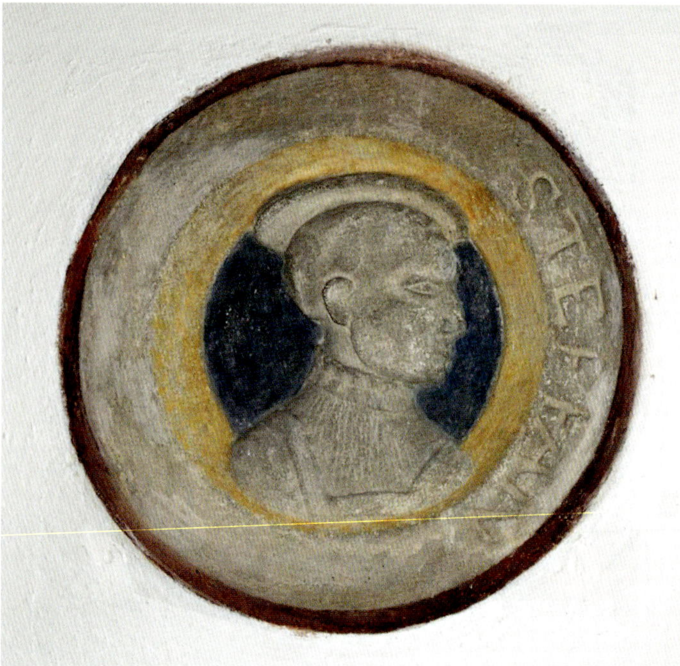

Fig. 75 Jáchymov, Church of St. Joachim and St. Anne, portrait relief medallion of Stephan Schlick secondarily set into the sacristy wall. Created in 1541, a fragment of the tombstone of Lorenz Schlick's first wife, Katherine of Vartenberk. Photograph by J. Royt (2019).

the emblem and inscription are almost completely worn away, leaving only disconnected remnants of letters. The tombstone was created in memory of the first imperial secretary of the court chamber, Kaspar Geitzkofler of Greifenegg, who died on 15 October 1575 in Karlovy Vary at the age of 44 and was brought to Jáchymov for burial in the dean's church.

Another tombstone, made of red marble in 1613 and measuring 1.95 x 1.05 metres, is set in the wall between the west portal and the altar of St. Joseph. There is a plaque with an insription at the top and an ornate emblem in a quadruple circle at the bottom. The lettering, partly illegible, reads: '…*Monats Oktrobris gegen morgen umb / Ein Uhr Anno 1613*…' and there is a quotation from Isaiah, c. 26.

The current neo-Gothic interior furnishings date from the period between 1876 and 1884 and were made by the Viennese sculptor Lehner. The elaborately-carved wooden altars and pulpit are painted and partially gilded.

The Jáchymov cemetery church, previously the **parish and hospital church of All Saints**, which was built in 1516–1520 and then covered with a flat ceiling in 1533, was abundantly decorated with works of art. (Fig. 76) This date is inscribed on one of the buttresses. The church is a single-nave rectangular building directly adjoing a chancel. It is covered by a high gable roof, which is slanted above the polygonal chancel and topped with a cupola tower. It is the oldest preserved half-timbered church in the western Ore Mountains. In 1520, a bell was cast for the church in the Jáchymov foundry of Hans Wildt. In the same year the organ was delivered, made by the organ builders Blasius and Antonius Lehmann of Bautzen.[269]

269) Jan Klípa – Michaela Ottová (ed.), *Bez Hranic*, 671; Lubomír Zeman, "Objekty s hrázděnou konstrukcí saského typu v západním Krušnohoří," in: *Historický sborník Karlovarska* 10 (2004), 42–61; Lubomír Zeman, *Stavební vývoj města Jáchymova*, 29–30.

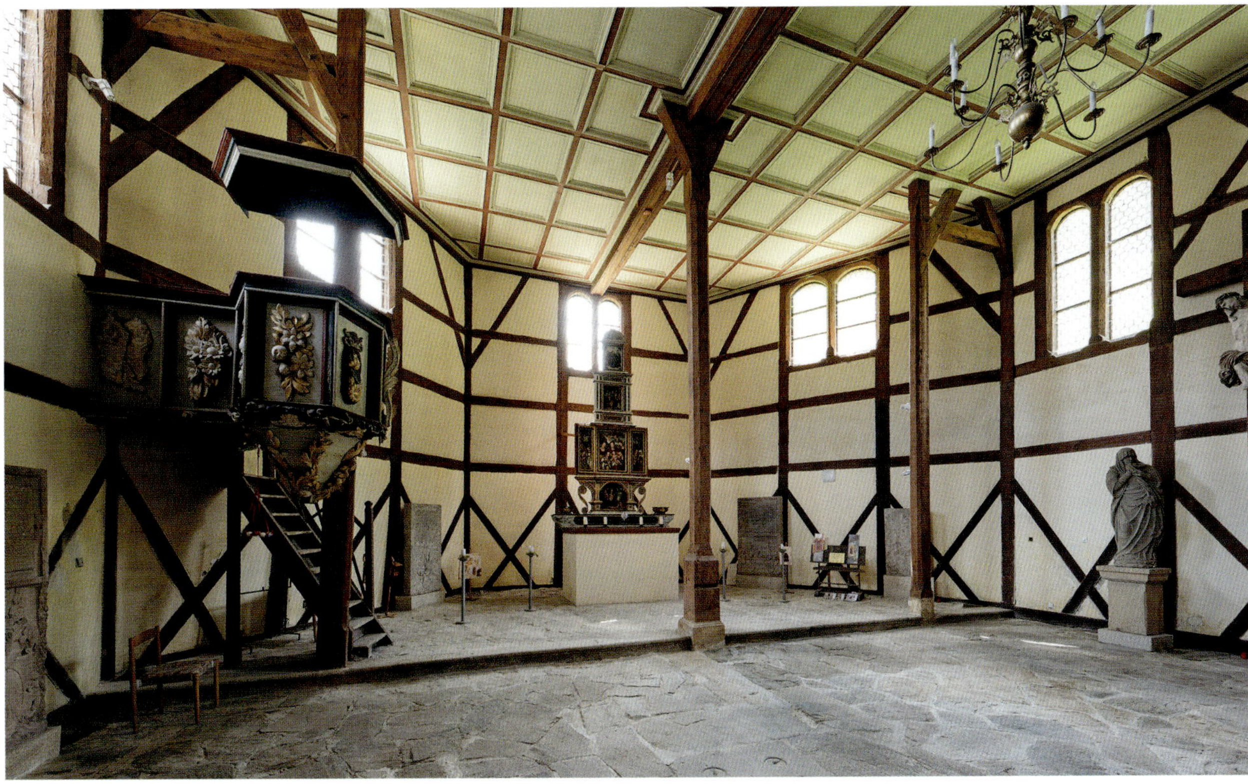

Fig. 76 Jáchymov, Church of All Saints, interior of the church with the main altar. Photo by J. Peer (2019).

Around 1519, a retable with the main theme of the Betrothal of St. Catherine was made for its high altar. (Fig. 77) Interestingly, three artists of different orientation were involved in its creation. On the inside of the left movable wing is the Annunciation and on the inside of the right movable wing is the Visitation. (Fig. 78)

The panel with the Annunciation bears the emblem of the altar's commissioner – the well-known Jáchymov governor and mintmaster, Heinrich von Könneritz (1483–1551). The Visitation panel bears the emblem of his wife. On the outside of the left wing is the figure of St. John the Evangelist, while the outside of the right wing depicts St. James the Elder. The two-part retable bears a depiction of the Death of the Virgin Mary at the bottom and the Coronation of the Virgin Mary at the top, both modelled on Albrecht Dürer's drawings (from the cycle The Life of the Virgin Mary, 1510). The predella shows the Adoration of the Magi. The central panel, which is of the highest artistic quality, was acquired by the commissioner of the altar directly from Cranach's workshop, as it is a replica of a panel lost during the war from the Kaiser Friedrich Museum in Berlin. The Adoration of the Magi must be the work of a painter versed in the Upper Rhine painting style. The altar is complemented by white-painted Baroque statues of St. Joseph and St. Joachim.[270]

Könneritz was also the donor of the altar in the funeral chapel in Lobstädt, which he commissioned from Cranach's workshop. An important monument of the church is the stonework

270) Jan Klípa – Michaela Ottová (ed.), *Bez Hranic*, 672–674; Magdaléna Hamsíková, *Recepce díla Lucase Cranacha*, 271–273.

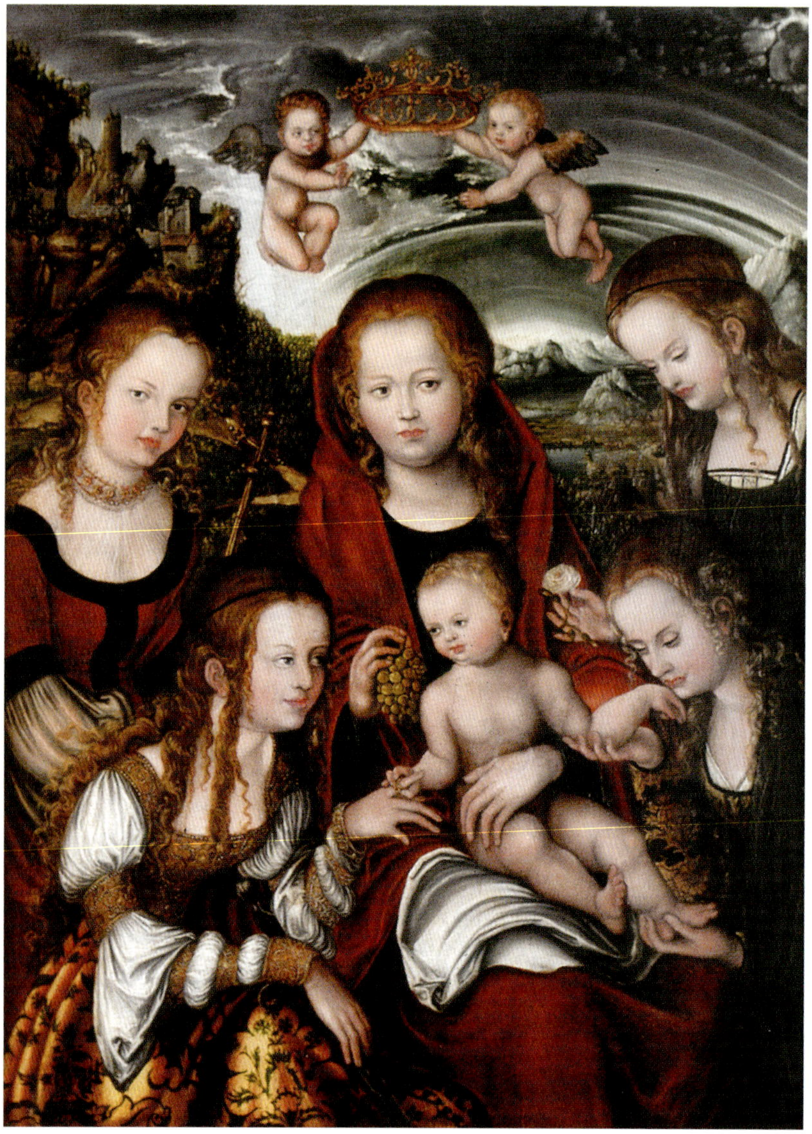

Fig. 77 Jáchymov, Church of All Saints, detail of the main altar with the central panel with the motif of the Visitation of the Virgin Mary. Cranach's workshop (central panel only), early 16th century. Photograph by J. Royt (2019).

of Calvary with the Virgin Mary and St. John the Evangelist, created by the Dresden sculptor Christoph Walter in 1544. It was moved to its current location from the shrine in the enclosure wall in front of the church. Originally, the Calvary probably stood in the cemetery.

There are a number of tombstones and painted epitaphs from the second half of the 16th and the first half of the 17th century in the church interior, which were commissioned by wealthy mining officials and shaft owners. A richly decorated epitaph of J. Pullacher from 1598, which served as a side altar, was placed against the left lateral wall. In the central part of the altar was a painting of the Laying in the Grave by an artist familiar with the painting style of the Low Countries. The predella depicts the deceased adoring the Lamb of God, and two miners. On the right wall of the chancel a side altar was placed that was made from an epitaph of an unknown family from 1598. Its dominant theme is a painting of the Resurrection of Christ (sig. A. F. 1598) that betrays the painter's inspiration by Italian Mannerism. The lower part of the painting shows the coats of arms of the Uttmann and Lerchenfeld families.

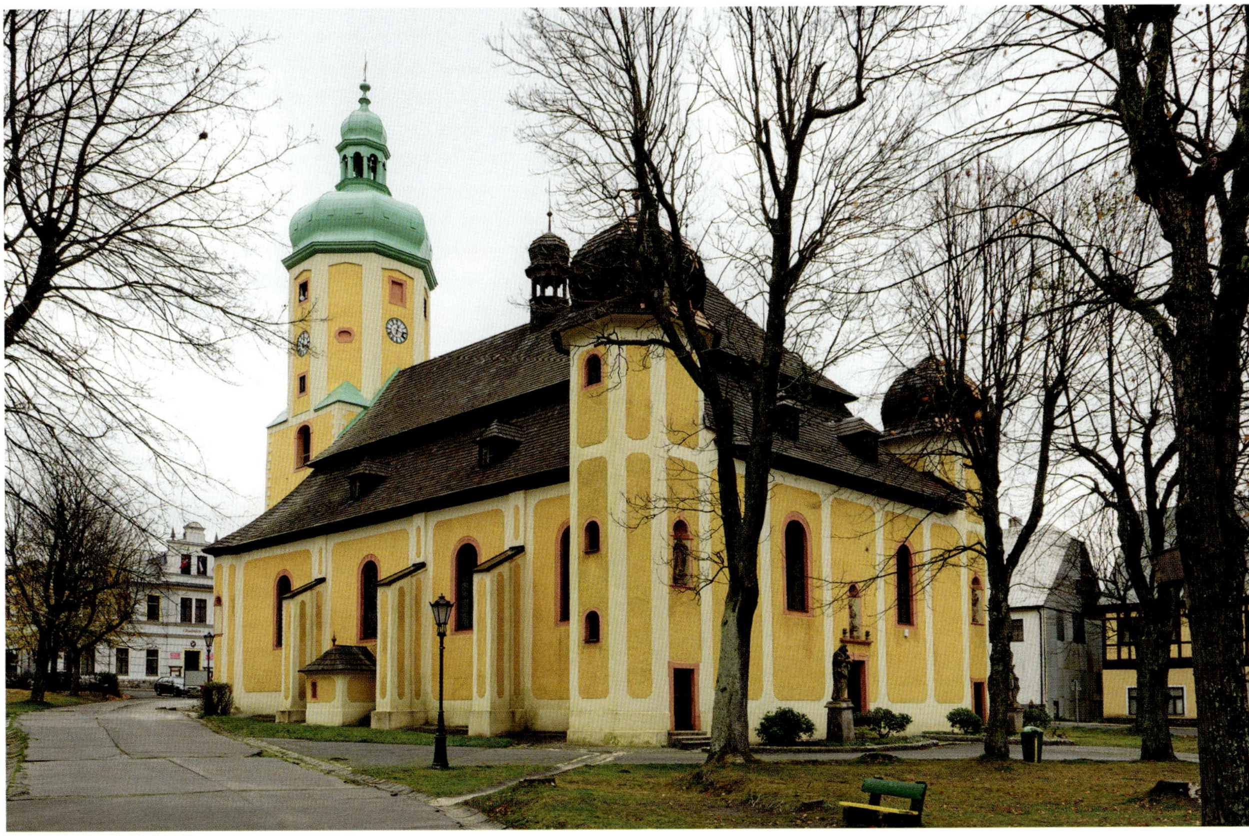

Fig. 78 Horní Blatná, Church of St. Lawrence, general view from the west. Construction 1593–1594, tower added 1605–1607, rebuilt in Baroque style around 1754. Photograph by J. Peer (2019).

The epitaph of the rich mine owner Pavel Beer the Elder from 1604 was placed on the long southwestern wall of the nave. A painting depicting the Conversion of St. Paul is set into it. The predella shows male and female members of the Beer family adoring the crucifix. A predella of the epitaph of the mintmaster Ruprecht Pullacher (died 1563) also used to be hung on that wall. The upper part of the epitaph was transferred to the Church of St. Joachim, where it burnt down in a fire in 1873. A Renaissance epitaph of the children of the mintmaster Centurius Lengenfelder from 1610 was hung on the gallery parapet. The epitaphs of Susanna Schedlich (1638) and Jacob Schedlich (1665) date from the transitional period between the Renaissance and the Baroque.[271]

Another example of a church that was built from scratch by the Lutherans is **St. Lawrence's Church in Horní Blatná**. (Fig. 79) The current church was built on the site of an older wooden church that stood on a stone foundation, which collapsed in 1542 as a result of the undermining of the building by the Holy Spirit shaft. Between 1593 and 1594, a massive stone church was built, originally without a frontal tower, which was added between 1605 and 1607.

271) Richard Schmidt, *Soupis památek historických a uměleckých*, 45–68; Emanuel Poche et al., *UPČ 1*, 564–565; Jan Royt, "Horní město Jáchymov, reformace a umění," in: *Gotické umění a jeho souvislosti I.*, *Ústecký sborník historický 2001*, 351–359; Jan Royt, *Gotické deskové malířství v severozápadních Čechách* (Praha: 2015), 60; Anton Boehm, *Gedächtnis Beitrag über die k. freye Bergstadt Joachimstahl, 1. Teil 1525–1699*, 297–304.

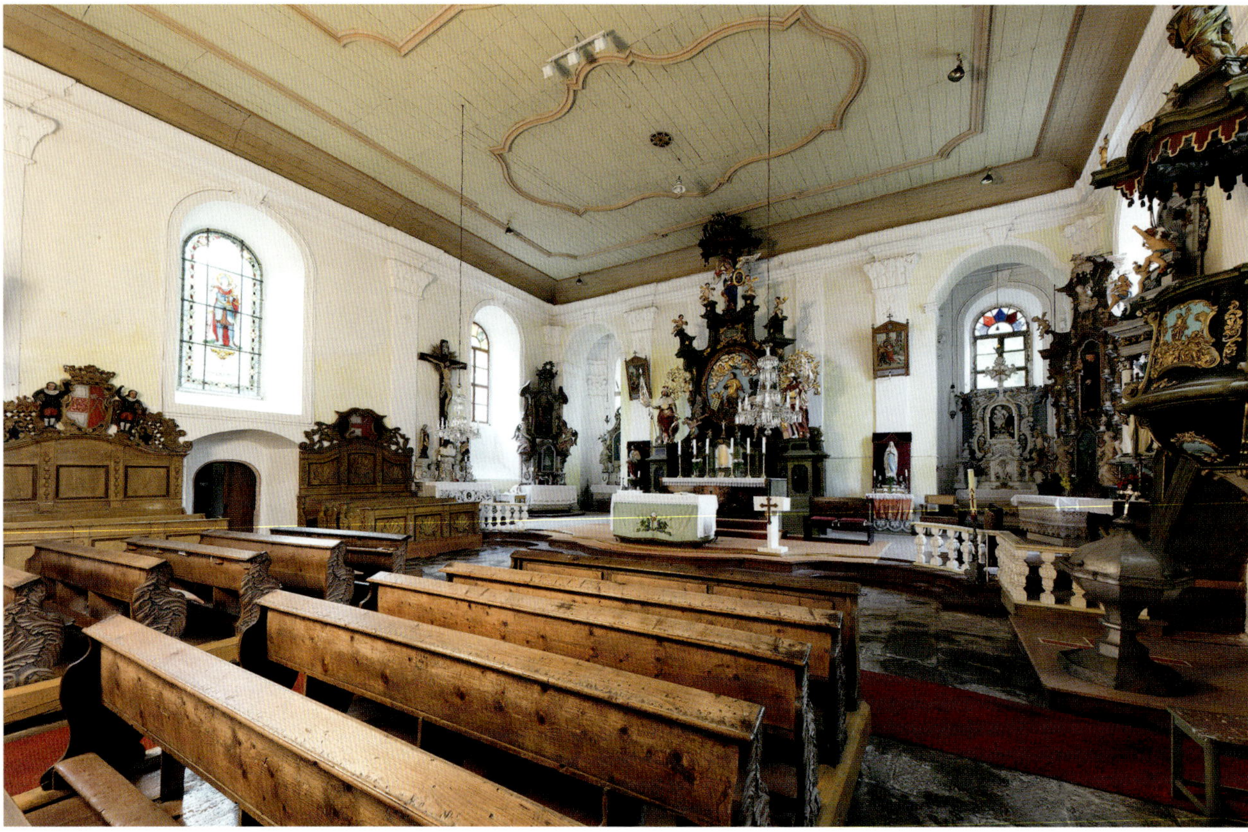

Fig. 79 Horní Blatná, Church of St. Lawrence, interior view from the west. Photograph by J. Peer (2019).

The church was built according to Saxon models, but its appearance and layout resemble more the late Renaissance sacral buildings of the Saxon Renaissance. For that reason, it does not belong in the broader category of historicising churches of Gothic that are common in the Ústí nad Labem (Aussig) region. The church in Horní Blatná is a flat-roofed single-nave building with a two small spires in the corners. (Fig. 80) In terms of layout and an almost square-shaped nave, the church looks strikingly like a Renaissance fortress with corner towers. The shape of the tower is also in keeping with Renaissance design principles, in that it is a polygonal shape on a square ground plan.

Another interesting detail is the fact that the church remained Protestant until 1686, when it was reconsecrated as a Catholic church by order of the Archbishop of Prague. The only reminder of the original Lutheran church is the tin baptismal font, renovated according to an inscription in 1680. (Fig. 81) The late Baroque statue of St. Anne, the patron saint of miners, and the patronage bench decorated with figures of miners from after 1700 are reminders of the village's mining history.[272] (Fig. 82)

In addition to the sacral buildings already mentioned, which have been at least partially preserved in their original state, or otherwise their appearance can be found in the preserved descriptions, there were churches and chapels in many towns and villages, whose architectural

272) Emanuel Poche et al., *UPČ 1*, 402.

Fig. 80 Horní Blatná, Church of St. Lawrence, tin font from the original equipment of the Lutheran congregation. Photograph by J. Peer (2019).

Fig. 81 Horní Blatná, Church of St. Lawrence, patronal bench with figures of miners. Photograph by J. Peer (2019).

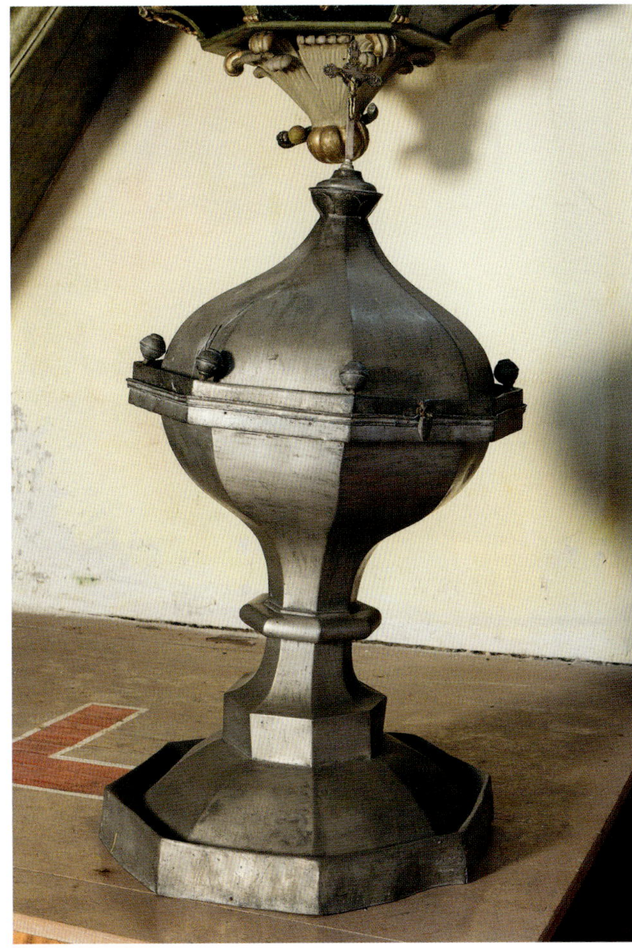

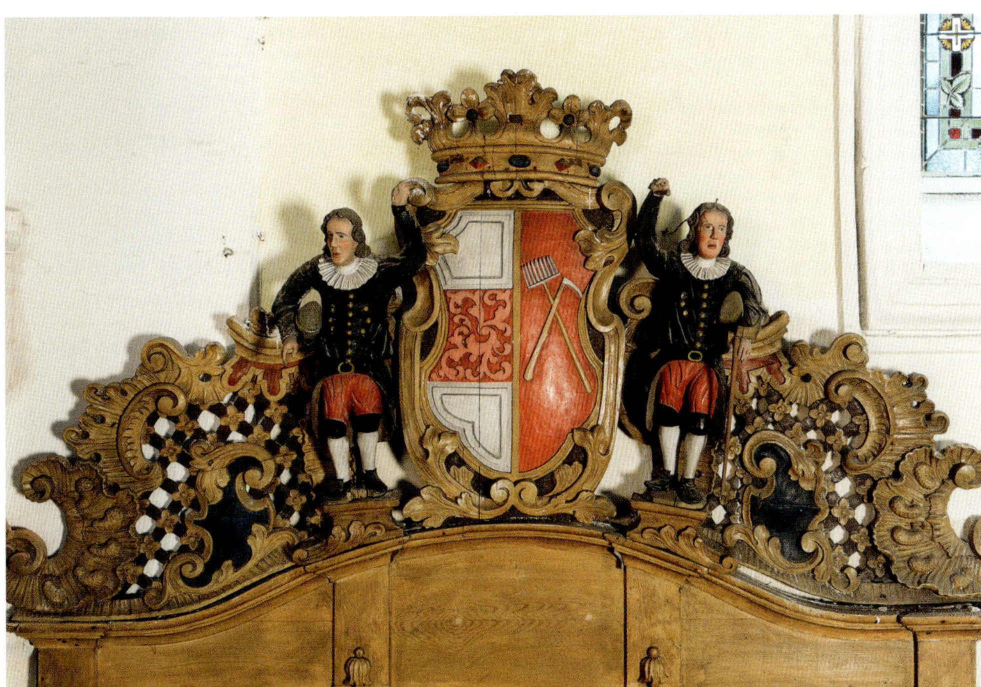

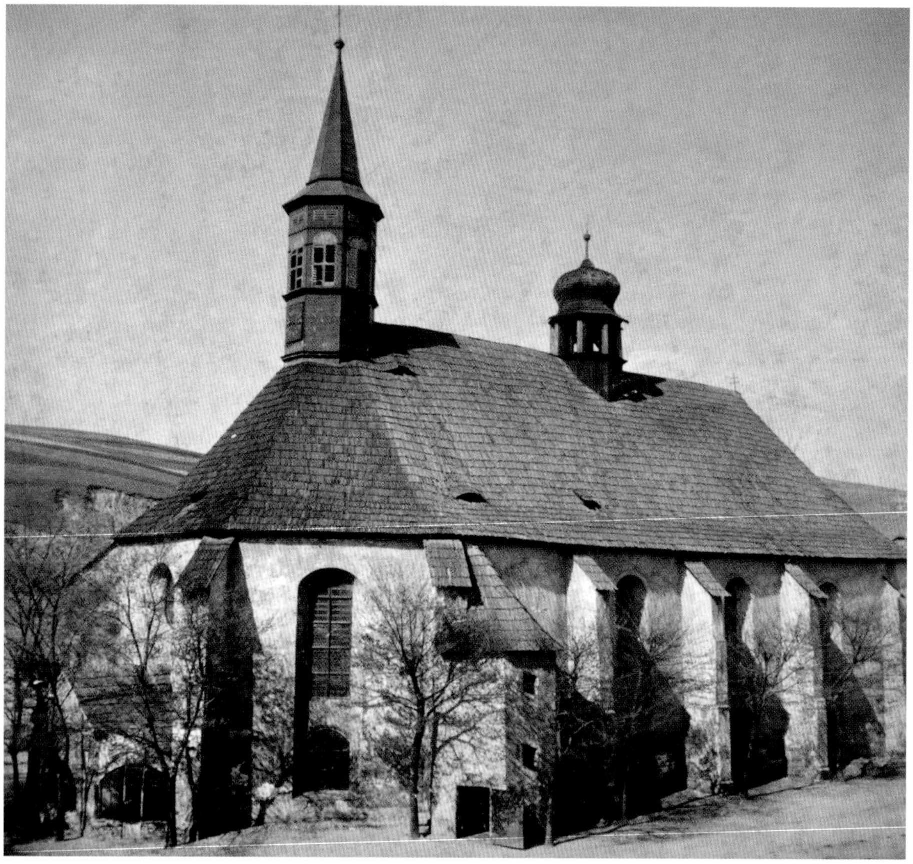

Fig. 82 Kraslice, Church of Corpus Christi, old Renaissance church before reconstruction in the late 19th century. Construction 1614–1619, replaced by a new building 1892–1896. Photos from the book Prokop, V. – Smola, L., Sokolovsko – Umění památky a umělci do roku 1945. Loket 2014.

appearance from the most famous period of mining activity in the Erzgebirge is either not preserved at all, or has been fatally changed by later reconstructions. In many of the transformed buildings, however, marginal parts of the original form or individual interior furnishings have been preserved, which provide a window on the glorious mining past.

The complex and turbulent historical development of the mining towns also had a bearing on the religious life of their people. A majority of the population quickly converted to the Reformed religion with a preference for Lutheranism, which resulted in the rebuilding of older churches.

A good example is the **Church of St. Martin at Nejdek**, commissioned by Peter Plick and built between 1341 and 1364.[273] This High-Gothic church was reconstructed around 1513, when the Schlicks owned the town. From 1562 until 1624, the church was used for Lutheran services. The last Lutheran parish priest, Valentin Löw of Adorf, left Nejdek in 1624. But it took until 1627 for a new Catholic parish priest, Georg Braun, to be installed, owing to the complicated process of re-Catholicisation. The church had a brief Protestant period in 1631, when the Protestant clergyman Zachary Adle held services in the church, following the Saxon invasion of Bohemia. After the departure of the Saxons, the church became definitively Catholic.[274]

273) Josef Pilz, *Geschichte der Stadt Neudek* (Neudek: 1923), 30.
274) Ibid., 76–79.

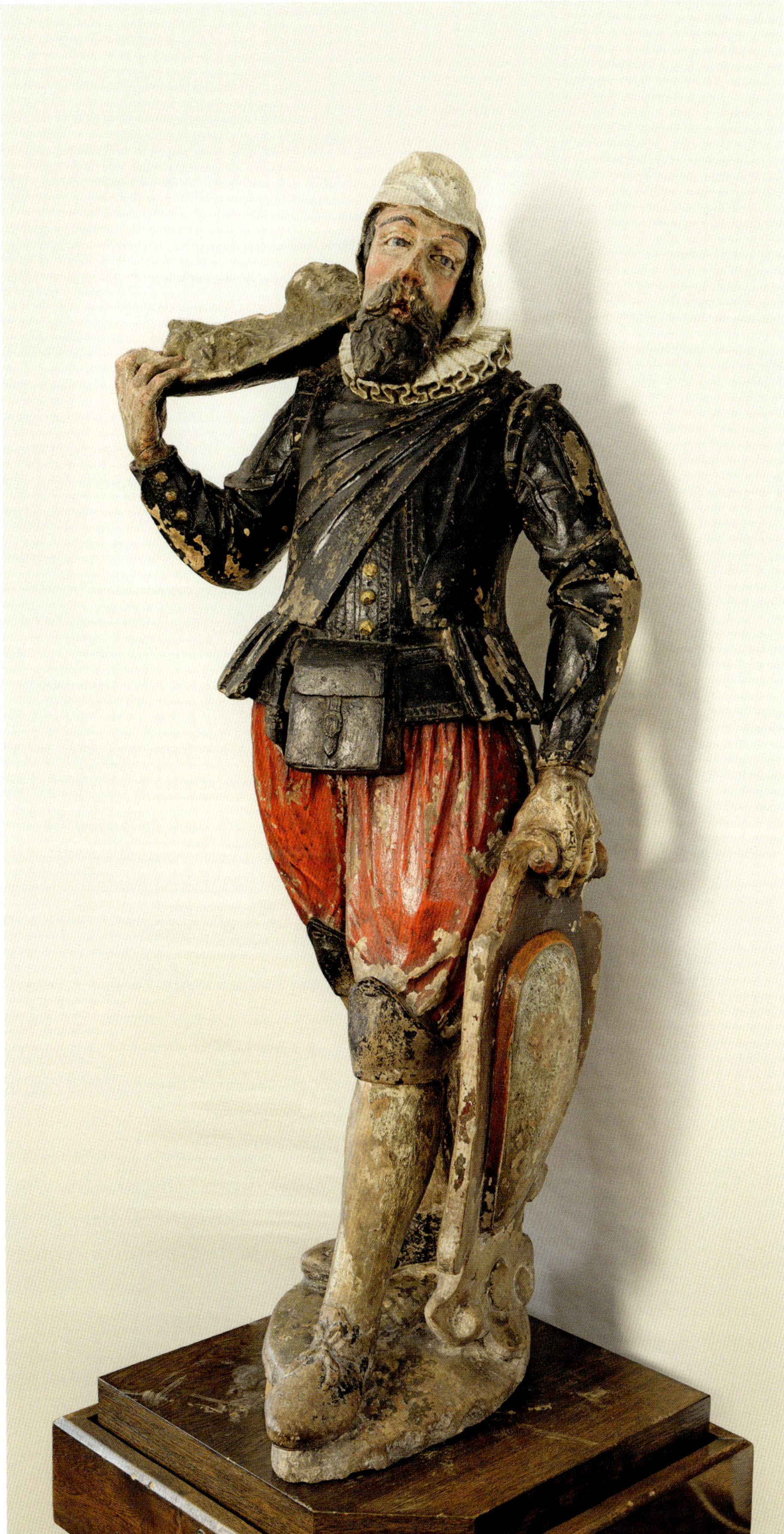

Fig. 83 The figure of a miner made of marlite from the pulpit of the old Renaissance Church of Corpus Christi in Kraslice. Photograph by J. Peer (2019).

The present appearance of the church dates back to 1755/1756. Some members of the Schlick family, such as Christoph Schlick, were buried inside the church. The main altar of the church was brought to Nejdek in 1779 from the closed Servite church in Prague. The church also contains statues of the patrons of miners, St. Joachim and St. Anne, and the altar of St. John of Nepomuk.[275]

The town of **Kraslice** went through a similar series of events. The oldest sacred building in the town was the **miners' church of the Corpus Christi**, which had been built as a fully wooden structure in the 14th century. (Fig. 83) By the end of the 16th century, however, it had become so structurally unsound that a decision was made to replace it with a new building. A collection for a new church was announced in Saxony. Since the townspeople subscribed to Lutheranism, the new church was built as a Lutheran place of worship with galleries. The foundation stone was laid on 10 July 1614 and the church was completed in 1619.[276]

A chapel of the Corpus Christi was established by the church. Galleries were put it the interior, with square wooden fillings on the parapets, decorated with biblically themed paintings. The church had a remarkable mining-themed pulpit. The parapet of the pulpit with the figures of the evangelists was supported by the figure of a miner made of gaize (now in the museum in Sokolov). (Fig. 84) It was commissioned in 1624 by the rich miner Johann Meyenschein from Nuremberg. In the 1880s, the church building began to show structural defects and had to be demolished and replaced by a new church. This was built in the Neo-Romanesque style between 1892 and 1896.

In the village of **Sněžná,** not far from Kraslice, stands the **pilgrimage church of St. James**.[277] As early as 1505, a wooden chapel was mentioned, which overlooked the provincial road leading via Luby (Schönbach) to Cheb (Eger). A small church, whose origins might date back to the 13th century, St. James was in the care of the Waldssasen monks. From the 1540s on, the church had a Lutheran pastor. After the Lutherans left the country, the church was returned to the Catholics and processions of pilgrims from Kraslice are known to have taken place there after 1671. In 1721 the wooden church was demolished and replaced by a simple, single-nave building. Inside, a late Gothic statue of St. James was venerated. The pilgrimage tradition was started and supported by the owner of the estate, Johann Hartwig Nostitz, who ordered his subjects to make a religious pilgrimage to Sněžná on Saturday 25 July 1671, the Feast of St. James the Great.[278] The Baroque pilgrimage was one of the phenomena of revived Catholicism after White Mountain, which was especially relevant in places where the majority of the population was Lutheran. Johann Hartwig Nostitz hailed from an Upper Lusatian noble family that had settled in Bohemia in the 17th century, where he acquired large estates that had been confiscated after White Mountain. He soon secured important court positions and was also a recipient of the Order of the Golden Fleece. His vast fortune enabled

275) Emanuel Poche et al., *UPČ 2*, 458.

276) Michal Rýneš, "Historie sakrálních staveb hornických měst středozápadního Krušnohoří" (diploma thesis, University of West Bohemia, Plzeň, 2015), 51.

277) Emanuel Poche et al., *UPČ 3*, 378; https://pamatkovykatalog.cz.

278) Vladimír Prokop – Lukáš Smola, *Sokolovsko*, 383–387.

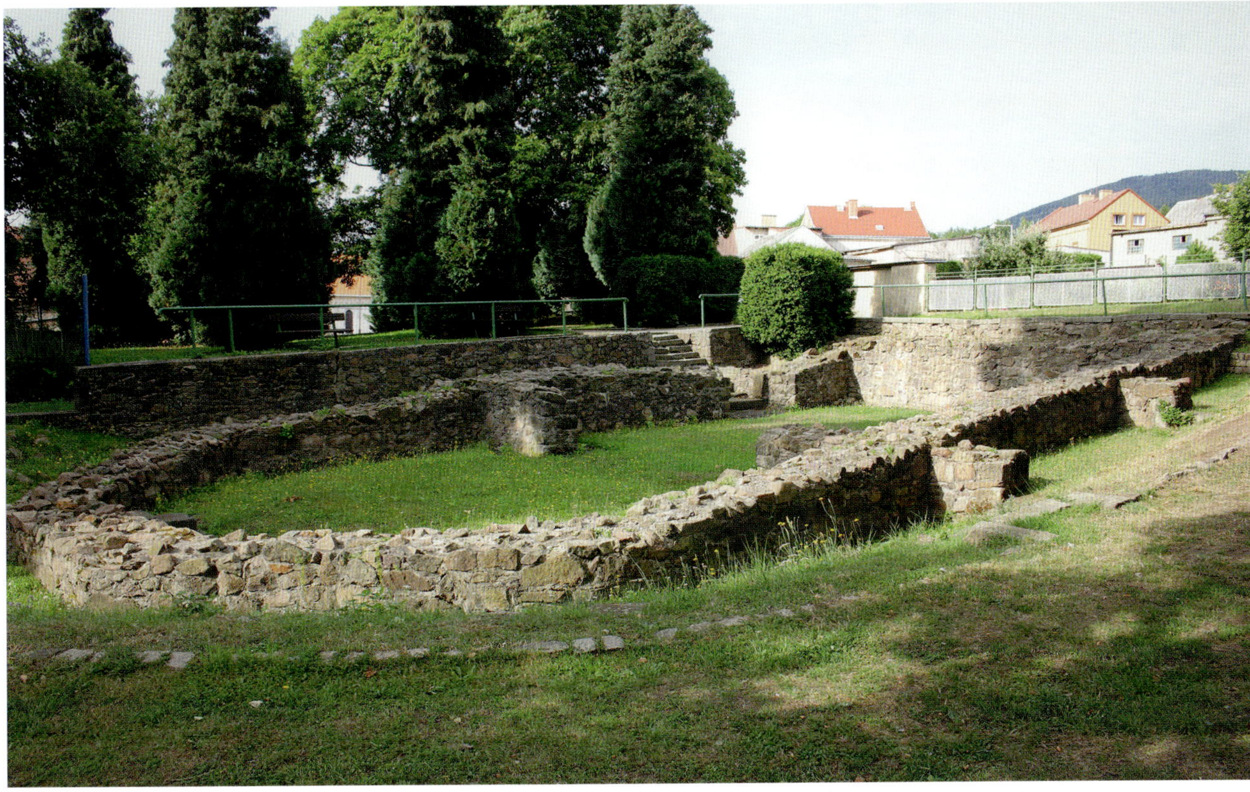

Fig. 84 Hrob, foundations of the demolished Lutheran church. Construction 1614, demolished 7 December 1617. Photographs by T. Šimková (2017).

him to invest in the construction of the Nostitz Palace in Prague, where he established an enormous picture gallery and, as an art collector and connoisseur, bought works created by famous contemporaries, such as Karel Škréta and Michael Leopold Willmann.[279]

The subject population of **Hrob** (Klostergrab) also attempted to build a Protestant church. The story of its construction and subsequent demolition had special relevance that foreshadowed the events at the start of the Thirty Years' War, although other religious monuments in the town deserve close attention as well.

In the 16th century, the miners of Saxon origin in Hrob were mostly Reformationists. Their campaign to build their own place of worship in the town, which was owned by Catholic nobility as part of the estate of the monastery of Osek (Ossegg), culminated in 1614. In that year, the Protestant population of Hrob built a church using construction material that belonged to the monastery, and they built it on land that was also owned by the monastery. By order of the Archbishop of Prague, Johann Lohelius, the church was torn down by the governor of Osek on 7 December 1617. The people of Hrob and the Protestant nobility saw this as a violation of the Letter of Majesty of Rudolf II, which guaranteed religious freedom in the country. The demolition of the Protestant church in Broumov was also viewed in the same way, and both

279) Petra Vokáčová, *Příběhy o hrdé pokoře: aristokracie českých zemí v době baroka* (Praha: 2014), 377; Lubomír Slavíček, *Chvála sběratelství, katalog výstavy* (Praha: 1993), 91.

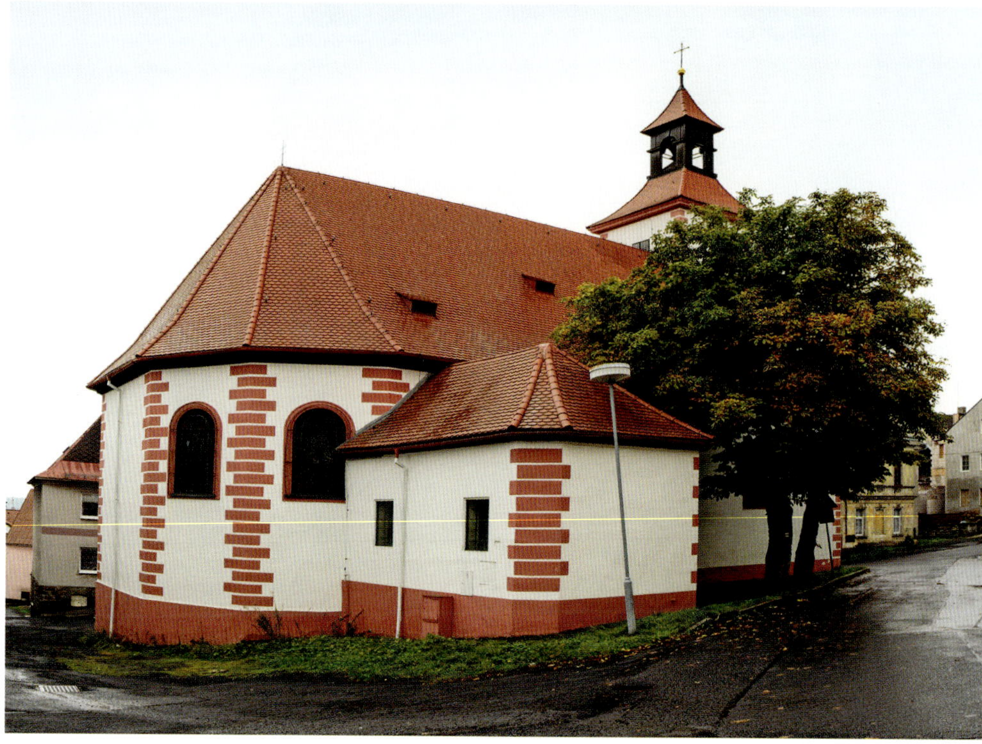

Fig. 85 Abertamy, Church of the Fourteen Holy Helpers, general view from the east. Built in 1534, rebuilt in Baroque style in 1735–1738. Photograph by J. Peer (2019).

events helped spark the second Prague defenestration of 1618 and the subsequent Estates Uprising.[280] (Fig. 85)

Next to the demolished Protestant church, the foundations of which are still apparent in the centre of the town after a modern era restoration, there was an older municipal **church in Hrob dedicated to the patron saint of miners, St. Barbara**. Its building history dates back to the 13th century. It was damaged during the Hussite wars and then rebuilt relatively soon after that. A major Renaissance reconstruction, financed by the Prague Archbishop, Zbyněk Berka of Dubá, took place between 1595 and 1602.[281] The new church was meant to be the centre of the counter-Reformation in a town whose population was mostly Lutheran, with only four families professing to be Catholic.

In 1632, the church was burnt down by the retreating Saxons, but it was rebuilt in 1637.[282] A single-nave building with a polygonal chancel, it was rebuilt in the pseudo-Gothic style in the 19th century. Only a bapsistery survives from the mediaeval church, while the altarpiece painting by Václav Vavřinec Reiner stands out among the Baroque furnishings.

280) Jan Kilián, *11. 12. 1617 – Zboření kostela v Hrobu: Na cestě k defenestraci* (Praha: 2007).

281) Lucie Kracíková – Olga Novosadová, *Stavebně historický průzkum: Hrob – farní kostel sv. Barbory* (Česká Lípa: NPÚ ÚOP v Ústí nad Labem, 2001), Sbírka stavebně-historických průzkumů, sign. 359/A.

282) Michal Urban et al., *Horní města – Ústecký kraj*, 70; Emanuel Poche et al., *UPČ 1*, 470; detailed information available online at: http://mapserver.ujep.cz.

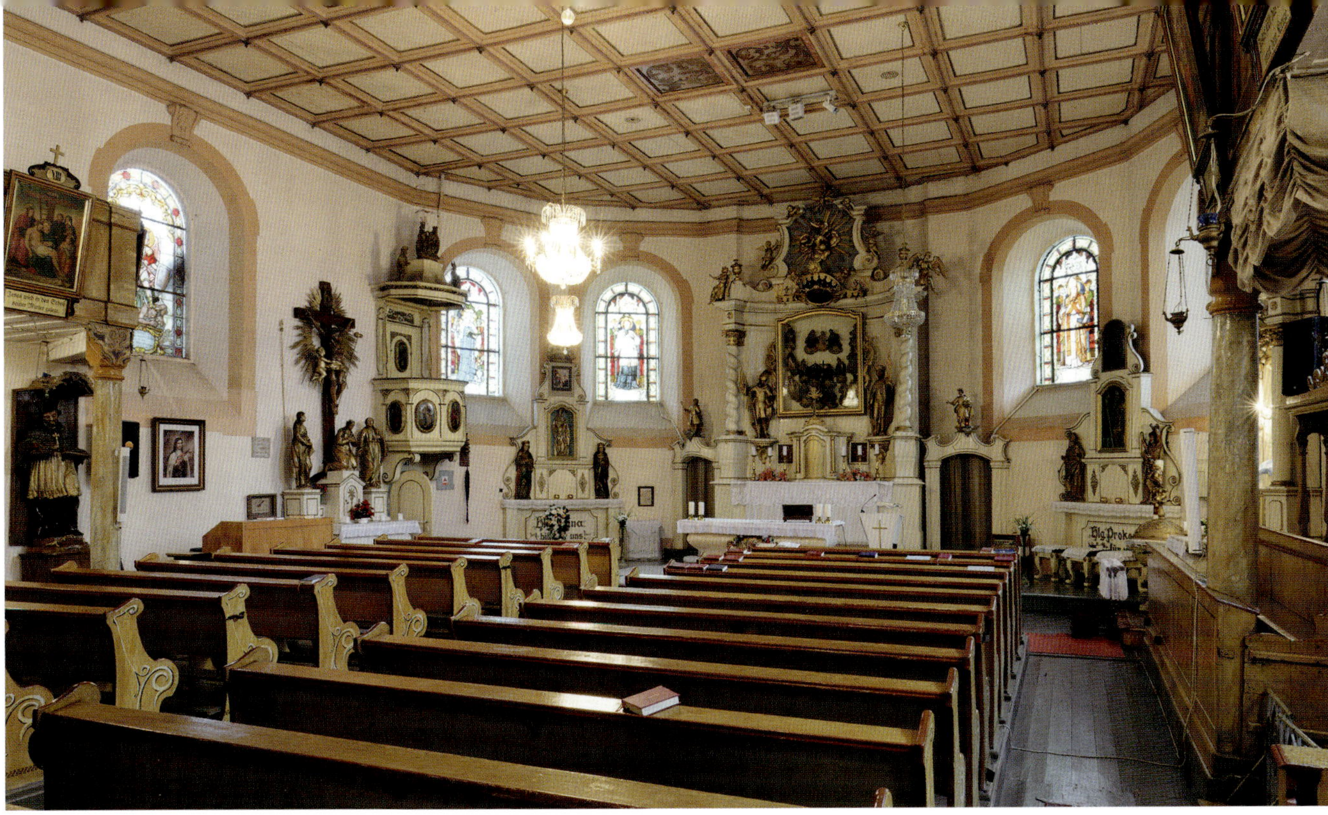

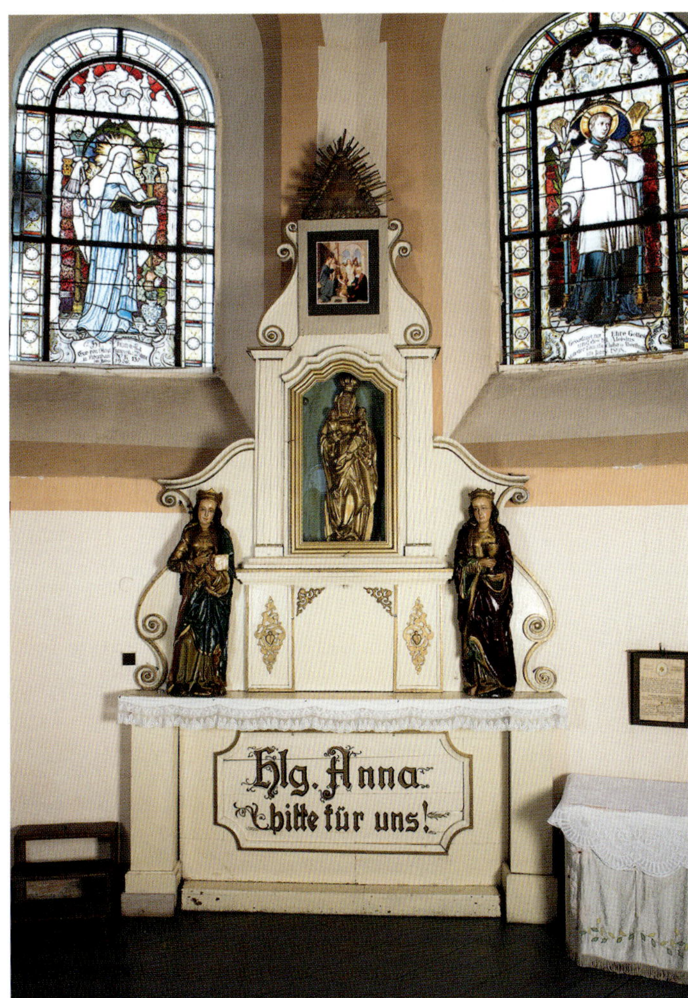

Fig. 86 Abertamy, Church of the Fourteen Holy Helpers, interior with original preserved furnishings. Photograph by J. Peer (2019).

Fig. 87 Abertamy, Church of the Fourteen Holy Helpers, altar with a statue of St. Anne. Photograph by J. Peer (2019).

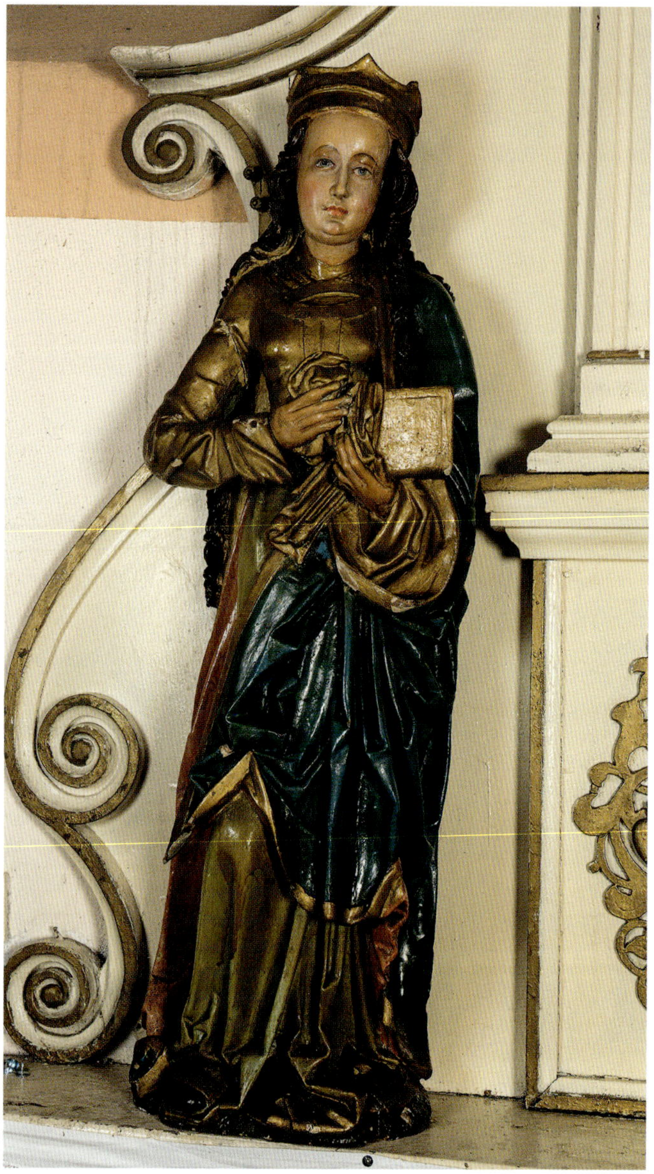

Fig. 88 Statue of St. Catherine (?) from Abertamy. Origin around 1520. Photo by J. Peer (2019).

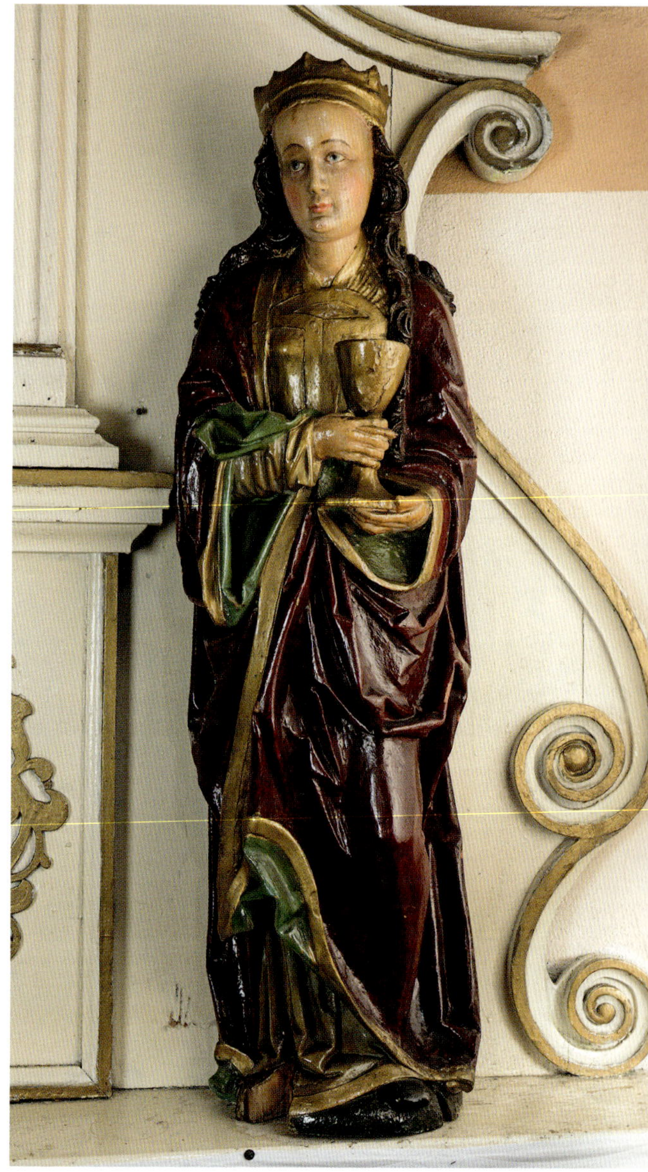

Fig. 89 Statue of St. Barbara of Abertamy. Origin around 1520. Photograph by J. Peer (2019).

In **Vejprty**, the only sacral building that 'remembers' the golden age of mining is the **Miners' Church of St. Martin**. It was built around 1550 and mentioned in sources for the first time in 1551. The construction of the single-nave church with a polygonal chancel was probably initiated by the chief magistrate Paul Spindler. Until 1616, the church served the Lutheran congregation. Two bells were made in 1612, during the Reformation, by brothers Zacharias and Gabriel Hilger. The church furnishings date from around 1700.[283]

A church dedicated to the **Fourteen Holy Helpers** was built in **Abertamy** (Abertham) around 1534, in the midst of a booming mining area near the entrance to the most important

283) Michal Urban a kol., *Horní města – Ústecký kraj*, 279; Emanuel Poche et al., *UPČ 4*, 185; detailed information available online at: http://mapserver.ujep.cz.

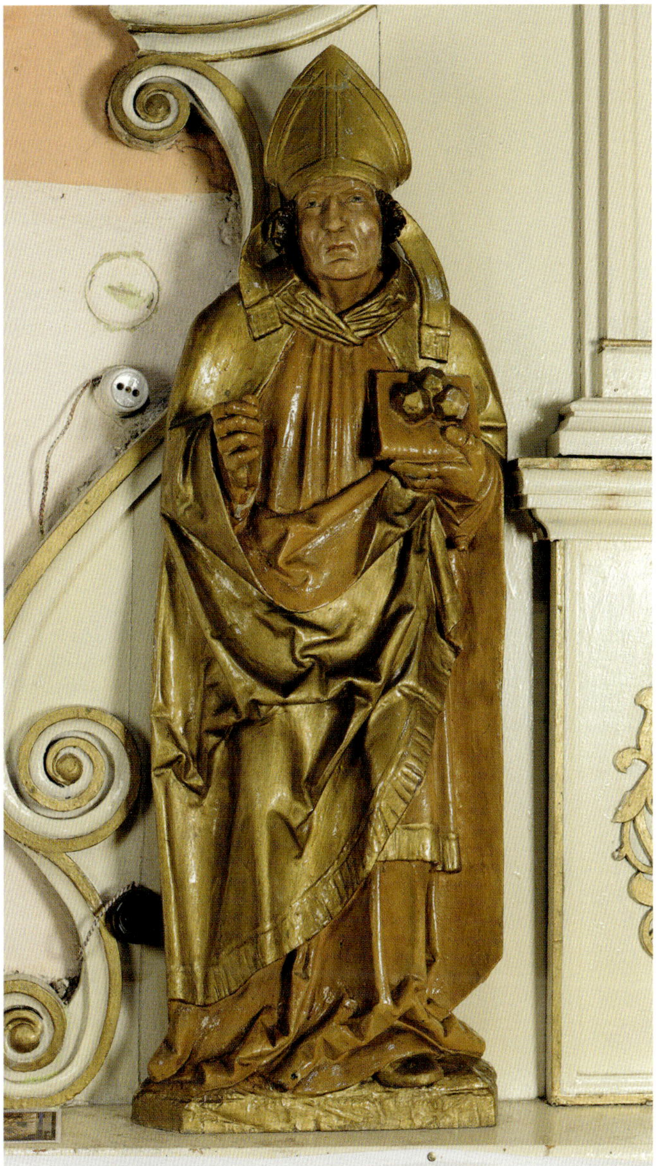

Fig. 90 Statue of St. Nicholas of Abertamy. Origin around 1520. Photograph by J. Peer (2019).

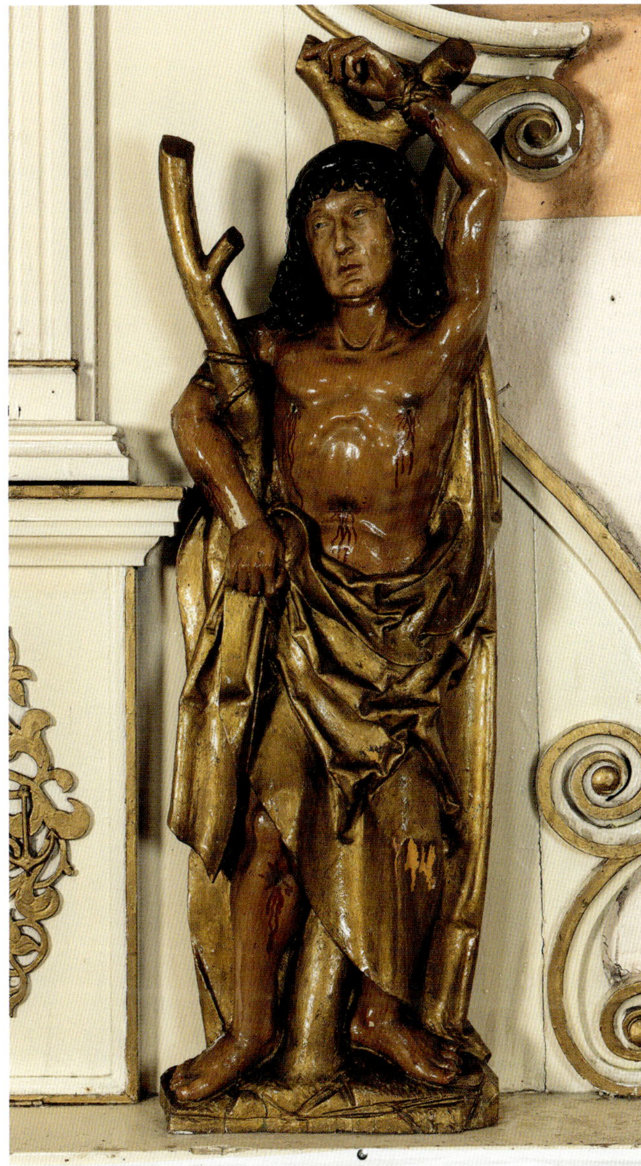

Fig. 91 Statue of St. Sebastian of Abertamy. Origin around 1520. Photograph by J. Peer (2019).

local adit, dedicated to St. Lawrence. (Fig. 86) The dedication to the Fourteen Holy Helpers is clearly of a later date, in the Baroque era, because at the time of its origin the miners were of Lutheran faith. As with other mining towns, the Lutheran church was originally wooden. Between 1735 and 1738, it was rebuilt in Baroque style.[284] (Fig. 87)

Several late-Gothic sculptures have been preserved from the original church furnishings. On the lateral altar, to the left of the high altar, there is a statue of St. Anne (c. 1520) in a glass case. (Fig. 88)

284) Emanuel Poche et al., *UPČ 1*, 23; detailed information available online at: http://mapserver.ujep.cz/SN_CZ.

On the left side of the communion table stands the statue of a saint, possibly St. Catherine, holding a book (c. 1520). On the right is St. Barbara with a chalice in her hand (c. 1520). The communion table of the lateral altar has a display of statues of St. Nicholas. (c. 1520) and St. Sebastian (c. 1520). (Fig. 89–91)

On the south wall of the nave, closer to the church entrance, there is a large statue of the Madonna on a console (c. 1510). (Fig. 92)

The statue of St. John the Evangelist has been lost. The roof of the pulpit bears a late Gothic relief of the Coronation of the Virgin Mary (c. 1510), (Fig. 93) accompanied by statues of St. Linhart (a bishop wearing a mitre, with a prisoner at his feet) and St. Wendel (or possibly St. Sebaldus).

The choice of saints makes it obvious that these are patrons common in the mining community (St. Anne, St. Nicholas, St. Barbara, St. Sebastian). In the Baroque period, St. Procopius

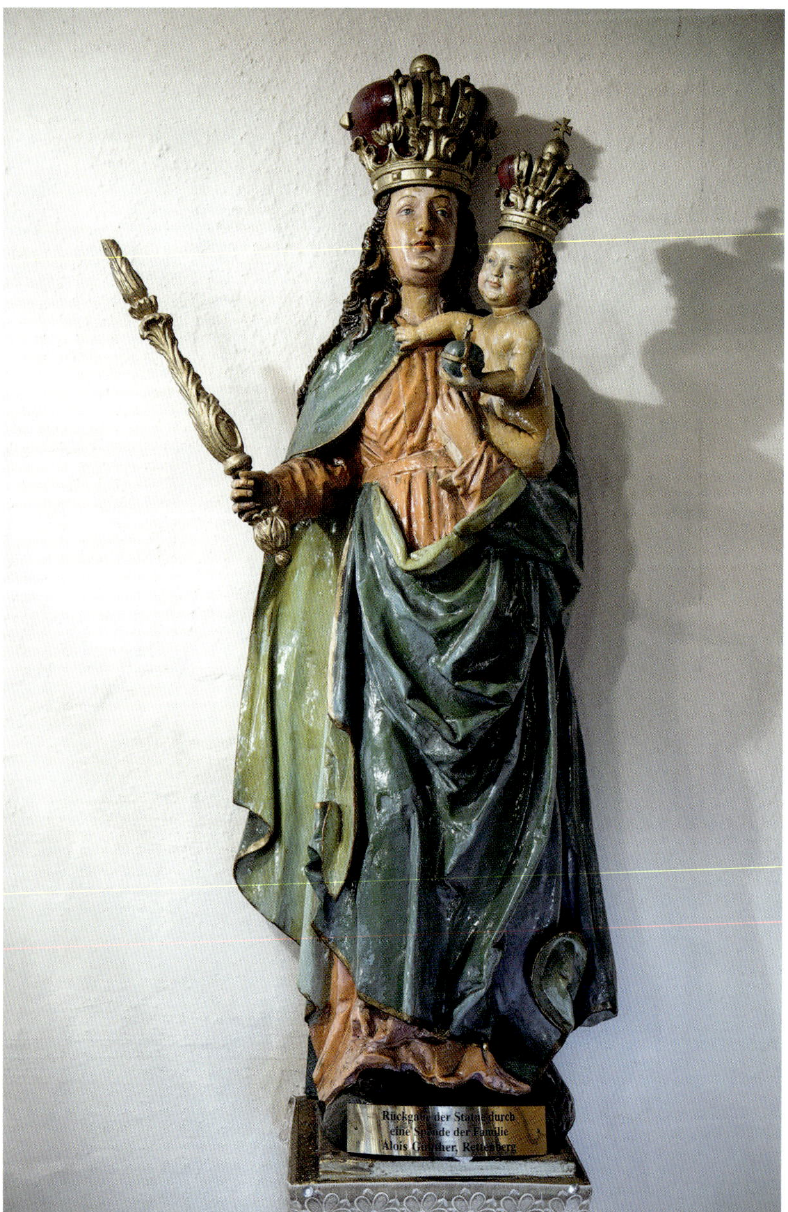

Fig. 92 Madonna and Child of Abertamy.
Origin around 1510. Photograph by J. Peer (2019).

Fig. 93 Gothic relief with the Coronation of the Virgin Mary on the roof of the pulpit in Abertamy. Created around 1510. Photograph by J. Peer (2019).

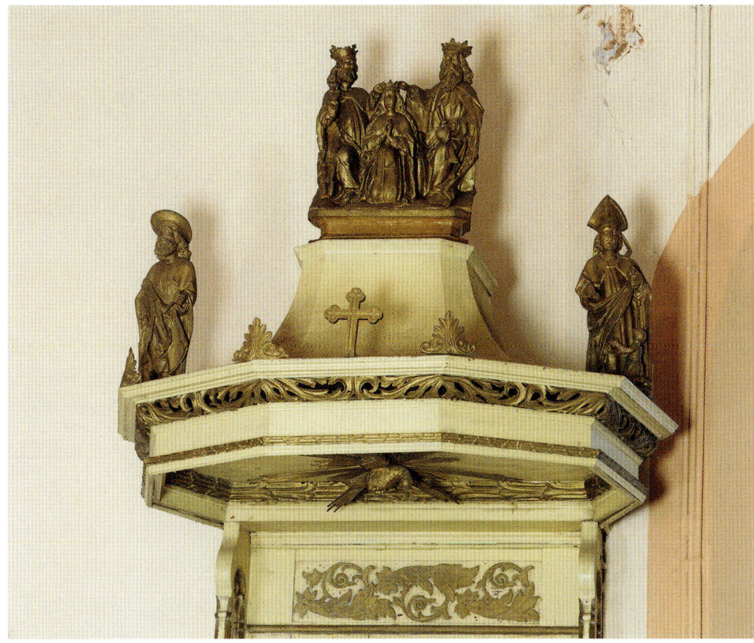

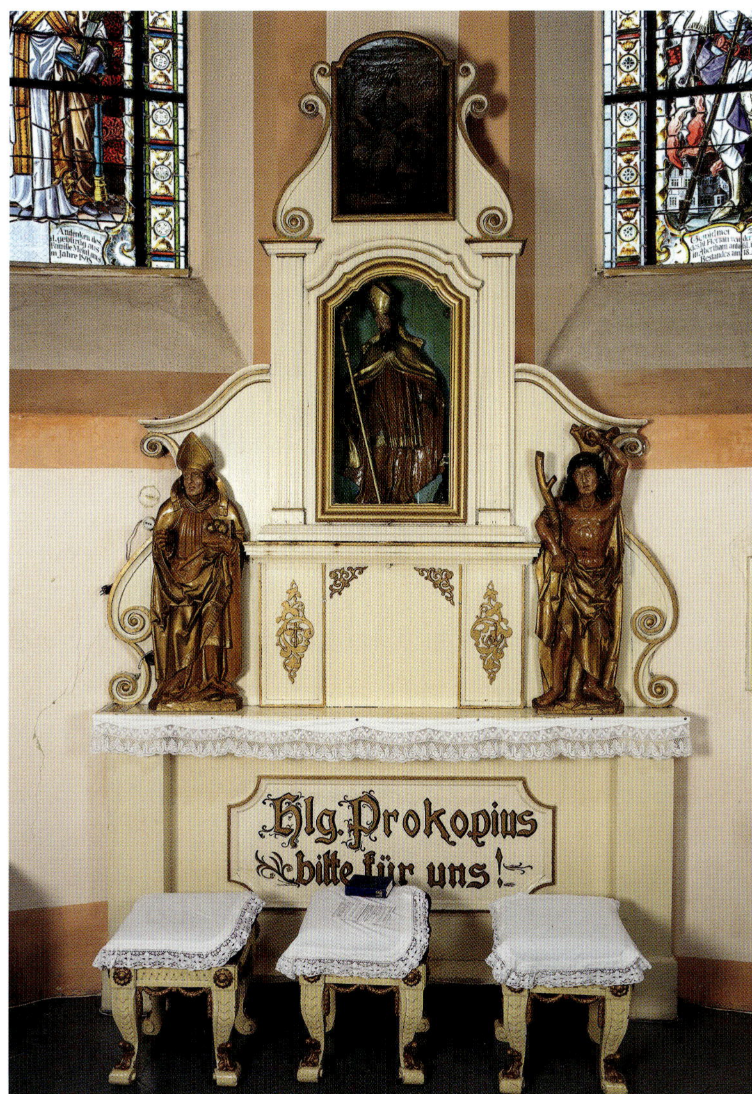

Fig. 94 Abertamy, Church of the Fourteen Holy Helpers, altar of St. Procopius with the central statue of the saint. Photograph by J. Peer (2019).

was added, whose statue appears in a glass case on the right lateral altar in the apse of the church. (Fig. 94)

The high altar displays Baroque statues of the Fourteen Holy Helpers, whose cult spread from the Frankish pilgrimage site of Vierzenheilligen and is already documented in Kadaň at the end of the 15th century.[285]

The Tombstone of Johann Preiss, 1680

The cast-iron tombstone of the Abertamy juror Johann Preiss is located in the west wall of the cemetery, where it was moved between 1902 and 1903 from the original Abertamy cemetery, located about 300 metres north of the present cemetery. The dimensions of the cast-iron plaque are 185 x 108 cm and there is a single-line inscription in cursive running the length of the perimeter that reads: 'Alhier ruhet in Gott Hr. Johann Preiss. Er ward gebohrn den 15 Febr. Ao 1609, lebete in Ehestand 50 Jahr, zeugete 8 Kinder, starb den 20. Juli Ao 1680 seines Alters 71 Jahr, 22 W. 2 Tag, ward Berggechworener 23 Jahr.' The centre of the plaque is decorated with the head of a cherub, below which are two biblical quotations in an oval field: Jan 11:25 and Job 19:25–26.[286]

The **wooden chapel dedicated to St. Anne**, a patron saint of miners, is known to us from a historical record made in 1537 in **Pernink** (Bärringen), owned at the time by the Schlicks. This chapel, which also dates back to the turbulent times of the early days of mining, was replaced in 1714 by a stone church dedicated to the Holy Trinity (consecrated in 1716). The original dedication of the mining church is commemorated today by the Baroque altar of St. Anne.[287]

A Lutheran church was also built in the centre of the square in **Oloví** (Bleistadt), where the Schlick family followed the Renaissance urban design. The existence of the church is documented as early as 1524, and the original wooden church was rebuilt between 1597 and 1603.[288] The church was built to accommodate the Lutheran congregation, with a wide, single nave suitable for preaching the Word of God, a polygonal apse, and an octagonal tower on the west side.

The list of pastors who worked there during the Reformation included: Bartolomeus Kroiez (1570), Nikolaus Ruhardus (1574), NikolausTrodel (1581), Andreas Fladter (1563 and 1590), Valentin Löw (1574) and David Troll (1599). It was used for Lutheran services until 1624, when counter-Reformation campaigns were launched, as a result of which many

285) Petr Hlaváček, *Čtrnáct svatých Pomocníků: k pozdně středověké spiritualitě elit a její christocentrické dimenzi* (Praha: 2014); Štepánka Chlumská – Lenka Helfertová, "Oltář Čtrnácti sv. Pomocníků z Kadaně: průzkum a restaurování malířské výzdoby archy a jejich přínos pro možnosti autorského určení a stanovení míry dochování originálu," in: *Josef Opitz a umění na Chomutovsku a Kadaňsku 1350–1590* (Chomutov: 2015), 247–260.

286) Josef Grimm, "Nejstarší abertamské památky pocházejí z let 1680 a 1706," in: *Měsíčník Krušné hory západ* 3, No. 7 (July 2014), 10; Michal Urban, "Abertamy mají další kulturní památku," in: *Měsíčník Krušné hory západ* 5, No. 7 (July 2016), 17.

287) Emanuel Poche et al., *UPČ* 3, 39.

288) Václav Kotěšovec, *Pohledy do historie měst a obcí Kraslicka* (Ostrov: 2011), 154–155.

Lutheran miners left the country. It was not until 1650 that a Catholic clergyman was installed in the rectory. The first parish priest was the Dominican Father Vincent Wilsbach.[289]

The church was newly dedicated to St. Michael the Archangel. It was reconstructed several times during the 17th and 18th centuries, e.g. in 1679 when a clock tower was added. The structural condition of the church was reportedly dismal, and in 1894 plans to demolish it and build a new church began to take shape.[290]

In 1897 (or 1898) the old church was torn down, but some of its original furnishings were preserved. In place of the old church a new building was built in a historicising style. Two original Renaissance stained-glass windows from the Lutheran church have been preserved, reverently set into the new windows and bearing the coats of arms of the Beheim family from Nuremberg. They were made in 1603 and donated to the church by the brothers Paul, Christopher, and Friedrich Beheim. The most precious monument, probably from the time of the church's foundation, is the Assumption on the Crescent, created between 1510 and 1520 in the workshop of Master of the Týnice Annunciation, now stored in the church's depository.[291]

Baroque burgher tombstones

Three gravestones set in the retaining wall below the church probably came from the original church. One of them was made for Johann Peter Stritzl (1698), who was a burgher of Oloví, burgermeister and choirmaster of the literary fraternity.

Assumpta of Oloví

This is a late Gothic statue with polychromatic decoration from the early 16th century. It is stylistically close to the Master of the Týnice Annunciation, whose workshop is believed to have been in Pilsen. A crown and sceptre were added to the statue in the Baroque period. It was probably originally placed in a Gothic altarpiece, later in a Baroque lateral altar and most recently in a pseudo-Gothic altarpiece.

Měděnec is also one of the towns situated on the plateaus of the Ore Mountains. A **wooden church dedicated to the Virgin Mary** was probably built there soon after the foundation of the village, first documented in sources in 1581. Until 1641, it served the large Lutheran community.[292] The Lutherans remained in the village for quite a long time after the issue of the Renewed Land Ordinance. They eventually left in 1641, whereupon the church became Catholic.

The dilapidated church was replaced by a new church built between 1803 and 1814. A statue of the Madonna from the second half of the 15th century probably comes from the original wooden church and was later deposited in the Baroque Chapel of the Immaculate Conception

289) Detailed information available online: http://mapserver.ujep.cz/SN_CZ/PDF_2/Cirkevni/36412_002.pdf.
290) Vladimír Prokop – Lukáš Smola, *Sokolovsko*, 578–581.
291) Lois Eißner, *Bleistadt, einst königlich freie Bergstadt 1523–1973* (Schwandorf: 1973), available at https://gpecher.de.tl; Emanuel Poche et al., *UPČ* 3, 529.
292) In 1641, 115 Protestants and only 27 Catholics lived in the town.

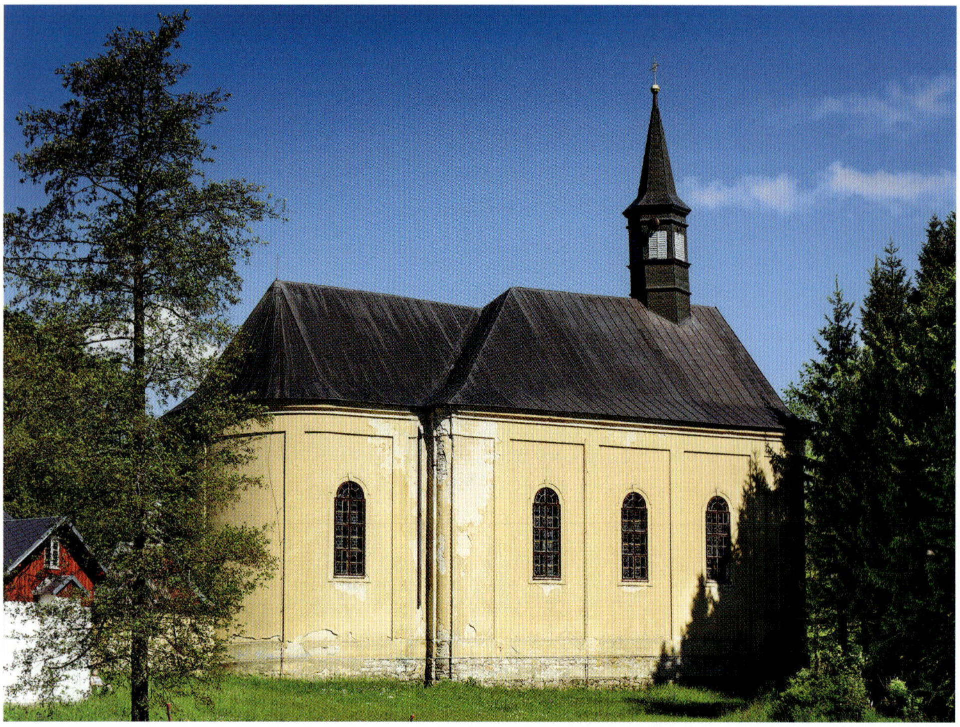

Fig. 95 Přebuz, Church of St. Bartholomew, view from the north. The original church was built in the first half of the 16th century, rebuilt in the Renaissance style in 1578, the present late Baroque appearance dates from 1787. Photograph by J. Peer (2019).

of the Virgin Mary. The chapel stands on the Měďník (Kupferhubel) hill and was built by Franz Julius, Duke of Sachsen-Lauenburg in 1672.[293]

A wooden church, dedicated to **St. Bartholomew**, was also built on a slight elevation above the Rolava (Rohlau) River in the mining town of **Přebuz** (Frühbuss). (Fig. 95) The earliest record of its existence dates back to 1555, and a rectory is mentioned in 1567. The rebuilding of the church probably took place in 1578, as there is a record in the Přebuz land register that a certain Georg Lorenz delivered stone for the church renovation.

A late Gothic baptistery (c. 1500), carved from Přebuz granite, probably comes from the original mediaeval and Renaissance church. (Fig. 96)

The church was thoroughly rebuilt in the 18th century in the Baroque style. It was constructed with the financial contribution of the Nostitz family between 1778 and 1787, by the Sokolov builder Johann Andreas Leistner. (Fig. 97)

The most precious monument of the church is a spectacular wooden polychrome crucifix created around 1500. It was probably originally placed in the triumphal arch between the chancel and the nave. The church bell was cast in tin bronze in 1565 by the master Wolfgang Hilger of Pernink.[294] (Fig. 98)

As in other mining towns, the first church in **Boží Dar (Gottesgab)** was built of wood. It was dedicated to **St. Anne**, a patron saint of miners. We know nothing about its appearance,

293) https://www.pamatkovykatalog.cz.

294) Vladimír Prokop – Lukáš Smola, *Sokolovsko*, 588–591; Lubomír Zeman, *Městečka na dlani – Karlovarský kraj* (Praha: 2017), 124; Václav Kotěšovec, *Pohledy do historie měst a obcí Kraslicka*, 171.

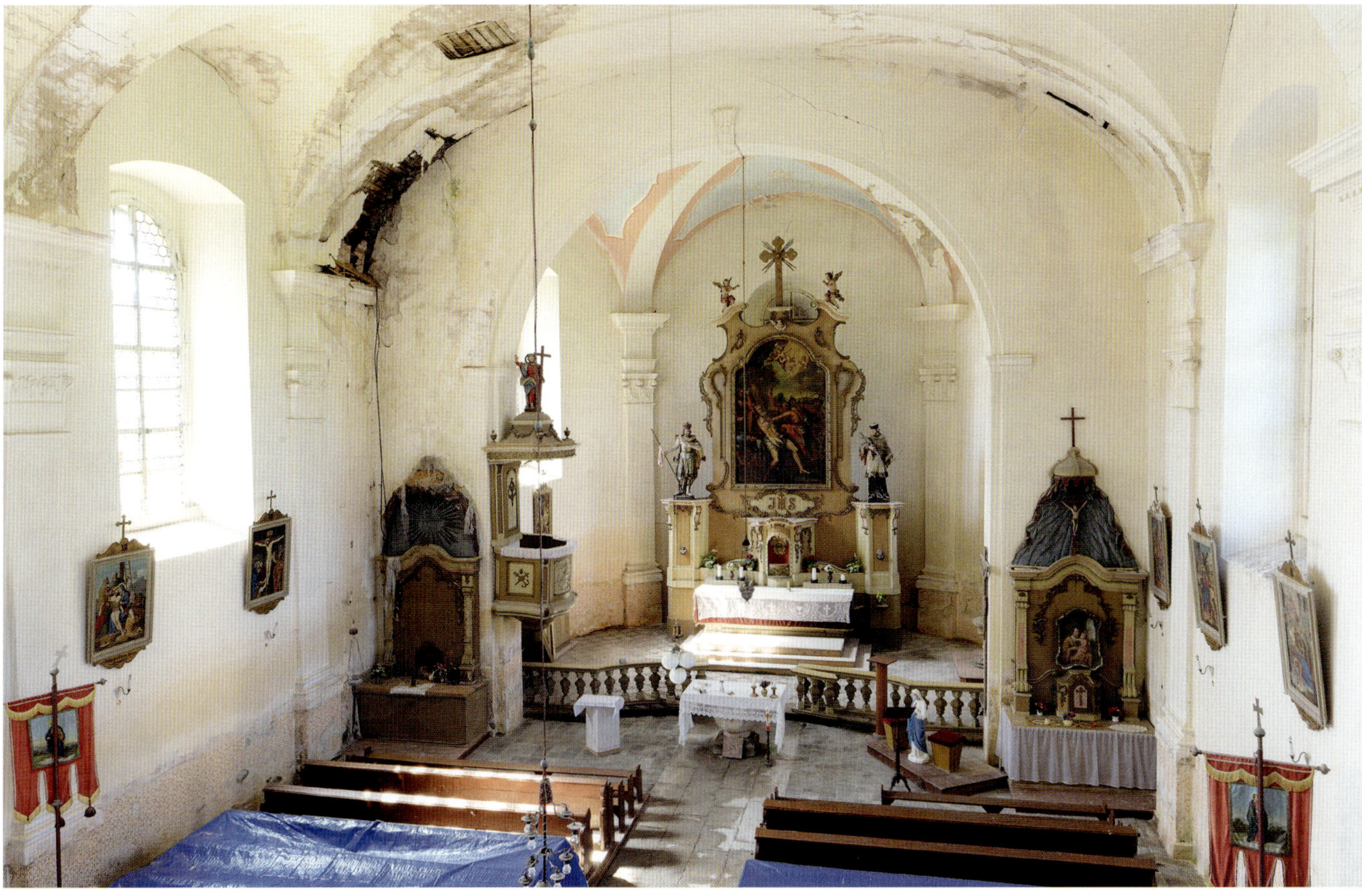

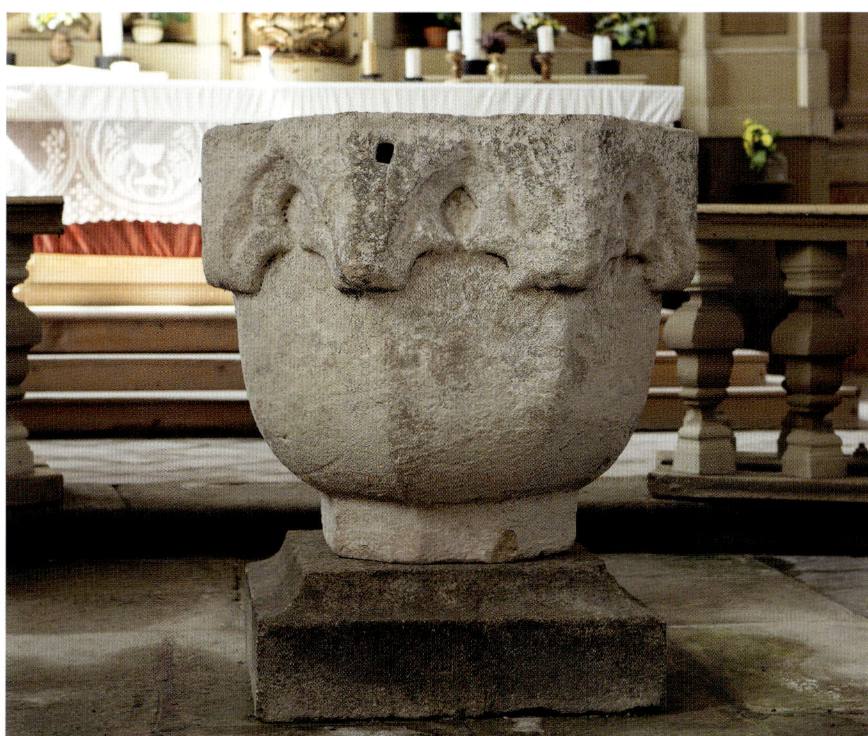

Fig. 97 Přebuz, Church of St. Bartholomew, view of the interior of the church from the west. Photograph by J. Peer (2019).

Fig. 96 Přebuz, Church of St. Bartholomew, original late Gothic font from the old church. It was built around 1500. Photograph by J. Peer (2019).

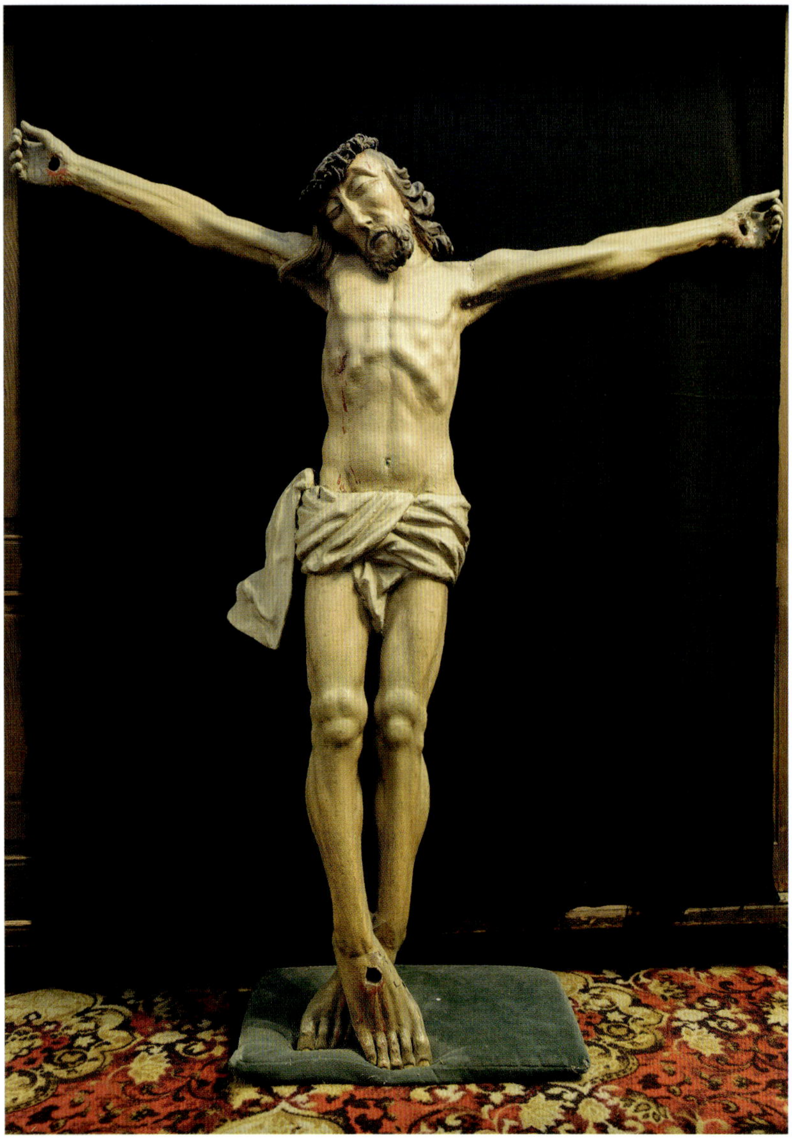

Fig. 98 A polychrome late Gothic crucifix from the original furnishings of the old church in Přebuz. It originated around 1500. Photograph by J. Peer (2019).

because it was replaced by a new church in 1593. In 1594, the new church received three bells made by the Jáchymov bell maker Hans Wildt. The tin baptismal font was cast in 1612 by the Jáchymov metalsmith Leonhard Dür. The design of the Renaissance church from the end of the 16th century has not been preserved, either, as it was rebuilt by Filip Heger in the style of Classical Baroque in 1772.[295]

Another mining town situated at high altitude, **Hora Sv. Šebestiána** (Sebastianberg),[296] rests on the barren ridge of the Ore Mountains. Little of the original Renaissance and Baroque buildings of the generously laid out town survived, due to the many military invasions and fires.

295) Richard Schmidt, *Soupis památek historických a uměleckých*, 3–14.

296) Ladislav Bílek – Ladislav Jangl – Jan Urban, *Dějiny hornictví na Chomutovsku* (Chomutov: 1976), 36; Emanuel Poche et al., *UPČ 1*, 398; Vlastimil Ružek, "Dějiny obce Hora sv. Šebestiána," in: *Památky, příroda, život* 10 (1978), No. 2, 43–45; No. 3, 85–86; No. 4, 101–102; Zdena Binterová, *Od Hory sv. Šebestiána po Krásnou Lípu* (Chomutov: 2000), 4–22; Michal Urban et al., *Horní města Krušných Hor – Karlovarský kraj*, 36–55.

The most devastating fire ravaged the town in 1854. On the site of the burnt-down Renaissance church, which had originally been Lutheran, the **Church of St. Sebastian** was built between 1874 and 1877, by the Chomutov builder Josef Dausch. It was torn down in 1967.

The dominant landmark of **Hora Sv. Kateřiny** (Katharinaberg) is the **church dedicated to St. Catherine**, the patroness of the town. It stands on the site where the original, possibly wooden, church probably stood in the mid-16th century. The local Lutherans built a spacious church in the same place between 1607 and 1612, which became Catholic in 1628 after the last Lutheran pastor left for Seiffen in Saxony. The bell in the church tower – from 1606, by Pavel Munich of Louny – is a relic from the original church. The description on the bell's cap mentions the names of the mining master Jiří Sattler and the parish priest Šimon Weber. The Jesuits from Chomutov worked here as part of a re-Catholicisation mission. A major late Baroque reconstruction of the church took place between 1785 and 1786, when the excellent ceiling paintings were also created. A tower was added, and the church furnishings date from the same period. There are many statues of the mining patrons, St. Anne and St. Joachim. In front of the church stands a column with a scultpure of the Pietà, created in 1729. In 1714 a Marian column with a statue of the Virgin Mary the Immaculata was erected in the square. A chapel with a statue of St. John of Nepomuk dates from the second half of the 18th century.[297]

297) Emanuel Poche et al., *UPČ 1*, 397–398; Reinhold Reichel, *Nástropní malby farního kostela v Hoře Sv. Kateřiny v Čechách* (Marienberg: 2000).

The mining towns and their monuments presented so far have been preserved in a more or less authentic form. The case of **Přísečnice** (Pressnitz) is different. It was an important mining town that was demolished to make room for a dam in the 1970s. Přísečnice used to be located in the Ore Mountains near Kadaň.[298]

The first written reference to the town dates back to 1335. Its development depended on the mining of iron and silver ore, and ore containing arsenic, cobalt, nickel, bismuth and, to a lesser extent, copper. There are reports from the middle of the 15th century about hammer mills owned by the Lords of Šumburk (Schönburg). In 1459, the owners of the Hasištejn (Hassenstein) estate, the Lobkowicz family, obtained the privilege to mine within a three-mile radius of Hasištejn, an area which included Přísečnice.[299] In 1546, King Ferdinand I bought the village of Přísečnice and promoted it to a mining town, granting it a coat of arms complete with the symbols of mining – the hammer and pick.[300] In the course of time, mining activity waxed and waned, with the 16th century being the golden age of mining. In the first half of the 17th century, problems arose in the mining operations. The mines were dug so deep that they reached the level of the drainage adit of Dům rakouský (The House of Austria). Additional drainage costs had to be factored in. The area around the town was also affected by the events of the Thirty Years' War, especially in connection with the Battle of Přísečnice in 1641.[301]

After the Thirty Years' War, only mines with sufficiently rich ore deposits were reopened. At that time, the drainage adit reached the length of 3,600 metres. From the middle of the

298) Emanuel Poche et al., *UPČ 3*, 188–189.

299) Jiří Crkal – Martin Volf, "Počátky a vývoj osídlení horního města Přísečnice," in: *Archaelogia historica* 41, 2 (2016), 1–2, 273–287; Jiří Crkal – Martin Volf, "Počátky města Přísečnice," in: Regina Smolnik (ed.), *ArchaeoMontan 2013* (Dresden: 2014), 95–108; Zdena Binterová, *Přísečnice zatopená, ale nezapomenutá* (Chomutov: 2004); Jiří Crkal, "Tvrz a zámek v Přísečnici," in: Jana Kuljavceva Hlavová – Oldřich Kotyza – Milan Sýkora, *Hrady českého severozápadu* (Most: 2012), 18.

300) Alena Pejcharová, "Těžba rud v okolí Přísečnice – historie a dopady na životní prostředí" (bachelor thesis, Jan Evangelista Purkyně University in Ústí nad Labem, 2010), 30.

301) Michal Kasl, "Bitva u Přísečnice," in: *Památky, příroda, život* 16/4 (1984), 108–109; Lukáš Sláma, *Krušné hory ve švédském sevření. Poslední tažení Jana Banéra 1641* (Praha: 2020), 139–181.

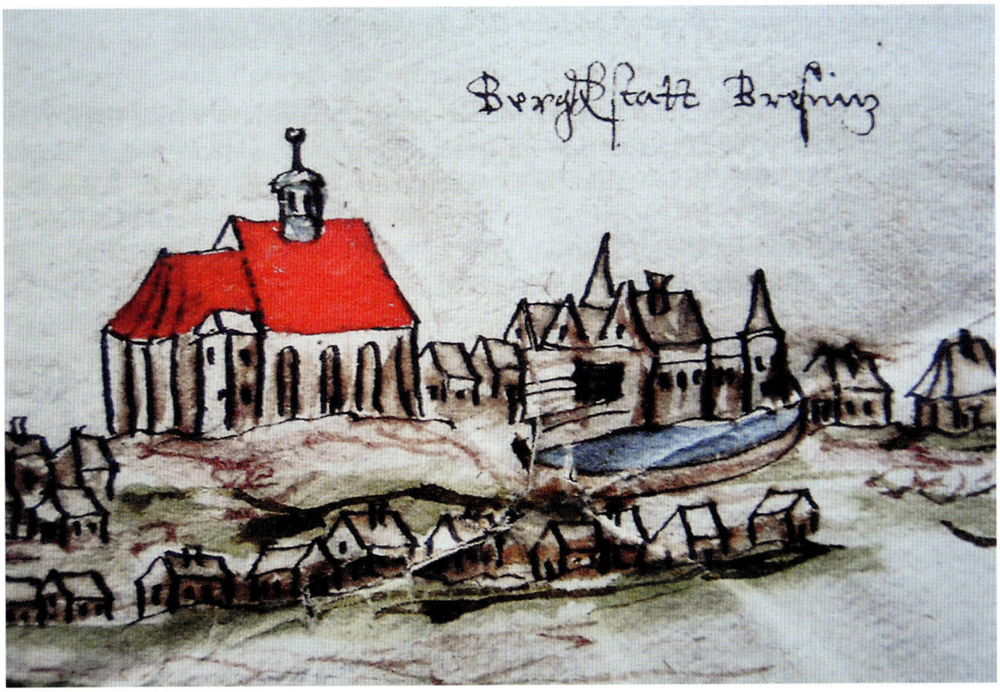

Fig. 99 Přísečnice, the Church of the Assumption of the Virgin Mary on a section of an archival map of the settlement. Photo © National Archives.

17th century, the adit and its branches were driven at the expense of the king, who kept half of the silver and all the iron ore. Although many silver deposits were found, mining entrepreneurs were reluctant to open new mines and the king did not have enough money to do so. Only the municipality operated a mine. So as to retain the status of a mining town, it operated the following mines: Tři labutě (Three Swans) and Požehnání boží (Lord's Blessing), the latter of which was abandoned in 1661. In 1687, when the only mine in operation was Nebeské vojsko (Heavenly Host), only about 21 kg of silver was extracted.[302]

Mining activity was not revived until the beginning of the 18th century, when fourteen mines were opened, which produced a total of 188 kg of silver in 1711 and 1712. However, by the 1720s mining was in significant decline, and in 1771 the town's smelting site was closed, leaving only the Maria Kirchenbau mine open. The hereditary adit of Dům rakouský was extended by a branch named Lederburská čelba, which was used to drain the iron ore mines near Mezilesí. Minor attempts to resume mining were made in 1812 (a mine called Josef na Heegbergu) and, later still, between 1881 and 1885, but were completely unsuccessful.[303]

The most notable example of sacred architecture in the town was the **Church of the Assumption of the Blessed Virgin Mary**, built by the market square in 1583. (Fig. 99) It took over the role of a parish church after the older Church of St. Nicholas, which at that point was turned into a cemetery church. The dedication to St. Nicholas demonstrates the popularity this saint enjoyed in the mining towns. Between 1759 and 1767, the church was rebuilt in the

302) Alena Pejcharová, *Těžba rud v okolí Přísečnice*, 30.
303) Ibid., 32.

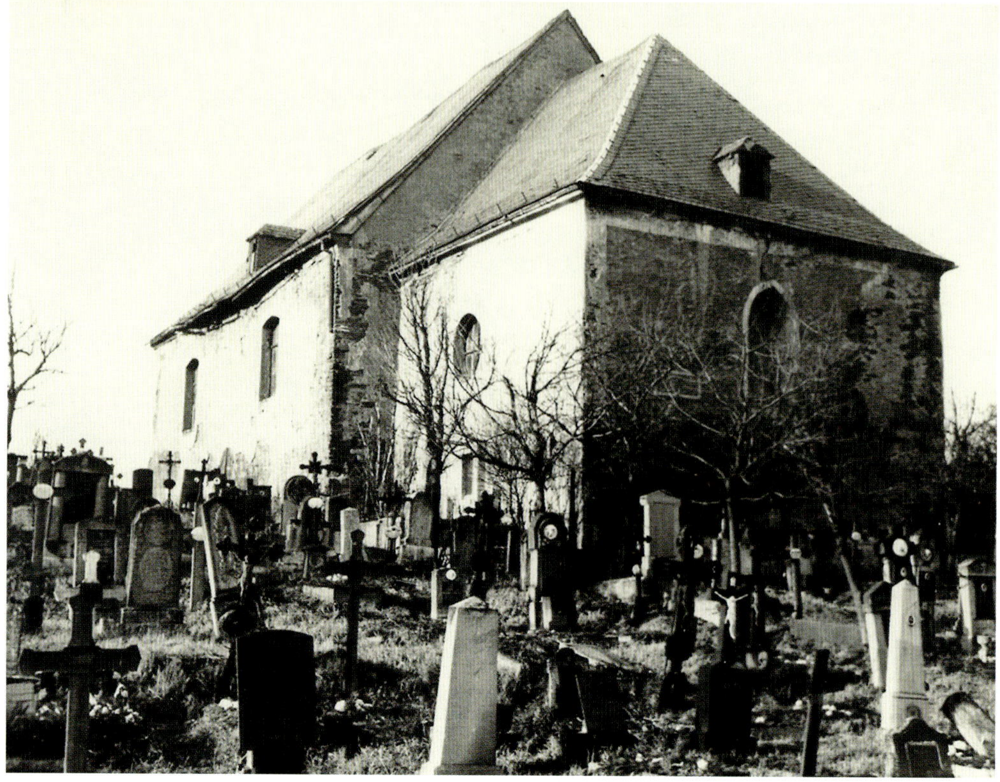

Fig. 100 Přísečnice, Church of St. Nicholas in 1961. Photo © National Heritage Institute.

Baroque style, and minor renovations were also made in the following centuries. The church was torn down before 1974 because of the Přísečnice Dam construction project, even though it stood outside of the flooded area.[304] Shortly before the demolition, an archeological survey was conducted in the church.[305]

The mediaeval **Church of St. Nicholas**, which was probably founded by the Lords of Šumburk (Schönburg) who had owned Přísečnice since 1351, is also gone. (Fig. 100) The founder of the Lobkowicz family, Mikuláš I Chudý Lobkowicz (Niklas Lobkowicz), was probably buried in the church by the altar of St. Dorothea in 1435. Mikuláš had owned a part of Přísečnice since 1418. In 1510, the body of the famous humanist Bohuslav Hasištejnský of Lobkowicz was laid to rest in the church. Unfortunately, his body could not be identified during the archaeological survey in 1973.[306]

In 1775, the church underwent a reconstruction and in 1811, it was renovated after a town fire. It was eventually demolished in 1963 because it was allegedly hampering traffic.[307] The

304) Martin Čechura, *Zaniklé kostely Čech* (Praha: 2012), 228–229.

305) Luděk Krčmář, "K zániku kostela Nanebevzetí Panny Marie v Přísečnici," in: *Muzejní a vlastivědné práce: Časopis Společnosti přátel starožitností* 45/115, No. 3–4 (2007), 214–217; Markéta Laurenčíková – Jan Gaža, *Zaniklé kostely na Chomutovsku po roce 1945* (Chomutov: 2001), 13.

306) Jaroslav Pachner – Hugo Sedláček, *Opevněné kostely na Chomutovsku* (Chomutov: 2013), 42–48; Lukáš Gavenda, "Páni Hasištejnští z Lobkovic na sklonku středověku" (diploma thesis, Charles University, 2008), 74.

307) Martin Čechura, *Zaniklé kostely Čech*, 228.

cenotaph of Mikuláš Chudý and the tombstone of Bohuslav Hasištejnský were transferred to the Church of St. James the Greater in Louchov. This church was also part of the Lobkowicz estate in Přísečnice from the very beginning and is also the oldest church in the Ore Mountains. However, since it was in a very poor condition, both important sepulchral monuments found a more suitable home in the Church of the Fourteen Holy Helpers in Kadaň.

Fig. 101 Horní Slavkov, Pluh's house (Pflughaus). Construction 1510–1512, extension in the 1660s. Photograph by J. Peer (2019). →

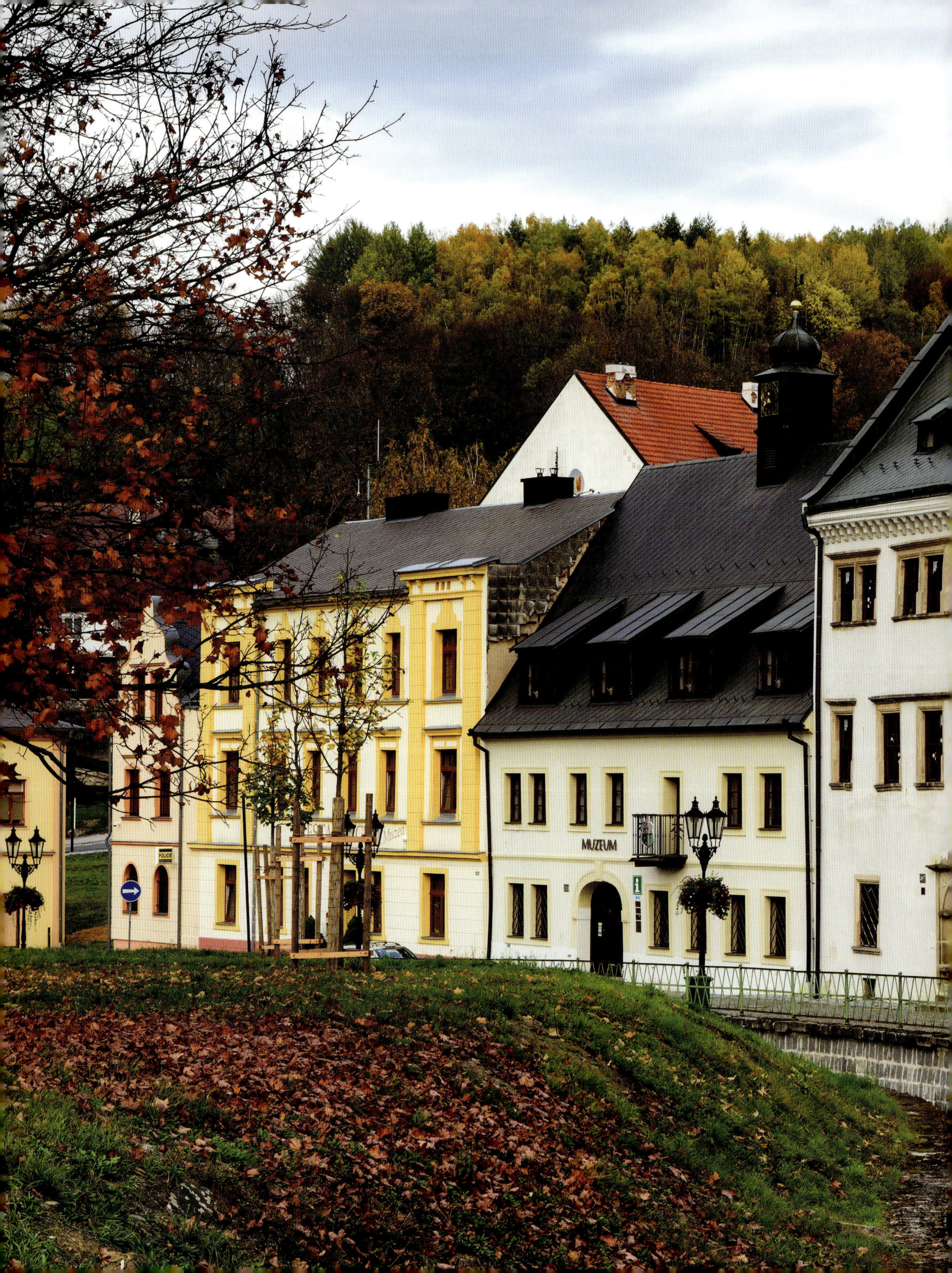
MUZEUM

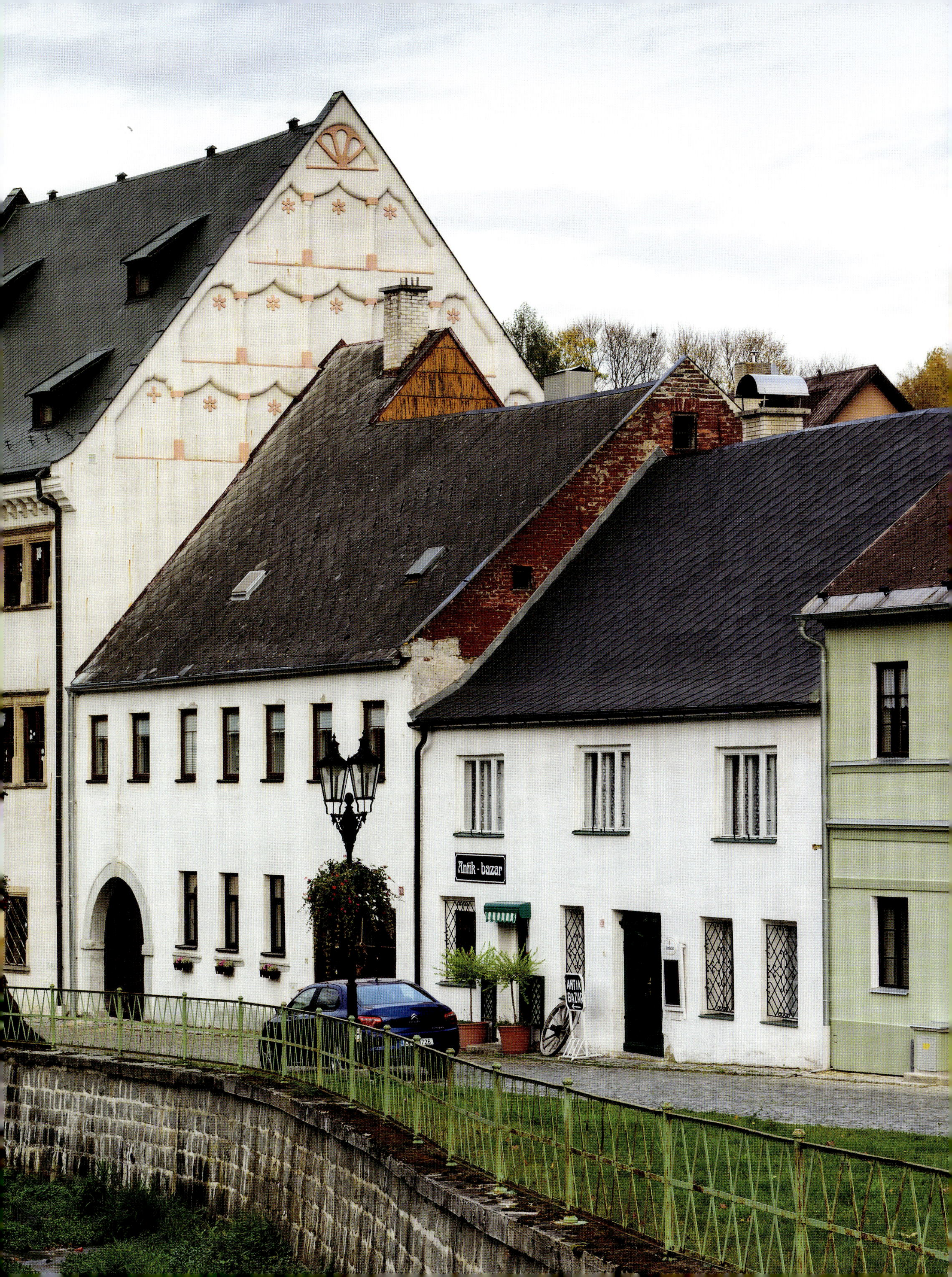
Antik - bazar

THE MINING TOWNS OF SLAVKOV FOREST

The group of important mining towns also includes Horní Slavkov (Schlaggenwald), Krásno (Schönfeld), and Čistá-Literbachy (Lauterbach), which no longer exists. These towns were situated in the Slavkov Forest, an area directly adjacent to the mining region of the Ore Mountains.

One of the notable mining towns in northwest Bohemia was undoubtedly **Horní Slavkov** (Schlaggenwald). Its original urban plan and most of its historical houses cannot be found today.[308] The town is located in the northeastern part of the Slavkov Forest and became known primarily for tin mining, although silver, copper and lead were also mined there. The oldest record of the town's existence dates from 1322, and soon after that, in 1335, it was populated by miners from Saxony. A town seal from 1351 is mentioned, which indicates that Horní Slavkov was probably already a town at that time and most of its population were German-speaking settlers.[309]

Horní Slavkov was a serf town until the mid-16th century. In 1489, Ernst von Gleichen, who owned the Bečov estate, reinstated its rights. In 1495, the town passed into the hands of the Pflugs von Rabenstein and soon after that, rich silver and tin lodes were discovered, which brought prosperity to both the estate and the town.[310] Credit for this should go to Johann Pflug von Rabenstein, who was Court Marshal from 1533 until 1537, and his nephew Stephan, who took over the estate because Johann had no direct descendants.[311] Shortly before 1547, Horní Slavkov was granted town privileges, but in 1547 the town was confiscated from Stephan Pflug due to his involvement in the uprising against the Habsburgs. Subsequently, Emperor Ferdinand I promoted Horní Slavkov to a royal mining town,[312] whose coat of arms includes the traditional mining tools and is accompanied by a pair of miners. At that time, the town had a population of about 5,000 people.

308) Emanuel Poche et al., *UPČ 2*, 417–418; Vladimír Prokop – Lukáš Smola, *Sokolovsko*, 97–164.

309) Anton Gnirs, *Eine Bergchronik der Städte Schlaggenwald und Elbogen* (Elbogen: 1926).

310) Rudolf Prosch, *Abriss der Geschichte der alten, einst kaiserlich freien Bergstadt Schlaggenwald* (Schlaggenwald: 1938), 7.

311) Ibid., 8.

312) Ibid., 16.

Fig. 102 Horní Slavkov, Pluh's house, entrance portal to the house with a secondarily carved dating. Photograph by J. Peer (2019).

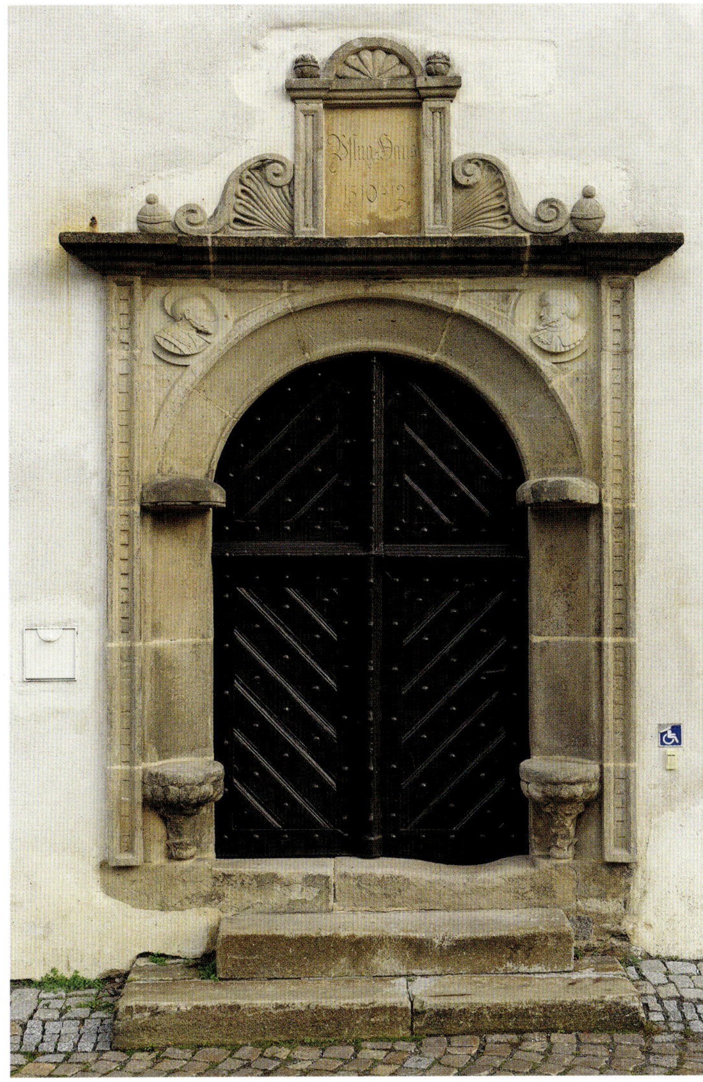

The Pflugs left a distinct mark on the town. Their manor house built between 1510 and 1512 in the Saxon Renaissance style and now called Pluhův dům (Pflughaus), still stands. However, only the cellars and part of the ground floor date from the early 16th century. The rest of the house was not completed until the 1660s.

It is a two-storey building with high side gables, articulated by blind arcades. The Niedermann house, which used to stand in the same block of buildings and was torn down in 1962, had a similar design. Its interiors were decorated with murals, which have been documented by restoration researchers. Today, the reconstructed house also contains a set of late Gothic faux-vaults, while the rooms on the first floor are enclosed by richly decorated beamed ceilings. A distinctive feature of the house is the entrance portal with seats and circular medallions in which the portrait busts of the owners are rendered in low relief. The date was carved in the portal superstructure later, in the 19th century.[313] (Fig. 102)

313) Jan Muk, *Stavebně historický průzkum, čp. 497, Horní Slavkov* (Praha: NPÚ ÚOP v Lokti, 1971), Oddělení EDIS, sign. SHP 000013; Hana Hanzlíková, *Podrobný stavebně historický průzkum (zhodnocení nálezové situace), čp. 497, Horní Slavkov* (Plzeň: NPÚ ÚOP v Lokti, 2003), Oddělení EDIS, sign. SHP 000014.

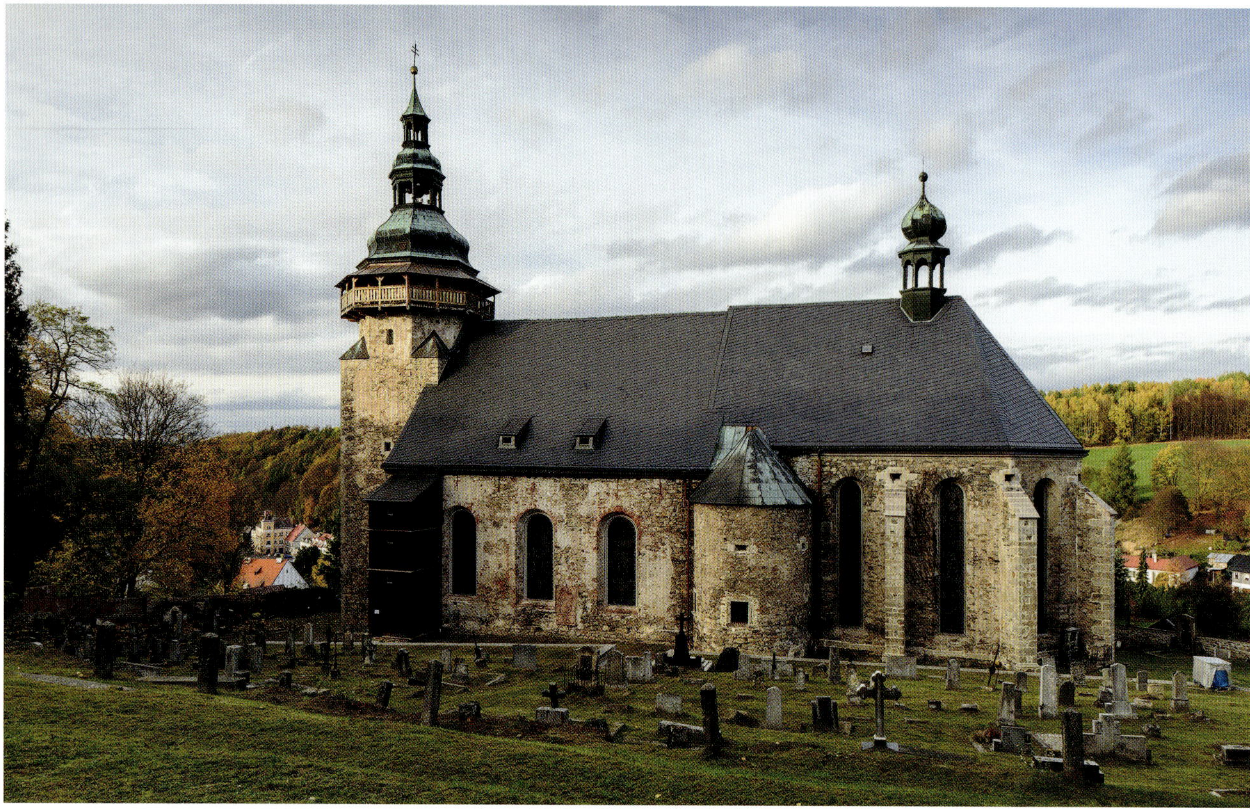

Fig. 103 Horní Slavkov, Church of St. George, general view from the south. First mention 1380, general reconstruction 1517–1520 – builder Hans Krug and Michal Wohl.

Johann Pflug von Rabenstein paid for the major reconstruction of the older **Church of St. George**, which is documented to have already existed in 1380. Older literature dates the church even further back in history, to the year 1242. (Fig. 103) The reconstruction was implemented by the builder Hans Krug (Rog) from 1517 until 1520[314] and it was finished by the builder Michal (Michal Wohl). According to tree-ring analysis, the wood for the truss was felled between 1518 and 1523.[315] The Chapel of the Holy Sepulchre is mentioned in 1520.

The church was surrounded by a high enclosure wall with a bastion. This gave it a fortress-like character, similar to the church in Banská Štiavnica. Since the town had no fortifications, the church could serve as a passive defence station for the town's population. A little later, the space above the vault of the chancel was equipped with shooting loopholes. The fortress-like character was accentuated by the three towers that were added to the west façade, and by the south and north end of the chancel. Exactly when the south tower was demolished is not known, but the north tower was continually being repaired from the 16th century onwards due to recurring structural problems caused by unstable foundations. It was eventually demolished in 1739, up to the level of the masonry line of the main nave.[316]

314) Rudolf Prosch, *Abriss der Geschichte*, 50.

315) Listed in dendrochronology database. Available online at: https://docs.google.com.

316) Jan Anderle, *Stavebně historický průzkum, kostel sv. Jiří v Horním Slavkově* (Plzeň: NPÚ ÚOP v Lokti, 2012), Oddělení EDIS, sign. SHP 000018.

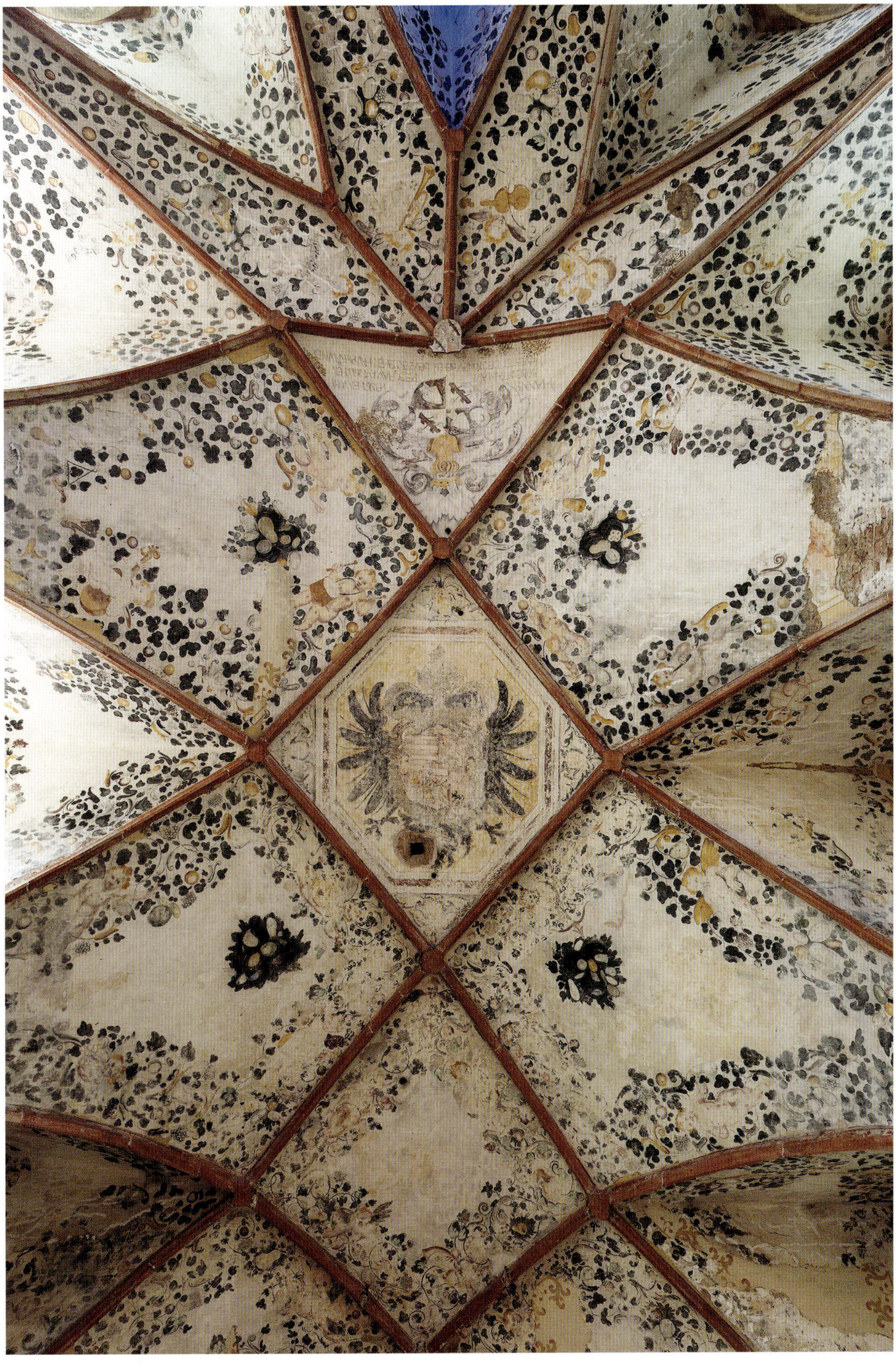

Fig. 104 Horní Slavkov, Church of St. George, net vault of the church. Photograph by J. Peer (2019).

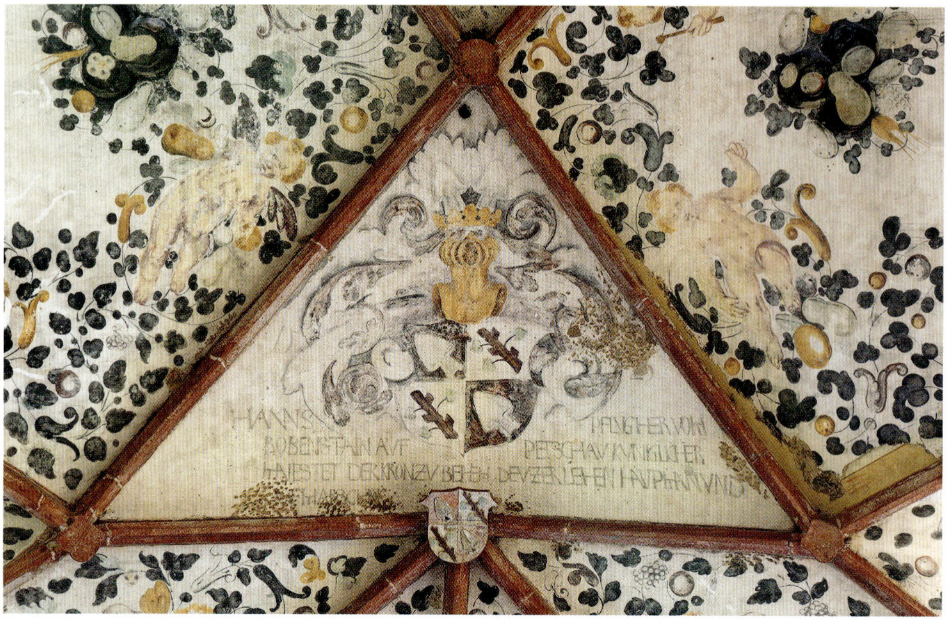

Fig. 105 Horní Slavkov, Church of St. George, coat of arms of Jan Pluh of Rabštejn on the vault of the church. Photograph by J. Peer (2019).

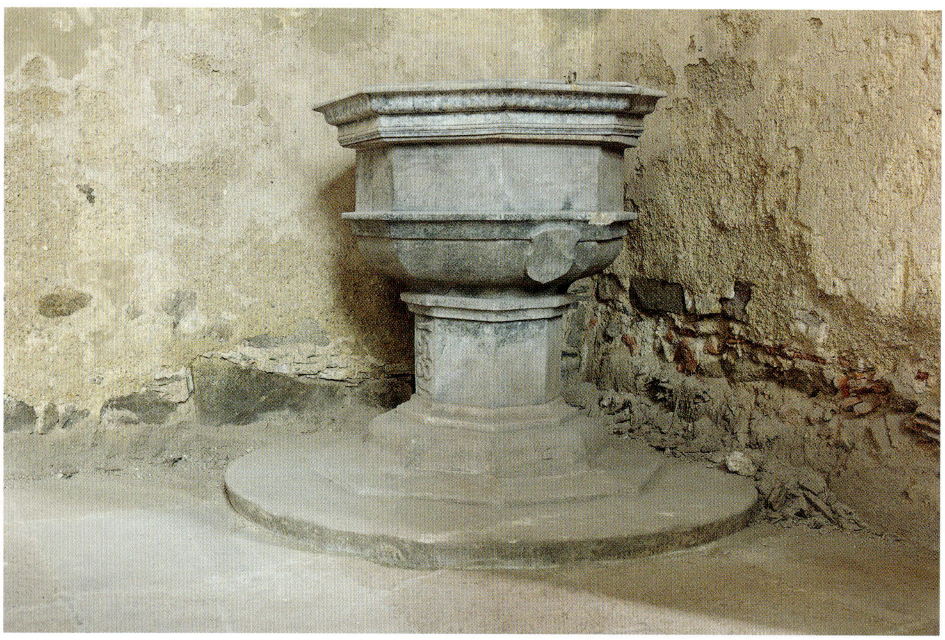

Fig. 106 Horní Slavkov, Church of St. George, Renaissance baptistery of the church. Created in 1581. Photograph by J. Peer (2019).

Not much has been preserved in the church from the late mediaeval and Renaissance periods. The net vault of the chancel is decorated with ornamental murals (vegetal motifs, putti with musical instruments), (Fig. 104) which were commissioned by Johann Pflug von Rabenstein, as revealed by his coat of arms and a German inscription with the date 1525 in the vault. The date probably refers to the time the construction was completed and the bells were installed.[317] (Fig. 105)

317) Rudolf Prosch, *Abriss der Geschichte*, 50.

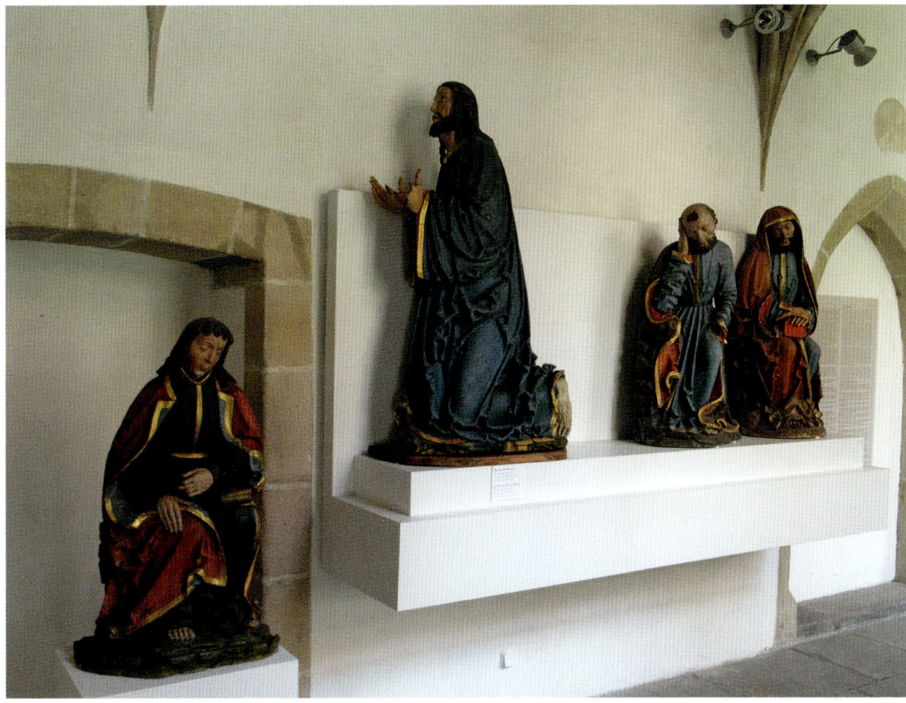

Fig. 107 Gothic Olivet Mountain from the Church of St. George in Horní Slavkov. Photo © Museum of Religious Art of the Plzeň Diocese.

The murals were uncovered and restored after a fire at the church in 1964.[318] They probably originated around 1530. The closest artistic parallels of these paintings can be found on the walls of the second floor of the upper palace of the Bečov Castle, which were probably commissioned by Katharina von Haslau, the wife of Johann Pflug von Rabenstein.

The holy water stoup (c. 1500) and the baptismal font (from 1581) probably come from the late mediaeval and Renaissance periods. (Fig. 106)

A late Gothic Mount of Olives with wooden polychromatic statues of a praying Christ and three apostles (now kept in the Museum of Religious Art of Pilsen Diocese) (Fig. 107) can be found on the ground floor of the tower.

They were made around 1520 and have been attributed to Hans Witten. Also of mediaeval origin (c. 1500) is the monumental and naturalistic statue of the Crucified Christ (now in the Museum of Religious Art of Pilsen Diocese), which was originally placed in the church's triumphal arch. It was damaged in the fire at the church in 1964. The Gothic Asumpta on the crescent (from around 1400) was venerated in the church until the fire in 1713, when it was destroyed. The shape of the statue is known from a Baroque copy made after the fire, which stood in the antechamber of the church and was later moved to the scapular altar in 1726. It was stolen in 1998 and subsequently destroyed.

An important monument from the early Renaissance is the so-called Häsler lantern (a funerary lamp). (Fig. 108) It was originally part of the grave of Georg Häsler (d. 1561), administrator of the mining authority, but later it was moved to the staircase leading to St. George's Church. (Fig. 109)

318) Petr Bareš – Jiří Brodský, *První etapa restaurátorských prací na nástěnných malbách v klenbě presbyteria hřbitovního kostela v Horním Slavkově* (NPÚ ÚOP v Lokti, 1969), Oddělení EDIS, sign. RZ 00596.

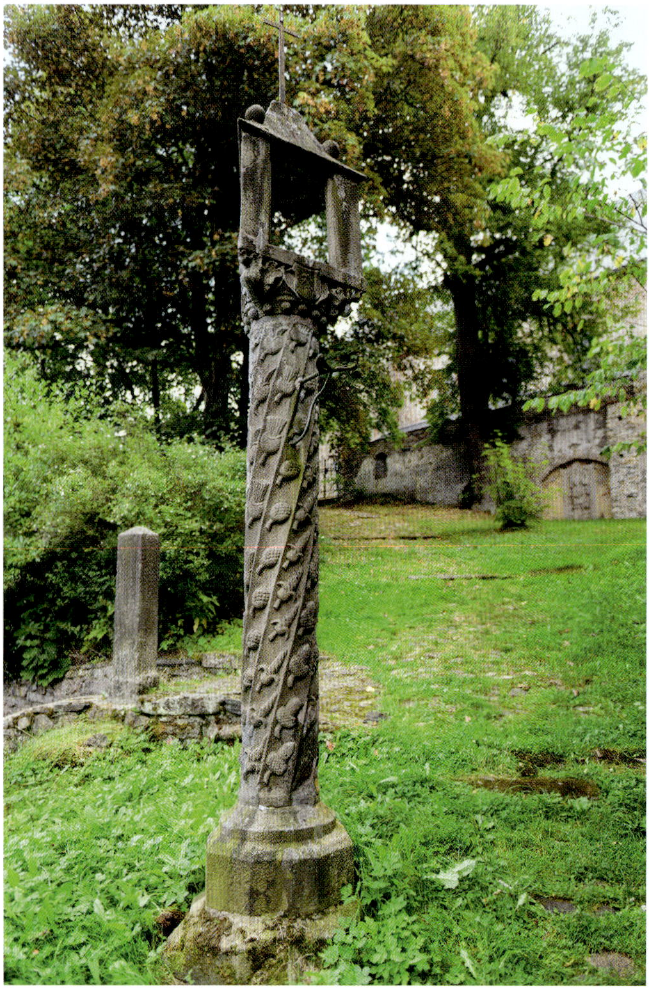

Fig. 108 So-called Häsler's lamp (Totenleuchte) from Horní Slavkov. Created in 1561. Photograph by J. Peer (2019).

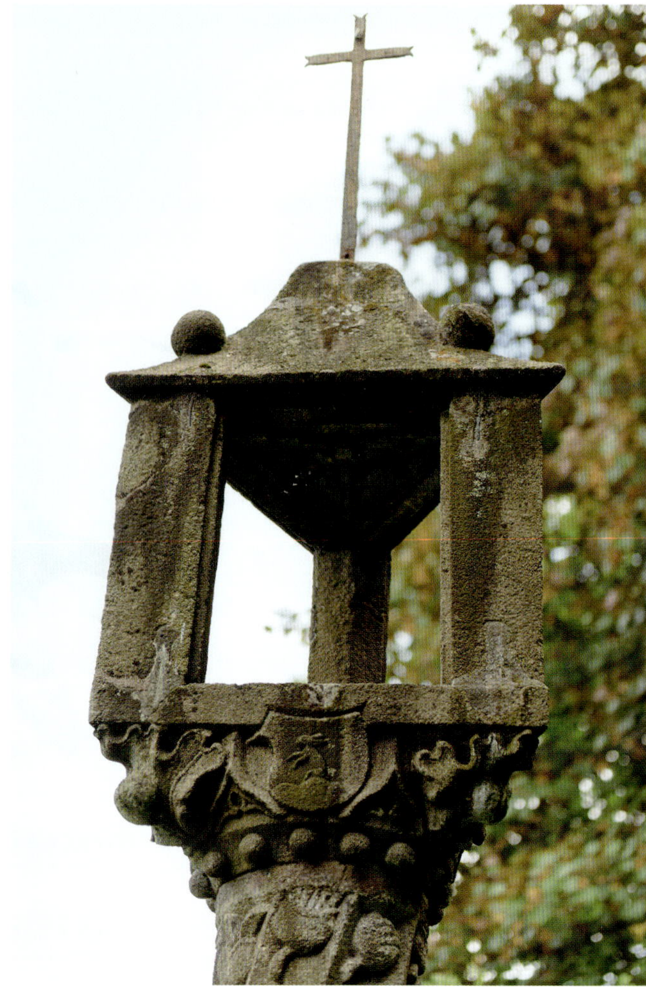

Fig. 109 Upper part of the so-called Häsler's lamp (Totenleuchte) from Horní Slavkov. Created in 1561. Photograph by J. Peer (2019).

The Baroque town hospital with the Church of St. Anne is also of mediaeval origin. The church and hospital existed as early as 1542, when the bells were reportedly moved here. It was burned to the ground in a devastating fire in 1713 and was subsequently rebuilt.

The striking Renaissance town hall, built in the style of the Saxon Renaissance, showed off the town's wealth. It was located in the upper, south-eastern part of what is today Republic Square. It replaced the older town hall, which used to stand below St. George's Church but soon ceased to suit the flourishing city. Therefore, in 1521, the town bought the late Gothic house of Michael Waldt and, after minor alterations, established a town hall there.

A major reconstruction of the house into a new Renaissance town hall took place between 1583 and 1586. The project was carried out by the northern Italian builder Matthäus Merklein.[319] It was an oblong, two-storey building with an attic that had triangular gables rising above a cornice decorated with an arched frieze. The gabled roof was topped with a turret

319) Anton Gnirs, *Topografie der historischen und Kunst-Denkmale*, 297.

Fig. 110 Krásno, Church of St. Catherine, old church pictured before the fire in 1848. The original church was built in the second half of the 14th century, rebuilt in the Renaissance style in 1553, the current appearance comes from the reconstruction in 1858–1859. Reproduction from the book Prokop, V. – Smola, L., Sokolovsko – Umění, památky a umělci do roku 1945. Loket 2014.

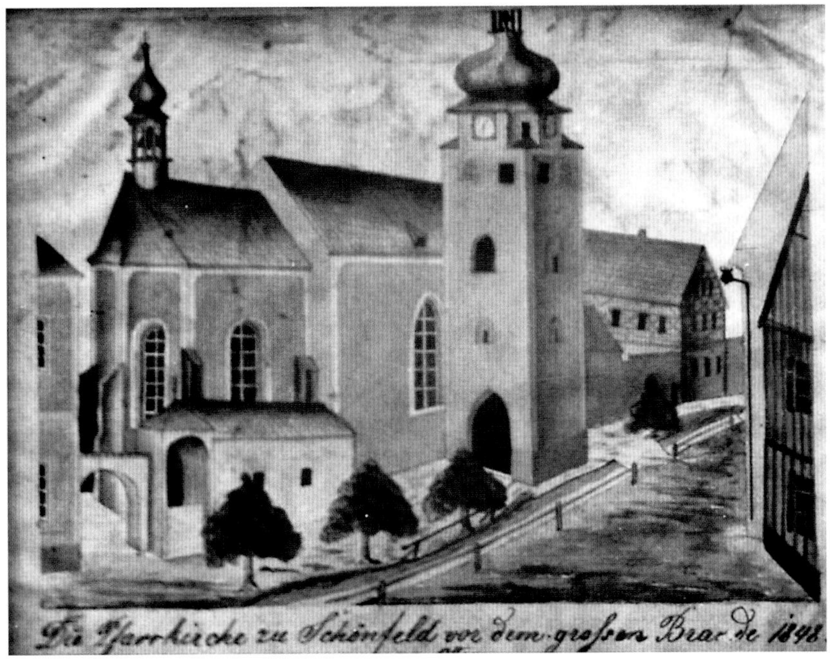

with a lantern.[320] The town hall housed the town archives and some monuments relating to the municipal government. Everything was destroyed in a fire at the town hall in 1978, whereupon the town hall was unnecessarily demolished. The town had a number of fine houses from the late mediaeval and Renaissance periods.

There was a Latin school in Slavkov, as in other larger mining towns. It operated from 1554 until 1624[321] in a building with a top floor built in 1525 opposite the parsonage. After graduating, successful local students went on to universities abroad, especially Wüttenberg. Notable students included the clergyman, historian and astronomer Zacharias Theobald, the preacher and orientalist Christophor Crimesius, and the poet and humanist Nicolaus Thodaenus.

In the 16th century, the Pflugs of Rabenstein contributed significantly to the devlopment of the mining town of **Krásno** (Schönfeld),[322] which had been founded at the turn of the 12th and 13th centuries by miners mainly from Meissen. The settlement is sometimes referenced in sources as Dreilinden. The town focused on the mining of tin and tungsten. Tin and tungsten mining boomed in the mid-14th century and, to a much greater extent, again in the second half of the 15th century and first half of the 16th century.

The credit for the second stage of development goes also to the Pflugs of Rabenstein, who ensured that Krásno be promoted to a town in 1529. In 1547, Emperor Ferdinand I granted the town a coat of arms with mining symbols.

The urban plan of Krásno is similar to that of the other mining towns. The houses were built along the Dlouhá Stream flowing through a long, shallow valley. At the turn of the 16th

320) The appearance of the town hall is preserved in photographs deposited in the archives of the NPÚ ÚOP in Loket. A digital version available at: https://iispp.npu.cz.

321) Rudolf Prosch, *Abriss der Geschichte*, 52–53.

322) Emanuel Poche et al., *UPČ* 2, 141; Vladimír Prokop – Lukáš Smola, *Sokolovsko*, 390–413.

and 17th centuries, 250 houses are documented in the town. The oldest building is house No. 11 with a late Gothic portal with a coat of arms bearing the symbols of mining.

The most noteworthy religious building in the town was the **parish church of St. Catherine**, which was built at the upper end in the narrowest part of the square. (Fig. 110) The earliest mention of the church dates from 1404. There was a major reconstruction at the end of the 15th century, and again in 1553. The church was laid out as a single-nave building with a polygonal chancel and a massive tower with a polygonal top. The older church was significantly damaged by fire in 1848, at which time the nearby half-timbered parsonage was completely destroyed.

After the fire, the remnants of the church were temporarily roofed over and served as a provisional place of worship until 1856. The existing church dedicated to St. Catherine of

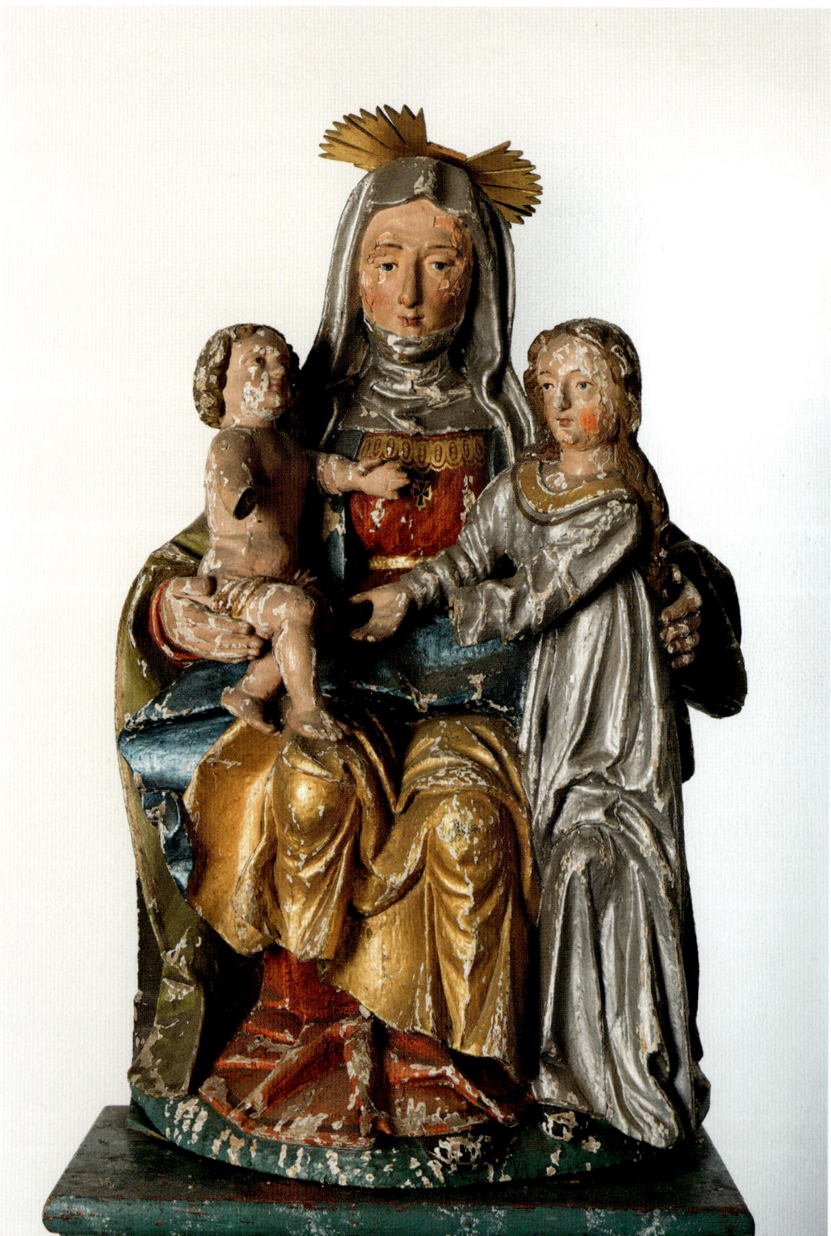

Fig. 111 Statue of St. Anne with Madonna and Child of Krásno. Created around 1520. Photograph by J. Peer (2019).

Fig. 112 Krásno, Church of St. Catherine, general view from the east. Photograph by J. Peer (2019).

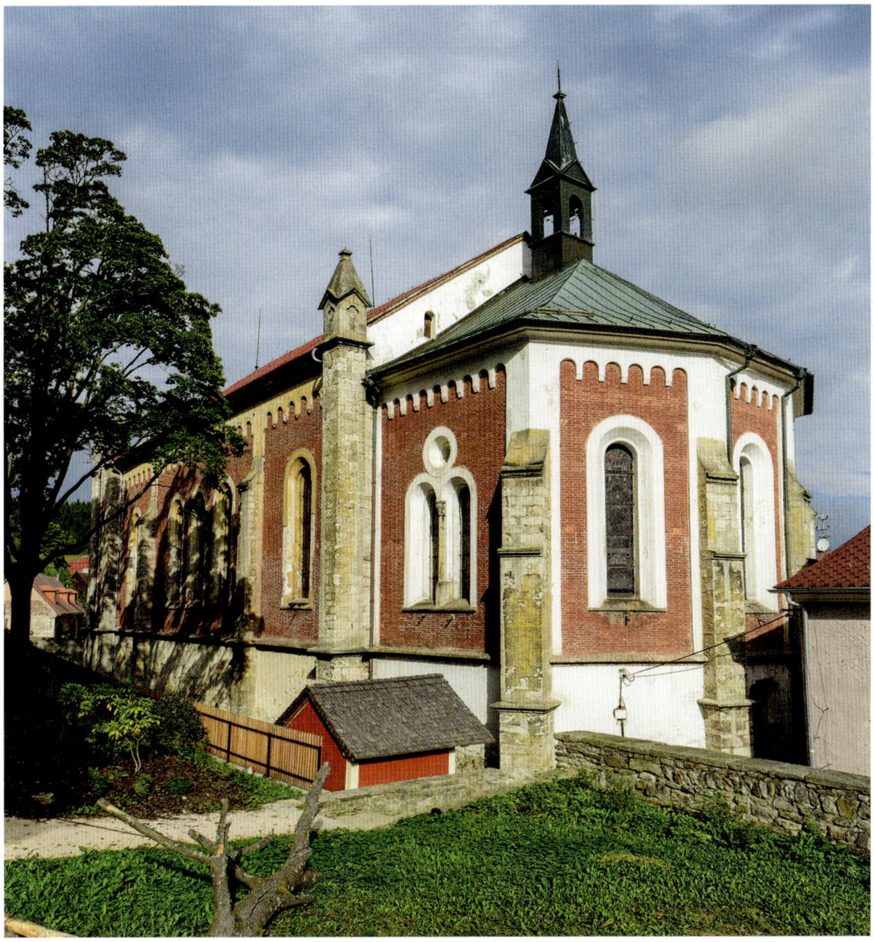

Alexandria was built between 1858 and 1859 in the Neo-Romanesque style by the Loket builder Josef Scherbaum, using parts of the outer walls from the previous church building.[323] (Fig. 112 , Fig. 113)

A late Gothic statue (c. 1520) of St. Anne, a patron saint of miners, probably comes from the original church furnishings. (Fig. 111) From 1782, the grace statue of the Virgin Mary of Krásná was venerated in the church, made by the local carpenter Zimmerhackel in 1677 from the wood of a linden tree that had fallen down during a storm. The statue was then placed in a hollow carved into another linden tree until 1782. The Chapel of the Assumption of the Virgin Mary was built near the tree in 1710. The consistory investigated the miracles associated with the statue, and announced in 1720 that while the statue was not miraculous, it could be venerated by the faithful for its beneficent effects.

Unfortunately, the historical architectural heritage of the town was ravaged by a huge fire that broke out on 7 July 1848. Among the buildings that were sadly lost in the fire were the late Gothic half-timbered town hall and the municipal tower from 1539.

323) https://www.pamatkovykatalog.cz.

Fig. 113 Krásno, Church of St. Catherine, general view of the interior from the west. Photograph by J. Peer (2019). →

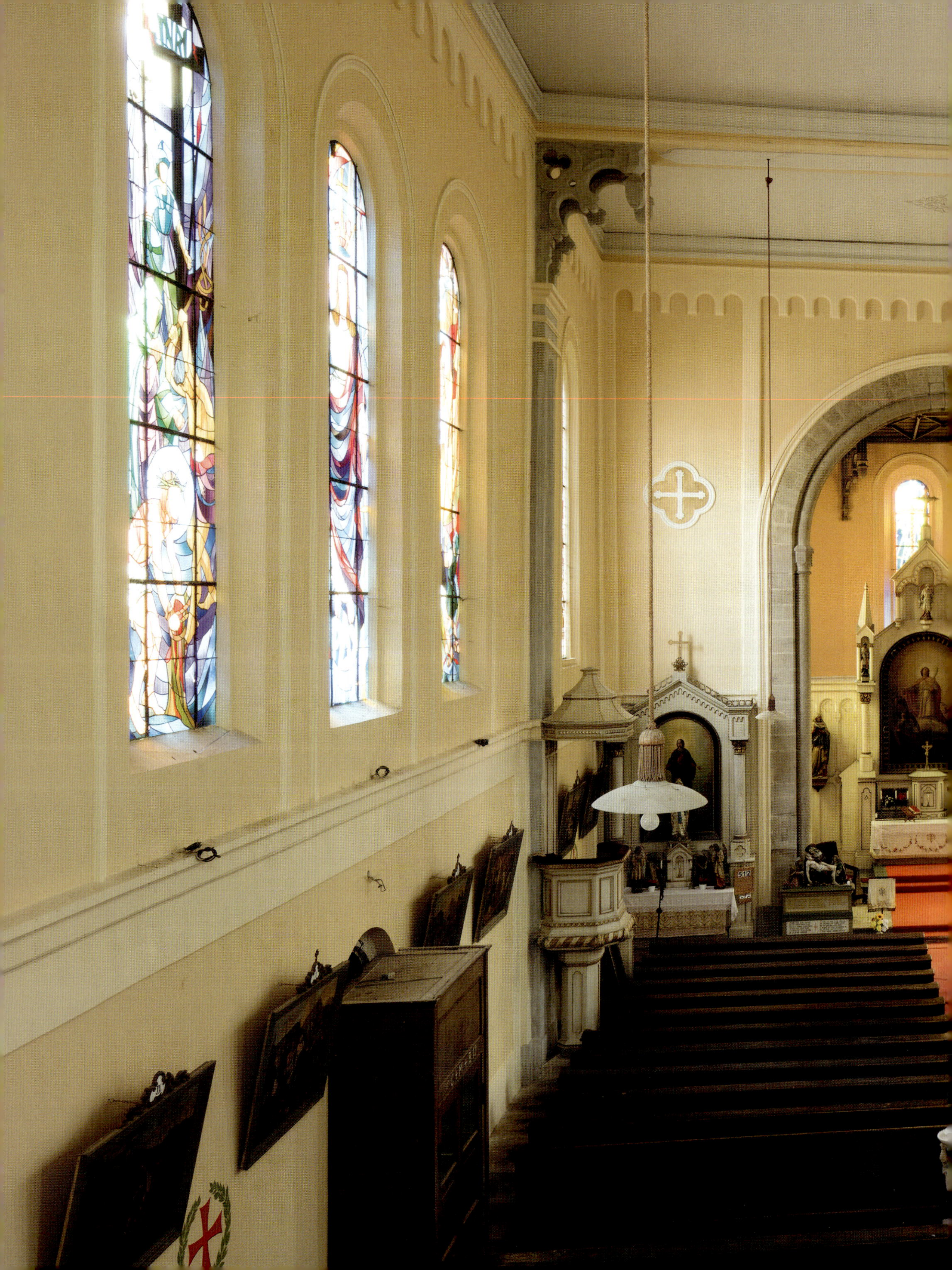

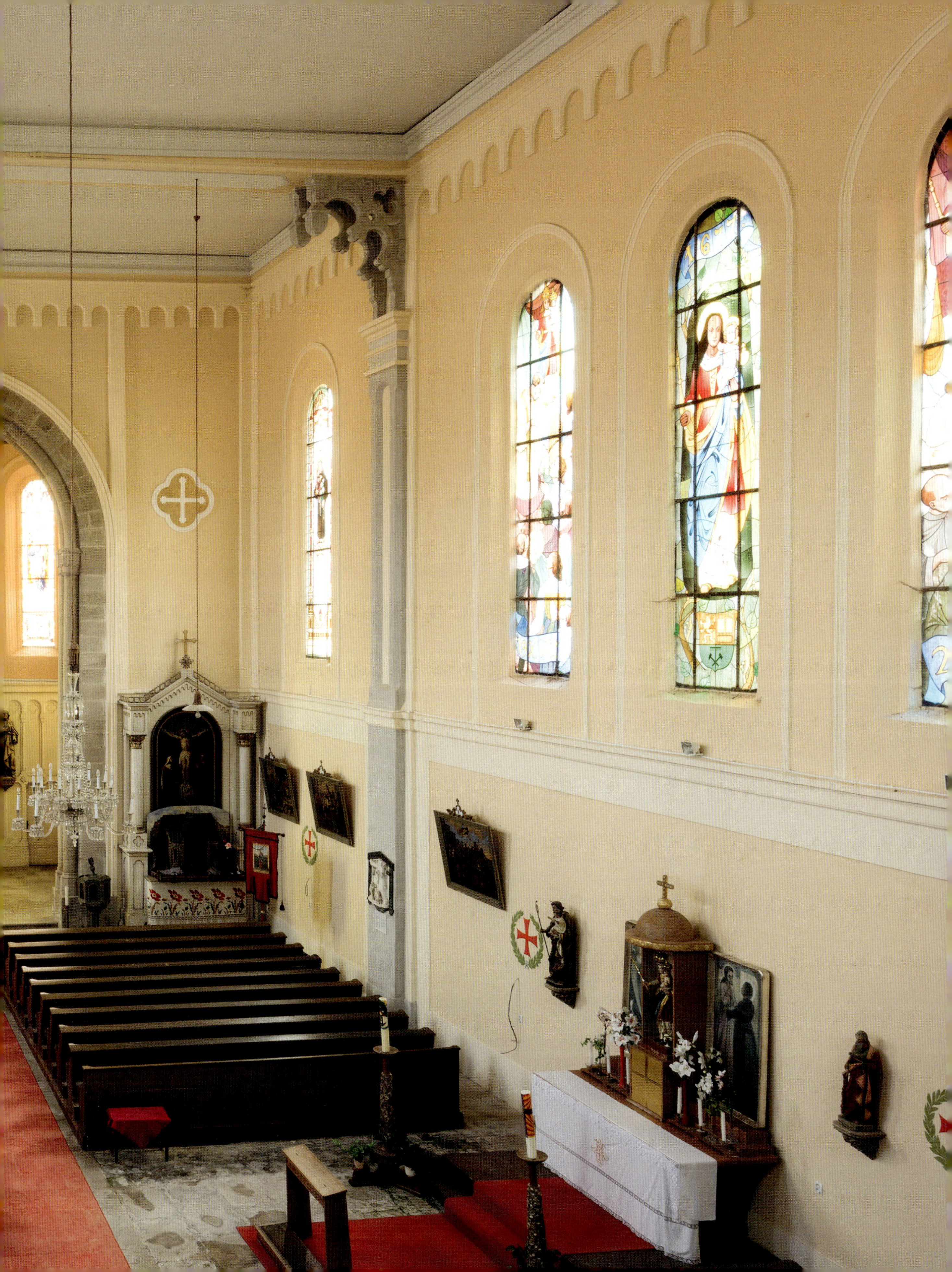

REVIEW OF SOURCES, LITERATURE AND INTERNET SOURCES

EDITION

Ježek, Bohuslav – Hummel, Josef (ed.). *Jiřího Agricoly dvanáct knih o hornictví a hutnictví.* Ostrava: 2001.

Linka, Jan (ed.). *Václav Hájek z Libočan – Kronika česká.* Praha: 2013.

Müller, August (ed.). *Quellen- und Urkundenbuch des Bezirkes Teplitz-Schönau bis zum Jahre 1500.* Prag: 1929.

Tomek, Václav Vladivoj (ed.). *Registra decimarum papalium.* Praha: 1873.

LITERATURE

Adamcová, Kateřina – Gláserová-Lebedová, Zdenka – Kovařík, Viktor – Nejedlý, Vratislav – Zahradník, Pavel. *Mariánské, trojiční a další světecké sloupy a pilíře v Ústeckém kraji.* Praha: 2012.

Anderle, Jan. *Stavebně historický průzkum, kostel sv. Jiří v Horním Slavkově.* Plzeň: 2012, NPÚ ÚOP v Lokti, Oddělení EDIS, sign. SHP 000018.

Approaching East-Central Europe over the Centuries. Berlin – Wien: 2019.

Arnold, Klaus-Peter (ed.). *Kunsthandwerk der Gotik und Renaissance: 13. bis 17. Jahrhundert.* Dresden: 1981.

Badstübner, Ernst. *Bauten der Renaissance in Sachsen und Thüringen: Einführung und Erläuterungen.* Leipzig: 1965.

Balážová, Barbara. "Das Erinnerungsmal für Christoph Füssl aus dem Jahr 1561 und andere Wiener Sepulkralkunstwerke für die Bürger der mittelslowakischen Bergbaustädte." In: *Epigraphica & Sepulcralia 8*, 85–102. 2019.

Bamberg, Paul Adolf. "Die *Münzmeister in Annaberg.*" *Deutsche Münzblätter* 60/62 (1940/42): 411–421.

Bamberg, Paul Adolf. "Hieronymus Magdeburger, Peter Goldschmied und Jobst Leypold." *Berliner Münzblätter* 11/53 (1933): 129–138, 148–151.

Bareš, Petr – Brodský, Jiří. *První etapa restaurátorských prací na nástěnných malbách v klenbě presbyteria hřbitovního kostela v Horním Slavkově.* 1969, NPÚ ÚOP v Lokti, Oddělení EDIS, sign. RZ 00596.

Barge, Herman – Bodenstein von Karlstadt, Andreas. *Karlstadt und die Anfänge der Reformation.* Leipzig: 1905.

Bartoš, Vítězslav. "Přínos českých horníků emigrujících do Saska roku 1654, speciálně do Johanngeorgenstadtu." *Studie z dějin hornictví* 34 (2006): 98–102.

Baťa, Jan (ed.). *Codex Kuttenbergensis / Kutnohorský kodex.* Praha: 2008.

Batta, Štefan. "Stredoveké baníctvo a hutníctvo na rožňavskej Matercii," *Zborník Banského múzea* 14, 105–129. Martin: 1989.

Batta, Štefan. *Rožňavská Metercia.* Martin: 2001.

Bergwelten. Katalog výstavy k 500. výročí Georgia Agricoly. Chemnitz: 1994.

Bervic, Rudolf – Kocourková, Květoslava. *Krupka. Půl tisíciletí horního města.* Krupka: 1978.

Bílek, Jaroslav (ed.). *Ius regale montanorum aneb Právo královské hornikuov.* Kutná Hora: 2010.

Bílek, Ladislav – Jangl, Ladislav – Urban, Jan. *Dějiny hornictví na Chomutovsku.* Chomutov: 1976.

Binterová, Zdena. *Historie Vejprt.* Chomutov: 2007.

Binterová, Zdena. *Od Hory sv. Šebestiána po Krásnou Lípu*. Chomutov: 2000.

Binterová, Zdena. *Přísečnice zatopená, ale nezapomenutá*. Chomutov: 2004.

Binterová, Zdena. *Zaniklé obce Chomutovska V., Přísečnicko*. Chomutov: 1996.

Blaschke, Karlheins. "Altzelle: Ein Kloster zwischen Geistlichkeit und Herrschaft." In: Schattkowsky, Martina – Thieme, André (ed.). *Altzelle: Zisterzienserabtei in Mitteldeutschland und Hauskloster der Wettiner*, 89–99. Leipzig: 2002.

Blaschke, Karlheinz. "Egranus, Johannes Sylvius." *Neue Deutsche Biographie* 4 (Berlin: 1959): 341–342.

Bobková, Lenka. "Sasko v teritoriální politice českých králů do roku 1459." In: Kaiserová, Kristina (ed.). *Čechy a Sasko v proměnách dějin, Acta Universitatis Purkynianae, Philosophica et Historica I., Slavogermanica II.*, 49–67. Ústí nad Labem: 1993.

Boehm, Anton. *Gedächtnis Beitrag über die k. freye Bergstadt Joachimsthal: 1. Teil 1525–1699.*

Boháč, Zdeněk. *Poutní místa v Čechách*. Praha: 1995.

Böhmer, Johann Fridrich – Huber, Alfons (ed.). *Regesta imperii VIII*. Innsbruck: 1877.

Boublíková-Jáhnová, Juliána. "Znamenité umění a mnoho krásných článků pravého náboženství: jáchymovské biblické a Husovy medaile jako odraz luterství." *Dějiny a současnost* 39, No. 9 (2017): 14–17.

Boublíková-Jáhnová, Juliána. "Bitevní a smuteční medaile jáchymovských řezáčů Conze Welcze a Nickela Milicze." *Numismatický sborník* 29, No. 1 (2015): 60–69.

Boublíková-Jáhnová, Juliána. "Co se skrývá za jáchymovskou medailí s Davidem, Goliášem a Jonatanem? Medaile na přátelství od Wolfa Milicze podle grafik Hanse Sebalda Behama." *Časopis Společnosti přátel starožitností* 121, No. 2 (2013): 94–101.

Boublíková-Jáhnová, Juliána. "Jáchymovské medaile. Významný fenomén evropského medailérství 16. století." In: *Jáchymovský smolinec a kovové radium. Studie z dějin hornictví* 40 (2011): 59–65.

Boublíková-Jáhnová, Juliána. "K ikonografii a významu jáchymovských medailí s Janem Husem." *Numismatické listy* 47, No. 2 (1992): 33–41.

Boublíková-Jáhnová, Juliána. "Počátky medailérství v Čechách. Jáchymovské portrétní medaile hrabat Šliků." In: *Sborník Národního muzea v Praze*, Řada A, Historie 57, No. 1–2 (2003): 1–44.

Boukal, Jan. *Jakoubek z Vřesovic († 1462): Cesta chudého moravského rytíře k vládě nad severozápadními Čechami*. České Budějovice: 2016.

Braun, Edmund Wilhelm. "Concz Welcz, der Goldschmied zu St. Joachimsthal." *Kunst und Kunsthandwerk. Monatsschrift herausgegeben vom k. k. österreichischen Museum für Kunst und Industrie* XX, No. 11–12 (1917): 422–429.

Braun, Edmund Wilhelm. "Drei weitere signierte Arbeiten des Joachimsthaler Goldschmiedes Concz Welcz." *Kunst und Kunsthandwerk. Monatsschrift herausgegeben vom k. k. österreichischen Museum für Kunst und Industrie* XXIII (1920): 7–10, 212–216.

Braun, Edmund Wilhelm. "Zwei Buchsreliefs vom Joachimsthaler Goldschmied Concz Welcz." In: *Archiv für Medaillen- und Plaketten-Kunde* III, 3–4, (1921/22): 128–133.

Bräuer, Helmut. *Zur Mentalität armer Leute in Obersachsen 1500 bis 1800*. Leipzig: 2008.

Brodesser, Slavomír – Mainuš, František – Janák, Jan. *Celnictví v Československu: Minulost a přítomnost*. Praha: 1982.

Brodský, Pavel. "Vyobrazení kutnohorských havířů v českých pozdně středověkých rukopisech." *Poznańskie Towarzystwo Przyjaciól Nauk* 106 (1989): 94–97.

Brunner, Sabine. "Beziehungen zwischen Böhmen, dem Egerland und dem Vogtland vom Mittelalter bis zur frühen Neuzeit." In: Kaiserová, Kristina (ed.). *Čechy a Sasko v proměnách dějin, Acta Universitatis Purkynianae, Philosophica et Historica I., Slavogermanica II.*, 75–88. Ústí nad Labem: 1993.

Budinská, Jitka – *Jančárek, Petr* – Procházka Jiří. *Hrob. Dějiny města*. Teplice: *1982*.

Buňatová, Marie. *Pražští kupci na cestách*. Praha: 2013.

Burachovič, Stanislav. *Jáchymov v zrcadle času. Stručné dějiny prvních radonových lázní světa*. Karlovy Vary: 2007.

Buran, Dušan. *Studien zur Wandmalerei um 1400 in der Slowakei. Die Pfarrkirche St. Jakob in Leutschau und die Pfarrkirche St. Franziskus Seraphicus in Poniky*. Weimar: 2002.

Cais, Petr. *Archiv města Horní Blatná: 1535–1945 (1954) – Inventář*. Karlovy Vary: 2006.

Cais, Petr. "Odeslaná korespondence města Jáchymova: sonda do písemných kontaktů krušnohorského horního města v polovině 16. století." *Západočeské archivy* (2010): 81–90.
Cílek, Václav. *Kameny domova*. Praha: 2011.
Čechura, Jaroslav. "Velkostatek kláštera Osek v letech 1310–1419." *Časopis Národního muzea. Řada historická* 160, No. 1–4 (1991): 20–46.
Čechura, Martin. *Zaniklé kostely Čech*. Praha: 2012.
Černý, Jiří. "Ein Himmelsbrief oder eine Lutherschrift? Die Joachimsthaler Flugschrift ‚Ein Mandat Jesu Christi' aus dem Jahre 1524." In: Wakounig, Marija – Kuhnel, Ferdinand (ed.). *Approaching East-Central Europe over the Centuries*, 55–72. Berlin – Wien: 2019.
Čumlivski, Denko. "První dvě generace rodu pánů z Koldic usedlé v Čechách a jejich činnost: Těma (I.) z Koldic 1303 až Těma (II.) z Koldic 1383." Diploma thesis. Charles University, 1974.
Derner, Kryštof (ed.). *Středověké hornictví a hutnictví na Přísečnicku ve středním Krušnohoří*. Dresden: 2018.
Distelberger, Rudolf. "Gold und Silber, Edelsteie und Elfenbein." In: Seibt, Ferdinand (ed.). *Renaissance in Böhmen*, 255–287. München: 1985.
Durdík, Tomáš. *Encyklopedie českých hradů*. Praha: 2005.
Durdík, Tomáš. *Ilustrovaná encyklopedie českých hradů – Dodatky*. Praha: 2002.
Eißner, Lois. *Bleistadt, einst königlich freie Bergstadt 1523–1973*. Schwandorf: 1973.
Fajt, Jiří (ed.). *Europa Jagellonica 1386–1572. Umění a kultura ve střední Evropě za vlády Jagellonců – katalog k výstavě*. Praha: 2012.
Farský, Milan. "Co spojuje města Zlaté Hory a Dubí v Krušných horách? – Nové vysvětlení možného významu názvu Zuckmantel." *Acta onomastica* 58 (2017): 172–176.
Fiala, Jaroslav. "Stará česko-saská hranice mezi Jáchymovem a Božím Darem." *Historický sborník Karlovarska* 5 (1997): 32–50.
Fiala, Jaroslav. "Vzestup a pád města Ostrova v 17. století a útěk jeho obyvatel před vrchností." *Historický sborník Karlovarska* 6 (1998): 53–65.
Fiedler, Uwe – Thoß, Hendrik – Bünz, Enno (ed.). *Des Himmels Fundgrube: Chemnitz und das sächsisch-böhmische Gebirge im 15. Jahrhundert*. Chemnitz: 2012.
Frieder, Jentsch. "Rülein von Calw." Ulrich, *Neue Deutsche Biographie* 22 (Berlin, 2005): 222.
Gavenda, Lukáš. "Páni Hasištejnští z Lobkovic na sklonku středověku." Diploma thesis. Charles University, 2008.
Gnirs, Anton. *Eine Bergchronik der Städte Schlaggenwald und Elbogen*. Elbogen: 1926.
Gnirs, Anton. *Topographie der historischen und kunstgeschichtlichen Denkmale in dem Bezirke Karlsbad*. München: 1996.
Gnirs, Anton. *Topographie der historischen und kunstgeschichtlichen Denkmalen in dem Bezirke Karlsbad*. München: 1939.
Grimm, Josef. "Nejstarší abertamské památky pocházejí z let 1680 a 1706." *Měsíčník Krušné hory západ* 3, No. 7 (July 2014): 10.
Halama, Oto – Soukup, Pavel. *Kalich jako symbol v prvním století utrakvismu*. Praha: 2016.
Hallwich, Hermann. *Geschichte der Bergstadt Graupen in Böhmen*. Prag: 1868.
Hammer, Vera M. – Hanzer, Helene – Huber, Petr. "Der ‚Handstein' in der Mineralogischen Schausammlung des Naturhistorischen Museums Wien." In: *Der Anschnitt* 57, No. 5–6 (2005): 200–206.
Hamsíková, Magdalena. "Desková malba z bývalé klášterní obrazárny v Oseku." Diploma thesis. Charles University, 2004.
Hanzlík, Jan. "Město a jeho koncept." In: Karel, Tomáš – Kratochvílová, Alžběta (ed.). *Proměny montánní krajiny. Historické sídelní a montánní struktury Krušnohoří*, 76–81. Loket: 2013.
Hanzlíková, Hana. *Podrobný stavebně historický průzkum (zhodnocení nálezové situace), čp. 497, Horní Slavkov*. Plzeň: NPÚ ÚOP v Lokti, Oddělení EDIS, sign. SHP 000014. 2003.
Haragová, Vladěna. "Ikonografická rekonstrukce nástěnných maleb z kostela sv. Wolfganga v Doupově." *Památky západních Čech* 4 (2014): 20–35.
Haubertová, Květoslava – Hofman, Gustav – Lešnický, Ladislav. *Soupis západočeských urbářů*. Plzeň: 1993.
Hauserová, Milena. "Luteránský kostel." In: Karel, Tomáš – Kratochvílová, Alžběta (ed.), *Proměny montánní krajiny. Historické sídelní a montánní struktury Krušnohoří*, 82–89. Loket: 2013.

Hauserová, Milena. "Prostorové uspořádání jáchymovských domů." In: *Jáchymov. Architektonická perla Krušnohoří*, 46–47. Loket: 2009.
Heifurth, Gerhard. *Bergbaukultur im Erzgebirge*. Schneeberg: 1995.
Hejnic, Josef – Thiergen, Peter – Udolph, Ludger. "Die St. Joachimsthaler Lateinschulbibliothek nach dem Jahre 1620." In: *Res slavica: Festschrift für Hans Rothe zum 65. Geburtstag*, 529–535. Schöningh: 1994.
Hejnic, Josef. "Jáchymovská škola v 16. století. Problémy a úkoly." *Sborník Národního muzea v Praze, Historie* 40, No. 1 (1986): 29–40.
Hentschel, Walter. "Nosseni und die dritte Walther-Generation." In: Hentschel, Walter. *Dresdner Bildhauer des 16. und 17. Jahrhunderts*, 67–88. Weimar: 1966.
Hlaváček, Petr – Bílková, Milena. *Františkánské nebe v Kadani: renesanční příběh kláštera Čtrnácti sv. Pomocníků / Der Franziskanerhimmel in Kadaň: die Renaissancegeschichte des Klosters der Vierzehn heiligen Nothelfer* (Kadaň: 2018).
Hlaváček, Petr. *Nový Jeruzalém? Příběh františkánského kláštera Čtrnácti sv. Pomocníků v Kadani*. Kadaň: 2013.
Hlaváček, Petr. "St. Joachimsthal, Johannes Mathesius und der lutherische ‚Wallfahrtsort' Horní Blatná/ Platten (1559)." In: *Wallfahrt und Reformation / Pouť a reformace. Zur Veränderung religiöser Praxis in Deutschland und Böhmen in den Umbrüchen der Frühen Neuzeit*, 221–234. Frankfurt am Main: 2007.
Hoffmann, Yves – Richter, Uwe. *Entstehung und Blüte der Stadt Freiberg: die bauliche Entwicklung der Bergstadt vom 12. bis zum Ende des 17. Jahrhunderts*. Halle: 2012.
Hoffmann, František. "Rukopisné sborníky horního práva." In: *Studie o rukopisech* X (1971): 65–137.
Hoffmann, Michaela. *Mariaschein – Bohosudov: ein Wallfahrtsort im Donröschenschlaf*. Brno: 2005.
Hoffmann, Yves – Richter, Uwe. "Die Portalarchitektur der Spätgotik und Renaissance." In: *Denkmale in Sachsen. Stadt Freiberg 2*, 729–806. Dresden: 2003.
Hoffmann, Yves – Richter, Uwe. "Portale der Renaissance in Marienberg." In: *Sächsische Heimatblätter* 52, No. 3 (2006): 226–233.
Hofmann, Gustav. "K populačnímu vývoji Jáchymova v 16. století." In: *Studie z dějin hornictví* 19 (1987): 72–89.
Holečková, Zuzana. "Šlikovské mince v období 1519/20–1528 a počátky mincovnictví v Jáchymově." In: Klípa, Jan – Ottová, Michaela (ed.). *Bez hranic. Umění v Krušnohoří mezi gotikou a renesancí*, 678–682. Praha: 2015.
Holzhausen, Walter. "Die Blütezeit bergmännischer Kunst." In: Winkelmann, Heinrich (ed.). *Die Bergbau in der Kunst*, 113–248. Essen: 1958.
Hrdlička, Josef – Just, Jiří – Zemek, Petr (ed.). "Evangelické církevní řády pro šlechtická panství v Čechách a na Moravě 1520–1620." In: *Prameny k českým dějinám 16.–18. století*, Řada B, sv. VIII, 123–124. České Budějovice: 2017.
Hrubá, Michaela. "Historie Krušnohoří mezi středověkem a raným novověkem." In: Hrubá, Michaela – Ottová, Michaela – Royt, Jan. *Ars Montana. Umělecký a kulturní transfer v otevřeném prostoru česko-saského Krušnohoří na prahu raného novověku*, 13–45. Praha: 2016.
Hrubá, Michaela. "Horní města v Krušnohoří a počátky reformace." In: Klípa, Jan – Ottová, Michaela (ed.). *Bez hranic. Umění v Krušnohoří mezi gotikou a renesancí*, 647–649. Praha: 2015.
Hrubá, Michaela. "Jiří Popel z Lobkovic a prostředky rekatolizace na sklonku 16. století. Příspěvek k dějinám rekatolizace v severozápadních Čechách." in: *Ústecký sborník historický* (2000): 132–144.
Hrubá, Michaela. "Tradice horního práva v českých zemích a právní rámec těžby v Krušných horách." In: Hrubá, Michaela – Ottová, Michaela – Royt, Jan. *Ars Montana. Umělecký a kulturní transfer v otevřeném prostoru česko-saského Krušnohoří na prahu raného novověku*, 47–52. Praha: 2016.
Hrubý, Petr. "Bohuslav Felix Hasištejnský z Lobkovic. Rodinné a majetkové zázemní luteránského předáka v předbělohorských Čechách." in: *Ústecký sborník historický* (2000): 98–131.
Hrubý, Petr. "Středověká těžba stříbronosných rud ve 13. a 14. století na českém území." In: Derner, Kryštof (ed.). *Středověké hornictví a hutnictví na Přísečnicku ve středním Krušnohoří*, 31–37. Dresden: 2018.
Hrubý, Petr. "Vývoj pozemkové držby Bohuslava Felixe Hasištejnského z Lobkowicz." *Vlastivědný sborník Kralupska* 5, No. 1–2 (1998): 32–50.
Hrůza, Jiří. *Svět měst*. Praha: 2014.
Huber, Peter – Huber, Simone. "St. Joachimsthal." *Lapis* 6, No. 6 (1981): 19–26, 38–40.

Huber, Peter. "Die schönste Stuffe." In: *Gediegen Silber. Das Erz der Münzen, das Metall des Schmuckes, das Element mit dem Glanz. ExtraLapis* 8 (1995): 58–67.
Huber, Peter. "Faszination und Geschichte bergmännischer Handsteine." *Berichte der Geologischen Bundesanstalt* 41 (Wien, 1997): 99–104.
Huber, Peter. *Handsteine from Slovakia and Bohemia / Bergmännische Handsteine aus der Slowakei und Böhmen*. 13. internationals Erbe-Symposium, Banská Štiavnica: 15.-20. Juni 2015, Abstracts, 90–91.
Huczmanová, Andrea. "Na paměť Štěpána Šlika a celého jeho rodu. Program výzdoby kostela sv. Jáchyma v Jáchymově." In: *Nevidíme, co nevíme. Sborník příspěvků z mezinárodní konference studentů doktorských programů / We cannot see what we do not know. The proceedings of the international conference for doctoral students*, 45–52. Praha: 2018.
Huczmanová, Andrea. "Začátky dolování v Jáchymově, založení města a mincovní práva Šliků ve světle politických jednání a písemných pramenů." *Herditas minariorum* 3 (2016): 9–24.
Hylla, Alexandra. "Himlische Erz –Silberschmiedekunst des 16. Jahrhundert." *Der Anschnitt* 70, 3–4 (2018): 119–138.
Charvátová, Kateřina. "Hospodářství oseckého kláštera v první polovině 14. století. " *Československý časopis historický* 28 (1980): 239–258.
Chlumská, Štepánka – Helfertová, Lenka. "Oltář Čtrnácti sv. pomocníků z Kadaně: průzkum a restaurování malířské výzdoby archy a jejich přínos pro možnosti autorského určení a stanovení míry dochování originálu." In: *Josef Opitz a umění na Chomutovsku a Kadaňsku 1350–1590*, 247–260. Chomutov: 2015.
Janáček, Josef. *Dějiny obchodu v předbělohorské Praze*. 1955.
Janáček, Josef. "Die Fugger und Joachimstahl." *Historica* 6 (1963): 109–144.
Jančárek, Petr. "Ekonomické typy báňských měst českého Krušnohoří v předbělohorské době." *Folia Historica Bohemica* 16 (1993): 35–52.
Jančárek, Petr. "K problematice demografického vývoje Jáchymova v době předbělohorské." *Historická demografie* 2 (1968): 17–27.
Jančárek, Petr. *Města českého Krušnohoří v předbělohorské době. Příspěvek ke studiu jejich sociální struktury*. Ústí nad Labem: 1971.
Jančárek, Petr. "Řemeslná výroba v městech českého Krušnohoří v předbělohorské době." *Archaeologia Historica* 8 (1983): 85–94.
Jančárek, Petr. "Sociální struktura báňského města Kraslic na konci předbělohorského období." *Minulostí Západočeského kraje* 28 (1992): 127–174.
Jangl, Ladislav. *České horní právo a báňská historie*. Praha: 2010.
Jireček, Josef. "Celnictví české za 16. věku." *Časopis muzea Království českého* 41, No. 1 (1867): 3–32.
Jirsík, Tobiáš. "Česká větev rodů pánů z Koldic na dvoře Lucemburků." Bachelor thesis. Charles University, 2015.
Jirsík, Tobiáš. "Páni z Koldic a páni z Bergova na českém královském dvoře v 15. století." Diploma thesis. Charles University, 2018.
Jiskra, Jaroslav. *Těžba stříbrných rud v Jáchymově v 16. století s jáchymovskými osobnostmi a první báňskou školou: Georgius Agricola, Johannes Mathesius, Lazarus Ercker*, 100–106. Plzeň: 2008.
Just, Jiří. "Život luterského sboru. Jáchymov a Jan Mathesius." In: Just, Jiří – Nešpor, Zdeněk R. – Matějka, Ondřej, et al. *Luteráni v českých zemích v proměnách staletí*, 59–65. Praha: 2009.
Kaden, Herbert. "Der Altbestand "Bergordnungen und Bergrechtsschriften" der Bibliothek des Sächsichen Bergarchives Freiberg – Quelle zur Erforschung der Geschichte sächsischer Bergbehörden im 16. und 17. Jahrhundert." In: *Berichte der Geologischen Bundesanstalt* 35, 197–201. Wien: 1996.
Kalina, Pavel. *Benedikt Ried a počátky záalpské renesance*. Praha: 2009.
Kašpar, Pavel. "Šlikové a počátky dolování stříbra v Jáchymově." *Bulletin mineralogicko-petrologického oddělení* Národního muzea v Praze 12 (2004): 22–24.
Katz, Viktor. "Wolf Milicz, Nickel Milicz a Zachariáš Kempf. Příspěvek k dějinám jáchymovského medailérství 16. století." *Numismatický časopis* 2 (1926): 85–114.
Kaufmann, Thomas Dacosta – Borggrefe, Heiner – Fusenig, Thomas. *Art and architecture in Central Europe 1550–1620. An annotated bibliography. Studien zur Kultur der Renaissance 2*. Marburg: 2003.
Kilián, Jan. *11. 12. 1617 – zboření kostela v Hrobu: na cestě k defenestraci*. Praha: 2007.

Klápště, Jan. *Proměna českých zemí ve středověku*. Praha: 2005.

Kloub, Jaroslav. "Vývoj Kovářské do poloviny 17. století." In: *Comotovia 2015*, 107–131. Chomutov: 2016.

Knape, Joachim – Kocher, Ursula. "Niavis, Paul," In: *Neue Deutsche Biographie* (NDB), Band 19 (Berlin, 1999).

Knetlová, Hana. "Regulace překračování hranic v období rekatolizace Chebu v první polovině 17. století." In: *Navzdory hranici. Migrační procesy na česko-německém pomezí*, 32–44. Plzeň: 2013.

Knopf, Karl. *Die Wunderstadt St. Joachimsthal*. Leipzig: 1909.

Kocourek, Ludomír – Kocourková, Květoslava – Vilím, Karel. *Krupka z cínu zrozená*. Krupka: 2005.

Koláček, Josef. "Kolej sv. Ignáce v Chomutově anno Domini 1591." *Památky, příroda, život* 34/3 (2002): 1–15.

Kořán, Jan. *Přehledné dějiny československého hornictví. I. díl*. Praha: 1955.

Kořán, Jan. *Sláva a pád starého českého rudného hornictví*. Příbram: 1988.

Kotěšovec, Václav. *Pohledy do historie měst a obcí Kraslicka: Bublava, Jindřichovice, Kraslice, Oloví, Přebuz, Rotava, Stříbrná, Šindelová, Dolní Nivy. Praha: 2011.*

Kracíková, Lucie – Novosadová, Olga. *Stavebně historický průzkum: Hrob – farní kostel sv. Barbory*. Česká Lípa: NPÚ ÚOP v Ústí nad Labem, Sbírka stavebně-historických průzkumů, sign. 359/A, 2001.

Kratzke, Christine – Tepper, Tim. "Konrad Krebs." In: Bartetzky, Arnold (ed.). *Die Baumeister der "Deutschen Renaissance." Ein Mythos der Kunstgeschichte?*, 44–72. Beucha: 2004.

Kratzsch, Klaus. *Bergstädte des Erzgebirges: Städtebau und Kunst zur Zeit der Reformation*. München: 1972.

Kratzsch, Klaus. "Marienberg – eine Idealstadt der Renaissance." In: Hoffmann, Yves (ed.). *Herzog Heinrich der Fromme*, 233–245. Beucha: 2007.

Krčmář, Luděk. "K zániku kostela Nanebevzetí Panny Marie v Přísečnici." Časopis Společnosti přátel starožitností 45/115, No. 3–4 (2007): 214–217.

Krenkel, Paul (ed.). "Paulus Niavis, Iudicium Iovis oder Das Gericht der Götter über den Bergbau: ein literarisches Dokument aus der Frühzeit des deutschen Bergbaus." *Freiberger Forschungshefte* 3. Berlin: 1953.

Krutský, Norbert. "Hornická činnost kláštera Osek. K historii těžby a zpracování nerostných surovin." In: *800 let kláštera Osek / 800 Jahre Kloster Ossegg*, 314–328. Osek: 1996.

Krutský, Norbert. "Mariánské Radčice – poutní místo oseckých cisterciáků / Maria Radschitz – ein Wallfahrtsort der Ossegger Zisterzienser." In: *800 let kláštera Osek / 800 Jahre Kloster Ossegg*, 35–44. Osek: 1996.

Křížek, Vladimír – Sajner, Josef – Ryba, Bohumil (ed.). *Václav Payer: Pojednání o Karlových Varech z r. 1522*. Praha: 1984.

Kubátová, Ludmila (ed.). *Nejstarší dolové účty Horní Blatná I–II*. Praha: 1992.

Kubátová, Ludmila. *Neznámý rukopis Lazara Erckera 1569*. Praha: 1996.

Kubátová, Ludmila. *Statuta horního města Jáchymova z roku 1526*. Praha: 2012.

Kubátová, Ludmila. "Účast žen na dolování v Horní Blatné." *Studie z dějin hornictví* 35 (Praha, 2006): 48–57.

Kubátová, Ludmila. "Zuzana Erckertová – paní mincmistrová a mincmistryně." *Studie z dějin hornictví* 22 (1993): 26–28.

Kuča, Karel – Zeman, Lubomír. *Památky Karlovarského kraje*. Karlovy Vary: 2006.

Kuča, Karel. "Krušnohorská města, jejich zakládání a urbanismus." In: Kratochvílová, Alžběta (ed.). *Bohatství historického stavebního vývoje Krušnohoří*, 7–12. Loket: 2011.

Kuča, Karel. *Města a městečka v Čechách, na Moravě a ve Slezsku, III. Kolí–Mi*. Praha: 1998.

Kuča, Karel. *Města a městečka v Čechách, na Moravě a ve Slezsku, VII. V–Ž*. Praha: 2011.

Kuča, Karel. *Města a městečka v Čechách, na Moravě a ve Slezsku. II. H–Kole*. Praha: 1997.

Kuča, Karel. Poznámky ke kompozici ortogonálních městských lokací v Čechách. *Archaeologica historica* 20 (1995): 107–124.

Kudrnáč, Jaroslav. "Archeologický výzkum středověké těžby drahých kamenů u Ciboušova v Krušných horách." *Památky a příroda* X., No. 10 (1985): 594–603.

Kuthan, Jiří. *Královské dílo za Jiřího z Poděbrad a dynastie Jagellonců II*. Praha: 2013.

Kvapil, Jan. "Augustinus Sartorius: Mariánský Atlas, Praha 1717 (koncepce barokního patriotismu vytvořená oseckými cisterciáky)." in: *Ústecký sborník historický* (2000): 145–166.

Kvapil, Jan. "Severočeská pánev – Mariánská země? Překlad díla Atlas Marianus Wilhelma Gumppenberga do němčiny oseckým cisterciákem Augustinem Sartoriem." In: *Náboženské dějiny severních Čech*, 20–24. Ústí nad Labem: 1999.

Laurenčíková, Markéta – Gaža, Jan. *Zaniklé kostely na Chomutovsku po roce 1945*. Chomutov: 2001.

Lebocová, Gabriela – Kratochvílová, Alžběta. "Portály jáchymovských domů." In: Zeman, Lubomír (ed.). *Jáchymov, architektonická perla v ohrožení*, 48–56. Karlovy Vary: 2009.

Líbal, Dobroslav – Heroutová, Marie. *Krupka. Stavebně historický průzkum objektů*. Praha: s. p. NPÚ ÚOP v Ústí nad Labem, Sbírka SHP a NZ, sign. 515/A, 1978.

Líbal, Dobroslav. *Gotická architektura v Čechách a na Moravě*. Praha: 1948.

Lorenz, Hellmut. "Spätgotik und Renaissance in Mitteleuropa – ein ‚Stil zwischen den Stillen'?" In: *Die Länder der Böhmischen Krone und ihre Nachbarn zur Zeit der Jagiellonenkönige (1471–1526)*, 31–47. Ostfildern: 2004.

Macek, Jaroslav. *950 let litoměřické kapituly*. Kostelní Vydří: 1997.

Magirius, Heinrich – Kelm, Christian – Eisbein, Martin – Mühlfriedel, Martin – Mühlfriedel, Lucas. "Der Cranachaltar in der St. Wolfgangskirche zu Schneeberg." *Zeitschrift für Kunsttechnologie und Konservierung* 6 (1992): 298–314.

Magirius, Heinrich. *Schneeberg, St. Wolfgang*, 18–25. Passau: 1996.

Majer, Jiří. "Georgius Agricola (1494–1565). Život a dílo." *Dějiny věd a techniky* 27, No. 1 (1994): 1–19.

Majer, Jiří. "K hospodářskému a sociálnímu vývoji Jáchymova v 16. století." *Studie z dějin hornictví* 26 (Praha, 1995): 42–43.

Majer, Jiří. "Lazarus Ercker (1528/30–1594) a české hornictví." *Dějiny věd a techniky* 27, No. 3 (1994): 129.

Majer, Jiří. *Lesní cínové doly na Českosaském pomezí v 16. a na počátku 17. století*. Praha: 1965.

Majer, Jiří. *Rudné hornictví v Čechách, na Moravě a ve Slezsku*. Praha: 2004.

Majer, Jiří. "Zur Gründung, Wirtschafts- und Sozialgeschichte. / K založení, hospodářskému a sociálnímu vývoji horního města Jáchymova v 16. století." In: *St. Joachimsthal in der Zeit Georgius Agricola. Zur Geschichte einer Bergstadt im 16. Jahrhundert.* / Jáchymov v době Georgia Agricoly. K dějinám horního města v 16. století, 9–11, 63–64. Schneeberg – Karlovy Vary: 1994.

Makarius, Roman. *České horní právo I*. Ostrava: 1999.

Malina, Ondřej. "Poznámky k hornické krajině jáchymovského revíru." *Archeologie západních Čech* 9 (Plzeň, 2015): 147–163.

Małowist, Marian. "Górnictwo w średniowiecznej Europie Środkowej i Wschodniej jako element struktur społeczno-gospodarczych w XII–XV w." *Przegląd Historyczny* 63, No. 4 (1972): 589–604.

Martínková, Dana (ed.). *Z Koldic, Kolda. Tractatus mystici: Mystické traktáty*. Praha: 1997.

Matasová, Kateřina. "Vdovy v báňských městech Krušnohoří na přelomu středověku a novověku." Diploma thesis. Jan Evangelista Purkyně University in Ústí nad Labem, 2009.

Maxová, Ivana – Nejedlý, Vratislav – Slížková, Zuzana – Zahradník, Pavel. *Mariánské, trojiční a další světecké sloupy a pilíře v Karlovarském kraji*. Praha: 2004.

Meine-Schawe, Monika. *Die Grablege der Wettiner im Dom zu Freiberg. Die Umgestaltung des Domchores durch Giovanni Maria Nosseni. 1585–1594*. München: 1992.

Mencl, Václav. "Vývoj okna v architektuře českého středověku." *Zprávy památkové péče* 20, No. 6 (1960): 181–232.

Mikschik, Jan. "Johannes Mathesius a Jáchymov." Bachelor thesis. Charles University, 2014.

Mikulec, Jiří. "Jezuitská bratrstva v Chomutově." In: *Comotovia 2002*, 102–114. Ústí nad Labem: 2003.

Moesta, Hasso. *Erze und Metalle — ihre Kulturgeschichte im Experiment*. Berlin – Heidelberg – New York: 1983.

Morávek, Petr – Litochleb, Jiří. *Jílovské zlaté doly*. Jílové u Prahy: 2002.

Morávek, Petr et al. *Jílovské zlaté doly*. Praha: 2018.

Muk, Jan. *Stavebně historický průzkum, čp. 497, Horní Slavkov*. Praha: NPÚ ÚOP v Lokti, Oddělení EDIS, sign. SHP 000013, 1971.

Müller, Anton. *Kurze Geschichte der freien Bergstadt St. Joachimstal*. Joachimstal: 1926.

Müller, Karl Otto. *Quellen zur Handelsgeschichte der Paumgartner von Augsburg 1480–1570 (Deutsche Handelsakten des Mittelalters und der Neuzeit, Band 9)*. Wiesbaden: 1955.

Myslivečková, Hana. "Renesanční sepulchrální tvorba Jana Miliče (Johannese Milicze)." *Průzkumy památek* 15, No. 1 (2008): 150–158.

Němec, Richard. *Architektura – vláda – země. Rezidence Karla IV. v Praze a zemích Koruny české*. Praha: 2015.

Nemeškal, Lubomír. "Jáchymov v hospodářských dějinách 16. století." *Folia Historica Bohemica* 11 (1987): 213–232.

Nemeškal, Lubomír. *Jáchymovská mincovna v první polovině 16. století (1519/1520–1561). Význam ražby tolaru*. Praha: 1964.

Nemeškal, Lubomír. "Neue Erkentnisse zur Geschichte der Joachimsthaler Münzstätte in der Schlickschen Ära." *Numismatische Zeitschrift* 103 (1995): 75–80.

Neuberger, Karel. *Stříbrský rudní revír od minulosti po současnost*. Stříbro: 2018.

Novotná, Ludmila. "Fundátorka Anna Šliková, příspěvek k historii kostela sv. Wolfganga v Ostrohu." In: *Sborník muzea Karlovarského kraje* 18 (2010): 273–276.

Novotný, Michal. "Šlikové. Majetková struktura panství a společenské postavení rodu do roku 1487." Diploma thesis. Charles University, 2007.

Nový velký ilustrovaný slovník naučný IX. Praha: 1930.

Oßmann, Harald. *Stadtentstehung im Erzgebirge des ausgehenden 15. und der ersten Hälfte des 16. Jahrhunderts, geprägt durch die Renaissance. Resultat des Silberbergbaus*. Dresden: 2002.

Ottová, Michaela – Royt, Jan. *Kostel Nanebevzetí Panny Marie v Mostě v době konfesních změn (1517–1594)*. Ústí nad Labem: 2014.

Ottová, Michaela. *Sochařství 15. století v severních a severozápadních Čechách*. Praha: 2004.

Pánek, Jaroslav – Polívka, Miloslav – Warta, Karin. "Chomutovská divadelní hra z roku 1594: dramatický obraz náboženských, politických a národnostních rozporů v předbělohorské stavovské společnosti." In: *Comotovia 2002*, 31–78. Ústí nad Labem: 2003.

Pátková, Hana. "Bratrstva svatého Wolfganga v pozdně středověkých Čechách." In: *Za zdmi kláštera. Cisterciáci v českých dějinách*, 167–171. České Budějovice: 2010.

Pejcharová, Alena. "Těžba rud v okolí Přísečnice – historie a dopady na životní prostředí." Bachelor thesis. Univerzita Jana Evangelisty Purkyně v Ústí nad Labem, 2010.

Pelant, Jan. *Města a městečka západočeského kraje*. Plzeň: 1988.

Pilz, Josef. *Dějiny města Nejdku do roku 1923*. Nejdek: 2003.

Pilz, Josef. *Geschichte der Stadt Neudek*. Neudek: 1923.

Plachý, Petr – Soukup, Michal – Večeřa, Josef. "Stopy středověké těžby v horách nad Osekem, okres Teplice." In: *Arbeits- und Forschungsberichte zur sächsischen Bodendenkmalpflege*, 137–145. Kadaň: 2013.

Poche, Emanuel et al. *Umělecké památky Čech, IV*. Praha: 1976.

Poche, Emanuel et al.. *Umělecké památky Čech, I*. Praha: 1977.

Poche, Emanuel et al.. *Umělecké památky Čech, II*. Praha: 1978.

Pörnbacher, Hans. "Svatý Jan Nepomucký jako zemský patron Bavorska." In: *Svatý Jan Nepomucký 1393–1993*, 23–32. Praha: 1993.

Pospíšil, Aleš. "Gotický plán chrámu sv. Barbory v Kutné Hoře ze sbírky vídeňské Akademie výtvarných umění (č. 16 841)." *Průzkumy památek* 12, No. 1 (2005): 91–96.

Pospíšilová, Martina. "Narovnání o hory a kovy (1534)." In: Schelle, Karel – Tauchen, Jaromír. *Encyklopedie českých právních dějin IV.*, 21–22. Plzeň: 2016.

Potůček, Václav – Černohorský, Jiří. *Orientační malířský restaurátorský průzkum omítkových vrstev v interiéru kostela Nanebevzetí Panny Marie v Krupce; Restaurátorský průzkum a návrh na restaurování vitrajového prosklení oken kostela Nanebevzetí P. Marie v Krupce*. Dubí u Teplic: NPÚ ÚOP v Ústí nad Labem, Sbírka restaurátorských zpráv, sign. 1948/R, 2002.

Prescher, Hans, "Georgius Agricola und St. Joachimsthal/Georgius Agricola a Jáchymov." In: *St. Joachimsthal in der Zeit Georgius Agricola. Zur Geschichte einer Bergstadt im 16. Jahrhundert / Jáchymov v době Georgia Agricoly. K dějinám horního města v 16.* století, 23–24, 73–74. Schneeberg – Karlovy Vary: 1994.

Prokop, Vladimír – Smola, Lukáš. *Sokolovsko: umění, památky a umělci do roku 1945*. Sokolov: 2014.

Prosch, Rudolf. *Abriss der Geschichte der alten, einst kaiserlich freien Bergstadt Schlaggenwald*. Schlaggenwald: 1938.

Prošková, Iva. "Mariánská úcta v severozápadních Čechách: putování a zbožnost jako součást každodenního života barokních Čech." *Poohří* 5, 100–11. 2015.

Radostová, Šárka. "Socha trůnící Panny Marie Chlumské a její druhý život." In: *Ústecký sborník historický* (2004): 433–453.

Radová, Milada – Rada, Oldřich. *Kniha o sklípkových klenbách*. Praha: 1988.

Rak, Petr. "Městské lokace Šebestiána z Weitmile." In: *Ústecký sborník historický* 1–2 (2014): 7–28.

Rathe, Steffi. "Böhmische Exulanten in Sachsen. Dargestellt am Beispiel Erzgebirge." In: *Grenzüberschreitende böhmisch-sächsische Beziehungen. Widerspiegelung im Archivwesen und in der Landesgeschichte*, 89–91. 2002.

Riedl, Alfred. *Zur Geschichte der Kirchen in Graslitz*. Dettingen am Main: 1967.

Richter, Uwe – Schwabenicky, Wolfgang. "Der Beginn des Freiberger Bergbaus, die Grenzbeschreibung des Klosters Altzelle und die Entstehung der Stadt Freiberg." In: Aurig, Rainer et al (Ed.). *Burg, Straße, Siedlung, Herrschaft: Studien zum Mittelalter in Sachsen und Mitteldeutschland*, 311–330. Beucha: 2007.

Rödig, Josef – Porkert, Eduard. *Abertham u. seine Schule*. Abertamy: 1938.

Rojík, Petr. *Historie cínového dobývání v západním Krušnohoří*. Sokolov: 2000.

Royt, Jan. *Biblické příběhy na reliéfech Chrámu Nanebevzetí Panny Marie v Mostě*. Ústí nad Labem: 2011.

Royt, Jan. *Gotické deskové malířství v severozápadních a severních Čechách 1340–1550*. Praha: 2015.

Royt, Jan. "Horní město Jáchymov, reformace a umění." In: *Ústecký sborník historický* (2001): 351–359.

Royt, Jan. "Ikonografie Mistra Jana Husa v 15. až 18. století." In: *Hus na přelomu tisíciletí. Mezinárodní rozprava o českém reformátoru 15. století a o jeho recepci na prahu třetího milénia. Husitský Tábor, Supplementum* 1, 405–452. 2001.

Royt, Jan. "Ikonografie sv. Jana Nepomuckého." In: *Svatojanský sborník*, 53–63. Praha: 1994.

Royt, Jan. "Malíř Hans Hesse a Roudnický oltář." In: *Hans Hesse. Pašijový cyklus z kostela Narození Panny Marie v Roudnici nad Labem, katalog výstavy*, 16–17. Roudnice: 2011.

Royt, Jan. "Poutě a poutní místa v Čechách." In: *Cesty a cestování v životě společnosti / Reisen im Leben der Gesellschaft*, 309–314. Ústí nad Labem: 1995.

Royt, Jan. "The Mining Town of Jáchymov. Reformation and Art." In: David, Zdeněk V. – Holeton, David (ed.). *The Bohemian Reformation and Religious Practice* 5, No. 2, 305–311. 2005.

Royt, Jan. "Utrakvistická ikonografie v Čechách 15. a první poloviny 16. století." In: Prix, Dalibor (ed.). *Pro Arte. Sborník k poctě Ivo Hlobila*, 193–205. Praha: 2002.

Royt, Jan. "Voda omilostňující a voda trestající: ikonografie luteránských křtitelnic v Čechách." In: *In puncto religionis: konfesní dimenze předbělohorské kultury Čech a Moravy*, 163–174. Praha: 2013.

Rozkošná, Blanka – Jakubec, Pavel. *Židovské památky Čech: historie a památky židovského osídlení Čech*. Brno: 2004.

Růžek, Vlastimil. "Dějiny obce Hora sv. Šebestiána." In: *Památky, příroda, život* 10, No. 2 (1978): 43–45; No. 3: 85–86; No. 4: 101–102.

Růžičková, Nikola. "Město a jeho hornictví. Prameny k hornické činnosti ve vybraných knihách Horní Blatné a Krupky." In: *Krušné hory v centru zájmu montánní archeologie*, 111–117. Dresden: 2018.

Rýneš, Michal. "Historie sakrálních staveb hornických měst středozápadního Krušnohoří." Diploma thesis. University of West Bohemia, 2015.

Sakařová-Malá, Alena. *Jáchymovská mincovna od zavedení zlatníkové měny (1561) do konce jejího trvání (1671). Příspěvek k dějinám peněžního oběhu 2. poloviny 16. a první poloviny 17. století*. Praha: 1967.

Sandner, Ingo – Wilsdorf, Helmut – Kiesewetter, Arndt. *Spätgotische Tafelmalerei*. Dresden – Basel: 1993.

Sandner, Ingo. *Hans Hesse. Ein Maler der Spätgotik in Sachsen*. Dresden: 1983.

Sedláček, August. *Hrady, zámky a tvrze české, XIII*. Praha: 1937.

Sedláček, August. *Hrady, zámky a tvrze Království českého, XIV*. Praha: 1923.

Semrádová, Alžběta. "Kult sv. Anny v Čechách v období středověku a raného novověku. Katalog malířských děl." Diploma thesis. Charles University, 2018.

Schattkowsky, Martina. "Die böhmischen Besitzungen des Zisterzienserklosters Altzella (1162–1540)." In: *Folia Historica Bohemica* 6 (1984): 221–234.

Scheicher, Elisabeth et al. *Die Kunstkammer. Kunsthistorisches Museum. Sammlungen Schloss Ambras*. Innsbruck: 1977.

Schlesinger, Walter. *Die Landesherrschaft der Herren von Schönburg: Eine Studie zur Geschichte des Staates in Deutschland*. Münster – Köln: 1954.
Schlesinger, Walter. "Entstehung und Bedeutung der sächsisch-böhmischen Grenze." *Neues Archiv für Sachsische Geschichte* 59 (1938): 6–39.
Schmidl, Carl G. – Luft, Michal. *Geschichte der Stadt Weipert*. Komotau: 1890.
Schmidt, Richard. *Soupis památek historických a uměleckých v Království českém XL., Politický okres Jáchymovský*. Praha: 1913.
Schneider, Petr. "Krušnohorské medaile." In: Klípa, Jan – Ottová, Michaela (ed.). *Bez hranic. Umění v Krušnohoří mezi gotikou a renesancí*, 683–690. Praha: 2015.
Schneiderwinklová, Pavlína – Malina, Ondřej – Augustýnová, Markéta. "Archeologické nálezy z důlních areálů 16. století v Jáchymově." *Archaeologia historica* 43, No. 2 (2018): 537–557.
Schreiber, Georg. "Der Bergbau in Geschichte, Ethos und Sakralkultur." In: *Wissenschaftliche Abhandlungen der Arbeitsgemeinschaft für Forschung des Landes Nordrhein-Westfalen*. Wiesbaden: 1962.
Schreiber, Rudolf. *Der Elbogner Kreis und seine Enklaven nach dem dreissigjahrigen Kriege*. Prag: 1935.
Schug, Adolf. *Heimatbuch Landkreis Neudek*, 243–245. Augsburg-Göggingen: 1978.
Schunicht-Rawe, Anne – Alshut, Elmar (ed.). *Handbuch der Renaissance. Deutschland, Niederlande, Belgien*. Österreich – Köln: 2002.
Schwabenicky, Wolfgang. *Der mittelalterliche Silberbergbau im Erzgebirgsvorland und im westlichen Erzgebirge unter besonderer Berücksichtigung der Ausgrabungen in der osten Bergstadt Bleiberg bei Frankenberg*. Chemnitz: 2009.
Smolík, Josef. "Smlouva krále Ferdinanda I. s pány Šliky o hory a minci Jáchymovskou." *Památky archaeologické a místopisné* 20, No. 5 (1903): 333–340.
Smolnik, Regina (ed.). *Silberrauch und Berggeschrey. Archälogie des o mittelalterlischen Berghaus in Sachsen und Böhmen / Stříbrná horečka a volání hor. Archeologie středověkého hornictví v Sasku a Čechách*. Dresden: 2016.
Spěváček, Jiří. *Václav IV. (1361–1419). K předpokladům husitské revoluce*. Praha: 1986.
St. Joachimstahl in der Zeit Georgius Agricola. Zur Geschichte einer Bergstadt im 16. Jahrhundert / Jáchymov v době Georgia Agricoly. K dějinám horního města v 16. století. Schneeberg – Karlovy Vary: 1994.
Sternberg, Kaspar von. *Umrisse einer Geschichte der böhmischen Bergwerke, Band 2*. Prag: 1838.
Studničková, Milada. "Úvodní iluminace Smíškovského graduálu jako klíč k interpretaci rukopisu." In: Prix, Dalibor (ed.). *Pro Arte. Sborník k poctě Ivo Hlobila*, 183–189. Praha: 2002.
Sturm, Heribert – Müller, Anton. *St. Joachimstahl*. St. Joachimstahl: 1930.
Sturm, Heribert. *Die Bücherei der Lateinschule zu St. Joachimstahl*. St. Joachimstahl: 1929.
Sturm, Heribert. *Die St. Joachimsthaler Lateinschulbibliothek aus dem 16. Jahrhundert*. Stuttgart: 1964.
Sviták, Zbyněk. *Úvod do historické topografie českých zemí*. Brno: 2014.
Svobodný, Petr. "Die Spitäler in Böhmen und Mähren im Mittelalter und in der Frühen Neuzeit." In: Schleutz, Martin – Sommerlechner, Andrea – Weigl, Herwig – Weiß, Alfred Stefan (ed.). *Europäisches Spitalwesen. Institutionelle Fürsorge in Mittelalter und Frühen Neuzeit*, 351–380. Wien – München: 2008.
Sýkora, Milan. "Příspěvek k poznání pozdně gotických sídel Weitmilů v severozápadních Čechách." In: *Comotovia 2015*, 65–88. Chomutov: 2016.
Syndram, Dirk. *In fürstlichem Glanz. Der Dresdner Hof um 1600*. Mailand: 2004.
Šimek, Eduard. "Jáchymovská produkce drobné mince a peněžní oběh 16. a 17. století. Rozbor mincovních nálezů." *Numismatický sborník* 21 (2006): 165–180.
Šimková, Táňa. *Standardní nedestruktivní stavebně-historický průzkum: Krupka (Ústecký kraj, okres Teplice): kostel sv. Ducha (č. rej. 4273/5-2645)*. Ústí nad Labem: NPÚ ÚOP v Ústí nad Labem, Sbírka stavebně-historických průzkumů, sign. 1828/A, 2016.
Šimková, Táňa. *Stavebně-historické zaměření kostela sv. Prokopa v Krupce*. Ústí nad Labem: 2012, manuscript.
Šimková, Táňa. "Stavební vývoj kostela Nanebevzetí Panny Marie v Krupce." *Monumentorum Custos* (2014, 2015): 31–48.
Škabrada, Jiří. *Architektura českého venkova*. Praha: 2005.
Thieme, André. "Kloster Altzelle und die Besiedlung im mittleren Erzgebirgsvorland." In: Schattkowsky, Martina – Thieme, André (ed.). *Altzelle: Zisterzienserabtei in Mitteldeutschland und Hauskloster der Wettiner*, 101–139. Leipzig: 2002.

Thurnwald, Andrea K. "Kirchenstuhl und Katechismus. Der Wandel von Liturgie und Sachkultur in Franken." In: Ritter, Bauern. *Lutheranen*, 42–49. Augsburg: 2017.

Tieftrunk, Karel. *Odpor stavův českých proti Ferdinandovi I. L. 1547*. Praha: 1872.

Toms, Bohumil. "Historické důlní revíry na těžbu zlata a stříbra na Šumavě a v Pošumaví." *Zlatá stezka* 16 (2009): 201–232.

Tresp, Uwe. "Kooperation ohne Grenzen: die Wettiner, die Grafen Schlik und das sächsisch-böhmische Erzegebirge als Wirtschaftsregion." In: *Die Kronländer in der Geschichte des böhmischen Staates. VI, Terra – Ducatus – Marchionatus – Regio. Die Bildung und Entwicklung der Regionen im Rahmen der Krone des Königreichs Böhmen*, 210–225. Praha: 2013.

Trnka, Pavel. "Diplomatika a správa kláštera Teplá ve druhé polovině 15. století." PhD diss., Charles University, 2016.

Trnka, Pavel. "Finanční situace českého krále Vladislava Jagellonského v letech 1471–1490." Diploma thesis. Charles University, 2008.

Truöl, Kurt. "Die Herren von Colditz und ihre Herrschaft." In: *Mitteilungen des Geschichts- und Altertumsvereins zu Leisnig*, svazek 15. Leisnig: 1927.

Třeštík, Dušan. "Cesta Ibrahima ibn Jakuba do Prahy v roce 966." *Dějiny a současnost* 5/92: 9–13.

Ullmann, Ernst. *Renaissance deutsche Baukunst 1520–1620*. Leipzig: 1995.

Urban, Jan (ed.). *Jan Mathesius, Hornická postila s krátkou jáchymovskou kronikou*. Praha: 1981.

Urban, Jan. "Johanes Mathesius und seine Sarepta / Johanes Mathesius a jeho Sarepta." In: *St. Joachimsthal in der Zeit Georgius Agricola. Zur Geschichte einer Bergstadt im 16. Jahrhundert. / Jáchymov v době Georgia Agricoly. K dějinám horního města v 16. století*, 31–33, 80–81. Schneeberg – Karlovy Vary: 1994.

Urban, Jan. "Zpráva Jana Jiřího Greiselia o studijní cestě do Jáchymova v r. 1670." In: *Historický sborník Karlovarska* 1 (1993): 9–17.

Urban, Michal – Albrecht, Helmut. *Hornické památky Montanregionu Krušné hory / Erzgebirge*. Jáchymov: 2014.

Urban, Michal et al. *Horní města Krušných hor. Ústecký kraj*. Sokolov: 2015.

Urban, Michal. "Abertamy mají další kulturní památku." *Měsíčník Krušné hory – Západ* 5, No. 7 (July 2016): 17.

Valentová, Alice – Aplt, Jiří (ed.). *Hans Sachs. Aktovky*. Praha: 1964.

Vávra, Ivan. "Osecká cesta – hrobská cesta." *Historická geografie* 20 (1982): 187–201.

Viczencz, Bruno Pavol. *Vznik úcty a modlitby ke čtrnácti svatým pomocníkům*. Praha: 2019.

Vlček, Pavel. *Ilustrovaná encyklopedie českých zámků*. Praha: 2001.

Vokurka, Michal. "Sasko-lauenburští vévodové jako příklad aristokracie v Čechách 17. století." In: *Bohemiae Occidentalis historica* 3, No. 2 (2017): 5–29.

Volf, Martin – Zeman, Lubomír. "Krušnohorská architektura a urbanismus. Nové poznatky k počátkům horního města Jáchymova." In: *Dějiny staveb. Sborník příspěvků z konference Dějiny staveb 2016*, 220–228. Plzeň: 2016.

Vorel, Petr – Nemeškal, Lubomír. *Dějiny jáchymovské mincovny a katalog ražeb I. (1519/1520–1619)*. Pardubice: 2010.

Vorel, Petr (ed.). *Stavovský odboj roku 1547. První krize habsburské monarchie*. Pardubice: 1999.

Vorel, Petr. "Jáchymovské tolary z roku 1527 se jménem Jeronýma Šlika a jejich význam pro stanovení chronologie jáchymovských ražeb." *Numismatické listy* 68, No. 1–2 (2013): 56–69.

Vorel, Petr. "Jáchymovský mincmistr Mikuláš (Klaus) Kraus a jeho působení v obchodě s českým stříbrem v letech 1530–1535." *Theatrum historiae* 1 (2006: 69–81).

Vorlová, Hana. "Svatá Anna Samatřetí v gotické plastice Českých zemí. Soupis a ikonografie." Diploma thesis. Palacký University Olomouc, 2002.

Wagenbreth, Otfried. "Die bergrechtliche Situation in der Frühzeit des Bergbaus von Freiberg in Sachsen, 1168 bis etwa 1350." In: *Dolování stříbra a mincování v Jihlavě*, 64–68. Jihlava: 1999.

Wejwoda, Mark. "Das Erzgebirge – Grenzlinie oder Kontaktraum? Die sächsisch-böhmischen Beziehungen im 15. Jahrhundert." In: *Des Himmels Fundgrube. Chemnitz und das sächsisch-böhmische Gebirge im 15. Jahrhundert*, 133–143. Chemnitz: 2012.

Weng, Gerhard. "Paul Schneevogels (Paulus Niavis') Beziehungen zum Bergbau." In: Naumann, Friedrich (ed.). *Sasko-české vztahy v 16. století*. Chemnitz: 2001.

Westermann, Ekkehard – Denzel, Markus A. – Schwarz, Matthäus. *Das Kaufmannsnotizbuch des Matthäus Schwarz aus Augsburg von 1548*. Stuttgart: 2011.

Wolf, Jiří. "Horní kniha města Krupky z let 1512–1533 (1535)." *Archivní časopis* 57 (2007): 1–24.

Wolkman, Rudolf. *Böhmens Antheil an der deutschen Litteratur des XVI. Jahrhunderts 3*. Praha: 1894.

Zeman, Lubomír – Kratochvílová, Alžběta. "Kostel sv. Jáchyma v Jáchymově. První luteránský kostel v Čechách a jeho přestavba Josefem Mockerem." In: *Svorník 10. Sborník příspěvků z 10. specializované konference stavebně-historického průzkumu uspořádané 7. – 10. června 2011 v Jindřichově Hradci*, 189–199. Praha: 2012.

Zeman, Lubomír. *Historie stavebního vývoje a architektury města Jáchymova. 500 let města Jáchymova*. Jáchymov: 2016.

Zeman, Lubomír. "Stavební vývoj města Jáchymova." In: Zeman, Lubomír (ed.). *Jáchymov, architektonická perla v ohrožení*, 7–18. Karlovy Vary: 2009.

Zeman, Lubomír. "Zástavba a urbanismus krušnohorských horních měst." In: *Sborník muzea Karlovarského kraje* 18 (2010): 3–94.

Žemlička, Josef. *Království v pohybu. Kolonizace, města a stříbro v závěru přemyslovské epochy*. Praha: 2014.

INTERNET SOURCES

"Databáze datovaných objektů." In: *Dendrochronologie.cz* [online]. July 16 2020. Available at: https://docs.google.com.

"Horní Slavkov – Sloupková kamenná zádušní svítilna." *Památkový katalog* [online]. July 16 2020. Available at: https://pamatkovykatalog.cz.

"Horní Slavkov – radnice. Evidenční list kulturní památky." *Metainformační systém NPÚ* [online]. July 16 2020. Available at: https://iispp.npu.cz.

"Horní Slavkov – Radnice." *Památkový katalog* [online]. July 16 2020. Available at: https://pamatkovykatalog.cz.

"Krásno – Městský dům." *Památkový katalog* [online]. July 16 2020. Available at: https://pamatkovykatalog.cz.

"Krásno – Kostel sv. Kateřiny Alexandrijské." *Památkový katalog* [online]. July 16 2020. Available at: https://www.pamatkovykatalog.cz.

"Měděnec – Kaple Neposkvrněného početí Panny Marie." *Památkový katalog* [online]. July 16 2020. Available at: https://www.pamatkovykatalog.cz.

Naše světové dědictví – Hornická kulturní krajina Krušnohoří/Erzgebirge: Mapová aplikace projektu [online]. July 16 2020. Available at: http://fzp.maps.arcgis.com.

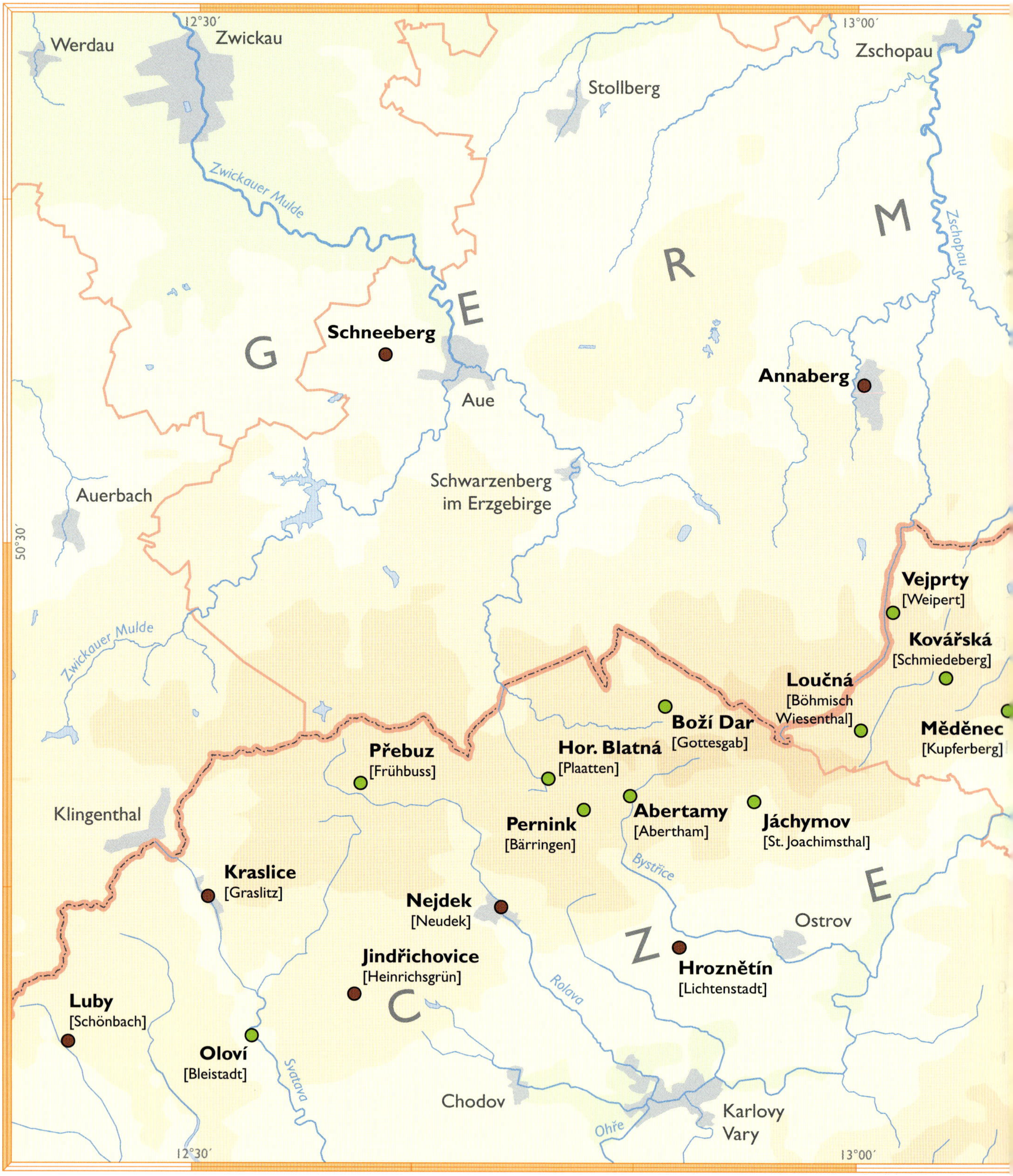
12°30′
13°00′
50°30′
Werdau
Zwickau
Stollberg
Zschopau
Zwickauer Mulde
Zschopau
G E R M
Schneeberg
Aue
Annaberg
Auerbach
Schwarzenberg
im Erzgebirge
Vejprty
[Weipert]
Kovářská
[Schmiedeberg]
Loučná
[Böhmisch
Wiesenthal]
Zwickauer Mulde
Boží Dar
[Gottesgab]
Měděnec
[Kupferberg]
Hor. Blatná
[Plaatten]
Přebuz
[Frühbuss]
Klingenthal
Pernink
[Bärringen]
Abertamy
[Abertham]
Jáchymov
[St. Joachimsthal]
Bystřice
Kraslice
[Graslitz]
Nejdek
[Neudek]
E
Ostrov
Z
Hroznětín
[Lichtenstadt]
Jindřichovice
[Heinrichsgrün]
C
Rolava
Luby
[Schönbach]
Oloví
[Bleistadt]
Svatava
Chodov
Karlovy
Vary
Ohře
12°30′
13°00′

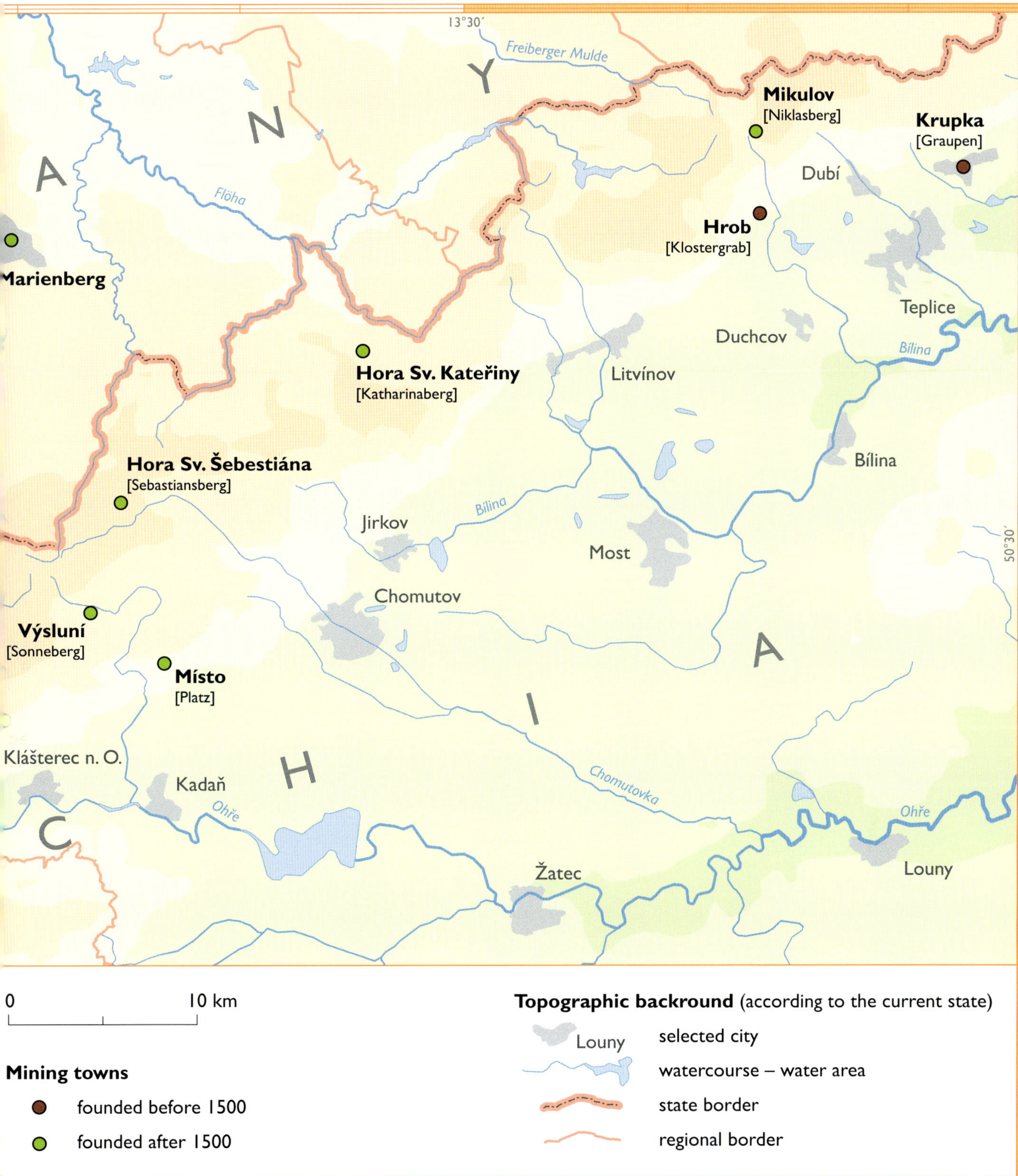
13°30′
Freiberger Mulde
Y
N
A
Flöha
Mikulov
[Niklasberg]
Krupka
[Graupen]
Dubí
Hrob
[Klostergrab]
Marienberg
Teplice
Duchcov
Bílina
Hora Sv. Kateřiny
[Katharinaberg]
Litvínov
Bílina
Hora Sv. Šebestiána
[Sebastiansberg]
Bílina
Jirkov
Most
50°30′
Chomutov
Výsluní
[Sonneberg]
Místo
[Platz]
A
I
Klášterec n. O.
Kadaň
H
Ohře
Chomutovka
Ohře
C
Žatec
Louny
0
10 km
Mining towns
founded before 1500
founded after 1500
Topographic backround (according to the current state)
Louny
selected city
watercourse – water area
state border
regional border